MAHATMA
GANDHI

MAHATMA GANDHI

Nonviolent Power in Action

Dennis Dalton

WITH A NEW PREFACE, AFTERWORD,
AND CHRONOLOGY BY THE AUTHOR

COLUMBIA UNIVERSITY PRESS   NEW YORK

COLUMBIA UNIVERSITY PRESS
Publishers Since 1893
New York   Chichester, West Sussex
cup.columbia.edu

Library of Congress Cataloging-in-Publication Data
Dalton, Dennis.
   Mahatma Gandhi : nonviolent power in action / Dennis Dalton.
      p.   cm.
   Reprint of 1993 edition. Includes new preface, afterword,
and chronology.
   Includes bibliographical references and index.
   ISBN 978-0-231-15958-6 (cloth : alk. paper) — ISBN 978-0-231-15959-3
(pbk. : alk. paper) — ISBN 978-0-231-53039-2 (e-book)
   1. Gandhi, Mahatma, 1869–1948. 2. Statesmen—India—Biography.
3. Nationalists—India—Biography. I. Title.

DS481.G3D215 2012
954.03'5092—dc23
[B]
                                                    2011029531

Columbia University Press books are printed on permanent and
durable acid-free paper.
This book is printed on paper with recycled content.
Printed in the United States of America

c 10 9 8 7 6 5 4 3 2 1
p 10 9 8 7 6 5 4 3 2 1

Photographs of Gandhi and letters were provided by Pyarelal Nayar
and S. K. De, then director of the Gandhi Memorial Museum and Library,
Rajghat, New Dehli. Special thanks to Pyarelal for his detailed comments
on and dating of these photos. Photographs of Lord Edward Irwin and
Reginald Reynolds were provided by the Nehru Memorial Museum and
Library, New Delhi. Photographs of Gangabehn and Ramjibhai Badhia
were donated by Mr. Arjubhai Badhia.

References to Internet Web sites (URLs) were accurate at the time of
writing. Neither the author nor Columbia University Press is responsible for
URLs that may have expired or changed since the manuscript was prepared.

CONTENTS

Contents

For my students, with thanks.
And to remember those
courageous and powerful few
who marched to Dandi
in pursuit of freedom.

A variety of incidents in my life have
conspired to bring me in close contact
with people of many creeds and many
communities, and my experience with all
of them warrants the statement that I have
known no distinction between relatives
and strangers, countrymen and foreigners,
white and colored, Hindus and Indians
of other faiths, whether Muslims, Parsis,
Christians or Jews. I may say that my
heart has been incapable of making any
such distinctions.

—*Gandhi*

The power of nonviolent action has been demonstrated amply
throughout the world since the second edition of this book in 2000. In that
year, nonviolent power succeeded dramatically in Eastern Europe, employed
by student groups like OTPOR in Belgrade to oust Slobodan Milosevic. But
the most striking evidence came in the Middle East, where activists led nonviolent mass action against the longstanding authoritarian regimes of Zin
El Abidine Ben Ali in Tunisia and Hosni Mubarak in Egypt. As the world
watched and worried in early 2011 that these revolts would degenerate into
violence, nonviolent power quickly deposed the despots. Pundits on both the
left and right failed to anticipate the success of "soft power" against these
entrenched governments; if considered at all, nonviolent action was quickly
discounted as impotent.

The most notable exception to these skeptics is the American political
theorist Gene Sharp. Against arguments that dictators like Milosevic and

Mubarak were impervious to the power of nonviolence, Sharp has consistently and cogently expounded strategies to overcome them. Since Sharp published *Gandhi Wields the Weapon of Moral Power* in 1960, he has steadfastly promulgated his theories (in works noted in the afterword). OTPOR activists in Serbia and protesters in Cairo have openly acknowledged their intellectual debt to Sharp's strategies for using mass nonviolent resistance to replace dictatorships with democracies.

Thus the idea of nonviolence has continued to circle the globe in improbable ways. From its origins in all of the great world religions, most significantly in the Hindu idea of *ahimsa* and Christ's Sermon on the Mount, it has leaped centuries to the interpretations of Thoreau and Tolstoy, to Gandhi's breakthrough in South Africa, and to the works of Martin Luther King Jr. and Gene Sharp in the United States. These are only a few obvious examples. Hundreds of writers have perpetuated the idea; millions have marched to bring it to life. Among all who have either theorized about this phenomenon or actively participated in civil disobedience against unjust authority, Gandhi's thought and leadership are unquestionably the most prominent.

Harold Laski, an eminent English political theorist and citizen of the empire that Gandhi was then in the process of overturning, observed when Gandhi arrived in London for the last time: "No living man has, either by precept or example, influenced so vast a number of people in so direct and profound a way."[1] This has also been the judgment of history if we compare Gandhi's enduring relevance to that of all the other leaders of major mass movements—violent without exception—during the twentieth century. Gandhi's claim to uniqueness rests both on the originality of his thinking about power and even more on his uncanny ability to put his theory into practice. Nonviolent power in action defined his career: the creative ways that he used it excite the world today. We can see human events, if only for a moment, through the lens that Gandhi above all others provided, without a bias toward the power of violence.

The aim of this study is to explain and understand the genius of Gandhi's singular achievement. Although the book recounts, especially in the third chapter, extensive criticism of Gandhi's leadership by his Indian contemporaries, I write for the most part with a strong sympathy for my subject. Most of the book is given to two lengthy case histories of his exercise of power: the mass civil disobedience campaign of 1930 and his fast for Hindu-Muslim unity in 1947. I chose these examples to show Gandhi at his best, using power strategically and wisely. In each case, the dramatic force of nonviolent power is highlighted because this is the purpose of the book: to offer lucid examples of how Gandhi connected his aim of liberation with the methods of nonviolent action.

As I have emphasized in the afterword, from the time that I arrived in India in 1960, I was fortunate to connect with Pyarelal and Sushila Nayar, the brother-sister team that served as Gandhi's personal secretary and physician, respectively. They were a remarkable pair of instructors, discussing in detail my questions and doubts about Gandhi, never turning away my queries about his personal and political life, whether concerning his conduct on the famous salt march (where Pyarelal was at his side) or matters of his health and diet. During the subsequent decades that I corresponded with both of them, in India and from London and New York, we exchanged manuscripts, including the ten-volume biography that they wrote together and the chapters of this book.

I will mention, after the Nayars, only a few of the many other Indian friends who provided me with their remarkable insights into Gandhi. First and foremost is S. R. Mehrotra, who from the beginning of my graduate studies in 1962 at the School of Oriental and African Studies (SOAS), University of London, guided me through the labyrinth of the old India Office Library files, explaining and interpreting records of the Raj in laborious detail. His awesome knowledge of the Indian National Congress has since been published; his recent discoveries behind Gandhi's writing of *Hind Swaraj* are featured in the afterword. For over fifty years, Sriram Mehrotra has been my steadfast mentor on Indian history.

Nirmal Kumar Bose served as Gandhi's Bengali interpreter and biographer during the period of partition and generously shared his understanding and serious criticisms of Gandhi during the final year of his life. K. K. Swaminathan and C. N. Patel, editors of Gandhi's *Collected Works*, allowed me to work with them on their scrupulous production of this opus and shared their intricate knowledge of difficult passages. In Delhi B. R. Nanda, author of several distinguished studies of Gandhi, gave vital assistance when he was director of the Nehru Memorial Museum and Library, as did S. K. De when he directed the Gandhi Library in Rajghat. Raghavan Iyer, analyst extraordinaire of Gandhi's philosophy, commented on my work from the period when he taught at Oxford University to later at the University of California. Bimal Prasad sponsored my research in India and arranged seminars at Jawaharlal University in Delhi, as did R. Kumar at the Indian Institute of Advanced Studies in Simla.

Finally, I have dedicated this book to those who accompanied Gandhi on his salt march because, along with Pyarelal, they tried in earnest to recreate that historic moment through their personal narratives. Dr. Haridas Muzumdar, one of the marchers, provided extensive written documentation as well as a series of interviews.

During the years that I studied and then lectured at SOAS (1962–1969), Hugh Tinker first supervised my doctoral dissertation on modern Indian political thought and then became a colleague. For decades after, he remained a close friend who read and criticized drafts of this entire book. No British or American historian helped me as much to appreciate the workings of the Raj because, unlike other English historians, he had served in the Indian Civil Service and then explained it in voluminous writings. W. H. Morris-Jones was the other Briton who helped me grasp British-Indian history and politics in the age of Gandhi, and he encouraged me for three decades to complete this book. It is a pleasure now to acknowledge the value of his comments on chapters 4 and 5 when they were first presented in seminars and conferences on the Partition of India at SOAS in 1965–1967 and 1974.

Professors Stephen Hay and James Hunt were American scholars and good friends who long focused their research and publications on Gandhi. They read and criticized preliminary drafts of chapters 4 and 5 when presented as papers at conferences in Mexico City and Toronto. Through their writings on Gandhi I have gained more perspective on his place in history. Barbara Stoler Miller, my colleague at Barnard College, offered important comments on Gandhi's use of the Vedic tradition when she read the introductory chapter of this book. The unflagging encouragement of Leonard Gordon during the last forty years should have been enough to spur my completion of a dozen books. As a preeminent historian of Bengali political leadership, he was not known for his sympathetic attitude toward Gandhi. But he concentrated his critical powers on this book, reading the entire manuscript at various stages of its evolution. His detailed suggestions of innumerable leads and sources could not have been more constructive. Legions of American students of India are indebted to Ainslie Embree for indispensable support, and I feel privileged to count myself among them. As noted in the afterword, Thomas Weber, an Australian scholar, not only made a close study of Gandhi's salt march but actually walked the entire route himself checking various points for historical accuracy. I appreciate the opportunity to have read his detailed account a decade ago in manuscript form.

It should be evident that those above who have read part or all of this study are not responsible for its lapses; the responsibility remains fully with the author. Anyone familiar with my writings on Gandhi over the last forty-five years may recognize parts of this book in previous incarnations. References to all of these early articles are given in the bibliography.

Research for this book was undertaken in India, London, and South Africa as well as throughout the United States. It received support from SOAS, University of London; the American Institute of Indian Studies; the American Council of Learned Societies; the American Philosophical Society; the Olin Foundation; Barnard College; and the Southern Asian Institute, Columbia University.

I gratefully acknowledge the assistance of the staffs of the India Office Library and Records, London; the British Library, London; the SOAS Library; the Nehru Memorial Museum and Library, Delhi, especially Mr. V. P. Joshi; the Gandhi Memorial Museum and Library, Delhi; the National Archives of India, Delhi; the Gandhi Library, Sabarmati Ashram, Ahmedabad, especially Mr. Kisanbhai Trivedi, Mr. Amrut Modi, Mr. Anil Patel, and Mr. Digant K. Dave; the Gandhi Ashram at Sevagram; the M. N. Roy Archives at the Indian Renaissance Institute, Dehra Dun, especially Mr. R. L. Nigam; the University of California Library at Berkeley; the University of Chicago Library; the King Library and Archives at the Martin Luther King Jr. Center for Nonviolent Social Change in Atlanta, Georgia; and the Barnard College and Columbia University Libraries in New York. In South Africa, the personal attention of Sushila Gandhi (the Mahatma's daughter-in-law) and her extended family in Durban is much appreciated, as well as the hospitality and instruction of Mr. A. D. Lazarus, an esteemed educator.

The special efforts of close friends on this project should be mentioned. Daniel Argov, Israeli historian of India, arranged for my research on Gandhi at the Hebrew University in 1966. Peter Juviler and Leslie Calman of the Barnard College Political Science Department team-taught courses with me in the 1970s and 1980s, listened to many of my lectures on Gandhi, and helped me with their countless comments to formulate what have become the main themes of this book. Jim Caraley, chair of my department for thirty years, was a consistent source of strength. And my brother, Terry, continues to be an unfailing source of wit. In addition to my students, who have provided me with remarkable reinforcement for over forty years—and this book is in part dedicated to them—two individuals have defined friendship for me by giving it in abundance: James Shokoff and Phillip Hubbart, professors of English and law, respectively.

Above all, and always there, is Sharron, my spouse of over fifty years. We met in Kathmandu and began our journey through India, England, New York, and the American West, her birthplace. She remains my fiercest critic and closest friend as we have tried to improve each other's books and teaching. Without India and Nepal we would have never met, so we remain in debt to those countries most. Our two sons, Kevin and Shaun, walked with us on our recreation of Gandhi's salt march, were adopted by Sushila Nayar when we lived in her home and she in ours, and experienced with us the wonders of South Asia. In turn, they have given us our four grandchildren: Mia and Sierra, Hadley and Blaise, and a new dimension on life. Finally, it is my pleasure to acknowledge the editorial assistance of Wade Weast and Michael Simon at Columbia University Press.

Notes

The epigraph to this preface comes from Gandhi's *Autobiography* in the *Collected Works of Mahatma Gandhi* (Delhi: Publications Division, Ministry of Information and Broadcasting, Government of India, 1961), 39:221.

1. Harold Laski, comment, *Daily Herald*, September 11, 1931.

If humanity is to progress, Gandhi is
inescapable. He lived, thought, and acted,
inspired by the vision of humanity evolving
toward a world of peace and harmony. We
may ignore him at our own risk.

—*Martin Luther King, Jr.*
The Words of Martin Luther King, Jr.
(New York: New Market Press, 1983), p. 71.

This book is dedicated to my students because its interpretations emerged from teaching experiences during the last four decades in South Asia, Britain, and America. A year after the book's publication, I went to Nepal as a Fulbright scholar and used it as a text in a political theory course at Tribhuvan University in Kathmandu, the very place where I had begun teaching in 1960. Students then and there, as always and elsewhere, taught me Gandhi's many meanings. This feedback continued when I returned to my classes in New York. From these exchanges, two aspects of Gandhi's originality appeared that I initially missed or understated, so I take this opportunity to discuss them here.

First, from 1904, a decade after he had arrived in South Africa, Gandhi said he discovered the sanctity or dignity of manual labor, insisting that all those in his community value working with their hands. He relates in his *Autobiography* how reading John Ruskin's *Unto This Last* inspired a conviction "that a life of labor, i.e., the life of the tiller of the soil and the handicraftsman is the life worth living," that heretofore "this idea had never occurred to me" (*Collected Works of Mahatma Gandhi*, 39: 239). Whatever Ruskin's initial influence, Gandhi developed this conception of work for his own purposes, to reinforce a growing egalitarianism that eventually distinguished his social reform program. Ruskin would not have recognized the philosophy of work that ultimately crystallized in India, where Gandhi used it to attack a caste hierarchy that systematically devalued manual labor.

Gandhi's originality on this point can be appreciated when one realizes its differences not only from Ruskin but especially from the social practices and vast intellectual traditions of India. If any single idea demonstrates or stamps Gandhi's credentials as a social reformer, it must be his theory and practice of work. The idea pervades his whole reform program, from abolition of untouchability to construction of village latrines and wells. His unique emphasis on public health and sanitation required social workers-cum-political volunteers to engage in labor that would routinely defy caste restrictions. In the hybrid conditions of his ashram communities this principle was pushed to the limit, initially creating severe tensions between caste Hindus and *harijans*.

In the common kitchen especially, as each member of the ashram performed his or her daily duties of food preparation and cooking, ancient norms of class and caste, sex and religion (as Muslims and Sikhs mixed with Christians and Hindus) provided endless grist for these mills of conflict resolution. Pyarelal Nayar, one of Gandhi's closest coworkers for twenty-eight years, liked to observe how much more of Gandhi's voluminous writings are devoted to management of his ashrams than to political campaigns because the former proved by far the toughest testing grounds for his "experiments with truth."

In a representative comment on labor made a year after returning from South Africa to India, Gandhi reviewed his program of social reforms, including spinning of cotton cloth and wearing of *khadi*. Then, speaking especially to an audience of Indian students, he concluded: "You may ask: 'Why should we use our hands?' and say 'the manual work has got to be done by those who are illiterate. I can only occupy myself with reading literature and political essays.' I think that we have to realise the dignity of labour.... I consider that a barber's profession is just as good as the profession of medicine." This must have seemed outrageous to his audience, first because according to caste proscriptions, a barber's work was meant for untouchables, and second, in colonized India, the medical profession, like law, promised entry into a Westernized elite.

But he was not finished. Only when these ideas are clearly understood, he insisted, "and not until then, you may come to Politics," practicing it not merely as a method of reform but as a creed of right principles infused with one's religious faith. "Politics, divorced of religion, have absolutely no meaning.... Politics are a part of our being" (*CWMG* 13: 234). This was Gandhi's statement in 1916, at the beginning of his thirty-year term of national leadership, and the demands that he made then were nothing short of revolutionary: profound changes in thinking about work, caste, religion, and politics, forming a nexus of ideas that young people must consider and adopt if they wanted to participate in the all-inclusive profession of politics.

Within four years of this speech, Gandhi was at the head of the first mass political movement in India's history. The extreme demands that he placed on political workers served not as an impediment but as an inspiration. In this new definition of politics as profession and creed, the performance of daily manual labor as a means to develop personal discipline, integrity, and identification with the peasantry became the litmus test for proof of nationalist citizenship.

The second aspect of Gandhi's originality as a political thinker and leader is the way that he forged connections, in theory and in practice, among the ideas of freedom, nonviolent power, and civic responsibility. This book's focus is on freedom (*swaraj*) and the power of nonviolence (*satyagraha*), but Gandhi usually connected these ideas with a concept of responsibility or moral obligation to improve society through nonviolent action. This connection is implied in the introduction and made explicit in chapter 5 (pp. 164–166), but it needs more clarification and development. Gandhi speaks often of how Indians must exercise responsibility to attain their freedom, and he conceives of this obligation in several ways.

First, he clearly distinguishes between liberty and license as the difference between true freedom (swaraj) and mere "independence" (p. 2). The latter suggests for him a lack of discipline and self-awareness, whereas swaraj requires of the citizen a growing sense of social unity. Second, following Thoreau, he argues that the quest for freedom incurs a definite political obligation or "the duty of disloyalty" when the state fails to represent the people's interests and needs. That is, "Disobedience of the law of an evil state is therefore a duty" (*CWMG* 43: 132–33). Finally, he moves beyond Thoreau by contending that the freedom struggle demands active participation in social reforms, i.e., no one is free until all are free from deprivation and discrimination. In the freedom struggle, volunteers or satyagrahis must dedicate themselves to the "uplift of all" (*sarvodaya*) by working in the range of reform programs noted above.

All citizens were obligated to keep the peace in times of civil strife. This duty became especially important in 1947 when India plunged into civil war as it gained independence from Britain. Chapter 5 details the history of Gandhi's leadership during this crucial period, but the conceptual connections among freedom, nonviolence, and civic responsibility merit reinforcement. The main point about civic duty is Gandhi's insistence that it was the clear and present obligation of the Hindu majority to protect India's Muslim minority. Hindus justified oppression of Muslims by arguing that in their newfound democracy, a majority had the right to prevail; this is what popular sovereignty meant. Gandhi countered with a liberal affirmation of minority rights and then went further by contending that majority rights should be earned through fulfillment of civic responsibility. In the great public squares of New Delhi, outside the chambers where India's new federal constitution was being written, Gandhi spoke urgently to his "Brothers and Sisters":

> What I am going to tell you today [June 28, 1947] will be something very special. I hope you will hear me with attention and try to digest what I say. When someone does something good he makes the whole world partake of the good. When someone does something bad, though he cannot make the world share his action he can certainly cause harm. The Constituent Assembly is discussing the rights of the citizen. As a matter of fact the proper question is not what the rights of a citizen are, but rather what constitutes the duties of a citizen. Fundamental rights can only be those rights the exercise of which is not only in the interest of the citizen but that of the whole world. Today, everyone wants to know what his rights are, but if a man learns to discharge his duties...if from childhood we learn what our dharma [sacred duty] is and try to follow it our rights look after themselves.... The beauty of it is that the very performance of a duty secures us our right. Rights cannot be divorced from duties. This is how satyagraha was born, for I was always striving to decide what my duty was.

On the next day, he resumed his theme, applying it directly to the problem of religious conflict:

> Yesterday I talked to you about duty. However I was not able to say all that I had intended to say. Whenever a person goes anywhere certain duties come to devolve on him. The man who neglects his duty and cares only to safeguard his rights does not know that rights that do not spring from duties done cannot be safeguarded. This applies to the Hindu–Muslim relations. Whether it is the Hindus living in a place or Muslims or both, they will come to acquire rights if they do their duty.... This is a paramount law and no one can change it. If Hindus consider Muslims their brothers and treat them well, Muslims too will return friendship for friendship.... The duty of the Hindus is to share with the Muslims in their joys and sorrows. (*CWMG* 88: 230, 236–37)

During the struggle for independence, Gandhi demanded that Indians accept responsibility for British colonization: they had allowed it to occur and could end it by doing their duty through satyagraha. When this struggle ended but brought civil war in its wake, Gandhi again insisted that his people accept and then exercise responsibility. How could they claim to enjoy their rights in a free India when failing in their duty to maintain peace and order? Swaraj through satyagraha still required the acceptance of social and political obligations for democracy to survive.

On August 15, 1997, as India celebrated fifty years of independence, an official ban was lifted on access to confidential documents of the British colonial government. Suddenly, thousands of pages contained in almost 800 separate files became available at the India Office Records collection in London (now located in the new British Library). These files comprise the carefully kept records of the Raj's secret service, or Indian Political Intelligence (IPI), described by archivists as "a shadowy and formerly non-avowed organization, within the Public and Judicial Department of the India Office in London, devoted to the internal and external security of British India." The IPI, reporting to Scotland Yard as well as to the India Office, maintained from 1916 to 1947 scrupulous surveillance of all "Indian revolutionaries," principally Gandhi and other leaders of the Indian National Congress. It reported on their movements, censored or proscribed objectionable Congressional or communist literature (including, for example, Gandhi's first tract, *Hind Swaraj*), and regularly intercepted and monitored personal and political correspondence. The newly opened files show that the mission of the IPI was amply met: the reports are highly detailed and documented, often thoughtful, perceptive, and elegantly written.

This fresh data substantiates a main thesis of chapter 4 on Gandhi's civil disobedience, that his use of nonviolent power effectively disarmed the Raj by creating a paralyzing ambivalence in their attempt at rule. It may appear that he achieved this with ease, but the records show that the British struggled hard to master the situation, agonizing over their predicament, searching for historical precedents when there were none, trying to determine the basic sources or dynamics of Gandhi's power. One lengthy report on Gandhi assesses the status of his leadership after the conclusion, in 1934, of prolonged civil disobedience. The tone throughout is exasperated and battle weary, resentful of "Gandhi's malevolent attitude" and "his determined retention of the civil disobedience weapon." Yet, citing an informant, the agent reports that there seems no way to stop him with "everyone hanging on Gandhi's smallest word (because he has the power).... *It is clear that nothing can be done without Gandhi, and, therefore, no one has the strength or courage to challenge him*" (parentheses and underlining in original). After citing several informants to substantiate further this analysis, the report distinguishes the "most striking fact" of Indian politics by 1936:

> Gandhi was much the master and director of Congress as ever and he had lost none of either his political astuteness or his inveterate hostility to British rule. Over and over again he intervened to save an open break between "reformists" and "revolutionaries" [liberal against violent factions within the Congress], and, in every such case, it was not difficult to see in the compromise that he brought about that, even when he appeared merely to have temporized, he had, in fact, kept Congress on the course chosen for it by him, deviating neither too far to the right, nor too far to the left, but steering all the time for the destination of mass revolution.

The British were clearly caught in a dilemma. On the one hand, they deplored Gandhi's "hostility" to their rule and his determined course of "mass revolution" that will end the Raj. On the other hand, Gandhi was surely preferable to the terrorists or communists on the extreme left because the British were never ambivalent about violent opposition. They deemed it hateful and crushed it unmercifully. They hesitated only with Gandhi because however "malevolent" his attitude, the method of nonviolence confounded them. Again and again, this intelligence agent presents the consuming question: how can the government effectively counter Gandhi's "dominating personality," "all-pervading influence," "appeal to the masses and the confidence of the commercial and professional classes," "while the whole of Hindu India regards him as a Saint who can do no wrong"? "Gandhi is the key-stone in the Congress movement," "Gandhi's triumph is a personal triumph...for his personality—to many his semi-divinity—has no rival in India" [Intelligence Bureau. Home Department. May 1, 1937.IOR/L/P&J/12/235]. British imperialism never found an answer to its Gandhi problem because it could not decipher the code to satyagraha, the secret of nonviolent power. Yet how ironic that an obscure English secret service officer should have described the Mahatma's power in terms that rival those of his most admiring hagiographers.

The analysis of British ambivalence that is presented in this book, especially in chapter 4, has been more recently developed in a trenchant study by D. A. Low, *Britain and Indian Nationalism: The Imprint of Ambiguity, 1929–1942* (1997). Low demonstrates through exhaustive use of British Indian sources and incisive analysis of all sides of the independence struggle that "the British frequently found themselves trapped in the coils of their own ambivalence." He explains how Gandhi's ingenious use of satyagraha served "to force their hand and make them grant India the swaraj it demanded in accord with their own self-avowed liberal values." From unprecedented case studies of Gandhi's interaction with the Raj, Low concludes that "It is now indeed possible to see that it was above all Gandhi's masterly grasp of the critical requirements of the Indian national movement in its momentous battle with India's profoundly ambiguous British rulers that gave him the towering position he came to hold in the Indian national movement" (pp. 31, 38–39). It may be seen, therefore, from Low's account as well as from the compelling data on this subject now available, that Gandhi succeeded because he wielded power in a unique manner. Alone among leaders of mass political movements in this century, he first conceived and then applied an entirely original method of action, satyagraha. Its use from 1906 to 1948 introduced a new mode of politics that Gandhi called "inclusive" rather than "exclusive." He demonstrated the power of this inclusivity when expressed, as it must be, through nonviolent action.

Old age is often unkind to political leaders, especially the most powerful or popular. They seem, like Churchill or many American ex-presidents, to outlive their usefulness. If they remain in power, like Mao and Nehru, they may preside over their own worst years. Gandhi in old age offers an instructive example of how nonviolent power may endure. In his late seventies, Gandhi's direct influence on Congressional policy declined as Nehru, Patel, and other leaders felt forced to accept the partition of India. Yet in other respects Gandhi's power grew, with his most dramatic and successful fasts in Calcutta and Delhi. The former, in September 1947, as Gandhi approached his seventy-eighth birthday, is examined in chapter 5. The latter, equally effective, occurred in January 1948, only two weeks before his assassination, and was devoted to the same cause, the resolution of Hindu–Muslim conflict, this time in India's strife-torn capital city.

Nicholas Mansergh, a British historian of the partition cited below, commented on Gandhi's use of power in these two fasts: "In this, the last year of his life, Gandhi's influence was transcendent.... It was his preaching of the doctrine of nonviolence more than any other single factor that stood between India and bloodshed on a frightful scale" (p. 159). The recently released files offer striking support of Mansergh's assessment. One lengthy report on Gandhi's conduct in Delhi after India gained independence ranks among the eloquent testimonies to his power. This is all the more remarkable because it was written by a senior representative of the government that Gandhi and his movement had just defeated. Mr. A.C.B. Symon, newly appointed high commissioner for the U.K. in India, writes with a tone and direction that suggest a resolution of earlier ambivalence. The report concurs with estimates of Gandhi's power offered by Lord Mountbatten around this time (e.g., pp. 233–34), but Symon provides details derived from firsthand observation of Gandhi's final four months in Delhi (September 9 to January 30), when he resided "in Birla House exactly opposite the Office of this High Commission":

> During these months Birla House became the focal point of political activity for all India. Day after day, the most important personages in the Dominion of India, as well as its most distinguished visitors, came to see the Mahatma here. Pandit Nehru and Sardar Patel, when they were not away from Delhi, were almost daily visitors. Next to these was Rajkumari Amrit Kaur, the Indian Christian Minister of Health as well as Maulana Kalam Azad, the Nationalist Muslim Minister of Education. Jai Prakash Narain and other Socialist leaders were also frequent visitors. Provincial Governors and Prime Ministers, too, always called on him when they visited Delhi and meetings of the All-India Congress Committee were invariably held in Birla House. Day after day people of all communities, rich and poor, came to visit him for guidance, assistance or consolation. Many of these were Sikh and Hindu refugees from Pakistan who had suffered personal bereavements and the loss of their homes. Day in and day out, too, Muslims of all classes of society, many of whom had also suffered personal bereavements in the recent disturbances, came to invoke his help. Normally too fearful even to leave their homes, they came to him because they had learned and believed that he had their interests at heart and was the only real force in the Indian Union capable of preserving them from destruction. Little groups of them, often belonging to the humblest classes of society, and including women, were frequently to be seen waiting outside the gates of Birla House until the Mahatma had time, as he always did, to listen to their requests. And each evening during these recent months congregations—again made up of all classes of society, including many members of the Indian Defence Services—assembled for his prayer meetings and listened to his daily exhortations that all races and creeds belonged to India; that all have the same rights; and that they must live in peace and amity together. There must be no retaliation on either side and conditions must be restored under which Muslims could return to safety to their homes in Delhi and non-Muslims to Pakistan.

It would be a mistaken impression, however, to suppose that Gandhi devoted these last months of his life exclusively to social and humanitarian tasks. Through this constant stream of visitors he was able to keep in remarkably close touch with Indian opinion and continued to play a most important role as the principal adviser of the Indian Government on all major political issues. Scarcely any important decision was taken without his prior advice, whether the subject was the movement and rehabilitation of refugees, Congress policy or the Kashmir issue. And when he disagreed with any decision taken it was not long, as in the recent case of the non-implementation of the Indo-Pakistan financial agreement, before he took determined and successful steps to have it revoked.... Gandhi entered upon what proved to be the last of his many fasts. His action immediately evoked expressions of goodwill from all over the world including Pakistan and on the third day of the fast the Indian Government as a gesture to him announced their willingness, in flat contradiction to their determination of a few days previously, to implement the recently concluded Indo-Pakistan financial agreements. Three days later on 18th January, Gandhi agreed to break his fast on receiving assurances from all communities in Delhi that Muslim life, property and religion would be both respected and protected.

The success of the Delhi fast would cost Gandhi his life. His effective pressure on the new Indian government to meet payments owed to Pakistan and on Hindus to cease persecution of Muslims persuaded his extremist Hindu assassins that they must wait no longer. Yet Gandhi's power was not finished: it was his murder, more than any other single event, that finally shamed his community into ending India's civil war. Symon concluded his report with this judgment: "Gandhi in these latter months genuinely came to believe that the future well-being of the Indian Union was entirely contingent on communal concord and that, if need be, he was prepared to sacrifice his life for this cause" [IOR/L/I/1/1379. A.C.B. Symon to Noel-Baker, New Delhi, February 4, 1948, British Commonwealth Affairs, No. 093].

After Gandhi made this sacrifice and the world rose to assess his life, Britons familiar with India tried earnestly to express how much had been lost. E. M. Forster, who had observed the Indian independence movement firsthand long before writing *A Passage to India*, contrasted Gandhi's "mature goodness" as a leader with the "blustering schoolboys" among his contemporary politicians. Forster concluded that Gandhi "was not only good. He made good, and ordinary men all over the world now look up to him in consequence.... 'A very great man' I have called him. He is likely to be the greatest of our century." Edward Thompson, an Oxford historian, wrote how after he had talked at length with Gandhi, "The conviction came to me, that not since Socrates has the world seen his equal for absolute self-control and composure...he will be remembered as one of the very few who have set the stamp of an *idea* on an epoch. That idea is non-violence, which has drawn out powerfully the sympathy of other lands." Then Thompson concluded with his hope and belief that "a sane and civilized relationship" might develop between Britain and India. "If that should come to pass, when the insanity now ravaging the world has passed away, then my country, as well as India, will look on this man as one of its greatest and most effective servants and sons" (*Mahatma Gandhi,* ed. S. Radhakrishnan, 1956).

Thompson thus foresaw the end that Gandhi most desired, the mutual redemption of England and India from their long and painful experience of colonialism. With satyagraha, Gandhi argued, there could be neither enemies nor losers, but only, in the end, victory for all. This is the demonstrable virtue of nonviolence.

Real swaraj *[freedom] is self-rule or self-control.*
The way to it is satyagraha: *the power of truth and*
love . . .

In my opinion, we have used the term
"*swaraj*" without understanding its real
significance. I have endeavoured to explain
it as I understand it, and my conscience
testifies that my life henceforth is dedicated
to its attainment.   —*M.K. Gandhi,*
Hind Swaraj, *1909*[1]

Mohandas Karamchand Gandhi (1869–1948) was called "Mahatma" ("Great Soul") because of his extraordinary achievements as leader
of the Indian movement for independence. Gandhi was not primarily a theorist but a reformer and activist. When pressed for a treatise on his philosophy, he protested that "I am not built for academic writings. Action is my
domain."[2] Yet he was guided by values and ideas that remained remarkably
enduring throughout his life. Chief among them were his unique concepts
of freedom and power, or, to use his terms, of swaraj and satyagraha. As
seen from his statement quoted above, these were closely connected ideas,
related to each other as means to end. He did, as he promised in 1909, devote his life to the pursuit of swaraj and he redefined the concept by insisting that individual freedom and social responsibility were no more antithetical than self-realization and self-restraint. In his pursuit of freedom he
transformed our conception of power through his practice of nonviolence

and satyagraha. Today the Mahatma has come to mean innumerable things to multitudes around the world. At least one of his important achievements was to show how the use of nonviolent power may clarify and enlarge our understanding of freedom.

Freedom as Swaraj: Redefinitions

In the heat of India's struggle for independence from British rule, the goal of swaraj was constantly invoked. It often meant simply freedom for India. But Gandhi argued that the word should mean more than political independence. When in 1931 he was asked to define the term precisely, he said it was not easily translated into a single English word. But he then went on to explain its meaning as it had evolved since the beginning of the nationalist movement:

> The root meaning of *swaraj* is self-rule. *Swaraj* may, therefore, be rendered as disciplined rule from within. . . . 'Independence' has no such limitation. Independence may mean license to do as you like. *Swaraj* is positive. Independence is negative. . . . The word *swaraj* is a sacred word, a Vedic word, meaning self-rule and self-restraint, and not freedom from all restraint which 'independence' often means.[3]

When Gandhi invoked ancient Vedic tradition in this way to define swaraj, he knew that it would allow for interpreting the idea of freedom in two distinct senses. Swaraj meant literally "self-rule" and could denote, in a strict political sense, a sovereign kingdom's freedom from external control.[4] Or it could mean freedom in a spiritual sense as being free from illusion and ignorance. From this perspective, one is liberated as one gains greater self-knowledge and consequent self-mastery. Obsessions with money or other means of domination become addictive forms of human bondage; freedom comes as we learn through self-discipline to rule ourselves. Thus *The Bhagavad-Gita*, Gandhi's primary text of Hinduism, saw the liberated individual as one who "acts without craving, possessiveness," and "finds peace" in awareness of the "infinite spirit," thereby being "freed from delusion."[5] The *Chandogya Upanishad*, like the *Gita*, defined freedom in a spiritual sense: "self-governing autonomy" and "unlimited freedom in all worlds," were the traits of swaraj in the sage. As in the *Gita*, this liberation evolved from a higher consciousness, an awareness of the unity of all being, the identity of oneself with the universal Self or *Atman*.[6]

This philosophy which related spiritual freedom or swaraj to a perception of the unity or oneness of life became the source of a vital stream of Gandhi's ideas: his conceptions of nonviolence, truth, and tolerance flow from it. And each of these important ideas, together with swaraj, denoted individual self-discipline. The traditional sage's "unlimited freedom" flowed from an enlightened self-restraint. Because the sage perceived a spiritual equality in the sacred connectedness of all life, an infatuation with power or drive to dominate others violated that vision; in their stead came self-control and an expansive sense of social duty. Thus *The Bhagavad-Gita* acclaimed the liberated sage as "the man of discipline" and affirmed that: "Arming himself with discipline, seeing everything with an equal eye, he sees the self in all creatures and all creatures in the self."[7] No lines from the *Gita* were more essential for Gandhi's idea of swaraj.

These were the meanings of swaraj—political and spiritual—that came from India's ancient tradition into the twentieth century to inspire the independence movement with a philosophy of freedom. But Gandhi was not the first Indian nationalist to interpret the idea of swaraj for the movement. The nationalist movement had begun in the late nineteenth century and India had its philosophers of freedom before Gandhi. Among these political leaders, swaraj at first implied no more than political liberty or national independence. Prominent leaders of the Indian National Congress like Bal Gangadhar Tilak and Dadabhai Naoroji meant by swaraj only this. In 1906, Naoroji, then elder statesman of the Indian National Congress, proclaimed the goal of swaraj as political autonomy in these terms:

> We do not ask any favours. We want only justice. Instead of going into any further divisions or details of our rights as British citizens, the whole matter can be comprised in one word—"self-government" or *Swaraj* like that of the United Kingdom or the Colonies.[8]

Soon after this, though, other Indian theorists developed further the meaning of swaraj. They argued along the lines stated later by Gandhi, that swaraj must mean more than just independence. "Self-rule" required what *The Bhagavad-Gita* and Upanishads demanded, knowledge of the individual self. Only this knowledge could produce a higher form of spiritual freedom, that is, freedom from the illusion of separateness and freedom to realize the universal Self. The aim of these theorists was not, of course, to discard the goal of Indian independence but to forge a synthesis of two meanings of freedom, political ("external") and spiritual ("internal") liberation.

Aurobindo Ghose and Bipin Chandra Pal, both Bengali theorists from the extremist faction of the Indian Congress, were the first to shape this synthesis that Gandhi eventually adopted. They insisted that swaraj was too sacred a word to be translated as the Western notion of political liberty. Ghose argued that "*Swaraj* as a sort of European ideal, political liberty for the sake of political self-assertion, will not awaken India." An ideal of "true *Swaraj* for India" must derive from the Vedantic concept of "self-liberation."⁹ Pal took the idea of swaraj still further by defining it as "the conscious identification of the individual with the universal." Its correct meaning derived not from Indian liberals like Dadabhai Naoroji but "in the Upanishads to indicate the highest spiritual state, wherein the individual self stands in conscious union with the Universal or the Supreme Self. When the Self sees and knows whatever is as its own self, it attains swaraj: so says the Chandogya Upanishad." Pal then contrasted this Vedantic conception of swaraj with the modern European notion of freedom, arguing as Ghose did the superiority of the classical Indian view:

"Indeed, the idea of freedom as it has gradually developed in Europe ever since old Paganism was replaced by Christianity with its essentially individualistic ethical implications and emphasis, is hardly in keeping with the new social philosophy of our age. Freedom, independence, liberty [as defined in Europe] are all essentially negative concepts. They all indicate absence of restraint, regulation and subjection. Consequently, Europe has not as yet discovered any really rational test by which to distinguish what is freedom from what is license." Western thought should learn from the Indian philosophy of freedom because it is not negative but positive: "It does not mean absence of restraint or regulation or dependence, but self-restraint, self-regulation, and self-dependence." This follows from the core principle that "the self in Hindu thought, even in the individual, is a synonym for the Universal."¹⁰

In this analysis of swaraj and freedom, the Bengali theorists set the ideological foundations for Gandhi's construction. As Pal, Ghose, and eventually Gandhi conceived it, the idea of swaraj had three distinct components. First, while it pretended to reject the European liberal concept of freedom as "negative," in fact it accepted that idea as one essential element of swaraj. Freedom for India, they believed, must include complete independence from England and after that guarantee the basic civil liberties that British liberalism had preached but denied Indians in practice. This was fundamental to their vision of an independent India. Gandhi later asserted that "Civil liberty consistent with the observance of non-violence is the first step towards *swaraj*. It is the breath of political and social life. It is the foundation of freedom. There is no room for dilution or compromise."[11]

Yet, if civil liberty was a necessary condition for swaraj, it could not be deemed sufficient: it lacked an essential correlate of social responsibility. Thus, the next part of their thinking about swaraj was a criticism of the liberal idea of liberty. They argued that Europeans saw the freedom of self-realization as mere self-aggrandizement, conceiving of freedom as unrestrained pursuit of selfish aims at the expense of others. So the Western notion of progress meant only a compulsive competition for material goods and never cooperation for a secure and just community. A corrective was needed and they prescribed a theory of freedom compatible with the value of self-restraint, and containing, as Pal intended, a decidedly positive quality.

This conceptualization of freedom bears some similarities with European political philosophers like Jean-Jacques Rousseau, G. W. F. Hegel, or T. H. Green, who formulated theories of "positive" freedom in the eighteenth and nineteenth centuries.[12] The Indians, however, consistently infused into their thinking about freedom insights from their own tradition. The "positive" freedom that they constructed argued that self-knowledge could lead to a discovery of human unity and thus reconcile the antagonism between individual and society so characteristic of the liberal concept of liberty. Ghose expressed this best:

> By liberty we mean the freedom to obey the law of our being, to grow to our natural self-fulfillment, to find out naturally and freely our harmony with our environment. The dangers and disadvantages of liberty [when conceived in the 'negative' sense] . . . are indeed obvious. But they arise from the absence or defect of the sense of unity between individual and individual, between community and community, which pushes them to assert themselves at the expense of each other instead of growing by mutual help . . . . If a real, a spiritual and psychological unity were effectuated, liberty would have no perils and disadvantages; for free individuals enamored of unity would be compelled by themselves, by their own need, to accommodate perfectly their own growth with the growth of their fellows and would not feel themselves complete except in the free growth of others. . . . Human society progresses really and vitally in proportion as law becomes the child of freedom; it will reach its perfection when, man having learned to know and become spiritually one with

his fellow-man, the spontaneous law of his society exists only as the outward mould of his self-governed inner liberty.[13]

In his extensive writing on freedom, Ghose contended that "the spirit of ancient Indian polity" inspired for our age a new perspective on political theory. Its cooperative rather than competitive approach to social life bred a secure self-discipline. The "spirit" of Indian culture, as distinct from its corrupt "forms" (manifest, for example, in the caste system), fostered a mature self-restraint and with it a harmony of political and social interests. Spiritual freedom meant liberation from attitudes of political or social separateness that foster ideologies of xenophobia and exclusivity. The idea of positive freedom or swaraj is thus inextricably interwoven with attitudes of inclusivity.[14] These two categories of "exclusivist" separatist thinking contrasted with an inclusivist perception of "unity in diversity" became essential to Gandhi's philosophy.

The importance of Bengali theorists like Ghose and Pal for the Indian idea of freedom should be recognized but not exaggerated. It was Gandhi who translated the theory of swaraj into political reality through a program and style of national leadership. But it was not just his activism that was unique. He shaped the theory of swaraj in at least three novel ways. First and foremost, he connected it with his conception of satyagraha or the power of nonviolence. Others like Pal had observed that swaraj signified a spirit of human unity but they did not then deduce from that a strategy of nonviolent change. The ancient Indian idea of *ahimsa* (literally, "not violent") posited the value that harming others was tantamount to injuring oneself but it took Gandhi to use this as an underpinning for political and social reform. He alone theorized that India's freedom could be attained only through nonviolence—that swaraj required the power of satyagraha—and simultaneously worked out ways to put it into practice.

Another distinctive feature of Gandhi's idea of swaraj was his persistent relation of the personal to the political. "*Swaraj* of a people," he declared, "means the sum total of the *swaraj* (self-rule) of individuals,"[15] and ". . . political self-government, that is, self-government for a large number of men and women, is no better than individual self-government, and therefore, it is to be attained by precisely the same means that are required for individual self-government or self-rule."[16] That is, personal self-rule or self-realization, attained through knowledge and examination of oneself, is the foundation of national independence. This view of swaraj demanded that the quest for India's freedom begin with each individual assuming personal responsibility for changing attitudes of intolerance and exclusivity. He stated succinctly this conception of swaraj when he wrote: "The outward freedom therefore that we shall attain will only be in exact proportion to the inward freedom to which we may have grown at a given moment. And if this is the correct view of freedom, our chief energy must be concentrated upon achieving reform from within."[17] "Outward" or "external" freedom is thus only one part of swaraj: political independence can be nothing more than a "means of measuring the freedom of the self within." The right aim of those "who wish to attain true freedom" should be "an improvement in the self."[18]

This idea of "inward freedom" associates swaraj with an internal journey or search for self-knowledge that liberates one from the sort of fear and insecurity that fuels both a desire to dominate or to be dominated. It was the willingness of Indians to cooperate with the British Raj out of fear that troubled Gandhi. The fruit of "internal freedom" is a personal liberation from fear. Raghavan Iyer captures the essence of swaraj in his trenchant analysis of the idea when he says that it involves "a demanding and continuous process of self-cultivation."[19]

This relates to Gandhi's own evolution as a leader and the profound changes of ideas and identity he experienced. "The pilgrimage to Swaraj" he said, "is a painful climb,"[20] and his own life can be viewed as an arduous journey. As such it may be compared with others who have suffered from racism and whose response might be seen as a personal struggle for freedom from fear and domination. The last chapter of this book compares Gandhi with Malcolm X. It examines the latter's autobiography as comparable to Gandhi's because both suggest a pilgrimage to self-realization. In this sense, Malcolm X personifies a quest for "inward freedom" that is at the heart of swaraj.[21]

The last point that Gandhi developed in his theory of swaraj was his insistence that social reforms were essential for India's freedom. When he asserted that "the movement for *Swaraj* is a movement for self-purification,"[22] he meant that individuals must take responsibility for a change of attitude to overcome three major problems in Indian society: Hindu-Muslim religious conflict, the evils of caste and untouchability, and economic inequality. Each of these areas of social corruption was an obstacle to swaraj and must be tackled coterminously with the fight for political independence.[23] "The sooner it is recognized" he said, "that many of our social evils impede our march towards *Swaraj*, the greater will be our progress towards our cherished goal. To postpone social reform till after the attainment of *Swaraj* is not to know the meaning of *Swaraj*."[24]

In relation to Gandhi's ideas about social reform, the analysis in this book focuses on the problems of caste and untouchability (chapter 2) and Hindu-Muslim conflict (chapter 5). His commitment to attaining social equality is evident in his personal example: he lived a life of simplicity. When he claimed that "The *Swaraj* of my dream is the poor man's *Swaraj*," and stressed his own identification with the poor, his word was accepted as authentic because of his consistency of thought and deed. Moreover, he built a movement that was social and not just political, around the need for self-sacrifice among its leaders: "Without a large, very large, army of self-sacrificing and determined workers, real progress of the masses, I hold to be an impossibility. And without that progress, there is no such thing as *Swaraj*. Progress towards *Swaraj* will be in exact proportion to the increase in the number of workers who will dare to sacrifice their all for the cause of the poor." [25] This economic aspect of swaraj was expressed in his idea of *sarvodaya* or "welfare of all," which asserted that "Economic equality is the master-key to non-violent independence."[26]

Satyagraha as a Form of Power

William Shirer went to India in 1930 as an American journalist to report on what he then saw as Gandhi's "peculiar revolution." Fifty years later he wrote a remarkable memoir about that visit. He described the civil disobedience campaign of that year in compelling terms and then concluded that satyagraha was Gandhi's "supreme achievement," which "taught us all that there was a greater power in life than force, which seemed to have ruled the planet since men first sprouted on it. That power lay in the spirit, in Truth and Love, in non-violent action."[27] Whether or not Gandhi in fact "taught us all" this lesson, the phenomenon of the power of satyagraha is there for all to know. And whether or not one accepts that this power derived from "Truth and love," the Indian independence movement remains one of the largest mobilizations of mass energy in history; it did excercise a form of power dramatically different from that of governments or armies or violent revolutions. This was because its leadership conceived of how to convert the power of nonviolence into political action.

Gandhi defined satyagraha as the power "born of Truth and Love or non-violence."[28] As early as 1909, he presented it as his method for attain-

8

ing swaraj. He believed, on the basis of his use of civil disobedience in South Africa from 1906 to 1914, that the power of nonviolent action identified with satyagraha was uniquely suited for achieving the "inward" as well as the "outward" freedom of swaraj. The word satyagraha was coined by Gandhi by joining the Sanskrit *satya* (truth) with *agraha* (holding firmly)[29] and the historical context of this derivation will be traced in the next chapter. He drew a sharp distinction between satyagraha and "passive resistance" because the latter allowed for "internal violence," the harboring of enmity and anger among resisters even when they commit no physical violence. Gandhi asserted that unlike passive resistance, "Satyagraha is gentle, it never wounds. It must not be the result of anger or malice."[30]

Much depends on the intent or motive of the *satyagrahi* (practitioner of satyagraha). Wrong motives occur when the intent is only to attain victory or satisfaction of a selfish interest. A *satyagrahi* concentrates on the common interest and strives not for retribution but to transform a conflict situation so that warring parties can come out of a confrontation convinced that it was in their mutual interest to resolve it. This was not unlike the scene in 1947 when without mutual recrimination the British left India after centuries of colonization. The way that the conflict was conducted, evidenced in the salt satyagraha examined in chapter 4, served to produce this result at the time of India's independence. Another example of the dynamics of satyagraha was the Calcutta fast, the focus of chapter 5. Here Gandhi's use of the fast transformed a Hindu-Muslim conflict so that the civil strife could end with a renewed commitment to peace.

Gandhi's conceptions of swaraj and satyagraha were both related to the emphasis that he placed on employing the right means to attain an end. This was another of the key ideas that he had expressed in *Hind Swaraj*. He argued there that: "the belief that there is no connection between the means and the end is a great mistake. Through that mistake even men who have been considered religious have committed grievous crimes. . . . The means may be likened to a seed, the end to a tree; and there is just the same inviolable connection between the means and the end as there is between the seed and the tree. . . . We reap exactly as we sow."[31]

Thus Gandhi can say that "Means and ends are convertible terms in my philosophy of life."[32] When it was rumored in late 1924 that he would be invited by the Soviet government to visit the USSR, he replied that he had been courted by Communists before, and reflected unfavorably on the Russian revolution:

I do not believe in short-violent-cuts to success. Those Bolshevik friends who are bestowing their attention on me should realize that however much I may sympathize with and admire worthy motives, I am an uncompromising opponent of violent methods even to serve the noblest of causes. There is, therefore, really no meeting ground between the school of violence and myself.[33]

Whenever he considered the kind of revolution that India needed, he stressed this emphasis on means as the basis of swaraj and satyagraha. As he planned the mass civil disobedience campaign that would be called the salt satyagraha, he went before the Indian people to argue his case in these terms:

No one will be able to stand in our way when we have developed the strength to win *swaraj*. Everyone's freedom is within his grasp. There are two alternatives before us. The one is that of violence, the other of non-violence; the one of physical strength, the other of soul-force; the one of hatred, the other love . . . If we want *swaraj*, we shall have to strive hard and follow one of these two courses. As they are incompatible with each other, the fruit, the *swaraj* that would be secured by following the one would necessarily be different from that which would be secured by following the other. . . . We reap as we sow.[34]

When Gandhi assumed leadership of the nationalist movement in 1919 he described satyagraha in terms of a metaphor that likened it to "a banyan tree with innumerable branches." The trunk of the tree, he said, consisted not only of nonviolence (*ahimsa*) but also of truth (*satya*).[35] So the last component of satyagraha to be introduced here is Gandhi's concept of truth. He begins with a warning to each of us: we must continually remind ourselves of our fallibility by recognizing our limitations. Human understanding is always imperfect and thus incapable of possessing absolute truth.[36] We may believe in truth or in God, or, as Gandhi did, in Truth as God. But we cannot possess complete knowledge of either and "the claim to infallibility would always be a most dangerous claim to make."[37]

Nonviolence therefore becomes imperative in any human conflict because there are inevitably partial and contending perceptions of truth. Leaders of nations are notorious for their claims to carry truth as they lead their people into battle. Gandhi offered his method to the world as a corrective: "*Satyagraha* . . . excludes the use of violence because man is not capable of knowing the absolute truth and, therefore, not competent to punish."[38] When Gandhi was questioned in 1920 by a Government tribunal about the volatile nature of civil disobedience, a British official asked: "However honestly a man may strive in his search for truth his notions of truth will be different" and would this not produce violent disorder? Gandhi replied that was precisely the reason why "non-violence was the necessary corollary," because without this India could not gain swaraj.[39] This answer hardly satisfied the British government in 1920. But it did underscore the integral relationship that Gandhi drew between truth and nonviolence. These remained the two overriding values that directed his quest for personal and political liberation. He usually spoke of truth in terms of a search: "Truth resides in every human heart, and one has to search for it there, and to be guided by truth as one sees it. But no one has a right to coerce others to act according to his own view of truth."[40] The essence of Gandhi's optimism about each person's pursuit of truth or of self-realization is here; equally significant is how nonviolence may be interpreted as both a guiding value and a warning, that we have no right to violate others.

When Gandhi compared satyagraha to "a banyan tree with innumerable branches," he extended the metaphor to include civil disobedience as one main branch; others were fasting for social reform or work in the villages to achieve economic change. In his metaphor, Gandhi saw satyagraha as an inclusive concept that embraced all forms of nonviolent action: social as well as political campaigns, the civil disobedience of the salt march or the fast for Hindu-Muslim harmony. Most of this book analyzes the dynamics of satyagraha and swaraj in specific historical contexts, as expressions of Gandhi's ideas of freedom and power in action. The next chapter concerns the initial development and application of these ideas as they emerged from Gandhi's early political leadership in South Africa.

CHAPTER ONE

Satyagraha Meets Swaraj: The Development of Gandhi's Ideas, 1896–1917

> None of us knew what name to give to
> our movement. I then used the term
> "passive resistance" in describing it: I
> did not quite understand the
> implications of 'passive resistance' as I
> called it—I only knew that some new
> principle had come into being.
> As the struggle advanced, the phrase
> "passive resistance" gave rise to
> confusion . . . I thus began to call the
> Indian movement "Satyagraha," that
> is to say the Force which is born of
> Truth and Love or non-violence.
>
> *—Gandhi, recalling events of*
> *1906–1907 in South Africa*[1]

Origins of Satyagraha in South Africa

At least as early as 1896, one may see in Gandhi's pamphlet, "Grievances of British Indians in South Africa," the embryo of the method he later called satyagraha: "Our method in South Africa is to conquer this hatred by love. . . . We do not attempt to have individuals punished but, as a rule, patiently suffer wrongs at their hands."[2] But the teaching of the past which he invoked at this time is the "precept of the Prophet of Nazareth, 'resist not evil';"[3] and the example of the present which he repeatedly praises is that of the British suffragettes.[4] During this initial period of protest his weekly issues of *Indian Opinion* recount and extol the lives of Mazzini, Lincoln, Washington, and Lord Nelson as supreme examples of selfless sacrifice in service of their countries.[5] When he criticized discriminatory government legislation, his worst charge was that the spirit of the laws seemed "un-British." Until 1906 the striking feature of his ideology is not merely his reliance upon Western examples and values but his dependence on them to the exclusion of anything Indian. The Mahatma, then, began his public career as a loyalist, totally committed to the values and institutions of the British empire.

But Gandhi is not the only example of a political leader who was radicalized in response to unyielding racist authority. Malcolm X was another and the specific reasons for their respective life changes will be compared in chapter 6. In Gandhi's case the dramatic shift from emulation to rejection of the oppressor came in late 1906, at age thirty-seven, when, as a lawyer trained in London to respect the imperial system, he suddenly realized the futility of working within it. It was then that the first meeting of swaraj and satyagraha occurred and the long relationship began. A small minority of fewer than 100,000 Indians in South Africa said goodbye to conventional political protest and embraced civil disobedience.

On August 22, 1906, the Transvaal Government Gazette published the Draft Asiatic Law Amendment Ordinance. This gave notice of new legislation: all Indians, Arabs, and Turks were required to register with the government. Fingerprints and identification marks on the person's body were to be recorded in order to obtain a certificate of registration. A fine of 100 pounds or three months' imprisonment could be imposed on those failing to register before a given date. Among the Indians, the ordinance became known as the "Black Act." Gandhi complained that the new law was not only discriminatory but also profoundly humiliating because Indians were treated as common criminals. After preparing the community through the press, Gandhi called a mass meeting of approximately 3,000 Transvaal Indians on September 11. The famous fourth resolution, prepared by Gandhi, was passed by the meeting. It called for resistance to the Registration Act through civil disobedience, including imprisonment if necessary. Gandhi made clear in moving the resolution that it was different than any passed by the Indians before: "It is a very grave resolution that we are making, as our existence in South Africa depends upon our fully observing it." He insisted that the action was so serious that it must be sealed by each individual with an oath before God, an unprecedented demand. "If having taken such an oath we violate our pledge we are guilty before God and man."[6]

Later Gandhi would refer to the events surrounding this meeting as the "advent of satyagraha." Elements appear here for the first time that became classic components of the method. First there is the *causa sine que non*, Gandhi's perception of an injustice as humiliating, depriving Indians of their dignity and self-respect. This is associated with fear and loss of individual autonomy. The remedy of achieving swaraj through satyagraha was conceived in 1906 and its essential ingredients are remarkably clear: the conviction that through a political movement each individual might achieve liberation from fear with a new sense of self-esteem and personal strength, autonomy, what is today called "empowerment."

The new method of action conceived at that September 11 meeting was initially described as "passive resistance." Within a year, Gandhi found that term objectionable. In a letter to the editor of the *Rand Daily Mail* dated July, 1907, Gandhi wrote: "It may appear ungrateful to have to criticize your moderate and well-meant leaderette on the so-called 'passive resistance' to the Asiatic Registration Act. I call the passive resistance to be offered by the Indian community 'so-called,' because, in my opinion, it is really not resistance but a policy of communal suffering."[7]

By this time, Gandhi had already begun to dislike the term "passive resistance," since it was a foreign one that implied principles he could not wholly accept. "When in a meeting of Europeans," he records in his *Autobiography*, "I found that the term 'passive resistance' was too narrowly construed, that it was supposed to be a weapon of the weak, that it could be characterized by hatred, and that it could finally manifest itself as violence, I had to demur to all these statements and explain the real nature of the Indian movement."[8] His ideal was active nonviolent resistance to injustice. Hatred and violence were incompatible with the method that he had conceived because his theory rested squarely on the principle of *ahimsa*, which he variously translated as "nonviolence," "love," and "charity." This idea of *ahimsa* he had taken from the Indian tradition, and particularly the Jain religion where it meant a strict observance of nonviolence.[9] Gandhi fused his own interpretation of this belief with ideas he found in Tolstoy and the Sermon on the Mount; the result was a principle that evoked rich religious symbolism and contributed to a dynamic method of action unique in Indian history.

Any doubts concerning Gandhi's conscious attempt to establish continuity with the Indian tradition in his search for a method of action may be dispelled by a look at the way in which he coined the term satyagraha, a word which had not heretofore existed.

> To respect our own language, speak it well and use in it as few foreign words as possible . . . this is also a part of patriotism. We have been using some English terms just as they are, since we cannot find exact Gujarati equivalents for them. Some of these terms are given below, which we place before our readers. . . . The following are the terms in question: Passive Resistance; Passive Resister; Cartoon; Civil Disobedience. . . . It should be noted that we do not want translations of these English terms, but terms with equivalent connotations.[10]

In this manner, Gandhi announced a contest in *Indian Opinion* for the renaming of "passive resistance." The thinking behind this idea of a contest is further explained as he describes the origins of his movement in South Africa: ". . . the phrase 'passive resistance' gave rise to confusion and it appeared shameful to permit this great struggle to be known only by an English name. Again, that foreign phrase could hardly pass as current coin among the community. A small prize was therefore announced in *Indian Opinion* to be awarded to the reader who invented the best designation for our struggle."[11] Gandhi's remark here that a "foreign phrase could hardly pass as current coin among the community" is noteworthy; equally significant is his candid admission, noted above, that "I did not quite understand the implications of 'passive resistance' as I called it. I only knew that some new principle had come into being." The "new principle" inspired both new deeds and thoughts and all first found expression in South Africa.

"What Gandhi did to South Africa," observes one of his biographers, "was less important than what South Africa did to him."[12] South Africa provided the laboratory for Gandhi's experiments; it proved an excellent testing ground, since many of the problems he later found in India occurred there in miniature. No Indian had confronted these problems in South Africa before: Gandhi was writing on a clean slate and he was able to try out almost any methods he chose.

Gandhi had formed beliefs before he arrived in South Africa. His *Autobiography* testifies to the lasting impression of childhood experiences, impressions, and lessons that were to affect the later development of the two ideas that would dominate his thought: truth and nonviolence.[13] Then almost three years were spent as a law student in London, during which time he discovered the Sermon on the Mount and came to understand the *Bhagavad Gita* through Sir Edwin Arnold's English translation.[14] Gandhi recalled that at this time, "My young mind tried to unify the teaching of the Gita, The Light of Asia and the Sermon on the Mount. That renunciation was the highest form of religion appealed to me greatly."[15] Religious and moral attitudes had thus begun to form in London. But they took definite shape only in South Africa. Moreover, he does not appear to have given any thought at all to political questions before his direct involvement with the problems of the Indian community in Natal. He remarked tersely in 1927, "South Africa gave the start to my life's mission."[16] This mission was one of self-realization but before he left South Africa he knew that it must involve a struggle for India's freedom as well. He had left Bombay for Durban in 1893 as a legal counsel for Dada Abdulla and Company; he returned to India twenty-one years later with a sense of mission, a reservoir of practical experience in social and political reform, and with the ideas that formed the basis of his political thought. That is what South Africa did for Gandhi.[17]

Hind Swaraj: A Proclamation of Ideological Independence

The main ideas that emerged from Gandhi's South African experience are contained in his short work, *Hind Swaraj*, easily one of the key writings of his entire career.[18] The original text, written in Gandhi's native language of Gujarati in 1909 during a return voyage from London to South Africa, was first published serially in Gandhi's newspaper *Indian Opinion*; later it went through numerous reprints, became a text for the Indian nationalist movement and was occasionally banned by the Government of India. In a significant comment on *Hind Swaraj* written in 1921, Gandhi stated the purpose behind the book.

> It was written . . . in answer to the Indian school of violence, and its prototype in South Africa. I came in contact with every known Indian anarchist in London. Their bravery impressed me, but I feel that their zeal was misguided. I felt that violence was no remedy for India's ills, and that her civilization required the use of a different and higher weapon for self-protection. The Satyagraha of South Africa was still an infant hardly two years old. But it had developed sufficiently to permit me to write of it with some degree of confidence . . . It [*Hind Swaraj*] teaches the gospel of love in the place of that of hate. It replaces violence with self-sacrifice. It pits soul-force against brute force.[19]

The aim of *Hind Swaraj* was to confront the anarchists and violence-prone Indian nationalists with an alternative to violence, derived from Gandhi's earliest experiments with satyagraha. Equally important is the book's concern with the concept from which it takes its title: this is Gandhi's first extensive statement on swaraj, his idea of freedom. The ideas he sets forth here provide the basis for much of his future thinking on both satyagraha and swaraj and the correspondence drawn between them.

Gandhi had written of swaraj before 1909; but he seldom referred to the term then, and conveyed only a limited awareness of the concept as it was developing in India. The first explicit use of swaraj in Gandhi's *Collected Works* occurs with a brief reference to Dadabhai Naoroji's Congress Presidential Address in 1906 that was cited above, in the introduction. Gandhi wrote in *Indian Opinion*:

> The address by the Grand Old Man of India is very forceful and effective. His words deserve to be enshrined in our hearts. The substance of the address is that India will not prosper until we wake up and become united. To put it differently, it means that it lies in our hands to achieve swaraj, to prosper and to preserve the rights we value . . . For our part we are to use only the strength that comes from unity and truth. That is to say, our bondage in India can cease this day, if all the people unite in their demands and are ready to suffer any hardships that may befall them.[20]

These few sentences contain the germs of the concept of freedom that Gandhi was soon to develop; and thirty-four years later he was still admonishing the Congress, and the Indian people, that swaraj "will not drop from heaven, all of a sudden, one fine morning. But it has to be built up brick by brick by corporate self-effort."

In the months following Naoroji's address, and before the writing of *Hind Swaraj*, while Gandhi rarely used the term swaraj he did develop his idea of freedom. Immediately before his departure for London in June 1909, Gandhi had spent three months in a Pretoria prison for civil disobedience. There he read The Gita, Upanishads, and the Bible, as well as Ruskin, Tolstoy, Emerson and Thoreau. He was impressed by Thoreau, and particularly by this passage from *On Civil Disobedience*: "I saw that, if there was a wall of stone between me and my townsmen, there was a still more difficult one to climb or break through before they could get to be as free as I was."[21]

Gandhi remarked on these lines that the individual who pursues truth through civil disobedience may be imprisoned but "his soul is thus free," and "taking this view of jail life, he feels himself quite a free being." He concluded that a right understanding and enjoyment of freedom "solely rests with individuals and their mental attitude."[22] A year later he wrote: "Whilst the views expressed in Hind Swaraj are held by me, I have but endeavoured humbly to follow Tolstoy, Ruskin, Thoreau, Emerson and other writers, besides the masters of Indian philosophy."[23]

When Gandhi left Capetown for London, then, the strands of his ideas on freedom, gleaned from both Indian and Western sources as well as from his own experience, were in his mind. The stimulus for weaving them together into a coherent pattern, and fusing them with a program of social action, came during his four months stay in London. Gandhi arrived on July 10, 1909; nine days earlier London had been shaken by the murder of Sir Curzon Wyllie by a young Indian terrorist, Madanlal Dhingra, who delivered at his trial a stirring speech on patriotism. The city was afire with discussions among anarchists, nationalists, and terrorists. Gandhi became intensely involved. He argued the views on satyagraha that were soon to become an integral part of his political and personal creed: India could gain her freedom only through nonviolence; terrorism would cause disruption and decay. From these conversations emerged the ideas set forth in *Hind Swaraj*.[24]

Hind Swaraj takes the form of a dialogue between "Reader" and "Editor." The former argues with haste and rashness terrorist ideas; the latter presents Gandhi's own case. At the outset, the Editor appears on the defensive. Then gradually he subdues the anarchist's storm. Ultimately the Reader yields to the force and novelty of an alternative that seems more revolutionary than his own position. As a statement of political thought *Hind Swaraj* has considerable limitations. It is a brief polemical tract more than a logical development of a serious and measured argument: written hastily, in less than ten days, it suffers from occasional disjointedness and egregious overstatement. Yet the essence of Gandhi's political and social philosophy is here and he could write in 1938, "after the stormy thirty years through which I have since passed I have seen nothing to make me alter the view expounded in it."[25]

The book opens with the Reader's attack upon the Indian Congress as "an instrument for perpetuating British rule." Moderates like Dadabhai Naoroji and G. K. Gokhale are indicted as unworthy "friends of the English." Gandhi rises to their defense: he insists that they, along with Englishmen like Hume and Wedderburn, deserve India's respect for their selflessness and for preparing the foundations of Indian Home Rule. The nature of Gandhi's argument is crucial. He neither identifies himself with the Moderates nor does he consider their position adequate: he argues only that their contribution was necessary to make further advance possible. "If, after many years of study," the Editor contends, "a teacher were to teach me something and if I were to build a little more on the foundation laid by that teacher, I would not, on that account be considered wiser than the teacher. He would always command my respect. Such is the case with the Grand Old Man of India [Naoroji]."[26]

The Reader reluctantly agrees and elicits from the Editor this reply: "Professor Gokhale occupies the place of a parent. What does it matter if he cannot run with us? A nation that is desirous of securing Home Rule cannot afford to despise its ancestors. We shall become useless, if we lack respect for our elders." "Are we, then, to follow him in every respect?" "I never said any such thing. If we conscientiously differed from him, the learned Professor himself would advise us to follow the dictates of our conscience rather than him."[27]

Thus, while the Moderates are defended in an almost reverential spirit, they are in practice set aside as "ancestors" who have played out their roles. The Congress appears in much the same manner, worthy of respect but no longer a dynamic organ of progress. "All I have to show," the Editor concludes, "is that the Congress gave us a foretaste of Home Rule [swaraj]."[28] And this indeed is all that he does show.

Gandhi's attitude toward the Congress, and the Moderates who in 1909 controlled the Congress, is clear. But he has not yet mentioned the Extremists. Aurobindo Ghose, B. C. Pal, B. G. Tilak, and Lajpat Rai were all Extremist leaders of considerable renown at this time, yet their names do not appear in *Hind Swaraj*. A passing, but revealing, reference is made to the Extremist group at the end of the second chapter. "Our leaders," the Editor observes, "are divided into two parties: the Moderates and the Extremists. These may be considered as the slow party and impatient party."[29]

"Slow" and "impatient": this is how Gandhi characterizes the two main sections of Indian political leadership in 1909. India cannot move ahead with slow leaders, but rash action may result in self-destruction. If the Moderates are left behind then the Extremists are irresponsible. It is no coincidence that the Editor often criticizes the Reader for his "impatience." *Hind Swaraj* is a direct reply to the Extremists, especially to the lunatic fringe of Indian anarchists and terrorists. Early in the book, then, Gandhi dismisses the leadership of both national parties in India as unviable. The moment has arrived for a statement of his own position: a philosophy and program of action that appear to gain the best of both sides, not through steering a mean course, but rather by moving forward to a new alternative and a fresh conception of freedom.

The Reader now poses the central question, "What is *swaraj?*" and the remainder of the book is occupied with a consideration of that question. The Reader gives his version of swaraj first: "As is Japan, so must India be. We must have our own navy, our own army, and we must have our own splendor, and then will India's voice ring through the world. . . . If the education we have received be any use, if the works of Spencer, Mill and others be of any importance, and if the English Parliament be the Mother of Parliaments, I certainly think that we should copy the English people. . . . It is, therefore, proper for us to import their institutions."[30]

The Editor disagrees:

> You have drawn the picture well. In effect it means this: that we want English rule without the Englishman. You want the tiger's nature, but not the tiger; that is to say, you would make India English. And when it becomes English, it will be called not Hindustan but Englishtan. This is not the Swaraj that I want. . . .
>
> It is as difficult for me to understand the true nature of Swaraj as it seems to you to be easy. I shall therefore, for the time being, content myself with endeavoring to show that what you call Swaraj is not truly Swaraj.[31]

The subsequent discussion, which occupies the middle section of the book, comprises Gandhi's notorious blanket condemnation of modern civilization. The argument is grossly overstated, often misguided, and in some instances, as with the sweeping denunciation of doctors and hospitals, lapses into pure fantasy.[32] The main point of this section is that all Western civilization should be shunned, for it "takes note neither of morality nor of religion."[33] All its trappings, from its parliamentary system of government to the whole of its industrial complex, are foreign to real civilization. If Indians are to attain swaraj, they must not imitate the Western example, but construct a civilization on the simple ethical and religious truths found in their own tradition.[34] "The tendency of the Indian civilization is to elevate the moral being, that of the modern Western civilization is to propagate immorality. The latter is godless, the former is based on a belief in God."[35]

This simplistic categorization of Indian and Western civilizations respectively as "moral" and "immoral," "soul force" *versus* "brute force," presented a wholesale indictment of modernity, worse, a polarization into an attitude of "us" against "them" redolent of what Gandhi would later deride as "violence of the spirit." *Hind Swaraj* in this respect reveals the high-water mark of his exclusivist ideology; that is, the depiction of social and political realities in antagonistic terms of unbridgeable dichotomies. Such an uncompromising view of human experience would later prove uncharacteristic of the Mahatma. Even in 1909, this portrayal of world cultures as mutually exclusive did not really befit a syncretic thinker like Gandhi, who had by that time been profoundly influenced by the ideas of Leo Tolstoy, John Ruskin, and Henry David Thoreau as well as British liberalism. Within ten years, Gandhi's exclusivist attitudes would evolve into an inclusivist approach evident in the way that his ideas were expressed toward the British in the salt satyagraha or toward Muslims in the Calcutta fast, as suggested in chapters 4 and 5. His inclusivism would ultimately become identified throughout the world and in the judgment of history as Gandhi's unique style of politics. Yet it is hard to imagine this mature inclusivist style without first passing through the youthful fire of *Hind Swaraj*, because the primary consolidation of his theory occurred there.

Although Gandhi never explicitly renounced any component of *Hind Swaraj*, he later modified his judgments of modern Western civilization, parliamentary democracy, and modern technology. In 1921 he accepted as an immediate, though not ultimate, goal, "Parliamentary Swaraj." "The least that Swaraj means," he said, "is a settlement with the Government in accordance with the wishes of the chosen representatives of the people."[36] Similarly with his views on machinery, he modified his stand, contending in 1924, "What I object to is the *craze* for machinery, not machinery as such. . . . I am aiming not at eradication of all machinery, but limitations."[37] By the 1920s his inclusivist thought had evolved into a vision of an ideal society that sought to meld elements of traditional Indian philosophy with the ideas of the Russian anarchists, Tolstoy and Peter Kropotkin. He envisaged a social order of small communities, each seeking attainment of individual freedom and social equality through mutual cooperation and respect. This was his theory of *sarvodaya*, the "Welfare of All," a society that had indeed achieved swaraj.

> In this structure composed of innumerable villages, there will be ever widening, never ascending circles. Life will not be a pyramid with the apex sustained by the bottom. But it will be an oceanic circle whose center will be the individual always ready to perish for the village, the latter ready to perish for the circle of villages, till at last the whole becomes one life composed of individuals, never aggressive in their arrogance but ever humble, sharing the majesty of the oceanic circle of which they are integral units. Therefore, the outermost circumference will not wield power to crush the inner circle but will give strength to all within and derive its own strength from it.[38]

A right form of civilization, Gandhi had concluded in *Hind Swaraj*, "is that mode of conduct which points out to man the path of duty. Performance of duty and observance of morality are convertible terms. To observe morality is to attain mastery over our mind and our passions. So doing, we know ourselves. The Gujarati equivalent for civilization means 'good conduct.' "[39] In striving to build this civilization, Indians will not only construct a free nation, they will come to realize swaraj within themselves. For just as a free civilization demands "mastery over our mind and our passions," so freedom for the individual consists of each person establishing self-rule. "If we become free, India is free. And in this thought you have a definition of Swaraj. It is Swaraj when we learn to rule ourselves. It is, therefore, in the palm of our hands. . . . But such Swaraj has to be experienced, by each one for himself."[40]

This is the core of Gandhi's idea of freedom. He was above all concerned with right obedience to one's self. Thirteen years after writing *Hind Swaraj* he declared, "The only tyrant I accept in this world is the 'still small voice' within."[41] For Gandhi, such tyranny was a necessary element of swaraj. It came never from a political system, but only from self-discovery: "Swaraj is to be found by searching inward, not by vainly expecting others, even our fellow-workers, to secure it for us."[42]

Several components of Gandhi's theory of swaraj were noted earlier, in the introduction: the connections between swaraj and satyagraha, the relationship drawn in the theory between the personal and the political, and the emphasis placed on specific social reforms. Now and in the next chapter, the analysis turns to Gandhi's development and implementation of the theory after his return to India in 1915. The movement in South Africa was small and restricted compared to the broad canvas of the Indian nationalist movement. Gandhi's theory now confronted possibilities for political and social change on a huge scale; his ideas would now be tested and refined in a demanding crucible of practice. Some of the modifications of *Hind Swaraj* were just noted, but in India a substantial development of his thought occurred as he quickly acquired more power in the freedom movement.

Gandhi's shaping of his idea of swaraj now took form in India in three main areas. First, he emphasized individual civil liberty as inherent to swaraj as he had not done before in South Africa, arguing that freedom must be viewed first as an individual and not a collective value. "Swaraj of a people," Gandhi affirmed, "means the sum total of the Swaraj (self-rule) of individuals."[43] He stressed the necessity of individual political and social freedom. "If the individual ceases to count what is left of society? Individual freedom alone can make a man voluntarily surrender himself completely to the services of society. If it is wrested from him, he becomes an automaton and society is ruined. No society can possibly be built on a denial of individual freedom. It is contrary to the very nature of man."[44]

As Gandhi's thought matured, he placed increasing emphasis upon non-violence, and saw its observance as closely linked with the preservation of liberty. He argued that "Civil Liberty consistent with the observance of nonviolence is the first step towards swaraj."[45] Yet Gandhi would not allow even this commitment to nonviolence to jeopardize free speech and action: "even those who believe in violence . . . will have the right to preach and even practise violence after we secure *swaraj* through non-violence."[46] He summed up his belief in the elementary importance of individual liberty near the end of his life, when he said that it is better to "be free and make mistakes than to be unfree and avoid them [for] the mind of a man who is good under compulsion cannot improve, in fact it gets worse. And when compulsion is removed, all the defects well up to the surface with even greater force."[47]

Second, although Gandhi carefully specified the conventional civil liberties of the press, speech, association, and religion as fundamental to swaraj, he held that the essence of freedom must constitute more than social, political or economic liberty.

> Let there be no mistake about my conception of Swaraj. It is complete independence of alien control and complete economic independence. So, at one end you have political independence; at the other, economic. It has two other ends. One of them is moral and social, the corresponding end is dharma, i.e., religion in the highest sense of the term. It includes Hinduism, Islam, Christianity, etc., but is superior to them all. You may recognize it by the name of Truth, not the honesty of experience, but the living Truth that pervades everything and will survive all destruction and all transformation. Moral and social uplift may be recognized by the term we are used to, i.e., non-violence. Let us call this the square of *swaraj*, which will be out of shape if any of its angles is untrue. We cannot achieve this political and economic freedom without truth and non-violence, in concrete terms without a living faith in God, and hence moral and social elevation.[48]

These were the four points on Gandhi's compass of swaraj: truth, non-violence, political and economic freedom; swaraj remained incomplete without the realization of each since each was interwoven with all.

As we have seen, Gandhi's conception of swaraj made a key distinction between "inner" and "outer" forms of freedom; this distinction involved a relegation of political freedom and national independence to a subsidiary position. But as the struggle for political independence quickened it became increasingly difficult for India's leaders to appreciate the advantages of "inner" freedom. Gandhi consistently emphasized the supreme value of a supra-political form of freedom but few other Indian political leaders shared his views on this issue. His difficulties are well expressed in this "Message to the Ceylon National Congress," delivered in 1927:

> It is, I know, a pleasurable pastime (and I have indulged in it sufficiently as you know), to strive against the powers that be, and to wrestle with the Government of the day, especially when that government happens to be a foreign government and a government under which we rightly feel we have not that scope which we should have, and which we desire, for expansion and fullest self-expression. But I have also come to the conclusion that self-expression and self-government are not things which may be either taken from us by anybody or which can be given us by anybody. It is quite true that if those who happen to hold our destinies, or seem to hold our destinies in their hands, are favorably disposed, are sympathetic, understand our aspirations, no doubt it is then easier for us to expand. But after all self-government depends entirely upon our own internal strength, upon our ability to fight against the heaviest odds. Indeed, self-government which does not require that continuous striving to attain it and to sustain it is not worth the name. I have therefore endeavored to show both in word and in deed, that political self-government, that is self-government for a large number of men and women, is no better than individual self-government, and therefore it is to be attained by precisely the same means that are required for individual self-government or self-rule, and so as you know also, I have striven in India to place this ideal before the people in season and out of season, very often much to the disgust of those who are merely politically minded.[49]

Gandhi argued, until the end of his life—not only before Indian independence but also in the months after—that swaraj must remain hollow and meaningless without the acquisition of "inward freedom," and for this a course of action should be followed through which Indians might gain sovereignty over themselves as well as over their nation. The example of the Calcutta fast, to be examined in chapter 5, provides a key case in point. Three weeks after India attained independence, Gandhi fasted for Hindu-Muslim harmony in the midst of civil war. India had still not achieved swaraj.

The origins of satyagraha in Gandhi's South African experience were traced above. A closer consideration may now be made of the relationship between satyagraha and swaraj. This primarily involves an examination of the various forms which satyagraha assumes in its development from an elementary method of civil disobedience to an all-embracing approach to moral, social, and political reform. Since Gandhi believed in the inseparable relationship of swaraj to satyagraha, a development in one was always paralleled, in his thought, by a similar development in the other: as a reformer he sought to keep his goal of swaraj firmly tied to his method of satyagraha.

The basic premise underlying the relationship between these two concepts is set forth in *Hind Swaraj*. There swaraj is defined as self-rule and satyagraha represents the way that individuals, through voluntary self-sacrifice, may gain control over themselves. The special function of satyagraha, when extended to the political realm, is to strengthen individuals' "soul-force" as they offer civil disobedience against the government. Satyagraha, remarks the Editor in *Hind Swaraj*,

is a method of securing rights by personal suffering; it is the reverse of resistance by arms. When I refuse to do a thing that is repugnant to my conscience, I use soul-force. For instance, the Government of the day has passed a law which is applicable to me. I do not like it. If by using violence I force the Government to repeal the law, I am employing what may be termed body-force. If I do not obey the law and accept the penalty for its breach, I use soul-force. It involves sacrifice of self.[50]

When one's spiritual power, or soul-force, becomes fully developed through self-sacrifice, one has mastered the technique and has attained swaraj. "Control over the mind is alone necessary [for the *satyagrahi*] and when that is attained, man is free."[51] The belief in achieving self-realization through voluntary self-sacrifice and suffering is embedded in the Indian tradition. Gandhi's innovation emerged with his relation of this ancient belief to the modern Indian call for social and political change. The government came to serve as the object on which the *satyagrahi* sharpened his horns of self-discipline. The aim of self-realization became inseparably linked with the political demand of independence. And, finally, because "there is just the same inviolable connection between the means and the end as there is between the seed and the tree,"[52] the only way to swaraj is through the power of satyagraha.[53] The fundamental correspondence between the goal of swaraj and the method of satyagraha was thus drawn before Gandhi left South Africa and rested upon the premises set forth in *Hind Swaraj*.

Return to India: First Test of Ideas

The development in Gandhi's thinking of the concepts of satyagraha and swaraj after his arrival in Bombay in January 1915 may be examined by a comparison of two of his writings. One of these was written in July 1914, immediately before his departure from South Africa; the other was delivered as a Presidential Address before the First Gujarat Political Conference in November 1917. The earlier writing was published in Gandhi's South African paper *Indian Opinion*, under the title "Theory and Practice of Passive Resistance." The discussion of satyagraha in this article remains substantially unchanged from that presented five years earlier in *Hind Swaraj*. Gandhi still uses the phrase "passive resistance" instead of satyagraha, even though he had coined the latter term seven years earlier. This suggests that at this point he continued to conceive of satyagraha in the limited sense of civil disobedience. He speaks of the method, in this writing, as "based upon the immutable maxim that government of the people is possible only so long as they consent either consciously or unconsciously to be governed."[54] Examples follow of the technique's efficacy in South Africa and all are instances of civil disobedience against the government.

A strikingly different note appears in the Gujarat Address and this difference may be attributed to the problems that confronted Gandhi after his return to India. He had known of these problems in South Africa but he does not seem to have worked out a method of approach there or fully anticipated their seriousness in India. Gandhi chose to abstain for one year after his arrival from the expression of political views and from all political activity. He wanted to learn of India's political and social problems and consider means of reform. When the period of abstinence ended he seems to have formed conclusions that guided his immediate efforts. The great single goal remained the achievement of swaraj. As before, it was seen in the Gujarat Address as a task that must begin with the acquisition of self-rule by the individual. "The first step to *swaraj* lies in the individual. The great truth, 'As with the individual so with the universe,' is applicable here as elsewhere. If we are ever torn by conflict from within, if we are ever going astray, and if instead of ruling our passions we allow them to rule us, swaraj can have no meaning for us. Government of self, then, is the first step."[55]

From this point, however, the meaning of swaraj expands. It embraces the moral and social aims that eventually form the basis of Gandhi's "Constructive Program," or agenda of social reforms. These were the aims that swaraj must encompass through the use of satyagraha: the abolition of un-touchability, improved health and hygiene in the cities and villages, tem-perance reform, Hindu-Muslim unity, *Swadeshi* (use of India-made prod-ucts), advancement of women, and establishment of closer contact between the educated elite and the villagers.[56] Many of these issues had been cham-pioned before by social reformers. Gandhi's contribution was, as a national political leader, to insist that these reforms were integral components of swaraj itself. No argument was to become more central than this to Gan-dhi's idea of freedom, and he now set it forth in the Gujarat Address:

> We may petition the government, we may agitate in the Imperial Council for our rights; but for a real awakening of the people, the more important thing is activities directed inwards. . . .
>
> One sometimes hears it said: "Let us get the government of India in our own hands; everything will be all right afterwards." There could be no greater superstition than this. No nation has gained its independence in this matter. The splendor of the spring is reflected in every tree, the whole earth is then filled with the freshness of youth. Similarly, when the spring of Swaraj is on us, a stranger suddenly arriving in our midst will observe the freshness of youth in every walk of life and will find servants of the people engaged, each according to his own abilities, in all manner of public activities.[57]

One instance of the "internal activity" to which Gandhi refers had oc-curred in Champaran. Gandhi had gone there, to the northwestern corner of Bihar, in April 1917, at the request of indigo sharecroppers to investigate their grievances with the planters. He began his inquiry but the local gov-ernment intervened and ordered him to leave Champaran immediately. He elected to offer civil disobedience. The Lieutenant-Governor of the prov-ince yielded by dismissing the case against him. Gandhi proceeded with his investigation and compiled a long indictment of the planters. A commission was eventually formed of planters and government officials; Gandhi repre-sented the peasants. The result was a successful settlement that moved Gandhi toward a position of national leadership.[58]

From the time of Gandhi's arrival in Champaran, however, he concerned himself with more than the legal aspects of the problem. The poverty of the area was immense and he soon launched his social reform program. Swaraj itself, he remarked on his arrival, depended upon the uplift of these vil-lagers.[59] A series of schools was constructed, village industries established, sanitation and personal hygiene programs begun, medical relief offered, and volunteers organized for the construction of wells and roads. Later he wrote with some regret of his efforts in Champaran, "It was my desire to continue the constructive work for some years, to establish more schools and to penetrate the villages more effectively."[60] This hope was not to be fulfilled. But Champaran had taught Gandhi valuable lessons: here, the manifold nature of satyagraha opened to him and he came to know the essential connection between social reform and the political aims of the nation. So he could conclude in his *Autobiography*: "The Champaran struggle was a proof of the fact that disinterested service of the people in any sphere ultimately helps the country politically."[61]

Gandhi came to the Gujarat Conference, then, fresh from his Champaran success and it is not surprising that his Presidential Address concludes with a development of his concept of satyagraha, as well as an expression of confidence in its powerful potential. He advocates satyagraha for the resolution of India's major social and religious problems as well as for political reform:

> On reflection we find that we can employ satyagraha even for social reform. We can rid ourselves of the many defects of our caste system. We can resolve Hindu-Muslim differences, and we can solve political problems. It is all right that, for the sake of convenience we speak of these things as separate subjects. But it should never be forgotten that they are all closely interrelated.
>
> This satyagraha is India's distinctive weapon. It has had others but satyagraha has been in greater use. It is an unfailing source of strength, and is capable of being used at all times and under all circumstances. It requires no stamp of approval from Congress. He who knows its power cannot but use it. Even as the eye-lashes automatically protect the eyes, so does satyagraha, when kindled, automatically protect the freedom of the soul.[62]

The significance of the 1917 Gujarat Address lies in the development which it signals of Gandhi's earlier ideas: a series of advances made in response to the political and social problems he encountered after his arrival in India. With this address, social reform found a permanent place alongside noncooperation. The fulfillment of swaraj is seen to rely upon "internal activity" or social reform. Satyagraha is recognized as a prime source of power for pursuing a wide range of reforms, the sovereign corrective of India's social as well as political ills. Henceforth the term "passive resistance," with its non-Indian and nonreligious associations, disappears because satyagraha has outgrown it. The theme of "swaraj through satyagraha" now dominates Gandhi's political thought, growing in theory as well as in religious symbolism. These ideas merge together into an inseparable relationship.

In *Hind Swaraj*, Gandhi had stressed the essential relationship of the means to the end. Twenty years later, asked to define his national goal, he placed even greater emphasis upon a method of right action: "After all, the real definition [of swaraj] will be determined by our action, the means we adopt to achieve the goal. If we would but concentrate upon the means, swaraj will take care of itself."[63]

By the time these thoughts were recorded in 1927, Gandhi had learned some hard lessons through his experiments with means. The next twenty years were to prove no easier, but only to test with increasing rigor this satyagrahi in search of swaraj.

CHAPTER TWO

Gandhi as Leader:
Nonviolence in Power

The task before nationalists is clear.
They have to win over by their
genuine love all minorities including
Englishmen. Indian nationalism, if it is
to remain non-violent, cannot be
exclusive.

                    —*Gandhi, 1921*[1]

By 1920, Gandhi's confidence in his method and mission had reached a high peak and on September 4, at a Special Session of the Indian Congress in Calcutta, he presented for adoption his idea of satyagraha against the Government. This method, set forth in the "Resolution on Non-co-operation," signified far more than just another Congress attempt at redress of grievances. It meant open rebellion.[2] As he said in moving the resolution, the step marked "a definite change in the policy which the country has hitherto adopted for the vindication of the rights that belong to it, and its honor."[3] The resolution was approved, and with it not only was a radical shift in national policy sanctioned but also a new leadership was created. Gandhi directed the satyagraha: it embodied, he told the Congress, "the results of my many years' of practical experience in non-co-operation."[4]

Mobilization of the Movement

Gandhi's consolidation of power at this point deserves study from the perspective of political movements. The twentieth century has given birth to mass political movements around the world. Whether Lenin's Bolshevik movement, Mao's Communist movement, Hitler's Nazi movement or Gandhi's nationalist movement, these political phenomena have all been characterized by at least three major forces: charismatic leadership, mass organization, and an ideological mode of thought that demands expression of ideas in action.[5] The success of each has depended upon how effectively these three elements have been combined. In Gandhi's case, the practical nature of the ideology of nonviolent noncooperation was stressed as the movement surged in 1920. India, Gandhi declared,

> must follow her own way of discipline and self-sacrifice through non-cooperation. It is as amazing as it is humiliating that less than one hundred thousand white men should be able to rule three hundred and fifteen million Indians. They do so somewhat undoubtedly by force but more by securing our cooperation in a thousand ways and making us more and more helpless and dependent on them as time goes forward. Let us not mistake reformed councils, mere law-courts and even governorships for real freedom or power. They are but subtler methods of emasculation. The British cannot rule us by mere force. And so they resort to all means, honorable and dishonorable, in order to retain their hold on India. They want India's billions and they want India's manpower for their imperialistic greed. If we refuse to supply them with men and money, we achieve our goal, namely, *swaraj*.[6]

Gandhi succeeded in a remarkably short period, from 1919 to 1922, in forging a mass movement "for real freedom or power" that was entirely unprecedented in India. This may be attributed to the way that he fulfilled the movement's needs of organization, leadership, and ideology. His most dramatic political achievement at this time was the transformation of the Indian National Congress into a political organization with a mass base. "I do not rely merely on the lawyer class," Gandhi said, "or highly educated men to carry out all the stages of non-co-operation. My hope is more with the masses. My faith in the people is boundless. Theirs is an amazingly responsive nature. Let not the leaders distrust them."[7]

And Gandhi knew that his faith was well founded. The one man who, before Gandhi, had combined mass appeal with power within the Congress had suddenly slipped from the scene. A month before the Special Calcutta Session Bal Gangadhar Tilak, formidable leader of the Extremist faction, died. This left the field open to Gandhi, and he quickly gained a hold on both the Congress and the masses that Tilak never approached. By 1921 there was, according to one study, "a spectacular growth of the Congress organization"; its recorded membership "increased enormously." Gandhi's extraordinary ability as a fund-raiser "made it possible to expand Congress activity on a scale hitherto inconceivable," and social reform programs flourished.[8] As Judith Brown has observed in her analysis of the organization of the country at this time, "Gandhi saw non-cooperation as a way of involving the whole spectrum of Indian society in a political movement." This worked through three distinct levels or "tiers of followers": the Western-educated elite; the "power brokers" or middle-level political operators in law, business, and agriculture; and, finally, the "dumb millions" (as Gandhi called them) or the silent majority of people without property.[9]

Gandhi's influence on this last group, particularly the vast poor peasantry, was substantial. A close analysis by Shahid Amin of how the peasants of Gorakhpur District viewed Gandhi reveals how quickly he was transformed into the Mahatma. By 1921 his message of swaraj as a personal as well as social and political revolution had dug deeply into the popular consciousness. Self-purification along with social reform merged into the "Constructive Program" that Congress promoted through its pervasive organization. Swaraj was interpreted as demanding changes in personal behavior that extended to family planning and diet. In Gorakhpur District, for example, an entire village altered its eating habits by giving up meat and fish as a step toward swaraj. Not only from the poor peasants, but also from all castes and classes in this region, the popular responses to Gandhi "were truly phenomenal."[10] The unprecedented quality of the Congress organization was matched by the consolidation of Gandhi's charismatic leadership. Some of the peasantry imagined the Mahatma having fantastic powers to defeat the Raj and envisaged swaraj as an imminent "millennium," the dawning of an age of absolute justice and social equality.[11]

At least part of this charisma came from Gandhi's skill as a communicator and especially his ability to use symbols and images in a language for and of the Indian people. Like a poet, Gandhi treated his past with affection, drawing from the Indian classics old words—*ahimsa, karmayoga, Ram Raj, tapasya, moksha*—and charging them with fresh meaning, until they became symbols of both past and future. Gandhi drew from Hinduism the core ideas that gave his thought continuity and coherence, yet he repeatedly reexamined that tradition for purposes of social reform. He sought to change through reinterpretation some of the main articles of faith in Hinduism. No Hindu text provided him more grist for this effort than his favorite source of sacred wisdom, the *Bhagavad Gita*. In a comment on the *Gita* that is characteristic of Gandhi's purpose as a reformer, he wrote:

> What, however, I have done is to put a new but natural and logical interpretation upon the whole teaching of the Gita and the spirit of Hinduism. Hinduism, not to speak of other religions, is ever evolving. It has no one scripture like the Quran or the Bible. Its scriptures are also evolving and suffering addition. The *Gita* itself is an instance in point. It has given a new meaning to *karma, sannyasa, yajna,* etc. It has breathed new life into Hinduism.[12]
>
> The *Gita* is not an aphoristic work; it is a great religious poem. The deeper you dive into it, the richer the meanings you get. It being meant for the people at large, there is pleasing repetition. With every age the important words will carry new and expanding meanings. But its central teaching will never vary. The seeker is at liberty to extract from this treasure any meaning he likes so as to enable him to enforce in his life the central teaching.[13]

"The seeker is at liberty to extract from this treasure any meaning he likes . . . " These words underline the whole nature of his approach. He went to his tradition with a purpose, to uncover ideas that would meet the demands of a modern India. He was engaged in a consciously selective effort; and no one was more aware than he of the extent of this selectivity. None of Gandhi's terms were infused with richer traditional Indian symbolism than the two key concepts of his thought, swaraj and satyagraha, and no one remained more sensitive to their meaning. When the members of Congress proposed, for purposes of greater clarity, to substitute the word "independence" for "swaraj" in future resolutions, Gandhi countered:

> I defy any one to give for independence a common Indian word intelligible to the masses. Our goal at any rate may be known by an indigenous word understood by the three hundred millions. And we have such a word in Swaraj first used in the name of the Nation by Dadabhai Naoroji. It is infinitely greater than and includes independence. It is a vital word. It has been sanctified by the noble sacrifices of thousands of Indians. It is a word which, if it has not penetrated the remotest corner of India, has at

least got the largest currency of any similar word. It is a sacrilege to displace that word by a foreign importation of doubtful value.[14]

As explained in the introduction, Gandhi liked the word swaraj because it had traditional Indian roots, and he seldom missed an opportunity to evoke the religious symbolism explicit in the ideas of both swaraj and satyagraha. "To the orthodox Hindus I need not point out the sovereign efficacy of *tapasya* [self-suffering]. And satyagraha is nothing but *tapasya* for Truth." And of swaraj he remarked, "Government over self is the truest Swaraj, it is synonymous with *moksha* or salvation."[15]

It seems paradoxical that while none of Gandhi's ideas were more liberally endowed with traditional symbolism than swaraj and satyagraha, none were more thoroughly misunderstood, both by his party and his people. The Congress followed him, on the whole, for his political experience and insights; the masses revered him as a Mahatma. Gandhi wanted understanding and appreciation of his thought rather than the reverence either of a saint or a politician. Yet, he must bear some of the responsibility for losing his followers along the way. The sheer vagueness and contradictions recurrent throughout his writing made it easier to accept him as a saint than to fathom the challenge posed by his demanding beliefs. Gandhi saw no harm in self-contradiction: life was a series of experiments, and any principle might change if Truth so dictated. Truth, moreover, had a habit of positing extraordinarily high moral standards. For those who had neither conducted the experiments nor acquired an unshakable faith in the premises behind them, Gandhi's ideas posed formidable demands.

One might worship Gandhi from afar as a Mahatma or—as the alternative that most Congressmen took—accept his judgments as "policy" but not as a "creed." Neither path was that of the *satyagrahi*, nor could either lead to what Gandhi called swaraj. Indeed, each undermined Gandhi's thought and message for neither could give him support when the going became rough. At the very end, when it was indeed the roughest, Gandhi stood, tragically, alone. He then fully realized his failure to persuade both the Congress leadership and the Indian people of the central meaning of his philosophy. "Intoxicated by my success in South Africa," he admitted in 1947, "I came to India. Here too the struggle bore fruit. But I have now realized that it was not based on nonviolence of the brave. If I had known so then, I would not have launched the struggle."[16] It is remarkable that an individual of Gandhi's insight did not appreciate this sooner. Indications of critical differences between his beliefs and those of Congress Extremists like B. G. Tilak and Aurobindo Ghose appear very early during his public career in India. Chief among these differences was that which concerned method; evidence of this occurs in Gandhi's controversy with Tilak a few months before the latter's death.

To Define Satyagraha: Gandhi's Differences with Tilak and Ghose

In 1920, when Gandhi outlined his program of total noncooperation with the Government, several key Congress leaders, especially B. G. Tilak, objected strongly to a boycott of the Government councils. He argued that Indian nationalists should seek entry to these councils, and then "wreck them from within." Gandhi, however, contended that it would be untruthful and therefore morally wrong to enter the councils under false pretenses. Such a deceptive move, even if politically advantageous, could only have undesirable consequences from an ethical point of view. This particular dispute reflected a broader area of disagreement on the questions of the relation of means to ends and of morality to politics. The crux of this difference came to light in the columns of Gandhi's *Young India*, in a revealing exchange of views with Tilak.

Gandhi began the discussion with a brief criticism of Tilak's view of politics: "L. [Lokamanya or "Revered of the People"] Tilak represents a definite school of thought of which he makes no secret. He considers that everything is fair in politics. We have joined issue with him in that conception of political life. . . . We believe that nothing but the strictest adherence to honesty, fair play and charity can advance the true interests of the country."[17]

Tilak immediately took issue with the remark and in a letter to *Young India* replied:

> I am sorry to see that in your article on "Reforms Resolution" in the last issue, you have represented me as holding that I considered "everything fair in politics." I write this to you to say that my view is not correctly represented therein. Politics is a game of worldly people, and not of sadhus [saints], and instead of the maxim अक्रोधेन जिने क्रोधं ["Overcome anger by loving kindness, evil by good."][18] as preached by Buddha, I prefer to rely on the maxim of Shri Krishna ये यथा मां प्रपद्यन्ते तांस्तथैव भजाम्यहम् ["In whatsoever way any come to Me, in that same way I grant them favour."][19] That

explains the whole difference and also the meaning of my phrase "responsive co-operation." Both methods are equally honest and righteous but the one is more suited to this world than the other.[20]

Gandhi answered:

I naturally feel the greatest diffidence about joining issue with the Lokamanya in matters involving questions of interpretation of religious works. But there are things in or about which instinct transcends even interpretation. For me there is no conflict between the two texts quoted by the Lokamanya. The Buddhist text lays down an eternal principle. The text from the Bhagvad Gita shows to me how the principle of conquering hate by love, untruth by truth, can and must be applied. If it be true that God metes out the same measure to us that we mete out to others, it follows that if we would escape condign punishment, we may not return anger for anger but gentleness even against anger. And this is the law not for the unworldly but essentially for the worldly. With deference to the Lokamanya, I venture to say that it betrays mental laziness to think that the world is not for sadhus. The epitome of all religions is to promote purushartha, and purushartha is nothing but a desperate attempt to become sadhu, i.e., to become a gentleman in every sense of the term.

Finally, when I wrote the sentence about 'everything being fair in politics' according to the Lokamanya's creed, I had in mind his oft-repeated quotation: शठ प्रति शाठ्यम् ["evil unto evil"][21] To me it enunciates bad law . . . . In any case, I pit the experience of a third of a century against the doctrine underlying शठ प्रति शाठ्यम् The true law is: शठं प्रत्यपि सत्यम् ["truth even unto evil"][22]

Tilak and Gandhi shared several aims and attributes in common and no one was quicker to observe these similarities than Gandhi himself. Nor was Gandhi sparing in his praise of Tilak's contribution to the independence movement. Yet the difference between them remained fundamental and Gandhi concluded their controversy with the laconic remark: "I am conscious that my method is not Mr. Tilak's method."[23] This contrast in method arising from a different way of looking at the relation of morality to politics corresponded with a different understanding of the meaning of swaraj. Tilak demanded home rule for India similar to that of Britain's other colonies within the Empire and used the term swaraj to exploit its traditional overtones. But as a concept it meant no more than political independence.

To many Congressmen, Tilak's definition of swaraj seemed clear and attainable. When Gandhi assumed leadership, however, it could no longer be understood in these simple terms. Nehru observed that in 1920, when Gandhi spoke of swaraj, he was "delightfully vague on the subject."[24] Other Congressmen, though, were not so delighted with Gandhi's vagueness and they continued to regard swaraj as nothing more than the replacement of British Raj by Congress Raj. Gandhi contributed to this misunderstanding of his position. In 1920, when he assumed leadership of the Congress, he promised "swaraj in one year." This proclamation was understandably met with a wild burst of enthusiasm among those ardent for independence. Early the following year, Gandhi tried to cool these expectations by insisting on "conditions of swaraj" or sweeping social reforms that would have to occur before Indians could expect to win "real freedom."[25]

Closely allied to Gandhi's differences with Tilak over the meaning of swaraj were his differences with Aurobindo Ghose over the meaning of satyagraha. By 1920, Gandhi's conceptualization of satyagraha had advanced significantly from his early formulation of the idea in South Africa. He increasingly characterized the idea as a form of power. In its most literal sense, it denotes "holding firmly to the truth," but Gandhi emphasized that power flows from "adherence to the truth," and so defined satyagraha as "truth-force" or "love-force." This form of power is capable not just of neutralizing violence but of transforming a situation, liberating reserves of energy in ways that acts of love or compassion often do. Gandhi assumed that the means of nonviolence are superior, both in a moral and practical sense, to the means of violence because there is a force contained in emotions of love and compassion that can be stronger, more effective, than those in hatred or in the desire to inflict harm. Often the former are not fully realized because they are not felt in thought as well as in deed. Gandhi sought to explain the full force of satyagraha when he wrote:

> The word *satyagraha* is often most loosely used and is made to cover veiled violence. But as the author of the word I may be allowed to say that it excludes every form of violence, direct or indirect, veiled or unveiled, and whether in thought, word, or deed. It is a breach of *satyagraha* to wish ill to an opponent or to say a harsh word to him or of him with the intention of doing harm. And often the evil thought or the evil word may, in terms of *satyagraha*, be more dangerous than actual violence used in the heat of the moment. *Satyagraha* is gentle, it never wounds. It must not be the result of anger or malice. . . . It was conceived as a complete substitute for violence.[26]

Gandhi sought to distinguish satyagraha from other terms like "passive resistance," "civil disobedience," and "non-cooperation." The latter two terms are components of satyagraha but passive resistance is not. As noted in the Introduction, passive resistance, like violent action, is diametrically opposed to satyagraha because passive resistance allows the resister to harbor feelings of hatred, anger,or fear toward the opponent. As such, Gandhi associated passive resistance with internal violence, or what he called *duragraha* (holding on to one's selfish, narrow interest rather than to truth and the common interest). Thus, passive resistance or *duragraha* unleashes forces of prejudice and exclusiveness, rather than attitudes of compassion and inclusiveness. Gandhi was sensitive to the common confusion between satyagraha and passive resistance. He distinguished them at length:

> Satyagraha, then, is literally holding on to Truth and it means, therefore, Truth-force. Truth is soul or spirit. It is, therefore, known as soul-force. It excludes the use of violence because man is not capable of knowing the absolute truth and, therefore, not competent to punish. The word was coined in South Africa to distinguish the nonviolent resistance of the Indians of South Africa from the contemporary "passive resistance" of the suffragettes and others. It is not conceived as a weapon of the weak.
>
> Passive resistance is used in the orthodox English sense and covers the suffragette movement as well as the resistance of the nonconformists. Passive resistance has been conceived and is regarded as a weapon of the weak. Whilst it avoids violence, being not open to the weak, it does not exclude its use if, in the opinion of a passive resister, the occasion demands it.[27]
>
> For the past thirty years I have been preaching and practicing *Satyagraha*. The principles of Satyagraha, as I know it today, constitute a gradual evolution. *Satyagraha* differs from Passive Resistance as the North Pole from the South. The latter has been conceived as a weapon of the weak and does not exclude the use of physical force or violence for the purpose of gaining one's end, whereas the former has been conceived as a weapon of the strongest and excludes the use of violence in any shape or form. . . . In the application of *Satyagraha* I discovered in the earliest stages that pursuit of truth did not admit of violence being inflicted on one's opponent but that he must be weaned from error by patience and sympathy. For what appears to be truth to the one may appear to be error to the other. And patience means self-suffering. So the doctrine came to mean vindication of truth not by infliction of suffering on the opponent but on one's self.[28]

Gandhi's clear attempt here to distinguish satyagraha from passive resistance signals his effort to distance himself not only from Tilak but also from

Aurobindo Ghose. As early as 1907, two years before Gandhi wrote *Hind Swaraj*, Ghose, a leading theorist of the Congress Extremist faction, developed an original ideology for his group that influenced subsequent thinking about the Indian nationalist movement. Ghose called his theory "the doctrine of passive resistance." He borrowed from the Irish Sinn Fein movement the word "boycott," and applied it to India, arguing that British rule "can be rendered impossible by successfully organized refusal of assistance."[29] This boycott of the British was urged in sweeping terms: not only of all British goods and services but also of the courts and administration, and especially tax resistance.[30] Ghose acknowledged the influence of the American colonists, but contended that passive resistance goes beyond "no representation, no taxation," to demand "no control, no assistance."[31] It insisted not only on the absolute duty of breaking unjust laws but also on "social excommunication" or ostracism of all Indians who obeyed the government.[32]

In his call for ostracism of Indian loyalists, Ghose marked a significant difference in his doctrine of passive resistance from Gandhi's theory of satyagraha. Ghose stated further the limits of passive resistance in a manner that conclusively separated his concept from Gandhi's:

> There is a limit however to passive resistance. So long as the action of the executive is peaceful and within the rule of the fight, the passive resister scrupulously maintains his attitude of passivity, but he is not bound to do so a moment beyond. To submit to illegal or violent methods of coercion, to accept outrage and hooliganism as part of the legal procedure of the country is to be guilty of cowardice, and, by dwarfing national manhood, to sin against the divinity within ourselves and the divinity in our motherland. The moment coercion of this kind is attempted, passive resistance ceases and active [violent] resistance becomes a duty. If the instruments of the executive choose to disperse our meeting by breaking the heads of those present, the right of self-defence entitles us not merely to defend our heads but to retaliate on those of the head-breakers. . . . The new politics, therefore, while it favors passive resistance, does not include meek submission to illegal outrage under the term; it has no intention of overstressing the passivity at the expense of the resistance. . . .
>
> The new politics is a serious doctrine and not, like the old, a thing of shows and political theatricals; it demands real sufferings from its adherents, imprisonment, worldly ruin, death itself, before it can allow him to assume the rank of a martyr for his country. Passive resistance cannot build up a strong and great nation unless it is masculine, bold and ardent

in its spirit and ready at any moment and at the slightest notice to supplement itself with active resistance. We do not want to develop a nation of women who know only how to suffer and not how to strike.

Moreover, the new politics must recognize the fact that beyond a certain point passive resistance puts a strain on human endurance which our natures cannot endure. This may come in particular instances where an outrage is too great or the stress of tyranny too unendurable for anyone to stand purely on the defensive; to hit back, to assail and crush the assailant, to vindicate one's manhood becomes an imperious necessity to outraged humanity. Or it may come in the mass when the strain of oppression a whole nation has to meet in its unarmed struggle for liberty, overpasses its powers of endurance. It then becomes the sole choice either to break under the strain and go under or to throw it off with violence.[33]

There is no evidence that Gandhi had read Aurobindo Ghose's writing on passive resistance when he wrote *Hind Swaraj* seven months later. However, some of Ghose's arguments were surely known by the Indian extremists in London with whom Gandhi debated issues of the nationalist movement during the summer of 1909. The key argument that he developed emphasized the *active power* of nonviolence as against Ghose's characterization of nonviolence as weak when faced with the force of violence.

Satyagraha vs. Duragraha: Power and Its Abuses

The idea of nonviolence as superior moral power is the key point that Gandhi sought to demonstrate in theory and practice after 1909, in South Africa and then in India. He countered Ghose's assertion that "we do not want to develop a nation of women" in gender terms, arguing that it was precisely the "feminine" nature of nonviolence that proved superior to the "brute force" associated with the "male aggression" of the British Raj.[34] He identified Ghose's idea of passive resistance with *duragraha* and argued an essential difference between *duragraha* and satyagraha. In 1917, two years before the first non-cooperation campaign began, Gandhi set the theoretical foundations for the coming movement in these terms:

There are two methods of attaining one's goal. *Satyagraha* and *duragraha*. In our scriptures they have been described, respectively, as divine and devilish modes of action. In *satyagraha*, there is always unflinching adherence to truth. It is never to be forsaken on any account. Even for the sake of one's country, it does not permit resort to falsehood. It proceeds

40

on the assumption of the ultimate triumph of truth. A *satyagrahi* does not abandon his path, even though at times it seems impenetrable and beset with difficulties and dangers, . . . Even an inveterate enemy he conquers by the force of the soul, which is love. We can cultivate such an attitude even towards the Government and, doing so, we shall be able to appreciate their beneficial activities and, as for their errors, rather than feel bitter on their account, point them out in love and so get them rectified. Love does not act through fear. Weakness there certainly cannot be. A coward is incapable of bearing love, it is the prerogative of the brave. Looking at everything with love, we shall not regard the Government with suspicion, nor believe that all their actions are inspired with bad motives. And our examination of their actions, being directed by love, will be unerring and is bound, therefore, to carry conviction with them. Love can fight; often, it is obliged to. In the intoxication of power, man fails to see his error. When that happens, a *satyagrahi* does not sit still. He suffers. He disobeys the ruler's orders and his laws in a civil manner, and willingly submits to the penalties of such disobedience, for instance, imprisonment and gallows. Thus is the soul disciplined.

In the event, no bitterness develops between the *satyagrahi* and those in power; the latter, on the contrary, willingly yield to him. They discover that they cannot command the *satyagrahi's* obedience. They cannot make him do anything against his will. And this is the consummation of *swaraj,* because it means complete independence. It need not be assumed that such resistance is possible only against civilized rulers. Even a heart of flint will melt in the fire kindled by the power of the soul. But *duragraha* is a force with the opposite attributes. . . .

Swaraj is useless at the sacrifice of truth. Such *swaraj* will ultimately ruin the people. The man who follows the path of *duragraha* becomes impatient and wants to kill the so-called enemy. There can be but one result of this. Hatred increases. The defeated party vows vengeance and simply bides its time. The spirit of revenge thus descends from father to son. It is much to be wished that India never gives predominance to this spirit of *duragraha.* . . . The *duragrahi*, like the oilman's ox, moves in a circle. His movement is only motion but it is not progress. The *satyagrahi* is ever moving forward. The *satyagrahi* and the *duragrahi* are both warriors. The latter, bereft of his arms, acknowledges defeat, the former never. He does not depend upon the perishable body and its weapons, but he fights on with the strength of the unconquerable and immortal *atma*.[35]

This, then, is the major flaw in *duragraha* or passive resistance: lacking concern for either truth or compassion, seeking its goal by any means necessary. It may for tactical reasons refrain from physical violence but it permits the sin of hubris: violence of the spirit—anger, contempt, malice, or arrogance. Unlike satyagraha it has no creedal commitment to *ahimsa* or a belief in the integral relationship between means and ends. Gandhi gave further development in 1925 to these principles in his book, *Satyagraha in South Africa*. There he recalled his reasons for conceiving the term satyagraha as distinct from passive resistance and argued at length the "great and fundamental difference between the two." He contended that satyagraha possesses a "strength" that passive resistance cannot approach because "there is no scope for love" in the latter: " . . . not only has hatred no place in satyagraha, but it is a positive breach of its ruling principle." While passive resistance may use harassment, or feel enmity, "in satyagraha there is not the remotest idea of injuring the opponent. Satyagraha postulates the conquest of the adversary by suffering in one's own person."[36]

After 1925 and until his death in 1948, Gandhi persistently returned to the basic differences between satyagraha and passive resistance. He did this not only to define more closely his concept of satyagraha but also because he feared that both the Indian National Congress and the Indian people had often misunderstood satyagraha. In July 1947, six months before his death, Gandhi addressed at length "the fundamental difference" between the Congress and himself:

> And what are the differences that matter? If you analyze them you would find only one fundamental difference to which all the others could be traced. Nonviolence is my creed. It never was of the Congress. With the Congress it has always been a policy. A policy takes the shape of a creed whilst it lasts, no longer. The Congress had every right to change it when it found it necessary. A creed can never admit of any change. . . . Let me make one thing clear. I have frankly and fully admitted that what we practiced during the past thirty years was not nonviolent resistance but passive resistance which only the weak offer because they are unable, not unwilling, to offer armed resistance.[37]

In sum, then, Gandhi believed that satyagraha was distinguished by a creedal commitment to nonviolence as opposed to an attitude of passive resistance or *duragraha* that advocated the use of nonviolent tactics because of an apparent pragmatic advantage. Gandhi came to believe toward the end of his life that India's civil war was a result of her failure to accept nonviolence as a creed rather than as a mere policy. He held Congress leaders responsible because they often lacked a creedal commitment to nonviolence. He warned that unless the Indian community scrupulously observed the integral relationship between means and ends, satyagraha "would be corrupted into *duragraha.*"[38]

In the last months of his life, after India had achieved independence, Gandhi worried about this corruption of satyagraha and how the coming of independence had seemed to introduce a "virulent poison" into India's political affairs. This poison induced her leaders to be concerned only with the "question of seizing power" whereby "every opportunity for attaining their object was seized by those who did not stop to consider that means and ends were convertible terms." "Whatever is done with a selfish motive cannot be called *satyagraha.*"[39]

The theory and practice of satyagraha as advanced by Gandhi represents a radically different process from *duragraha.* The former is not based on a zero-sum calculation of how much loss can be inflicted on the opponent. There is instead a scrupulous concern for the humanity of the adversary and its chief purpose is to elevate the conflict to a point where resolution will elicit the best from all parties and not reduce anyone to disgrace or humiliation. In an analysis of the difference between satyagraha and *duragraha,* Joan Bondurant writes: "*Duragraha* in its most common forms amounts to the intensification of pressure or the shifting of points of attack until a settlement is reached through capitulation or compromise . . . . *Duragraha* seeks concessions; *Satyagraha* sets out to develop alternatives which will satisfy antagonists on all sides."[40]

Bondurant emphasizes a key feature of satyagraha as against *duragraha* which distinguishes it: the attempt of the *satyagrahi* to develop a mutual psychologically supportive interaction through which real conflict resolution might be achieved. Bondurant observes: "Over against the harassment and distress commonly effected in *Duragraha* is set the fundamentally supportive nature of *Satyagraha.* As the *Satyagrahi* moves to bring about change in the situation through persuading his opponent to modify or alter the position under attack, he seeks to strengthen interpersonal relationships and interpersonal satisfactions through acts of support and service to the opponent."[41]

The theory of satyagraha, therefore, rests fundamentally on a certain view about "the capacity of man to change" by effecting a "context of reassurance" rather than of hostility, of mutual support rather than of alienation and anger. The ultimate goal is not to attain a decisive triumph, but "to achieve the transformation of relationships" that will genuinely resolve the conflict rather than simply postpone it to a later time.[42]

While the methods of both *duragraha* and satyagraha aim at the reconciliation of differences, the first approaches the conflict with no particular concern for inquiring into the truth of the issues, but only with imposing a solution short of violence. Satyagraha, conversely, presents itself as a way of bringing both parties to a realization of a common truth, and believes that political issues or positions must be relegated to this primary concern for arriving at the truth. Gandhi believed that the approach used by the *satyagrahi* must not assert the possession of an absolute or final truth, but rather willingly concede that he has not yet found it, for this will leave the whole process of conflict resolution open to inquiry. "I am but a seeker after truth," Gandhi liked to say. "I claim to be making a ceaseless effort to find it. But I admit I have not yet found it. To find truth completely is to realize one's self and one's destiny, that is, to become perfect. I am painfully conscious of my imperfections."[43]

A concept foreign to the theory of *duragraha* but intrinsic in the method of satyagraha is the relationship of the personal to the political, or of the individual's self-realization to the political program of change. The emphasis in satyagraha on the importance of swaraj or individual self-awareness means that in satyagraha there must be a strengthening of the individual's self-esteem and sense of moral worth. There is an individual moral energy directed at the problem of conflict that allows the process to be humanizing rather than dehumanizing. Gandhi recognized this relationship between satyagraha and swaraj when he wrote that the power of any political advance "lies in us. If we reform ourselves, the rulers will automatically do so."[44]

The point of achieving individual self-realization as a vital component of the political method of satyagraha is related to Gandhi's vision of the ultimate source of conflict resolution. He contended that the seeming diversity of individual interests could be ultimately reconciled in terms of a higher unity or consensus. This unity was expressed in a religious ethic of spiritual oneness. Raghavan Iyer has written that "Gandhi held to the Buddhist and Jain view that all sins are modifications of *himsa*, that the basic sin, the only sin in the ultimate analysis, is the sin of separateness."[45] Satyagraha, in contrast to *duragraha,* sought to invoke the universal element of love or truth within every individual. It was an elevating and creative force that could not effectively work in the absence of a creedal, life encompassing commitment. The concluding passage of Gandhi's *Autobiography* linked religion to politics in a way that also explains the relationship between swaraj and satyagraha:

> To see the universal and all-pervading Spirit of Truth face to face one must be able to love the meanest of creation as oneself. And a man who aspires after that cannot afford to keep out of any field of life. That is why my devotion to Truth has drawn me into the field of politics; and I can say without the slightest hesitation, and yet in all humility, that those who say that religion has nothing to do with politics do not know what religion means. Identification with everything that lives is impossible without self-purification; without self-purification the observance of the law of Ahimsa must remain an empty dream.[46]

The main point here is the difference between the logic of swaraj and satyagraha, as against the notion of *duragraha* or passive resistance as Aurobindo Ghose conceived it. In both theories, the basic idea is that power resides with the people, and if they realize this elementary political fact, they might attain their desired end without violence by withdrawing their support. Satyagraha, however, begins with a major effort to raise the consciousness of each individual in a quest for swaraj that will purify the nature and use of political power. As Gandhi frequently observed, political independence for India would be an empty goal if it were not accompanied by the swaraj of each Indian. When he realized in early 1947 that Indians had not attained personal swaraj, he forecast the social and political disaster of civil war. He wrote, six months before independence: "If this weakness continues, we shall have to go through rivers of blood once the British rule goes."[47]

Unlike *duragraha,* therefore, satyagraha insists on the swaraj of the individual as an integral part of truth-force. "There is a causal connection," Gandhi wrote, "between the purity of the intention of the individual and the extent of effectiveness of nonviolent action."[48] The effectiveness of *duragraha* cannot rely on such a condition because the idea of purity of intent and the necessary relationship of means to end is absent. For satyagraha the focus is on the inward capacity of the individual to uncover the dynamics of change, the process of swaraj. In *duragraha,* it is strictly a use of political power that must, within the confines of nonviolence, attain the desired end. Gandhi's emphasis on the integral connection between *satya* and *ahimsa* in satyagraha is missing in the idea of *duragraha* as well as the pivotal role played by his means-end theory.

The central significance of *ahimsa* for Gandhi is that through an authentic commitment to nonviolence, an individual may attain the highest spiritual awareness, may "see the universal and all-pervading Spirit of Truth" leading to "identification with everything that lives," as he said in his *Autobiography*. The opposite of *ahimsa* is *himsa*, meaning violence or pain caused to another being, and so signifying a sense of separateness or lack of identification with life. *Ahimsa* in the strict sense of traditional Hinduism is "the renunciation of the will to kill," but in Gandhi's broader sense, it is the moral cement binding satyagraha to swaraj. As Iyer observes, "*Ahimsa* is not a quality to be displayed to order, but an inward growth depending for sustenance upon intense individual effort, and it can be effectively taught only by living it. It is not a mere passive quality but the mightiest force man is endowed with."[49]

Whereas passive resistance, in Aurobindo's terms, conceived of correct action only as an absence of violence, and saw nonviolence as less powerful than violence, Gandhi asserted that the power of satyagraha was superior to either *duragraha* or violence. Satyagraha could be activated only through strict adherence to *ahimsa* because the real energy of the former came from the latter. This energy became expressed in the power of conversion. Thus while Aurobindo's doctrine of passive resistance admits the necessity and even the desirability of coercion to achieve its ends, satyagraha aims, through *ahimsa*, at "a replacement of coercion by persuasion resulting in the conversion of the violent opponent."[50] With its overwhelming emphasis on passive resistance as a way of humiliating and crippling the opponent, there is little recognition in *duragraha* of reason and conscience. But for satyagraha, "Gandhi's appeal to *Ahimsa* was ultimately an appeal to the conscience and reason of the individual, an affirmation of purity of means in the pursuit of any social or political goal."[51]

Satyagraha's Power Applied to Social Reforms

Gandhi believed that only the power of *ahimsa* could create a basic psychological transformation in the country. He particularly stressed three social reforms that would if attained signal "a real change of heart" among all Indians: these were Hindu-Muslim unity, the abolition of untouchability and *swadeshi* or the manufacture and use of Indian goods. The last he claimed required that Indians wear *khadi* or homespun cotton cloth made by the traditional *charkha* or spinning wheel. The simplicity of a person's dress could signify a certain commitment to social equality. In November 1921, at the height of the first campaign for independence, Gandhi called attention to the primacy of social reforms and their necessary connection to *ahimsa* and swaraj:

> Swaraj does consist in the change of government and its real control by the people, but that would be merely the form. The substance that I am hankering after is a definite acceptance of the means and, therefore, a real change of heart on the part of the people. I am certain that it does not require ages for Hindus to discard the error of untouchability, for Hindus and Muslims to shed enmity and accept heart friendship as an eternal factor of national life, for all to adopt the charkha as the only universal means of attaining India's economic salvation and finally for all to believe that India's freedom lies only through nonviolence, and no other method. Definite, intelligent and free adoption by the nation of this programme, I hold, as the attainment of the substance. The symbol, the transfer of power, is sure to follow, even as the seed truly laid must develop into a tree.[52]

This emphasis upon the Constructive Program did not mean an abandonment of civil disobedience as an integral form of satyagraha. Gandhi's faith in mass civil disobedience, however, was considerably shaken in 1922 by several acts of violence; no indictment distressed him more and forced a harder reexamination of satyagraha than that of Chauri Chaura.

In December 1921 and January 1922, Government action against the campaign of noncooperation intensified; thirty thousand noncooperators were imprisoned, volunteer organizations became illegal, and public meetings were dispersed. The National Congress convened at Ahmedabad in December 1921. Gandhi was appointed its sole executive authority, and he was pressed by various members to launch mass civil disobedience.[53] He realized that no weapon of satyagraha was more dangerous than this, yet he also believed it to be the duty of an individual to resist unjust rule. "I wish I could persuade everybody," he wrote on January 5, 1922, "that Civil Disobedience is the inherent right of the citizen. . . . At the same time that the right of Civil Disobedience is insisted upon, its use must be guarded by all conceivable restrictions. Every possible provision should be made against an outbreak of violence or general lawlessness."[54]

On February 1, he made the decision to begin mass civil disobedience in the single district of Bardoli; if it succeeded there, he would extend it throughout India. He immediately communicated this to Lord Reading the Viceroy, and warned him that unless the Government freed the noncooperators and lifted restrictions on the press, the action would be taken.[55]

Gandhi's demands were rejected, and Bardoli prepared for mass civil disobedience.

On February 5, a procession of nationalists formed in Chauri Chaura, a village in Uttar Pradesh; a number of constables attempted to intervene, and when the demonstrators turned on them they opened fire. Their ammunition soon becoming exhausted, they withdrew to a police station. The crowd set fire to the building and twenty-two officers were subsequently burnt alive or hacked to death in the midst of the mob's fury.[56] Gandhi received the news on February 8 and his reaction was immediate. He called a meeting of the Congress Working Committee and advised cancellation of civil disobedience; they disagreed with him but his will prevailed. He then imposed upon himself a five days' fast as a penance for the violence. When nationalists throughout the country rebuked him for his decision to call off the campaign he replied, "God spoke clearly through Chauri Chaura."

> No provocation can possibly justify the brutal murder of men who had been rendered defenseless and had virtually thrown themselves on the mercy of the mob. And when India claims to be nonviolent and hopes to mount the throne of Liberty through nonviolent means, mob-violence even in answer to grave provocation is a bad augury.
>
> The tragedy of Chauri Chaura is really the index finger. It shows the way India may easily go, if drastic precautions be not taken. If we are not to evolve violence out of nonviolence, it is quite clear that we must hastily retrace our steps and re-establish an atmosphere of peace, re-arrange our programme and not think of starting mass Civil Disobedience until we are sure of peace being retained in spite of mass Civil Disobedience being started and in spite of Government provocation.[57]

"We dare not enter the kingdom of Liberty," Gandhi concluded in this article entitled "The Crime of Chauri Chaura," "with mere lip homage to Truth and Non-Violence."[58]

February, 1922, was not, of course, the last time that Gandhi brandished the weapon of civil disobedience. Chapter 4 concentrates on his civil disobedience campaign of 1930. However, his use of civil disobedience after 1922 grew even more controlled and restricted, subject to careful planning and orchestration. Chauri Chaura taught him the complex nature of the task and the endless difficulties involved. After the noncooperation movement's first flush, then, Gandhi turned increasingly to social reform or related types of satyagraha in his struggle for swaraj. So as the world came to see Gandhi as a rebel against the Raj, he increasingly saw himself as a social reformer. He remarked in 1931, following the success of his political campaign:

> My work of social reform was in no way less or subordinate to political work. The fact is, that when I saw that to a certain extent my social work would be impossible without the help of political work, I took to the latter and only to the extent that it helped the former. I must therefore confess that work of social reform or self-purification of this nature is a hundred times dearer to me than what is called purely political work.[59]

Focus on Reform of Caste and Untouchability

A major social reform that concerned Gandhi was the injustice in the institutions of caste and untouchability. By 1933, Gandhi had come to state his purpose plainly: "It is the whole of Hinduism that has to be purified and purged. What I am aiming at . . . is the greatest reform of the age."[60] But this was Gandhi writing in 1933: such a direct challenge to traditional Hindu norms, especially regarding the institution of caste, was not evident in his pronouncements of fifteen years earlier. An analysis of his changing views on caste should be examined in detail, because they reveal so much about his whole approach to social reform and religion.

In South Africa, as early as 1909, Gandhi had publicly decried the caste system for its inequalities: its "hypocritical distinctions of high and low" and "caste tyranny" which had made India "turn [her] back on truth and embrace falsehood."[61] But however much Gandhi condemned inequality of castes in South Africa, shortly after he returned to India the emphasis fell on the generally beneficial aspects of caste, and a strong defense of it for its "wonderful powers of organization."[62] It is on the basis of his remarks on caste in this five-year period, from 1916 to 1921, that he acquired the reputation of orthodoxy; and certainly it is true that at this time he was most sensitive to that community of opinion. Caste prohibitions on interdining and intermarriage are upheld, since they foster "self-control"; and the system itself is regarded as a beneficial, "natural institution."[63]

Gradually Gandhi began in his comment on caste reform to use the term *varna* (or *varnashrama* or *varnadharma*). These denoted his conception of aspects of an idea social order based on ancient Hindu thought.[64] At first, in this relatively underdeveloped stage of his views, the idea of caste and *varna* are not distinguished.[65] Gandhi is at this point searching for an approach to caste that will allow him to reform it effectively from within, without alienating the orthodox. The remark that he makes at this time on the issue of intercaste marriage is suggestive of his attitude. He advises that a beginning should be made with intermarriage not between different *varnas* (the four brahmanical occupational classes), but among members of different subcastes. "This would satisfy the most ardent reformers as a first step and enable men like Pandi Malaviya [an orthodox Hindu] to support it."[66] The remark signals the approach he would take for almost another decade, an approach that continues to sanction prohibitions on intermarriage and interdining. Thus gradually he builds *varna* into a social ideal distinct from orthodox notions of caste.

After 1919, when Gandhi assumes effective control of the Congress, signs appear that he has begun the long process of gaining confidence as a national leader. He is now the "Mahatma," and while for some his credentials as a Sanatani or orthodox Hindu remain in question and his writings are still replete with defensive remarks, there is nonetheless evident now a surer sense of purpose. He urges the caste ideal as the right path to social harmony: "If we can prove it to be a success, it can be offered to the world as a leaven and as the best remedy against heartless competition and social disintegration born of avarice and greed."[67] This defense of caste, however, is significantly qualified in December 1920 by distinguishing between "the four divisions" (*varnas*) and "the subcastes," and also by stressing his earlier insistence on equality among the four orders:

> I believe that caste has saved Hinduism from disintegration. But like every other institution it has suffered from excrescences. I consider the four divisions alone to be fundamental, natural and essential. The innumerable subcastes are sometimes a convenience, often a hindrance. The sooner there is fusion the better. The silent destruction and reconstruction of subcastes have ever gone on and are bound to continue. Social pressure and public opinion can be trusted to deal with the problem. But I am certainly against any attempt at destroying the fundamental divisions. The caste system is not based on inequality, there is no question of inferiority, and so far as there is any such question arising, the tendency should undoubtedly be checked. But there appears to be no valid reason for ending the system because of its abuse. It lends itself easily to reformation. The spirit of democracy, which is fast spreading throughout India, and the rest of the world, will, without a shadow of doubt, purge the institution of the idea of predominance and subordination. The spirit of democracy is not a mechanical thing to be adjusted by abolition of forms. It requires change of the heart.[68]

Writing in October 1921, Gandhi reinforces the distinction between the four divisions and caste; significantly, he now begins to use the term *varna* quite consistently. With a view to the orthodox, he maintains his support of restrictions on interdining and intermarriage, for Hinduism "does most emphatically discourage interdining and intermarriage between divisions," in the interests of "self-restraint." Indeed, he goes so far as to say that "Prohibition against intermarriage and interdining is essential for a rapid evolution of the soul." This is the justification of caste practices that he later repudiated. "But," he continues, now suggesting his line of reform: "this self-denial is no test of *varna*. A Brahamana may remain a Brahamana, though he may dine with his Shudra. . . . The four divisions define a man's calling, they do not restrict or regulate social intercourse."[69]

The Gandhian technique is here in full swing: on the one hand, he holds that since *varna* is, as the orthodox contend, inherited, "I do not believe that interdining or even intermarriage necessarily deprives a man of his status that birth has given him." On the other hand, the two key pillars of caste, interdining and intermarriage, are neatly separated from the concept of *varnashrama*. It is precisely on this basis that Gandhi can argue, six years later, "*Varna* has nothing to do with caste. Down with the monster of caste that masquerades in the guise of *varna*. It is this travesty of *varna* that has degraded Hinduism and India."[70] This unambiguous castigation of caste began as early as January 1926,[71] and as caste comes under an increasingly scathing attack the ideal of *varna* moves in to fill the vacuum, replacing one traditional concept with another. The admixture of continuity and innovation that always characterized his style is evident in this passage—a statement that offers an outstanding example of Gandhi's use of language:

> When we have come to our own, when we have cleansed ourselves, we may have the four *varnas* according to the way in which we can express the best in us. But *varna* then will invest one with higher responsibility and duties. Those who will impart knowledge in a spirit of service will be called Brahamanas. They will assume no superior airs but will be true servants of society. When inequality of status of rights is ended, every one of us will be equal. I do not know, however, when we shall be able to revive true *varnadharma*. Its real revival would mean true democracy.[72]

Gandhi is thus able to urge on the orthodox a "democratic" ideal derived from the classical Indian tradition, while he opposes as "excrescences" those caste practices he has separated from *varna*. The *varna* ideal with which by 1927 he has replaced caste could hardly have been seen by the orthodox as a suitable substitute:

> Fight, by all means, the monster that passes for *varnashrama* today, and you will find me working side by side with you. My *varnashrama* enables me to dine with anybody who will give me clean food, be he Hindu, Muslim, Christian, Parsi, whatever he is. My *varnashrama* accommodates a Pariah girl under my own roof as my own daughter. My *varnashrama* accommodates many Panchama [fifth and lowest class, i.e., Untouchable] families with whom I dine with the greatest pleasure—to dine with whom is a privilege. My *varnashrama* compels me to bow down my head in all humility before knowledge, before purity, before every person, where I see God face to face.[73]

Gandhi's views on caste during this initial decade (1916–26) mark the period that the first real change in his position occurred: the crucial distinction between the caste system and *varnadharma* emerged then. Throughout this decade, he was constantly harassed by Hindu conservatives, especially in his reform of untouchability; and the pace as well as the content of his views on caste reform must be seen in the context of his response to the Indian orthodox as well as to Western liberalism.

The last two decades of his career (1927–47) represent a progressive movement toward a radical critique of caste. In September and October of 1927, Gandhi made two noteworthy speeches on *varna* at Tangore and Trivandrum where the orthodox elements were formidable. The emphasis in both speeches is on social equality, justified with an appeal, not to Western ideas, but to the traditional Hindu concept of *advaita*, or the spiritual oneness of all being. The caste system's most vicious feature, he argued, is that it has upheld the idea of inherited superiority. This is inconsistent with the spirit of Hinduism in general and the ideal of *varna* in particular: "There is nothing in common between *varnashrama* and caste." Gandhi concluded his Tangore speech with an expression of his idealist approach to social reform:

> You would be entitled to say that this is not how *varnashrama* is understood in these days. I have myself said times without number that *varnashrama* as it is at present understood and practiced is a monstrous parody of the original, but in order to demolish this distortion let us not seek to demolish the original. And if you say the idealistic *varnashrama* which I have placed before you is quite all right you have admitted all that I like you to admit. I would also urge on you to believe with me that no nation, no individual, can possibly live without proper ideals. And if you believe

with me in the idealistic *varnashrama*, you will also strive with me to reach that ideal so far as may be.[74]

Not until 1932, does the vestige of orthodoxy seen in his support of caste restrictions on intermarriage and interdining disappear. These restrictions are now criticized as being "no part of the Hindu religion," serving only to "stunt Hindu society."[75] Writing in 1935 on this issue under the title "Caste Has To Go," he insists that "in *varnashrama* there was and should be no prohibition of intermarriage or interdining."[76] His views on intermarriage, once loosened, culminated in the announcement of 1946 that "If anybody was not prepared to marry a Harijan Gandhi would not bless that marriage."[77] "If I had my way I would persuade all caste Hindu girls coming under my influence to select Harijan husbands."[78]

Gandhi's reinterpretation of *varna* emphasizes his dominant concern for social equality and harmony. An egalitarian democratic society, one in which no one was oppressed or driven to envy by the privileged status of another, must develop a cooperative spirit where no energy would be wasted in a competitive pursuit of material gain; it would be turned instead into some form of social service. "The law of *varna* is the antithesis of competition which kills."[79] He conceptualizes an organic social order:

> The four *varnas* have been compared in the Vedas to the four members of the body, and no simile could be happier. If they are members of one body, how can one be superior or inferior to another? If the members of the body had the power of expression and each of them were to say that it was higher and better than the rest, the body would go to pieces. Even so, our body politic, the body of humanity, would go to pieces, if it were to perpetuate the canker of superiority or inferiority. It is this canker that is at the root of the various ills of our time, especially class war and civil strife. It should not be difficult for even the meanest understanding to see that these wars and strifes could not be ended except by the observance of the law of *varna*.[80]

If Gandhi's approach to the reform of caste changed in the early 1930s from cautious reform to radical opposition, his attitude toward the institution of untouchability remained consistent: he was always unequivocally against it.[81] His abhorrence of how India treated its untouchables was felt since childhood and he often expressed this during his South African experience.[82] After his return to India, his campaign against the institution of untouchability became a major plank in his reform platform. In a speech of early 1916, he condemned untouchability in the strongest possible terms as "an ineffaceable blot that Hinduism today carries with it. . . . This miserable, wretched, enslaving spirit of untouchableness." "It is, to my mind, a curse that has come to us, and as long as that curse remains with us, so long I think we are bound to consider that every affliction that we labor under in this sacred land is a fit and proper punishment for this great and indelible crime that we are committing."[83]

Gandhi welcomed untouchable families into the community that he formed in Ahmedabad called Sabarmati (later Satyagraha) ashram. He had a particularly close relationship there during the 1920s with a Harijan couple, Ramijibhai and Gangabehn Badhia. These two and their family became vital contributors to that community. Ramjibhai, a skilled weaver when he joined the ashram in 1920, was known as "Gandhiji's guru in khadi weaving." Along with his son and son-in-law, he was among the seventy-nine volunteers chosen to join Gandhi on the salt march. Gandhi repeatedly cited Ramijibhai as an exemplary freedom fighter, a model for all Indians to follow.[84] He soon came to see the fight against untouchability as an integral part of satyagraha, and its resolution as a prerequisite for swaraj. This necessary relationship of swaraj to the abolition of untouchability that Gandhi saw was seldom, however, seen by others. Thus one correspondent wrote to *Young India*:

> I am unable to understand the relation between the existence of this evil and the establishment of *Swaraj*. After all, "unapproachability" is only one of the many evils of the Hindu society. . . . How is this an impediment to the obtaining of *Swaraj* and why do you make its removal a condition precedent to our fitness for *Swaraj*? Is it not possible for this to be set right when *Swaraj* is obtained, if not voluntarily, at least by legislation.[85]

Gandhi replied:

> *Swaraj* for me means freedom for the meanest of our countrymen. If the lot of the Panchama [untouchable] is not improved when we are all suffering, it is not likely to be better under the intoxication of *Swaraj*. If it is necessary for us to buy peace with the Mussalmans as a condition of *Swaraj*, it is equally necessary for us to give peace to the Panchama before we can with any show of justice or self-respect talk of *Swaraj*. I am not interested in freeing India merely from the English yoke. I am bent upon freeing India from any yoke whatsoever. I have no desire to exchange

"king log for king stork." Hence for me the movement of *Swaraj* is a movement of self-purification.[86]

These last few sentences contain a vital element of Gandhi's conception of freedom: the conviction that tyranny over another inevitably corrupts the character of the tyrant, and so enslaves the tyrant himself. "We have become 'pariahs of the Empire' because we have created 'pariahs' in our midst. The slave owner is always more hurt than the slave. We shall be unfit to gain *Swaraj* so long as we would keep in bondage a fifth of the population of Hindustan."[87]

Again, speaking in 1928 on the reform of untouchability he asked, "Shall we not have the vision to see that in suppressing a sixth (or whatever the number) of ourselves, we have depressed ourselves? No man takes another down a pit without descending into it himself and sinning in the bargain. It is not the suppressed that sin. It is the suppressor who has to answer for his crime against those whom he suppresses."[88]

Despite these arguments, many Congressmen remained unconvinced of the connection between swaraj and the abolition of untouchability. At the Forty-First Congress of 1926, Mr. S. Srinivasa Aiyengar delivered the Presidential Address; after paying high tribute to Gandhi's thought, he turned to the gospel of swaraj: "Our foremost duty is to keep constantly before our eyes the vision of *swaraj*, what it is, what it requires of us, and what it will not permit us."[89]

Aiyengar, however, then moved on to ideas decidedly at variance with Gandhi's position. He described the use of *khadi* and the abolition of untouchability as "vital aspects of our national movement." But, he contended,

> Neither foreign nor domestic critics are right when they assert that untouchability is a formidable obstacle for *swaraj*, or that its removal will automatically bring about *swaraj*. We cannot wait for *swaraj* till it is removed anymore than we can wait till caste is abolished. . . . I would deprecate the iterated rhetorical stress on untouchability as a serious impediment to *swaraj*.[90]

Gandhi was quick to note this comment on untouchability in Aiyengar's address, and he soon answered it in *Young India*:

> There is, too, confusion regarding Swaraj. The term Swaraj has many meanings. When Sjt. Iyengar says that removal of untouchability has

nothing to do with Swaraj, I presume he means that its existence can be no hindrance to constitutional advance. It can surely have nothing to do with dyarchy or greater and effective powers being given the legislatures. . . .

Real organic Swaraj is a different question. That freedom which is associated with the term Swaraj in the popular mind is no doubt unattainable without not only the removal of untouchability and the promotion of heart unity between the different sections but also without removing many other social evils that can be easily named. That inward growth which must never stop we have come to understand by the comprehensive term Swaraj. And that Swaraj cannot be had so long as walls of prejudice, passion and superstition continue to stifle the growth of that stately oak.[91]

This was the aspect of untouchability Gandhi disliked most: the "walls of prejudice, passion and superstition" it created, prohibiting "promotion of heart unity between the different sections." Gandhi uses, for the first time in this passage, the term "organic Swaraj" and this holds a special significance: it suggests a freedom that seeks to include a sense of social harmony. "Organic" as opposed to "constitutional" or "parliamentary" swaraj included individual civil liberty and national independence, but it also sought to go beyond these to a realization of "heart unity."

Gandhi wanted, then, to establish an organic swaraj, a solid spirit of social unity, in three major areas on Indian society: among the untouchables and the various castes; between Hindus and Muslims; and, finally, he wished to overcome the considerable gap that had grown between the rural, traditional, largely illiterate villagers, on the one hand, and the urban, Westernized, educated classes on the other. Gandhi interpreted this last aspect of social separateness as another form of untouchability.

To me, the campaign against untouchability has begun to imply ever so much more than the eradication of the ceremonial untouchability of those who are labelled untouchables. For the city dweller, the villagers have become untouchables.[92]

The ulcer of untouchability has gone so deep that it seems to pervade our life. Hence the unreal differences: Brahamana and Non-Brahamana, provinces and provinces, religion and religion. Why should we not all be children of one Indian family and, further, of one human family? Are we not like branches of the same tree?[93]

I have not hesitated to say with great deliberation that, if we, Hindus, do not destroy this monster of untouchability, it will devour both Hindus

and Hinduism. And when I ask you to purify your hearts of untouchability, I ask of you nothing less than this—that you should believe
in the fundamental unity and equality of man. I invite you all to forget
that there are any distinctions of high and low among the children of one
and the same God.[94]

These ideas gained dramatic force in September 1932 when Gandhi fasted
to shock his society out of its indifference to the evils of untouchability and
also to persuade the Government to deal more constructively with it. Not
everyone appreciated this fast, perhaps least of all Dr. B. R. Ambedkar, an
articulate leader and member of the untouchable minority, whose criticisms
of Gandhi are noted in the next chapter.[95] However, Gandhi's fast so inspired the novelist Mulk Raj Anand that he joined Gandhi's ashram and
then wrote an enduring work of Indian fiction entitled *Untouchable* (published in 1935). Anand saw in Gandhi's action a striking truth: that the practice of untouchability had divided Indian society with a persuasive sense of
exclusiveness and against this Gandhi's inclusive spirit had spread unity and
uplifted members of the *harijan* community. Anand conveyed this through
the character of his *harijan* hero, Bakha, who meets the Mahatma in these
circumstances:

At once the crowd, and Bakha among them, rushed towards the golbagh.
He had not asked himself where he was going. He hadn't paused to think.
The word "Mahatma" was like a magical magnet, to which he, like all the
other people about him, rushed blindly. The wooden boards of the foot-
bridge creaked under the eager downward rush of his ammunition boots.
He was so much in a hurry that he didn't even remember that he was an
Untouchable, and actually touched a few people. But not having his
broom and basket with him, and the people being all in a flurry, no one
noticed that a sweeper-boy had brushed past him.

At the foot of the bridge, by the tonga and motor-lorry stand, the road
leading to the fort past the entrance of the golbagh looked like a regular
racecourse. Men, women and children of all the different races, colors,
castes and creeds, were running towards the oval. There were Hindu
lallas from the piece-goods market of Bulandshahr, smartly dressed in
silks; there were Kashmiri Muhammadans from the local carpet factories,
immaculately clad in white cotton; there were the rough Sikh rustics from
the near-by villages swathed in handspun cloth, staves in their hands and
loads of shopping on their backs; there were fierce-looking red-cheeked
Pathans in red shirts, followers of Abdul Gaffar Khan, the frontier Gandhi; there were the black-faced Indian Christian girls from the Salvation

Army colony, in short, colored skirts, blouses and aprons; there were people from the outcastes' colony, whom Bakha recognized in the distance, but whom he was not too anxious to greet; there was here and there a stray European—there was everybody going to meet the Mahatma, to pay homage to Mohandas Karam Chand Gandhi. But he became aware of the fact of being a sweeper by the contrast which his dirty, khaki uniform presented to the white garments of most of the crowd. There was an insuperable barrier between himself and the crowd, the barrier of caste. He was part of a consciousness which he could share and yet not understand. He had been lifted from the gutter, through the barriers of space, to partake of a life which was his, and yet not his. He was in the midst of a humanity which included him in its folds, and yet debarred him from entering into a sentient, living, quivering contact with it. Gandhi alone united him with them, in the mind, because Gandhi was in everybody's mind, including Bakha's. Gandhi might unite them really. Bakha waited for Gandhi.

Gandhi did not disappoint: Bakha saw "something beautiful" in his face, "something intimate and warm about him. He smiled like a child." After he heard Gandhi's speech, an appeal to break down the social barriers of intolerance and make society "open to the Untouchables,"

> Bakha stood on the branch of the tree spellbound. Each word of the concluding passage seemed to him to echo as deep and intense a feeling of horror and indignation as his own at the distinction which the caste Hindus made between themselves and the Untouchables. The Mahatma seemed to have touched the most intimate corners of his soul. 'To be sure, he is a good man,' Bakha said."

This was the moment of conversion:

> Bakha felt thrilled. A tremor went down his spine. That the Mahatma should want to be born as an outcaste! That he should love scavenging! He adored the man. He felt he could put his life in his hands and ask him to do what he liked with it. For him he would do anything."[96]

Freedom with Equality: Swaraj and Sarvodaya

Anand's story depicts the multiple sources of Gandhi's charisma, the devotion inspired in a diverse mass of people. Gandhi reached Bakha with his empathy, an identification with feelings that "touched the most intimate corners of his soul," with words such as these, that Gandhi addressed to India in 1941:

> So far as Harijans are concerned, every Hindu should make common cause with them and befriend them in their awful isolation—such isolation as perhaps the world has never seen in the monstrous immensity one witnesses in India. I know from experience how difficult the task is. But it is part of the task of building the edifice of *swaraj*. And the road to *swaraj* is steep and narrow. There are many slippery ascents and many deep chasms. They have all to be negotiated with unfaltering steps before we can reach the summit and breathe the fresh air of freedom.[97]

Gandhi continually emphasized the necessity for identification with the villagers, who represented the masses of India, that their attitudes might be understood and their needs met.

> We must first come in living touch with them [the masses] by working for them and in their midst. We must share their sorrows, understand their difficulties and anticipate their wants. With the pariahs we must be pariahs and see how we feel to clean the closets [toilets] of the upper classes and have the remains of their table thrown at us. We must see how we like being in the boxes, miscalled houses, of the laborers of Bombay. We must identify ourselves with the villagers who toil under the hot sun beating on their bent backs and see how we would like to drink water from the pool in which the villagers bathe, wash their clothes and pots and in which their cattle drink and roll. Then and not till then shall we truly represent the masses and they will, as surely as I am writing this, respond to every call. "We cannot do all this, and if we are to do this, good-bye to Swaraj for a thousand years and more," some will say. I shall sympathize with the objection. But I do claim that some of us at least will have to go through the agony and out of it only will a nation full, vigorous and free be born.[98]

This call for service did not begin in modern India with Gandhi. He had said that he wished to serve India's villagers "because I recognize no God except the God that is to be found in the hearts of the dumb millions . . . and I worship the God that is Truth or Truth which is God through the service of these millions."[99] Swami Vivekananda, an influential Hindu reformer, had set forth the same idea a generation earlier, and Gandhi knew this. Even the word which Gandhi used, *Daridranarayan*, to mean the divinity of the poor and needy, had been used by Vivekananda and the Bengali nationalist leader C. R. Das.[100] But Gandhi did not derive this gospel of service from Das or Vivekananda alone. He had found it in numerous sources: the Sermon on the Mount, Tolstoy, texts and saints of the Indian tradition, and in the recollection of simple childhood experiences. Gandhi imbibed these influences and directed the lessons he learned toward problems of the Indian villager. Then he repeatedly connected his goal of village uplift, which he called *Sarvodaya* or social equality, to the other reforms. But it was his insistence on their connection to swaraj that bears emphasis: he asserted in 1924 that "truthful relations between Hindus and Muslims, bread for the masses and removal of untouchability. That is how I would define *swaraj* at the present moment. . . . Realization of the goal is in exact proportion to that of the means [of satyagraha]. This is a proposition that admits of no exception."[101]

Gandhi, moreover, was not the only major political leader of his time to call attention to the crucial importance of the Indian villages. C. R. Das in his Congress Presidential Address of 1922 had urged, as a requisite of Swaraj, the "organization of village life and the practical autonomy of small local centres." Village communities must not exist as "disconnected units" but rather be "held together by a system of co-operation and integration." "I maintain that real Swaraj," Das declared, "can only be attained by vesting the power of Government in these small local centres"; and he suggested that the Congress "draw up a scheme of Government" based on this principle.[102]

As a result of this recommendation, an *Outline Scheme of Swaraj* was drafted by C. R. Das and Bhagavan Das,[103] and presented to the Congress in early 1923. This plan urged the creation, after independence was granted, of a highly decentralized form of government, "a maximum of local autonomy," and "a minimum of control by higher centres."[104] The organ of administration would be the *panchayat*, organized into village, town, district, provincial, and All-India units of government.[105] The purpose behind this scheme was the uplift of India's villages; and "the idea underlying this condition is that which has been discussed and emphasized before, the idea of spiritualizing politics by changing the whole culture and civilization of society from its present mercenary to a missionary basis."[106] Gandhi, then, was not unique among Congress leaders in his approach to the villages. His contribution lies in the sustained emphasis he gave to this aspect of his Constructive Program and in his use of traditional symbols and concepts for a problem that had psychological as well as political and economic roots.

Gandhi had perceived what most early Congress moderates had ignored: not only that traditional language and symbols were needed to involve the people in the national movement, but also that the educated had to overcome a substantial psychological barrier to achieve any rapport at all with the peasantry. He directed his efforts toward both aspects of this problem. He approached the villagers through the use of the Indian tradition with his vision of *sarvodaya*. The endless pleas for village sanitation, personal hygiene, and basic education came to them this time, not from just another Westernized social reformer, but from a Mahatma. Gandhi remained equally concerned, however, with the other group he tried to persuade, the educated Westernized Indians. No single major proposal that Gandhi made during his period of Congress leadership induced greater ridicule than that concerning the use of the spinning wheel and the wearing of *khadi*. Gandhi asked Congressmen to wear the homespun cloth and to devote a certain amount of time each day to the spinning of yarn. The proposal was set forth in Congress resolutions and many members paid lip service to it. Few seemed to appreciate Gandhi's purposes in advocating it.

"I can only think of spinning," Gandhi wrote, "as the fittest and most acceptable sacrificial body labor. I cannot imagine anything nobler or more national than that, for we should all do the labor that the poor must do and thus identify ourselves with them and through them with all mankind."[107] The wearing of *khadi* by each Indian Gandhi felt to be a privilege which should "make him proud of his identity with every drop of the ocean of Indian humanity."[108] The spinning wheel was seen as "the cement to bind the masses to us national servants,"[109] the instrument for "creating an indissoluble bond between the rich and poor,"[110] and "the symbol of social service of the highest order."[111] Few examples illustrate better than the spinning wheel Gandhi's reliance upon the force of a symbol.

Gandhi believed not only in a free, but also a harmonious and equal social order of *sarvodaya*. His campaign against untouchability was, above all, a movement to create a common feeling among castes and untouchables; his struggle for Hindu-Muslim unity sought a harmony of religious sympathies; and his attempt to advance the use of *khadi* and the spinning wheel was an effort at bridging the gulf between groups of educated Indians and the majority in the villages. Gandhi forever remained an apostle of harmony, but at the basis of this was the value of compromise. From a lesson learned early in his South African experience, he concluded, "All my life through, the very insistence on truth has taught me to appreciate the beauty of compromise. I saw in later life that this spirit was an essential part of *satyagraha.*"[112]

Satyagraha—the power of nonviolence—remained the *sine qua non* for the attainment of swaraj and *sarvodaya*—freedom and equality alike. Only nonviolent means could produce the desired end, a free and equal social order. Gandhi's belief in *ahimsa*, which he variously translated as "love" and "charity" as well as "nonviolence," was for him a religious persuasion. "Experience has convinced me," he concludes in his *Autobiography*, "that there is no other God than Truth. And if every page of these chapters does not proclaim to the reader that the only means for the realization of Truth is Ahimsa, I shall deem all my labor in writing these chapters to have been in vain. . . . this much I can say with assurance, as a result of all my experiments, that a perfect vision of Truth can only follow a complete realization of Ahimsa."[113] Nonviolent means were not only truthful but efficacious. "You need not be afraid," he replied in 1925 to an Indian terrorist who had challenged the workability of his method, "that the method of nonviolence is a slow long drawn out process. It is the swiftest the world has seen, for it is the surest. You will see that it will overtake the revolutionaries whom you imagine I have misjudged."[114] He could say this because he knew that his appeal as a leader never lay merely in his evocation of the great ideals of freedom and equality, truth and nonviolence. His impact came from a singular ability to express these ideas in action.

CHAPTER THREE

Critiques of Gandhi from His Contemporaries: Rabindranath Tagore and M. N. Roy

To me all these demands of Mahatma Gandhi
seemed not only extreme, but even crude and
irrational. It appeared to me that his entire
ideology was driven by a resolve to abandon
civilized life and revert to a primitive
existence.

I thought that he was preaching the rejection
not only of European civilization, but of
Hindu civilization as well. I could see that he
had not the slightest understanding of the
higher features of Hindu culture, and of its
complexity.

—*Nirad Chaudhuri recalling his view
of Gandhi in 1921*[1]

A balanced view of Gandhi's theory in practice should consider
the voices of some of his critics. And he has had many, both during his long
political career and after his death. Among the most penetrating assessments of his thought and leadership were from those who actually knew
him. Rabindranath Tagore and M. N. Roy were theorists in their own right
and well acquainted with Gandhi. Their critiques differed substantially, yet
they shared the deep skepticism of Nirad Chaudhuri, the gifted author and
contemporary of Gandhi. This chapter will be devoted largely to judgments
of Gandhi by Tagore and Roy but it begins with a sample of the striking

range of critical reactions that the Mahatma managed to evoke from his contemporaries.

It is sometimes assumed that since Gandhi fought for noble causes such as the abolition of untouchability and developed a worldwide reputation as a saint he stood above criticism. On the contrary, some of the harshest condemnation came from Indian contemporaries who saw him either as a traitor to orthodox Hinduism for his attack on the caste system or as a caste Hindu who pretended to defend untouchables but in actuality advocated phony reforms that preserved all the evils of caste. The latter position was taken by Dr. B. R. Ambedkar, a leader of the untouchables, as mentioned in the previous chapter. Ambedkar knew Gandhi, disliked him intensely, and regarded his influence on India as wholly pernicious. "Few know," he declared, "what tragedies the Untouchables as well as the country have had to go through on account of the illusions of Mr. Gandhi." Among these destructive illusions was Gandhi's idea of *varna*, discussed above, which was touted as a reform of caste whereas "It is simply a new name for the caste system and retains all the worst features." Ambedkar was himself an untouchable and viewed Gandhi's claims to be an "honorary *harijan*" as a pretentious and condescending insult. "The Untouchables must still hold that the best way to safeguard themselves is to say 'Beware of Mr. Gandhi,' " because his entire philosophy was primitive and irrational. If followed, it meant "back to squalor, back to poverty and back to ignorance for the vast mass of the people."[2]

This criticism from Gandhi's Indian compatriots was matched by that of his English rulers. Winston Churchill has earned a permanent place in Gandhiana for his characterization of the Mahatma, in 1931, as a "seditious Middle Temple lawyer, now posing as a fakir . . . striding half-naked up the steps of the Viceroyal palace . . ."[3] Yet, even more extensive and vituperative than Churchill's was the criticism of Lord Archibald Percival Wavell, the penultimate Viceroy of India, who held office from October, 1943 to March 1947. The years that Lord Wavell ruled India required many difficult and delicate negotiations with rival Indian parties, especially with the leaders of the Indian Congress and the Muslim League, as Wavell strove earnestly but fruitlessly to avoid partition of the country into two nations, India and Pakistan. Of all the leaders that he met, Wavell liked Gandhi the least. Indeed, it is clear from his detailed journal that he loathed the Mahatma. After a series of lengthy sessions with him, Wavell confided in his diary of September 26, 1946, ". . . Gandhi at the end exposed Congress policy of domination more nakedly than ever before. The more I see of that old man, the more I regard him as an unscrupulous old hypocrite; he would shrink from no violence and blood-letting to achieve his ends, though he would naturally prefer to do so by chicanery and a false show of mildness and friendship."

Wavell never doubted that the Raj had served India well and Gandhi was its arch enemy: "His one idea for 40 years has been to overthrow British rule and influence and to establish a Hindu raj; and he is as unscrupulous as he is persistent." He condemned Gandhi's character and motives as much as his ideas. Thus his favored adjectives for the Mahatma are "malignant" and "malevolent" although his most colorful single sentence (and there are several to choose from) is perhaps this: "He is an exceedingly shrewd, obstinate, domineering, double-tongued, single-minded politician; and there is little true saintliness in him." Even as he heard the news of Gandhi's assassination, the most that Wavell could manage was this sober query: "I always thought he had more of malevolence than benevolence in him, but who am I to judge, and how can an Englishman estimate a Hindu? Our standards are poles apart."[4]

Wavell's judgments of Gandhi are not typical of the Raj mainly because they are so clear and unequivocal. Most of Gandhi's British rulers came forth with opinions that were decidedly ambivalent and perplexed. Representative of this ambivalence was the estimate of Lord Edward Irwin, a Viceroy of uncommon insight who was nonetheless befuddled by Gandhi, as will be argued at length in the next chapter. The sort of misunderstanding that came from high quarters of the Raj was expressed as early as 1917 by Edwin S. Montague, then Secretary of State for India, who did not see Gandhi as politically dangerous: "He is a social reformer; he has a real desire to find grievances and to cure them, not for any reasons of self-advertisement, but to improve the conditions of his fellowmen . . . . He dresses like a coolie, forswears all personal advancement, lives practically on the air, and is a pure visionary." Gandhi, Montague concluded, was only interested in "helping the Government to find a solution" for certain social problems and represented no political threat to the Raj.[5]

On the other side arose a legion of articulate Indian sympathizers who from their beginning came not to criticize Gandhi but to extol his virtues. The first of these was his mentor among Congress Moderates, G. K. Gokhale, who, as was noted above, Gandhi had damned with faint praise in *Hind Swaraj.* Only months before that tract appeared, Gokhale presented

Gandhi to India in these terms: "He is a man who may be well described as a man among men, a hero among heroes, a patriot amongst patriots, and we may well say that in him Indian humanity at the present time has really reached its high watermark."[6]

Thirty-five years later, near the end of Gandhi's long public career, Jawaharlal Nehru, soon to become independent India's first prime minister, reflected back on the turning point of the nationalist movement. With an unparalleled eloquence that deserves to be quoted at length, Nehru wrote what remains as perhaps the most moving assessment of what Gandhi achieved:

> And then Gandhi came. He was like a powerful current of fresh air that made us stretch ourselves and take deep breaths, like a beam of light that pierced the darkness and removed the scales from our eyes, like a whirlwind that upset many things but most of all the working of people's minds. He did not descend from the top; he seemed to emerge from the millions of India, speaking their language and incessantly drawing attention to them and their appalling condition. Get off the backs of these peasants and workers, he told us, all you who live by their exploitation; get rid of the system that produces this poverty and misery.
>
> Political freedom took new shape then and acquired a new content. Much that he said we only partially accepted or sometimes did not accept at all. But all this was secondary. The essence of his teaching was fearlessness and truth and action allied to these, always keeping the welfare of the masses in view. The greatest gift for an individual or a nation, so we had been told in our ancient books, was *abhaya*, fearlessness, not merely bodily courage but the absence of fear from the mind. Chanakya and Yagnavalka had said, at the dawn of our history, that it was the function of the leaders of a people to make them fearless. But the dominant impulse in India under British rule was that of fear, pervasive, oppressing, strangling fear; fear of the army, the police, the widespread secret service; fear of the official class; fear of laws meant to suppress, and of prison; fear of the landlord's agent; fear of the moneylender; fear of unemployment and starvation, which were always on the threshold. It was against this all-pervading fear that Gandhi's quiet and determined voice was raised: Be not afraid.
>
> Was it so simple as all that? Not quite. And yet fear builds its phantoms which are more fearsome than reality itself, and reality when calmly analyzed and its consequences willingly accepted loses much of its terror.
>
> So, suddenly, as it were, that black pall of fear was lifted from the people's shoulders, not wholly, of course, but to an amazing degree. As fear is

close companion to falsehood, so truth follows fearlessness. The Indian people did not become much more truthful than they were, nor did they change their essential nature overnight; nevertheless a sea change was visible as the need for falsehood and furtive behavior lessened. It was a psychological change, almost as if some expert in psychoanalytical method had probed deep into the patient's past, found out the origins of his complexes, exposed them to his view, and thus rid him of that burden.

There was that psychological reaction also, a feeling of shame at our long submission to an alien rule that had degraded and humiliated us, and a desire to submit no longer, whatever the consequences might be.[7]

Tagore Versus Gandhi on the Meanings of Freedom and Power

Not all Indians were as appreciative of Gandhi as Nehru, as the example of Dr. Ambedkar showed. In fact, Indian critics of the Mahatma abound by 1920, and they come from a wide range of perspectives. Only two of these perspectives will be presented here, one from an artist, India's renowned poet, Rabindranath Tagore (1861–1941), the other from a prominent Marxist, M. N. Roy (1887–1954). Both are Bengali brahmins with elitist views on their society that lead them to share the criticisms of Gandhi expressed by Nirad Chaudhuri. While in most other respects Tagore and Roy could not be more different as social theorists, they are united in their strong criticism of Gandhi's thought and leadership.[8]

Tagore was awarded the Nobel Prize for Literature in 1913, and remained throughout his life a formidable presence on the Indian scene. From a well-known family and personally famous because of his Nobel Prize, he could not be dismissed like M. N. Roy, as a misguided Communist. Gandhi could afford to ignore Roy: he was forced to confront Tagore. In 1921, Gandhi took account of Tagore's criticisms, and replied with all the deference due to India's poet laureate: "I regard the Poet as a sentinel warning us against the approach of enemies called Bigotry, Lethargy, Intolerance, Ignorance, Inertia and other members of that brood."[9]

Tagore, however, would not be mollified. The Poet chose to challenge the dominant political belief of his age and of modern Indian politics, the gospel of nationalism. Gandhi had extolled the ideal of universal harmony but he had not singled out Indian nationalism as a threat to that ideal. His criticism was rather reserved for the western nation-state system. Tagore asserted that in principle there was no distinction: "Nationalism is a great menace," he declared, and with this generalization Gandhi may have agreed. But Tagore added: "It is the particular thing which for years has been at the bottom of India's troubles."[10] Tagore not only proclaimed this position in unequivocal terms, he also made the theme of individual freedom *versus* the nation-state a central feature of his social and political thought. His critique of nationalism and of its various manifestations in modern India became an indictment of Gandhi's leadership.

Tagore's case against nationalism was originally made against the West. At its base was his disillusionment over the events of the Boer War. Appalled with the brutality and futility of that struggle and sensing the deeper implication of the attitudes it represented, Tagore expressed his feelings in a sonnet composed on the last day of the nineteenth century:

> The last sun of the century sets amidst the bloodred clouds of the West
> and the whirlwind of hatred.
> The naked passion of self-love of Nations, in its drunken delirium of
> greed, is dancing to the clash of steel and the howling verses of
> vengeance.
> The hungry self of the Nation shall burst in a violence of fury from its
> own shameless feeding.
> For it has made the world its food . . . .[11]

The book of poems concludes with a warning to India to "keep watch," and,

> Be not ashamed, my brothers, to stand before the proud and the
> powerful
> With your white robe of simpleness.
> Let your crown be of humility, your freedom, the freedom of the soul.
> Build God's throne daily upon the ample bareness of your poverty
> And know that what is huge is not great and pride is not everlasting.[12]

The events of the early twentieth century only increased Tagore's fear of nationalism and his desire for international harmony. In his famous poem *Gitanjali* of 1912, he yearned for an age of freedom,

> Where the mind is without fear and the head is held high;
> Where the world has not been broken up into fragments by narrow
> domestic walls.[13]

With the outbreak of the First World War, all Tagore's fears seemed to him confirmed. His cry of protest came in three lectures on nationalism delivered in 1916. These comprised a frontal attack on an idea which had then reached its apogee, and Tagore directed this attack against nationalism throughout the world: he called his lectures "Nationalism in the West," "Nationalism in Japan," and "Nationalism in India." The primary concern that dominates these lectures is that of the suppression of individual freedom by the cult of nationalism. "This nationalism," he begins, "is a cruel epidemic of evil that is sweeping over the human world of the present age, and eating into its moral vitality."[14] In Japan, "the voluntary submission of the whole people to the trimming of their minds and clipping of their freedom by their government, which through various educational agencies regulates their thoughts, manufactures their feelings" has led to an acceptance of an "all-pervading mental slavery with cheerfulness and pride because of their nervous desire to turn themselves into a machine of power called the Nation."[15] In the West, nationalism has corrupted the colonizers no less than the colonies. "Not merely the subject races," Tagore told America, "but you who live under the delusion that you are free, are everyday sacrificing your freedom and humanity to this fetish of nationalism, living in the dense poisonous atmosphere of world-wide suspicion and greed and panic."[16]

Tagore was most distressed not with the prevalence of nationalism in the West, but with its infection of India. The idea was a Western importation, but Tagore realized that his own countrymen, and especially his Bengali contemporaries, had developed it into a peculiar Indian type. Bankimchandra Chatterjee, Swami Vivekananda, B. C. Pal, and Aurobindo Ghose were the main philosophers of early Indian nationalism. Ironically, as Tagore was in America, preaching against nationalism, C. R. Das, a prominent Congress leader at that time, was telling his Indian audiences, "I find in the conception of my country the expression also of divinity. With me nationality is no mere political conception, borrowed from the philosophy of the West. . . . I value this principle of nationality as I value the principle of morality and religion."[17]

The greatest disservice nationalism had rendered India, Tagore argued, was to have directed the country's attention away from its primary needs. "Our real problem in India," Tagore contended, "is not political. It is social."[18] The nationalist urge leads to a pursuit of political goals to the neglect of pressing social problems. Neither the Congress Moderates nor the Extremists realized this critical need. The former had "no constructive idea," no sense that "what India most needed was constructive work coming from within herself."[19] They lost power "because the people soon came to realize how futile was the half policy adopted by them."[20] The Extremists pretended to root their program in traditional Indian truths but, in reality, they were nothing but advocates of Western nationalism. "Their ideals were based on Western history. They had no sympathy with the special problems of India. They did not recognize the patent fact that there were causes in our social organization which made the Indian incapable of coping with the alien . . . the domination in India of the caste system, and the blind and lazy habit of relying upon the authority of traditions that are incongruous anachronisms in the present age."[21] Nationalism cannot prompt a social and moral reform of the nature that is needed; rather, it will only whet the popular appetite for increased political warfare. The real task before India is that of building a good society, and "society is the expression of those moral and spiritual aspirations of man which belong to his higher nature."[22] If India pursues political independence to the exclusion of all else, she may attain a sovereign state; it will be one, however, in which the old social and moral maladies are not purged but magnified. Above all, a narrow quest for political liberty will only obscure India's real goal, which must always remain that of moral and spiritual freedom for the individual in society:

> Our social ideals create the human world, but when our mind is diverted from them to greed of power then in that state of intoxication we live in a world of abnormality where our strength is not health and our liberty is not freedom. Therefore political freedom does not give us freedom when our mind is not free. An automobile does not create freedom of the movement, because it is a mere machine. When I myself am free I can use the automobile for the purpose of my freedom.
>
> We must never forget in the present day that those people who have got their political freedom are not necessarily free, they are merely powerful. The passions which are unbridled in them are creating huge organizations of slavery in the disguise of freedom. Those who have made the gain of money their highest end are unconsciously selling their life and soul to rich persons or to the combinations that represent money. Those who are enamored of their political power and gloat over their extension of domain over foreign races gradually surrender their own freedom and humanity to the organizations necessary for holding other peoples in slavery. In the so-called free countries the majority of the people are not free, they are driven by the minority to a goal which is not even known to them. This becomes possible only because people do not acknowledge moral and spiritual freedom as their object. They create huge eddies with their passions, and they feel dizzily inebriated with the mere velocity of their whirling movement, taking that to be freedom. But the doom which

is waiting to overtake them is as certain as death for man's truth is moral truth and his emancipation is in the spiritual life.

The general opinion of the majority of the present-day nationalists in India is that we have come to a final completeness in our social and spiritual ideals, the task of the constructive work of society having been done several thousand years before we were born, and that now we are free to employ all our activities in the political direction. We never dream of blaming our social inadequacy as the origin of our present helplessness, for we have accepted as the creed of our nationalism that this social system has been perfected for all time to come by our ancestors. . . . This is the reason why we think that our one task is to build a political miracle of freedom upon the quicksand of social slavery. . . . Those of us in India who have come under the delusion that mere political freedom will make us free have accepted their lessons from the West as the gospel truth and lost their faith in humanity. We must remember whatever weakness we cherish in our society will become the source of danger in politics. The same inertia which leads us to our idolatry of dead forms in social institutions will create in our politics prison-houses with immovable walls. The narrowness of sympathy which makes it possible for us to impose upon a considerable portion of humanity the galling yoke of inferiority will assert itself in our politics in creating the tyranny of injustice.[23]

Many of the ideas Tagore voices in the above passage are in profound agreement with those of Gandhi. They agree ultimately on the primary need for social reform in India, as well as on the essential meaning of swaraj. Tagore's unique position concerned Indian nationalism: he attacked it as an unmitigated evil that could only thwart the quest for swaraj. This inevitably sparked a controversy with India's arch-nationalist, Mahatma Gandhi.

"Indian nationalism is not exclusive, nor aggressive, nor destructive. It is health- giving, religious and therefore humanitarian."[24] This is Gandhi replying to Tagore's criticisms and the view he expressed here accurately represents his general position on Indian nationalism. It may rightly be argued that Gandhi did not advocate many of the forms of nationalism that had sprung up around 1900 in Bengal. Gandhi did not see the nation as a transcendent entity, possessed of a soul and a form of freedom of its own, apart from its individual human components. He thought of swaraj in terms, first, of the individual, and then of society. Yet, although Gandhi was not an exponent of nationalism after the fashion of B. C. Pal or C. R. Das, his ideas did support other forms of nationalism, which he frankly endorsed, and which, as Tagore soon discovered, posed threats to individual freedom.

In March 1919, Gandhi called upon the people of India to observe April 6 as a mass *hartal*: a day of fasting, public meetings, and suspension of labor. The intent was to mobilize popular opposition to the government's enactment of the Rowlatt Bills; the effect of the *hartal* was to demonstrate the considerable power potential of the noncooperation program. On April 12, Tagore wrote to Gandhi from his home of Shantiniketan urging him to exercise caution in the use of noncooperation. The letter represents the first written evidence of Tagore's qualms over Gandhi's emerging political leadership. "Power in all its forms is irrational," Tagore began, "it is like the horse that drags the carriage blind-folded." He expressed his concern over recent acts of government repression, and questioned the good that could result from pressing the campaign further. "I have always felt," he continued, "and said accordingly, that the great gift of freedom can never come to a people through charity. We must win it before we can own it. And India's opportunities for winning it will come to her when she can prove that she is morally superior to the people who rule her by their right of conquest." The present noncooperation movement, he implied, did not seem to him representative of India's moral superiority, and he concluded this letter with these telling lines: "I pray most fervently that nothing that tends to weaken our spiritual freedom may intrude into your marching line, that martyrdom for the cause of truth may never degenerate into fanaticism for mere verbal forms, descending into the self-defence that hides itself behind a moral name."[25]

Tagore sailed for England and America early the next year. While abroad, he seems to have made up his mind as to whether Gandhi's movement had in fact "degenerated into fanaticism for mere verbal forms," hiding itself "behind a moral name." "I wish I were the little creature Jack," he wrote from Chicago in reference to the noncooperation campaign, "whose one mission is to kill the Giant Abstraction, which is claiming the sacrifice of individuals all over the world under highly tainted masks of delusion."[26] In July 1921, he returned to India, after fourteen months abroad, to confront the campaign at its peak. His battle against "the Giant Abstraction" soon began in earnest.

On August 29, Tagore delivered at a Calcutta public meeting an address entitled "The Call of Truth." A remarkable commentary, it offered both a trenchant criticism of Gandhi's leadership and an eloquent defense of individual freedom with which Gandhi, above all Indian leaders of this time, had identified himself. Tagore begins his remarks with a proposition shared by Gandhi: it is in our nature to struggle for the self-realization and freedom of swaraj. This must remain an individual's highest aim, to gain knowledge and mastery of one's self.[27] Reiterating a maxim that both he and Gandhi had stressed for the last decade, Tagore said, "They who have failed to attain Swaraj within themselves must lose it in the outside world too."[28] Political independence was a great *desideratum*, but it was not swaraj. Nor could it promote swaraj if not accompanied by a transformation of an individual's moral values. Tagore often expressed his ideas through metaphor. In "The Call of Truth" he drew on this medium to set forth his conception of the relation of social and moral to political reform. The metaphor is his own, but the idea was shared by Gandhi:

> When we turn our gaze upon the progress of other nations, the political cart-horse comes prominently into view—on it seems to depend wholly the speed of the vehicle. We forget that the cart behind the horse must also be in a fit state to move; its wheels must have the right alignment, its part must have been properly assembled. The cart is the product not simply of materials on which saw and hammer had worked; thought, energy and application have gone into its making. We have seen countries that are outwardly free, but as they are drawn by the horse of politics the rattle rouses all the neighborhood from sleep and the jolting makes the limbs of the passengers ache; the vehicles break down repeatedly on their way and to put them in running order is a terrific business. Yet they are vehicles of sort, after all. The fragments that pass for our country not only lack cohesion but are comprised of parts at odds with one another. To hitch it to anger or avarice or some other passion, drag it along painfully with much din and bustle, and call this political progress! How long could the driving force last? Is it not wiser, then, to keep the horse in the stable for the time and take up the task, first, of putting the vehicle in good shape?[29]

From this passage may be anticipated the nature of the criticism that follows: it consists, in effect, of Tagore turning Gandhi's own arguments against him. While abroad, Tagore says, he had heard nothing but high praise of the noncooperation movement. He had come to believe from this that India was at last on the path to "real liberation."[30] Then, in a chilling paragraph, he tells of what he found on his return to India: "So, in the excited expectation of breathing the air of a new-found freedom, I hurried back to my homeland. But what I have seen and felt troubles me. Something seems to be weighing on the people's spirit; a stern pressure is at work; it makes everyone talk in the same voice and make the same gestures."[31]

This climate of opinion, Tagore believed, was a manifestation of nationalism at its worst. "Slave mentality" of this nature rather than alien rule, is "our real enemy and through its defeat alone can swaraj within and without come to us."[32] Gandhi's directives, which urged among other things the manual spinning of yarn and burning of foreign cloth, were not being weighed by critical minds; rather, they had been accepted as dogma. And, "As dogma takes the place of reason, freedom will give way to some kind of despotism."[33] Tagore himself remained highly critical of Gandhi's directives. He found Gandhi's dicta on spinning and cloth-burning negative and destructive. "Swaraj is not a matter of mere self-sufficiency in the production of cloth. Its real place is within us, the mind with its diverse power goes on building swaraj for itself."[34] Gandhi's tenets of swaraj and *swadeshi* struck Tagore as medieval in their compulsive desire for simplicity; they closed doors to economic advance. In their rabid advocacy of a narrow form of *swadeshi* they cramped Indian attitudes into a restrictive provincial mold, inhibiting the mind's "diverse power" to go on "building swaraj for itself." "As everywhere else, swaraj in this country has to find its basis in the mind's unfoldment, in knowledge, in scientific thinking, and not in shallow gestures."[35] Gandhi's approach to social reform, Tagore contended, would not stimulate the "mind's unfoldment," but rather restrict its development and lead to its atrophy. On a national level this approach would result in a deplorable attitude of isolationism and hostility toward the rest of the world. "The Call of Truth" ends with a characteristic appeal to answer the "urgent call" of "universal humanity" by shedding the limitations of narrow nationalism, and recognizing "the vast dimensions of India in its world context."[36]

"Henceforth, any nation which seeks isolation for itself must come into conflict with the time-spirit and find no peace. From now onward the plane of thinking of every nation will have to be international. It is the striving of the new age to develop in the mind this faculty of universality."[37]

The Gandhi-Tagore controversy thus focused on two aspects of the meaning of swaraj or of freedom in its fullest sense. Tagore argued, first, that on a domestic level, Indians had placed themselves in bondage through their unthinking acceptance of dogma. They idolized a leader who, however saintly, had harnessed their blind allegiance to a gospel of retardation rather than growth. A second and related feature of Gandhi's teaching was its implications on an international level. Gandhi's ideas, Tagore argued, had fostered, for the most part, an unhealthy sense of separateness that foolishly spurned the knowledge and advances of the Western world. Each of these attitudes inhibited India's growth and thus restricted her freedom.

Gandhi responded to the first of Tagore's charges that he did not wish to produce a "deathlike sameness in the nation," but rather to use the spinning wheel to "realize the essential and living oneness of interest among India's myriads."[38] Spinning was not intended to replace all other forms of activity, but rather to symbolize "sacrifice for the whole nation."

"If the Poet span half an hour daily his poetry would gain in richness. For it would then represent the poor man's wants and woes in a more forcible manner than now."[39] Spinning for Gandhi, then, was a symbolic form of identification with the masses. Tagore, however, remained suspicious of any such abstract appeal and tended to identify this symbolism with aspects of Indian nationalism. Moreover, when Tagore accused Gandhi of narrow provincialism, the latter replied, "I hope I am as great a believer in free air as the great Poet. I do not want my house to be walled in on all sides and my windows to be stuffed. I want the cultures of all the lands to be blown about my house as freely as possible. But I refuse to be blown off my feet by any."[40] And when Tagore warned him of the inevitable danger inherent in his nationalism, Gandhi argued, "My patriotism is not exclusive; it is calculated not only not to hurt any other nation but to benefit all in the true sense of the word. India's freedom as conceived by me can never be a menace to the world."[41]

Yet, despite these assurances, Gandhi could express extreme sentiments of Indian nationalism. "The interests of my country," he once wrote, "are identical with those of my religion,"[42] and, on another occasion, "The attainment of national independence is to me a search after truth."[43] As Gandhi held nothing more sacred than his religion and the quest for truth, it is clear how highly he placed the interests of his country and the struggle for Indian Independence. Tagore detected in such feelings a threat to individual freedom. That he himself was reviled by his countrymen for his heretical criticism of the noncooperation movement and accused of everything from high treason to an inveterate jealousy of Gandhi suggests that his fear of "the Giant Abstraction" was not altogether unjustified.

Gandhi did contribute, as a political leader and thinker, to the growth of Indian nationalism as much as any figure of this century. Nowhere does he seem to recognize the implicit danger in nationalism to individual freedom, as well as to India's own free development vis-à-vis the rest of the world. On the contrary, he dismissed all attacks on Indian nationalism, not only

from Tagore but also from his Western friends, as totally without foundation. Charles Andrews, his closest British friend, wrote to Gandhi with
shock and dismay in September 1921 concerning the burning of foreign
cloth. "The picture of your lighting that great pile," Andrews said, "including beautiful fabrics, shocked me intensely. We seem to be losing sight of
the great beautiful world to which we belong and concentrating selfishly on
India, and this must (I fear) lead back to the old bad selfish nationalism. If
so, we get into the vicious circle from which Europe is now trying so desperately to escape."[44]

Gandhi replied, "In all I do or advise, the infallible test I apply is, whether the particular action will hold good in regard to the dearest and the near-
est."[45] He then concludes, "Experience shows that the richest gifts must be
destroyed without compensation and hesitation if they hinder one's moral
progress."[46] On this point of view, Tagore made a telling critique: "Experience . . . has led me to dread, no so much evil itself, as tyrannical attempts
to create goodness. Of punitive police, political or moral, I have a whole-
some horror. The state of slavery which is thus brought on is the worst form
of cancer to which humanity is subject."[47] Tagore, almost alone in his time,
insisted not only that there may be more than one path to "moral progress,"
but also that the greatest obstacle to be found on each of them was the
"slave mentality" that characterized nationalism.[48]

What was the strength and weakness of Tagore's critique of Gandhi?
Tagore's invaluable contribution came with his clear exposition of swaraj as
meaning more than political independence, as demanding basic social change
and self-realization. Gandhi had of course recognized this but Tagore drove
the point home with his case against the culture of nationalism, when he
championed personal freedom against political correctness. He had the
courage to denounce Gandhi's doctrines when they lapsed into dogma or
duragraha. Yet both Tagore's theory and practice fell short of a method of
political and social change. Enveloped in a system of imperialism and social
injustice, he remained a powerful critic with no potential for exercising real
political power. If his hold on swaraj was firm, his grasp of satyagraha was
weak. To have one without the other is a blow to both, as will be suggested
in chapter 6 with the analysis of Malcolm X and Martin Luther King, Jr.
Gandhi's contribution lies not only in his idea of freedom as swaraj but
as well in his unique conception of the power of satyagraha and the connections that he forged between them. This is his claim to greatness and
Tagore's criticisms do not touch it.

Gandhi's further response to Tagore's criticism of nationalism came with his theories of decentralization and democracy. He argued that the state often represented the greatest obstacle to our realization of swaraj and that we may decrease the scope of political violence and increase the sphere of individual freedom and voluntary action, by decentralizing for a limited democratic state. Gandhi viewed "with the greatest fear" the increasing centralization of power in most states because this "does the greatest harm to mankind by destroying individuality which lies at the root of all progress."[49] Therefore, "if India is to evolve along nonviolent lines, it will have to decentralize," because "centralization as a system is inconsistent with a nonviolent structure of society."[50] Gandhi did not delineate the precise functions that would be retained by a democratic central authority. The main point is that he advocated for Indian democracy "the maximum possible decentralization of the political and economic power and resources of the state."[51]

Unlike Tagore, Gandhi set forth a theory of democracy as a central part of his political thought. He built this on his idea of swaraj, asserting that "The spirit of democracy cannot be imposed from without. It has to come from within."[52] The recurrent theme in his thinking about democracy as also with swaraj, is the necessity of achieving freedom with discipline and self-restraint: "Democracy disciplined and enlightened is the finest thing in the world. A democracy prejudiced, ignorant, superstitious will land itself in chaos and be self-destroyed."[53] This is an abiding danger, that "democracy degenerate into mobocracy."[54] Another theme running through his democratic theory is his preoccupation with the right use of power. If power is wielded by either an authoritarian state or a mobocracy, civil disobedience against it becomes imperative. A legitimate form of power is then exercised but people must understand that in any system, despotic or democratic, "the truth is that power resides in the people." It may be "entrusted for the time being to those whom they may choose as their representatives" but "The parliaments have no power or even existence independently of the people."

If this basic truth is realized then the most democratic and decentralized state will still carry a corrective within it of satyagraha to remedy abuses of power. At any sign of mob rule, responsible citizens may administer a dose of civil disobedience because that is the real "storehouse of power." Gandhi asks that we "imagine a whole people unwilling to conform to the laws of the legislature and prepared to suffer the consequences of non-compliance!

They will bring the whole legislative and the executive machinery to a standstill . . . no police or military coercion can bend the resolute will of a people, out for suffering to the uttermost. And parliamentary procedure is good only when its members are willing to conform to the will of the majority."[55] If Gandhi's advocacy of democracy carries this warning to the government of a continuing sanction for mass civil disobedience, it also admonishes the citizenry of its collective responsibility, for "Every citizen, therefore, renders himself responsible for every act of his government," and when the government goes astray, "it becomes his duty to withdraw his support."[56]

This, then, is the fullness of Gandhi's response to Tagore. It also represents a defense against similar criticisms made by M. N. Roy, as suggested in the analysis of Roy below. All three are concerned with abuses of power by political leaders but among them only Gandhi was in a position to exercise substantial power through satyagraha. Gandhi's defense is that in both theory and practice he remained wholly committed to democracy: "I claim to be a democrat both by instinct and training."[57] The democratic ideal that he espouses correlates with his theory of swaraj, or freedom with restraint, and of satyagraha, as a continuing legitimization of civil disobedience; it shows that he wants power wielded wisely or responsibly controlled in a democracy.

M. N. Roy's Critique: Coming to Terms with the Mahatma

Manabendra Nath Roy was born in 1887 into a Bengali *brahmin* family in a village outside of Calcutta.[58] Twenty-eight years later, as a terrorist revolutionary, he left India for an adventurous career in the Communist international movement. These initial twenty-eight years in Bengal were decisive for the shaping of his personality and thought. Three components of this early experience deserve mention. First, there was the influence of Roy's brahmanical family background and outlook. This inspired and reinforced his penchant for theory, his elitism, and his strong moral outlook.[59] Second, there was Roy's early, intense belief in Hinduism. His religious frame of mind, like his brahmanical spirit, never left him, but prodded him on in his quest for "those abiding, permanent values of humanity."[60] Third, in this first generation of his life, the ideology of Indian nationalism exerted an immense influence on Roy as it did on many of his contemporary Bengali intellectuals and students.

"An ideology," writes Edward Shils, "is the product of man's need for imposing intellectual order on the world. The need for ideology is an intensification of the need for a cognitive and moral map of the universe. . ."[61] Roy's quest for an adequate ideology began during his youth in Bengal. It continued throughout his next phase as an orthodox communist and later as a Marxist revisionist. Then, later, having abandoned Marxism for what he called "Radical Humanism," his search intensified for "a cognitive and moral map of the universe." It ended not in satisfaction but only with his death in 1954. Yet, in this last phase of his thought, Roy had come closer to the fulfillment of his needs, to realization of his identity through the construction of an ideology, than he had ever approached in his earlier phases. If the outlines of Roy's cognitive and moral map had been determined in his youth by a brahmanical outlook, a Hindu creed, and the nationalist experience in Bengal, then unlike Gandhi, he never came to terms with the demands of his early formative period and remained alienated from his Indian tradition.

The year 1915 is a key one in the Gandhi-Roy story. In that year, Roy, as a terrorist schooled under Jatin Mukherjee and Aurobindo Ghose, left Calcutta on a revolutionary mission to obtain German arms for the struggle against the Raj. In that same year, Gandhi returned to India after twenty-one years in South Africa. As Gandhi achieved his extraordinary rise to power in the Congress during the 1920s, Roy acquired his reputation of being "undoubtedly the most colorful of all non-Russian Communists in the era of Lenin and Stalin."[62] From 1915 to 1930, Roy moved about on various revolutionary missions, from Mexico to Berlin, and then Paris, Zurich, Tashkent, and Moscow. In Mexico, Roy was converted to Communism and reputedly helped form the first Communist Party there. In Moscow, he contributed to revolutionary strategy for communist activity in the colonial areas.[63] In Europe, he rose to a position of authority in the Comintern, published a series of books and pamphlets on Marxist theory, and edited a communist newspaper. The achievements of both Gandhi and Roy during this period were spectacular, but in complete contrast.

Yet, for all their respective achievements, there was never anything like a balance of power between these two figures. It was always Gandhi and never Roy who dominated the Indian nationalist movement with his unparalleled genius for mass leadership. Whereas Roy would struggle for decades to gain power in India and fail, Gandhi acquired authority quickly and kept it. While Roy remained preoccupied with Gandhi's power, the Mahatma rarely mentions Roy in his writings or speeches.[64] When Roy returned from prison to the political scene in the late thirties, Gandhi took scant notice of him. Roy was both a cultural and political outsider and suffered as a result. Gandhi, after his return to India in 1915, became rooted in the nationalist tradition and developed a style of political behavior that gained for him personal confidence as well as political power. Thus, while Roy, out of touch with his tradition, never ceased in his effort to come to terms with Gandhi, the Mahatma, secure in his surroundings, could remain aloof. In this sense, a consideration of Roy's view of Gandhi becomes part of a larger question, that of the relationship of the Indian intellectual to the people.[65]

The first detailed Marxist critique of Gandhi appeared in Roy's early book, *India in Transition*, written in Moscow in 1921. The book grew out of discussions that Roy had with Lenin and other communist figures at the Second Congress of the Communist International. At this Congress, Roy had argued, contrary to Lenin, that communist policy in the colonial areas must be to support proletarian rather than bourgeois movements. Lenin contended that bourgeois nationalist organizations like the Indian Congress could be considered revolutionary, and since no viable Communist parties existed, these organizations deserved the support of the International. Roy replied that the Indian Congress and similar agencies could only betray the revolution: an Indian proletariat existed, and must be mobilized behind a communist vanguard. Liberation from imperialism could come only under communist leadership. The Roy-Lenin controversy was clearly over fundamental issues and would have implications for communist strategy in the future.

Roy later reflected back upon his differences with Lenin and concluded that "The role of Gandhi was the crucial point of difference. Lenin believed that, as the inspirer and leader of a mass movement, he was a revolutionary. I maintained that, a religious and cultural revivalist, he was bound to be a reactionary socially, however revolutionary he might appear politically."[66] In Roy's view, "The religious ideology preached by him [Gandhi] also appealed to the medieval mentality of the masses. But the same ideology discouraged any revolutionary mass action. The quintessence of the situation, as I analyzed and understood it, was a potentially revolutionary movement restrained by a reactionary ideology."[67] "I reminded Lenin of the dictum that I had learnt from him: that without a revolutionary ideology, there could be no revolution."[68] These arguments formed the basis of the position on Gandhi that was developed by Roy in *India in Transition*.

"The most serious defect of *India in Transition*," wrote a leading biographer of Roy "is its underestimation of Mahatma Gandhi's political potential."[69] Roy begins his critique of Gandhi in this book with the confident assertion that Gandhism has now "reached a crisis" and its "impending wane . . . signifies the collapse of the reactionary forces and their total alienation from the political movement."[70] Roy's confidence was rooted in the classic Marxist belief in the inexorable march forward of western civilization. Gandhism was seen as a temporary obstacle in the path of history, which would soon be swept aside: not by the Raj, but by the masses themselves, once they became conscious of the progressive movement of history. Whatever Gandhi may tell the masses, "post-British India cannot and will not become pre-British India." Therefore, "Here lies the contradiction in the orthodox nationalism as expressed of late in the cult of Gandhism. It endeavors to utilize the mass energy for the perpetuation or revival of that heritage of national culture which has been made untenable by the awakening of mass energy. . . . Therefore, Gandhism is bound to be defeated. The signs of the impending defeat are already perceptible. Gandhism will fall victim to its own contradictions."[71]

Roy admits that under Gandhi's leadership, through the effective use of *hartal* and noncooperation, "For the first time in its history, the Indian national movement entered into the period of active struggle."[72] Yet, here as elsewhere Roy remains confined within his Marxist categories. Gandhi's success in 1920, he says, simply revealed that "the time for mass-action was ripe. Economic forces, together with other objective causes had created an atmosphere" which propelled Gandhi into power. Roy tried to drive home his argument against Lenin by stressing the potential role of the Indian proletariat, portraying it as an awakened and thriving revolutionary force. But Roy's view of the proletariat was as fanciful as his anticipation of "the imminent collapse of Gandhism."[73] In each of these miscalculations, one sees repeated the error of a dogmatic application of Marxist doctrine to an inappropriate political context.

However, Roy's mistakes cannot be attributed entirely to his doctrinaire Marxism. Rather, his Marxism may be explained as part of a desperate search for an ideology, which was in turn prompted by a quest for a new identity. The identity that Roy sought in the critical period of his youth, was that of an urbane, cosmopolitan type, entirely at home with western civilization, fully equipped to appreciate and assist in its historical forward movement. Yet, he required as well an ideology that would allow him to criticize those aspects of western civilization which were responsible for the subjugation of his own people. The ideology must serve to liberate him from the sense of inferiority instilled by imperialism and at the same time arm him in his struggle for the liberation of India. Marxism suited this purpose exactly. His total affirmation of Marxism, therefore, followed immediately after his total rejection of nationalism, and from this there emerged his total denial of Gandhi as a lasting political force in India. In this sense, *India in Transition* offers a clear example of an intellectual determined to reject his tradition. Not only Gandhi, but also extremist leaders like Tilak and Aurobindo, who only five years earlier had commanded Roy's allegiance, are now dismissed with contempt as examples of "petty-bourgeois humanitarianism."[74] For the next ten years, until his imprisonment in 1931, Roy struggled to affirm himself in his new identity as an international Marxist revolutionary.

Throughout the twenties, as Roy rose to the peak of his authority in the Comintern, he refined and elaborated the view of Gandhi he had set forth in 1921. A series of excellent articles and pamphlets by Roy and his first wife Evelyn were devoted to Gandhism. In *One Year of Non-Cooperation*, for example, the Roys distinguish five "grave errors" or "great defects" of Gandhism. The "most glaring defect" is the absence of an intelligent program of economic reform. Next, there is Gandhi's "obstinate and futile" emphasis on social harmony instead of a frank recognition of the real necessity of class conflict. Then, they find a senseless "intrusion of metaphysics into the realm of politics." The revolt against the British Raj, they emphasize, "is a question of economics, not metaphysics." Further, they deplore Gandhi's reactionary view of history, his desire "to run from the Machine-age back to the Stone Age." Finally, they criticize the total lack of any revolutionary quality in Gandhi's approach to social change; they see only a "weak and watery reformism, which shrinks at every turn from the realities of the struggle for freedom."[75] The entire critique is made with exceptional clarity and forcefulness, and it, together with other writings by the Roys on Gandhi, represents the most incisive communist criticism of him during this period.

For a variety of reasons Roy fell out of favor with Moscow, and in December 1929 he was officially expelled from the Communist International. He reacted by persuading himself that he could seize control of the revolutionary movement in India and a year later he returned home. He was soon arrested and he remained a political prisoner of the Raj until November 1936. These five hard years in jail witnessed a substantial change in Roy's ideology and this eventually had its effect upon his view of Gandhi.

While in prison, Roy, like Gandhi and Nehru, read and wrote voluminously. His three volumes of "prison diaries" refer often to Gandhi. Indeed, it might be argued that there is no better index to the extent to which Gandhi's presence dominated the Indian scene than the jail reflections of his harshest critic.[76] Roy had apparently inherited from his early nationalist experience and brahmanical background a moralist's predilection for seeing the world in categorical terms of right and wrong. Gandhi shared with Roy a strong taste for moralizing expressed in a dominant concern for the moral values of society. Eventually, in his Radical Humanist phase, the moralist in Roy prevails, just as it always had prevailed in Gandhi, and Roy abandons Marxism because he finds it devoid of ethics. However, even as early as the thirties, a first glimpse of the way in which Roy's moral outlook erodes his Marxism can be seen in his prison diaries. This appears in his reflections on the two concepts of freedom and revolution. Both of these ideas were to become key themes of Radical Humanism, and the basis of their later development is found here, in the diaries.

When Roy wrote about freedom and revolution as an orthodox Marxist in the twenties, he conceived them as economic categories. Freedom would come with the necessary changes in the economic mode of production, and revolution would be achieved through a violent seizure of power by the Party and the masses. Swaraj meant no more than independence from British rule. Now, in the thirties, Roy begins to perceive other dimensions in these two ideas. In regard to freedom, he says that his aim is to "indicate the way to real spiritual freedom offered by the materialist philosophy."[77] For the first time in Roy's writings, the supreme goal of "spiritual freedom" is distinguished from the lesser aims of "political freedom, economic prosperity and social happiness."[78] It is significant that Roy, a Marxist, by using the term "spiritual freedom" departs from Marxist language. Yet, he does not adopt either Gandhi's or Tagore's use and meaning of swaraj. This is presumably because he considers himself not only a critic of Gandhi but also outside the Hindu tradition that both Gandhi and Tagore personify. Moreover, a significant change in Roy's concept of revolution is evident in his increasing preference for the term "Indian Renaissance," which means for him a "philosophical" and "spiritual" as well as economic revolution. His concluding essay, "Preconditions of Indian Renaissance,"[79] in the second volume of the jail diaries emphasizes the need for a new philosophical and moral outlook in India.

The above analysis of Roy's prison diaries is not meant to suggest that a reader of these volumes in the thirties, with no possible knowledge of the way Roy's thought would develop, could have perceived the affinities between Gandhi and Roy that eventually appeared. However, since these ideas can be found in the diaries in embryonic form, it is apparent that Roy's movement toward a Gandhian way of thinking did not occur overnight. What did occur was a long and painful intellectual journey in which Roy gradually yielded, point by point, to the force of an ideological tradition until substantial similarities with Gandhi and with earlier Bengali nationalists were established. Moreover, if it were not for Roy's untimely death, the journey toward reconciliation with Gandhi might well have continued further.

If there was a long-term movement in Roy's thinking about freedom and change that drew him closer to Gandhi, there were also sharp contrasts between these two men during the 1930s and 1940s. The ruthlessness of Roy's attack on Gandhi in the diaries reaches a climax in an essay entitled "India's Message." The critique begins with a contemptuous dismissal of Gandhism as a political philosophy. Far from positing a philosophical system, Roy finds in Gandhism only "a mass of platitudes and hopeless self-contradictions" emerging from "a conception of morality based upon dogmatic faith." As such, it is religion not philosophy; and a religion that has become politicized and thus serves as "the ideological reflex" of India's "cultural backwardness" and "superstition."[80]

Roy's attack on Gandhi in 1922 was largely content to write Gandhism off as a medieval ideology at the mercy of inexorable economic forces. Now, a decade later, Roy concentrates on the moral virtues that Gandhi idealized and refutes them at length. Roy argues that "admirable virtues" like "love, goodness, sacrifice, simplicity, and absolute nonviolence" when preached to the masses by Gandhi only serve to emasculate them. Overthrow of the ruling classes becomes impossible, and the result can only be "voluntary submission of the masses to the established system of oppression and exploitation."

The worst of Gandhi's tenets is his "cult of nonviolence," the "central pivot" of his thought, "holding its quaint dogmas and naive doctrines together into a comprehensive system of highly reactionary thought." Far from serving any noble purpose, *ahimsa* in politics only tends to support the forces of violence and exploitation. "Therefore, those who preach nonviolence [to and for] . . . the exploited and oppressed masses, are defenders of violence in practice." If Gandhi's nonviolence were practiced, capitalism would remain entrenched and "the Juggernaut of vulgar materialism" would emerge triumphant. "Love, the sentimental counterpart of the cult of nonviolence, thus is exposed as mere cant." Finally, Roy asserts that Gandhi's values are based on "blind faith" and offer only "the message of medievalism" that idealizes "the savage living on the tree." In this way Gandhi inhibits real progress, which Roy sees in terms of the "dynamic process" of "modern civilization" that "must go forward." For Roy, then, the light is in the West: in the forces of rationalism, technology, modern science, and "an economy of abundance."[81] Roy maintained this latter position until the end, and it will always distinguish him sharply from Gandhi.

Soon after his discharge from prison, Roy decided that the sole route to political success in India lay in cooperation with the Congress. This meant a much more conciliatory attitude toward Gandhi. Subhas Bose had opposed Gandhi in the Congress with some initial success, but Roy, unlike Bose, had neither mass appeal nor a strong regional base of power in Bengal. Therefore, Roy made a brief but futile attempt to rise in the Congress through cooperation with the Gandhians. His article of this period entitled "Gandhiji, A Critical Appreciation" reflects this spirit of conciliation. He begins with the claim that "I appreciate Gandhiji's greatness better than any of his ardent admirers." Gandhi, he says, is a great "political awakener" of the masses and the highest tribute that one can pay him "would be to regard and respect Gandhiji as the embodiment of the primitive, blind, spontaneous spirit of revolt of the Indian masses." While Roy does mention, incidentally, that Gandhism may in the future come to stifle the revolution rather than promote it, he concludes that at present "let us admire, respect, and properly appreciate him for the great services that he has rendered to the struggle for freedom."[82] This article does not present a sincere statement of Roy's view of Gandhi at this time. As his personal correspondence shows,[83] Roy regarded Gandhi in this period as his arch-enemy, who should be destroyed as quickly as possible. The significance of this "critical appreciation" by Roy lies in its indication of the extent to which Roy, in his effort to influence the Congress, was prepared to compromise his real view of Gandhi as a hopeless medieval reactionary. In the months ahead, Roy made a desperate attempt to gain power, but he failed miserably. No single factor was more responsible for this than his utter inability to come to grips, not merely with Gandhi, but with the nationalist culture that Gandhi represented and to which Roy remained so much an outsider.

In 1946, Philip Spratt, a close associate and strong admirer of Roy wrote an appreciative foreword for Roy's latest series of speeches, which were published under the significant title of *New Orientation*. Spratt reviewed Roy's position on Gandhi and then concluded: "Roy was highly critical of Gandhism from the very start, in 1920, and has never altered his opinion. . . . Yet it is true, I think, that he has failed to make his criticisms intelligible to the Indian reader. His approach to Gandhism seems that of an outsider, an unsympathetic foreigner. He has never tried to get under the skin of the Mahatma or his admirers and see where that extraordinary power comes from."[84]

This remark constitutes a good indication of the nature of Roy's difficulties with Gandhi during a generation of observation and criticism. Yet, at the moment of Spratt's writing, significant changes were occurring in Roy's thinking about the nature of power and freedom, revolution and history, politics and leadership. And with this fundamental reassessment of basic issues, which Roy called his "New Orientation," there followed a change of view of Gandhi.

Several factors influenced Roy's sweeping intellectual reappraisal in 1946. First, Roy's Radical Democratic Party, established in opposition to the Congress, was resoundingly defeated in the Indian general elections held throughout the country in the spring of 1946. If the historical importance for India of these general elections was to demonstrate that the Muslim League represented the Muslims and the Congress the Hindus, then their importance for Roy was to show that his party, given the nation's polarization, represented no one. It meant the end of his political career. A second factor that affected his thinking concerned the direction and behavior of the world communist movement under Stalin. The brutal aspects of Stalinist leadership were becoming clear; Roy had long been under attack from the Communist Party of India and neither practical nor theoretical reconciliation with Communism was possible. Roy expressed the nature of his dilemma in stark terms when he told his followers that they must beware of "two psychoses" prevalent in India, those of Communism and nationalism. "Radicalism," he declared, "is not camouflaged Communism. We shall have to get over the major nationalist psychosis as well as the minor Communist psychosis, if we believe that we have something new to contribute to the political thought and practice, not only for our country, but of the world as a whole."[85]

An ideologist abhors nothing more than a moral vacuum, or what Roy liked to deplore as the "moral cultural crisis"[86] of his time. For this suggests basic uncertainty over the rightness and wrongness of fundamental moral values, and it is the element of moral certainty that the ideologist seeks above all else. In this respect, Gandhi was no less an ideologist than Roy; but whereas Gandhi had achieved certainty on such matters during his experience in South Africa, Roy underwent a series of such crises, the last and most serious in 1945–46. The final phase of his life, from 1946–53, represents a period of gradual resolution in which Roy delved deeply into his personal resources, trying to form a coherent pattern of thought to meet the demands before him. Roy, while trying to purge himself of the "nationalist psychosis," nevertheless moved far away from Marxism into a way of thinking significantly akin to Gandhi.

On August 16, 1946, while Roy, residing in Dehra Dun, was appraising and reappraising his New Orientation, and Gandhi was busily commenting on Nature Cure from Sevagram, there occurred in Calcutta unprecedented communal riots (to be discussed in chapter 5). These events had a profound effect upon Roy's view of Gandhi.

Gandhi's reaction to the Calcutta killings, unlike that of Nehru or Jinnah, was to perceive immediately the disastrous social implications and then to act courageously, in an attempt to quell the violence. Just as the Amritsar massacre twenty-seven years earlier had shocked Gandhi into realizing the injustice of the Raj, so the Calcutta killing forced him to see the abyss of violence within his own society. The ensuing fifteen months, culminating in his assassination, contain some of the finest hours of his entire career. During this period, he scored two brilliant triumphs for his method of satyagraha in his Calcutta and Delhi fasts against communal violence. Less dramatic than these, but equally impressive, were his "walking tours" in Noakhali and his ingenious use of the prayer meeting to restore trust in a series of strife-torn villages. These final acts moved nearly everyone in India to a higher appreciation of Gandhi's greatness. Roy in this case was no exception.

"What changed Roy's attitude [toward Gandhi]," writes Philip Spratt, "was Gandhi's campaign against the communal massacres, which came at the time of his own final disillusionment with Communist political methods." Spratt observes the similarity in Roy's and Gandhi's mutual opposition to partition, and the common spirit of their response to the communal riots. He remarks that on hearing the news of Gandhi's assassination, "Roy was deeply moved . . . henceforth a new respect for Gandhi showed in his writing."[87] There was indeed a striking change in Roy's attitude toward Gandhi following the assassination. In two articles of February and April,

1948, entitled "The Message of the Martyr" and "Homage to the Martyr," Roy sets forth for the first time the extent of his ideological agreement with Gandhi. He now discovers that Gandhi's revivalist nationalism was neither the essential nor the greatest element in Gandhi's teaching. "Essentially, [Gandhi's message] is a moral, humanist, cosmopolitan appeal. . . . The lesson of the martyrdom of the Mahatma is that the nobler core of his message could not be reconciled with the intolerant cult of nationalism, which he also preached. Unfortunately, this contradiction in his ideas and ideals was not realized by the Mahatma until the last days of his life." In Gandhi's final phase, what Roy repeatedly calls the "moral and humanist essence of his message" appeared, and it is precisely this which is "needed by India never so very urgently as today." Thus, Indians can do justice to their Mahatma when they learn "to place the moral and humanist core of his teachings above the carnal cult of nationalism and power-politics."[88]

There are those who argue that Roy's tributes to Gandhi after the assassination were merely sentimental outbursts, entirely inconsistent with the main line of his thought. This argument is mistaken for several reasons. First, when Roy was attacked by some of his readers for calling Gandhi a humanist and cosmopolitan, he admitted that he had written the article while "deeply moved" by the crime, "in an emotional state." But then he went on vehemently to defend his position, deploring the "insensitivity of the logical purists" who attacked him, and refusing categorically to retract a word that he had written. Gandhi, he insisted in this later article, "sincerely wanted politics to be guided by moral considerations," and his "endeavour to introduce morality into political practice was the positive core of Gandhism."[89] This made Gandhi, like Roy, a humanist. A second reason why this argument is mistaken has already been seen: glimpses of Roy's movement away from Marx and toward Gandhi can be found as early as in the prison diaries, and are clearly manifest two years before the assassination in the ideological changes of his "new orientation."

Finally, far from Roy's tribute to Gandhi being a sporadic outburst, his changed attitude takes a permanent form in his later writings: a "new respect" for Gandhi now infuses his thoughts.[90] This can be seen clearly in an article Roy wrote on Gandhi a full year after the assassination. In this piece, Roy pays respect to "the immortality of his [Gandhi's] message" and then sums up the significance of Gandhi's thought in these remarkable words: "Practice of the precept of purifying politics with truth and nonviolence alone will immortalize the memory of the Mahatma. Monuments of mortar and marble will perish, but the light of the sublime message of truth and nonviolence will shine forever."[91] The passage signifies a radical departure from Roy's earlier denunciation of Gandhi. Equally important, though, is the relationship Roy suggests here between the values of truth and non-violence on the one hand, and the goal of purifying politics on the other. For the formation of this conceptual relationship indicates a nexus of ideas in Roy's mind familiar to Gandhi's way of thinking, especially on the themes of politics and power, and the relation of the means to the ends of action.

"The implication of the doctrine of nonviolence," Roy now believes, "is the moral dictum that the end does not justify the means. That is the core of the Mahatma's message which is not compatible with power-politics. The Mahatma wanted to purify politics; that can be done only by raising political practice above the vulgar level of a scramble for power."[92] This passage represents the ideas Roy began to develop at a feverish pace in the last five years of his life. In a characteristically Gandhian manner, Roy wants now to purify politics by purging it of both the "struggle for power" and the party system itself. "Humanist politics," he says, must be a moral force; "it must get out of the struggle for power of the political parties."[93] Only in these circumstances can political power be transformed into moral authority. Leadership must come not from corrupt party bosses, but rather from "detached individuals, that is, spiritually free men [who] cannot be corrupted by power . . . it is possible for the individual man to attain spiritual freedom, to be detached and thus to be above corruption. Such men would not hanker after power."[94] This preoccupation with the right use of political power and the need for establishing a moral basis for leadership was, as Roy acknowledged, at the heart of Gandhi's thought.

What conclusions may be drawn from these critiques of Gandhi by two such sharply contrasting thinkers as Tagore and Roy? First, their responses to Gandhi illustrate the central position and pull of his thought and leadership. His ideas clearly dominated the movement for independence. Tagore and Roy are forceful but at the same time they are forced to acknowledge Gandhi's centrality. Second, these three figures—Tagore, Roy, and Gandhi—may be viewed as constituting together vital currents of ideas in the mainstream of contemporary Indian political thought. But there were numerous other Indian thinkers during this period. Some, like Nehru, Tilak, Pal, and Aurobindo Ghose, have been mentioned above; others, such as Jayaprakash

Narayan or Subhas Bose, have not.[95] However, all have this in common: each enters into a rich dialogue with Gandhi, usually sustained over decades. The cumulative result is a vigorous national discourse that more often than not finds itself tested in political practice. Whether one examines political dialogues in countries of East or West, twentieth-century India is remarkable for providing such a fertile soil for the production of political ideas that then bear fruit in action.

The extraordinary feature of this discourse, evident in the thought of both Tagore and Roy, is the focus that is maintained on the ideas of freedom, power, and change. Gandhi sets the terms and boundaries of this discussion with his theory and practice of swaraj and satyagraha. Tagore engages in the debate over swaraj, underscoring the key themes of freedom as self-realization, the problem of political power, and the necessity of social change. Roy brings to the dialogue a Marxist economic perspective but later shifts to an un-Marxist emphasis on "spiritual freedom," the corruption of power, and the importance of moral values in politics. The vitality and creativity of Gandhi's thought appears in his original formation of the relationship between swaraj and satyagraha. This achievement is due to Gandhi's unique ability to translate ideas into action. Neither Tagore nor Roy conceive a method of action that might use power to implement the value of freedom they so fervently advocate. Roy no less than Tagore is opposed to the evils of imperialism or of social injustice but his Marxist doctrine after decades of struggle proves impotent in practice. So it is precisely the connection between freedom and power that eludes both Roy and Tagore, even though they attack the problem of change from opposite directions. Gandhi's use of power, evidenced in his way of connecting swaraj and satyagraha in the context of the salt march and the Calcutta fast is the subject of the two chapters that follow.

CHAPTER FOUR

Civil Disobedience:
The Salt Satyagraha

The plan of civil disobedience has been
conceived to neutralize and ultimately
entirely to displace violence and enthrone
non-violence in its stead, to replace hatred
by love, to replace strife by concord.[1]

—*Gandhi, March, 1930*

On March 12, 1930, Mohandas Gandhi, age sixty years, left his
ashram at Sabarmati with seventy-eight followers, bound for the shores of
Dandi, a small village on the coast of Gujarat in western India. Thus began
the historic Dandi march and salt satyagraha, one of the most dramatic
events of modern Indian history. The march covered over two hundred
miles and lasted twenty-four days. Its specific object was to protest against
the tax the British Raj had placed on salt. Under the regulations of the India
Salt Act 1882, the government enforced a monopoly on the collection or
manufacture of salt, restricting its handling to officially controlled salt de-
pots and levying a tax of Rs1-4-0 (46 cents) on each maund (82 lbs.).[2] Gandhi defied this monopoly and so broke the law by simply collecting natural
salt from the seashore on April 6. The broader object of the march was to
spark a campaign of civil disobedience against the Raj in order to attain independence. The salt satyagraha, therefore, began with Gandhi's act at
Dandi, quickly spread throughout India as others followed his example, and

intensified with his arrest on May 5. It then continued for almost a year until direct negotiations between Gandhi and Lord Edward Irwin, the Viceroy, ended the campaign.[3]

Those are the bare facts of the salt satyagraha: but it needs first to be set in its historical context. The Lahore Congress, which met in December 1929, affirmed swaraj as India's national goal and sanctioned satyagraha or civil disobedience for 1930. But the Congress lacked any specific program of action, and so entrusted the campaign to Gandhi's imagination. As 1930 dawned, Gandhi returned to his home, the Satyagraha Ashram at Sabarmati (near Ahmedabad) for inspiration. By mid-February, the essential "formula" for civil disobedience had come to him.[4]

Influence of Bardoli's Tax Resistance on Gandhi's Subsequent Strategy

When Gandhi considered the location and manner of resistance, the Bardoli satyagraha of 1928 provided a key precedent. In Bardoli, a district in Gujarat, a limited campaign of tax resistance was waged in a small area of the state, but it had assumed all-India significance. The Bardoli district or *taluka* consisted of approximately 137 villages, with a total population of about 88,000 and an area of 222 square miles. In 1927, the *taluka* received an increase of 22 percent in its tax assessment from the Government of Bombay Revenue Department. After several months of random protest and agitation, the peasants began an organized satyagraha in February, 1928 under the direct leadership of Sardar Vallabhbhai Patel, acting under Gandhi's authority.[5] This was a tax resistance movement limited to a protest against the property tax increase that the Government had demanded. It asserted that the tax official's report recommending the increase was unjust and inaccurate. For several weeks the Government insisted adamantly that there was no need to reconsider the assessment. But pressure from the satyagraha eventually forced the Governor, Sir Leslie Wilson, to appoint an independent committee of enquiry and the committee's report favored the peasants' position. The final consequence, therefore, was a dramatic victory for Bardoli with only a small increase of revenue and a substantial blow to the Government's authority and credibility.

The degree of non-cooperation obtained by Patel and Gandhi in Bardoli was so extraordinary that it must rank as a textbook example of successful small-scale satyagrahas. Throughout the campaign, press coverage, even in the pro-Government *Times of India*, was extensive and sensational. The effects of the satyagraha were portrayed in the most graphic terms under the headline GOVERNMENT MACHINERY PARALYSED IN BARDOLI: REVOLT OF THE PEASANTRY.

The article, reported by a special correspondent in Bardoli, took note of:

> a situation there that is unique in the history of the British administration of India, and one that must sooner or later result in bloodshed or abdication by Government in the *Taluka*. The leaders of the no-tax campaign have succeeded in producing such a complete paralysis of the machinery of Government in the Taluka that not a finger can be moved, not a person stirs out of his house without their knowledge and consent. Even the officers of Government themselves are practically dependent for supplies, conveyance, etc., upon the good will of Mr. Vallabhbhai Patel and his "volunteers," . . . The power of the social boycott, the wide net of Mr. Patel's followers and informers, the complete success that has hitherto attended the campaign and the utter helplessness of the Government has given to the people a vivid realization of their power [which will produce] . . . a crisis that the country has rarely experienced.[6]

On July 4, one week before Leslie Wilson left Bombay for Simla and an urgent conference with Lord Irwin on Bardoli, the *Times of India* reported: BOLSHEVIK REGIME IN BARDOLI. MR. VALLABHBHAI PATEL IN THE ROLE OF LENIN:

> Iron discipline prevails at Bardoli. Mr. Patel has instituted there a Bolshevik regime in which he plays the role of Lenin. His hold on the population is absolute . . . . Though Mr. Patel is the chief figure at Bardoli, the brain behind the agitation is Mr. Gandhi, who from his Ashram at Sabarmati is in careful touch with the situation, while Patel himself constantly seeks his leader's advice.[7]

Government correspondence at this time confirms that the Bardoli situation was seen in desperate terms,[8] and some of the consequences of this for the Raj's reaction to the salt satyagraha will be observed below. However, the point here is that the campaign, due to the dramatic press coverage received, scored a propaganda victory out of all proportion to its size. The fame of Bardoli's triumph over the Government spread throughout India and Sardar Patel's prestige soared within the Congress.

Gandhi's reaction to the impact of Bardoli is instructive. After four years (1924–28) of relatively uneventful leadership, he found in Bardoli the key to his strategy for 1930. At first he was notably cautious about the wisdom

93

of Bardoli confronting the Government on this issue and relied on Patel's judgment. But as the serious purpose and determination of the peasantry became clear, Gandhi thrilled at the prospect of this combat with "Dyerism."[10] "Will the people of Bardoli stand this last trial?" he asked as the climax of the satyagraha approached. "They have already staggered Indian humanity. They have shown heroic patience in the midst of great provocation. Will they stand the greatest provocation that can be offered? If they will, they will have gained everything."[11] Shortly after this, Gandhi toured Bardoli with Patel and returned convinced that a rare demonstration of the effectiveness of satyagraha was being staged. He begins to write often on "lessons of Bardoli" and these signify the guidelines that apply later to the salt satyagraha. In early August, at the moment of the "settlement" with the Government he wrote:

> Bardoli is a sign of the times. It has a lesson both for the Government and the people; for the Government if they will recognize the power of the people when they have truth on their side and when they can form a nonviolent combination to vindicate it . . . . Nonviolent energy properly stored up sets free a force that becomes irresistible. So far as I have been able to see, there is no doubt that the settlement has been wrung from an unwilling Government by the pressure of a public opinion that was ever gathering force in geometrical progression.[12]

Shortly after he wrote to C. F. Andrews that the "Bardoli victory was indeed a victory for Truth and Nonviolence. It has almost restored the shattered faith in nonviolence on the political field."[13] Indeed, the Bardoli satyagraha did nothing less than restore Gandhi's own faith in the efficacy of nonviolent action in the quest for swaraj. He repeatedly returned in 1929 to the implications of Bardoli:

> The Government did not change its policy in the case of Bardoli, it was only compelled to yield under the pressure of organized resistance of the Bardoli peasantry and it is bound to do so again wherever such resistance is well organized.[14]
>
> It is only gradually that we shall come to know the importance of the victory gained at Bardoli . . . Bardoli has shown the way and cleared it. Swaraj lies on that route and that alone is the cure . . . .[15]
>
> It was just the extraordinary means discovered by non-cooperators [at Bardoli] that were employed by Sardar Vallabhbhai Patel with consummate skill and absolute faithfulness that influenced the Government, and it is just these extraordinary means which I would like the country to

adopt, and I know that it will reach its goal as surely as the simple peasants of Bardoli did.[16]

In February 1930, therefore, on the eve of the salt march, it was the example of Bardoli's success that remained foremost in Gandhi's mind. In Bardoli, he recalled:

> The forces of violence were hushed in the presence of nonviolent action. It remains to be seen how the all-India struggle for independence will shape. The law that governed the Bardoli struggle which centered around a local grievance will govern the greater struggle for independence. The partakers will have to be strictly nonviolent; they will have to visualize the grievance of slavery as the Bardoli peasant visualized the grievance of an unjust settlement; they will have to submit to the strictest discipline even as the Bardoli peasants did.[17]

The Bardoli example appealed to Gandhi, then, for several reasons. First, there was the moral drama of an oppressed peasantry fighting valiantly but nonviolently against an unjust government authority. This was precisely the style of combat that Gandhi savored. He was struck with the extraordinary discipline and courage that Patel's forceful leadership elicited from the Bardoli peasants. This inspired him to inject into the subsequent march the martial imagery of a nonviolent army armed with "truth-force." Moreover, the response of the Bardoli *taluka* encouraged him to utilize this same area and population for the salt march: not only did he march through many of the same villages that had been mobilized in 1928, but he also recruited heavily from this group. Finally, he had been struck by the Raj's response to Bardoli: the Government of Bombay had been overcome by the results of the settlement and frightened by the implications of the satyagraha.[18] Gandhi fully appreciated the meaning of this and sought now to exploit it further on an all-India basis. In all these respects, Bardoli was a key source of inspiration for what followed.[19]

If all of these factors produced substantial continuities between the Bardoli and salt satyagrahas, at least one large difference should be emphasized. This stemmed from the nature of Sardar Patel's kind of leadership, which dominated much of the Bardoli satyagraha and in certain respects contrasted sharply with that of Gandhi. The contrast suggests, in fact, a key difference between exclusive and inclusive types of leadership, the former associated with Patel and the latter with Gandhi. In Bardoli, Patel perceived the struggle persistently in terms of a "we-they" dichotomy, with the Government representing an enemy that was not to be trusted. For Patel, non-violence was a tactic that should be used to humiliate and demolish the adversary; it was a potentially effective way of exercising coercive power and scoring political victories. For Gandhi (as observed above), nonviolence was more than just a tactic, it was a creed. The implications of this difference between Gandhi and Patel become clearer as time passed, and became manifestly irreconcilable over the issue of the partition of India, examined in the next chapter.[20]

Yet, in an embryonic sense, the differences are apparent in a contrast between the two types of leadership in 1928 and 1930. Like Patel, Gandhi had an authoritarian tendency that found satisfaction in militant confrontations. His commitment to the creed of nonviolence, however, brought his inclusive attitude so forcefully into play that it transformed the nature of the confrontation. The opponent in the conflict was not perceived as "the enemy," in Patel's sense, to be beaten by tough tactics and superior power. Such a perception could lead to *duragraha*. Gandhi saw his adversary as someone whose sense of humanity could be awakened through the use of nonviolence. He trusted his opponent, believing that no individual was totally incapable of re-examining his own position to see a standard of justice. The logic of this view led to a sense of inclusiveness, evident both in the salt march and Calcutta fast.

The essential point concerns the nature of satyagraha and its integral connection with swaraj. The aim in satyagraha is not merely to prevail but to transform the conflict in such a way that all parties may be uplifted in the process by being brought closer to a sense of their common interest. The dynamics of the conflict resolution should humanize rather than degrade the participants. When this happens the means are consistent with the end and one moves toward swaraj. The Bardoli effort was certainly successful, yet Gandhi worried throughout about a slide into *duragraha* that would see the sole goal as winning against the Government by any means necessary. He resolved that the next satyagraha could do better than Bardoli: it would be pure *ahimsa*, reaching the Raj as effectively as the Indian people.

Preparation for Satyagraha: Debate and Decisions Over Issues and Methods

It might seem today as one reflects on the smooth execution of the 1930 civil disobedience campaign that the outcome of the whole operation was a foregone conclusion from the time Gandhi was charged by the Lahore Congress to lead the movement. In fact, there was uncertainty surrounding it from the outset, partly because in the months before the march Gandhi was receiving much advice from trusted friends who urged patience rather than provocation. Close political allies in Britain called for caution, imploring him not to risk rebellion but to accept the terms offered by the Government. Fenner Brockway, a staunch Labourite, cabled Gandhi: "Beg you cooperate [with Wedgwood Benn, Secretary of State for India] thus opening door friendship."[21] Horace Alexander, who would remain until Gandhi's death an intimate Quaker friend, wrote on behalf of the British Friends Peace Committee to implore cooperation with Irwin by attending the Round Table Conference to discuss future political reforms. It is, Alexander advised, "a sound pacifist rule that when two groups of men are preparing for war whether with or without weapons of violence the peacemaker must try to bring the leaders together in conference."[22]

Gandhi's old friend from South Africa, Henry S. L. Polak, was even more emphatic. In a series of letters and telegrams from London, Polak insisted that he knew the mind of Wedgwood Benn to be conciliatory, that Benn "has the solid backing of the [Labour] Cabinet," and "there is no doubt that there is a complete and fundamental change in the attitude towards the India problem on the part of the Labour Party. They most earnestly want a settlement in India and a very friendly one. They do not intend to take up the attitude of superiors towards inferiors." Polak commended Wedgwood Benn's "intense earnestness and sincerity," and concluded that the only rational and successful approach to Britain must be not civil disobedience but "mutual cooperation."[23]

This advice from abroad was reinforced by some of Gandhi's respected friends in India. On the eve of the salt march, M. A. Ansari, a Delhi Nationalist Muslim, wrote a lengthy letter to Gandhi pleading with him to desist. He reports a conversation with a friend, a "God-fearing and deeply religious Gujarati Hindu," who saw the outbreak of smallpox that had recently occurred in Gandhi's ashram as "a sign from God" that Gandhi must postpone civil disobedience. Ansari noted further that Muslims were generally not supportive, and that "your direct action today would only appeal to a very small section, i.e., those who are and have been always with you; but a considerable position of the Hindu population, an overwhelming number of Muslims and Sikhs would not be touched by your movement. Rather, these would be used as a counterfoil against you. The impatient and the impetuous youth of the country are sure to break out in violence. Your whole movement would then fail."[24]

At the same time that Dr. Ansari was diagnosing potential disaster and the youth as being a dangerous element, Asaf Ali, another Delhi Nationalist Muslim, saw the situation in more positive terms. "The youth of the country," he wrote Gandhi on February 25, "are anxious for a 'trial of strength,' both violent and nonviolent, driven by *economic* causes. But the Congress has yet to yoke their energy. . . ." [25] Gandhi had already determined on a "trial of strength" and it may be that the torrent of letters that he was now receiving from young people all over the country proved decisive.[26] One young woman, writing from Ahmedabad, presciently perceived the enthusiasm of women for the movement. She suggested organizing "a band of women as Peace-volunteers" who may inject a special element of nonviolence into the struggle because "Women who bring life into the world are the greatest haters of bloodshed, for life is too precious to them. Give the women a chance therefore to show what they can do."[27] Student leaders from a youth league in Madras wrote in terms that must have moved Gandhi:

> We are determined to join your campaign, but we are disallowed by our parents. So we have come to a definite conclusion that our holy nation's call is to be responded to more than our parents wish. We are under a firm belief that our service to humanity will outweigh the sin of disobeying our parents. [But] we must get an order from you. Please allow us to join your volunteer corps. We request you not to let our parents know that we have written you . . . . [28]

A young man writing from Bengal offered: "my humble services as a Satyagrahi in the coming struggle." He then managed to express precisely the ideas behind the campaign:

> Your decision to launch civil disobedience led me to believe that you are trying, once and for all, to establish the supremacy and efficacy of nonviolent methods over violent means. Politics in India today has been confused with an unholy mixture of nonviolence and violence. I regard nonviolence as a much greater and cleaner political weapon because nonviolence blesses him who wields it as well as him against whom it is wielded. In Bengal there is a school of politics who believe in violence, but terrorism is now an exploded theory in the West. If we could only establish the truth of our way in the public mind with our own blood, we will have achieved our end.

He added that he knew "hundreds of trained workers [who] will rally around our nonviolent banner. Women are anxious to join."[29]

These excerpts from the numerous letters that Gandhi received indicate that for at least some Indian students the message was clear and compelling. Satish Kalelkar, one of the students who was eventually selected to join Gandhi on the salt march, later reflected on that moment and said that before 1930, many college men and women had dismissed Gandhi as at worst a silly old fool or at best, "a saint who cannot lead us." But once the clarion call of civil disobedience was sounded, they suddenly felt that only Gandhi could lead them.[30] The details of the campaign, its main demands, and its precise method of attack could be left to the leader; what now emerged was an urgent appeal for the power of nonviolence. When Gandhi later remarked that he made his decisions on listening to his "inner voice," the appeal from India's youth must have come across loud and clear. Yet, trained and practiced as a lawyer, he was never one to defy the law lightly; and he worried over the criticism now expressed by Chimanlal Setalvad, a leader of India's Liberal Party: "if you inculcate in the minds of the younger generation the idea of direct action, the idea of disobeying laws, what will happen to your Swaraj when you get it?"[31] Gandhi responded to Liberals in India as Martin Luther King, Jr. would some thirty years later to liberals in America: that respectful obedience to law must always remain the norm, but that it remains the citizen's responsibility to discern and if necessary disobey nonviolently those laws that violate standards of morality and justice. It was a principle that both had learned from Thoreau.

Why did Gandhi choose the salt tax as the issue?[32] Its abolition had been advocated in India generally, and by Gandhi in particular, decades before the salt satyagraha. Gopal Krishna Gokhale, Gandhi's mentor, roundly condemned the salt tax in 1902 before the Imperial Legislative council in Bombay. Gokhale dwelt on the "unquestioned hardship"that the salt tax "imposes upon the poorest of the poor of our community."Then he buttressed his case by citing evidence from British officials who had themselves conceded as early as 1888 their "greatest reluctance" in imposing this particular tax. Gokhale quoted from none other than Lord Cross, Secretary of State for India, 1886–1892, who had then expressed "great regret" for placing this "burden on the poorest classes of the population, through the taxation of a necessity of life."[33] However sincere these officials were at the time, this was precisely the language that Gandhi was to adopt as he began to oppose the salt tax.In 1905, Gandhi wrote from South Africa that the tax should be abolished immediately, and the demand is repeated, though not stressed, over the years.[34] In his blanket indictment of British rule in *Hind Swaraj*, Gandhi makes a special point of commenting that "The salt-tax is not a small injustice."[35] By January 1930, the issue of the salt tax had been elevated to one of Gandhi's primary concerns, being listed as fourth in his eleven demands for basic reforms presented to Lord Irwin.[36] However, it was not until February 5, only five weeks before the march, that the press reported that Gandhi would undertake civil disobedience "in connection with the salt tax."[37] It struck even the most loyal of Gandhi's followers as a poor choice for an issue to fight the campaign. Manufacture of salt occurred mainly along the coast and it was difficult to imagine how a nationwide protest might be organized. When Gandhi proposed it to the Working Committee of the Congress in mid-February, the response was incredulity.[38]

Gandhi did not explain his position publicly until February 27. In the first extensive comment that he had ever made on the salt tax, he outlined the reasons for his choice of this particular tax in characteristically inclusive terms: "Next to air and water, salt is perhaps the greatest necessity of life. It is the only condiment of the poor. . . . There is no article like salt outside water by taxing which the State can reach even the starving millions, the sick, the maimed and the utterly helpless. The tax constitutes therefore the most inhuman poll tax that ingenuity of man can devise." The issue, then, had by now acquired its essential components: the indispensable moral emphasis, including special stress on the suffering of a "helpless" population, and the suggestion that resistance to the tax must touch virtually everyone, but certainly "the starving millions." In this article, Gandhi proceeds to wax eloquent on some of his favorite themes: the way in which Government monopoly of salt production and distribution has killed the native Bengal salt industry; the exorbitantly unfair charge of the salt tax compared to the cost of production; the ability of India to manufacture all the salt it needs without unnecessary foreign imports from Liverpool; and the insinuation that if an illegality exists in this instance, it rests with the Government and not those who must legitimately resist this immoral law:

> When therefore the time comes, civil resisters will have an ample opportunity . . . to conduct their campaign regarding the tax in a most effective manner. The illegality is in a Government that steals the people's salt and makes them pay heavily for the stolen article. The people, when they become conscious of their power, will have every right to take possession of what belongs to them.[39]

Gandhi's inclusive leadership in his choice of the salt tax is evident and has been noted by other commentators.[40] But the symbolism of the issue deserves to be underlined: the image appears of an outrageous injustice, in which already destitute millions are made to carry an unjust burden; a tax not on a superfluous item (such as tea), or on an object of privilege (land), but on a primary need, a commodity equivalent to air and water that belongs to all and which everyone has a natural right to consume. The Government "steals" and then exploits; "the people" must therefore assert their "right" and rise with all their "power" in order "to take possession of what belongs to them."[41]

If the issue of the salt tax represented an inclusive target, then the method of the march constituted an inclusive means of attacking it. The very notion of the march to Dandi exuded a "come, join me" call for recruitment. Gandhi's methodical procedure of walking through dozens of villages, pausing regularly to hold public meetings, and covering a remarkable distance of more than 200 miles in 24 days, may be seen, quite apart from the strength of the issue, as a massive political campaign. The gradual cumulative force of this leadership converted the streams of "volunteers" who converged around it into a human tide, quickly rising and eventually sweeping the movement to the sea. The way in which this floodtide grew, carrying such diverse elements in its flow, is phenomenal; but to understand its force, one must go to its source, the idea behind it.

How and when did the conception of a march form in Gandhi's mind? During his stay in South Africa, he had used the technique of the march before, in 1913. As part of a strike of Indian laborers, he had led a large contingent from Natal into the Transvaal. The "Great March" as it came to be called, took five days, from November 6 to 10 and involved 2,037 men, 127 women, and 57 children.[42] Its purpose was to register a mass protest against repressive legislation and to assert the self-respect of the Indian community. It was similar to the Dandi march in its dramatic use of a powerful means of nonviolent action, the dominant leadership of Gandhi, its ultimately successful outcome, and the mutual respect that eventually emerged between Gandhi and his chief adversary, in this case, General J. C. Smuts.

Yet there were significant differences between the two marches. The much larger size of the South African group gave it an unwieldy and untrained character that the press derided as a "pathetic Indian army" or "a long struggling line of weary and footsore travellers" that fell into the waiting arms of the police.[43] Moreover, the relatively short period of five days did not allow for the same buildup of suspense and publicity. Gandhi had not acquired an international reputation in 1913 and so the event received no attention in the world press. As the protesters moved through hostile territory, they must have felt, unlike the Dandi marchers, that they were unnoticed, certainly unacclaimed. However, the most striking difference between the two marches came with the contrasting responses of the respective governments. The South African government did not hesitate to arrest Gandhi on the first night of the march. Although he was subsequently released on bail, he was rearrested and the government thus demonstrated its unequivocal determination and total control of the situation. The campaign was deprived of its leadership and the protesters were sent back home. Only later, in the aftermath of the march, when the government went too far in its repression, did the movement ultimately succeed.

The overall contrast between the marches of 1913 and 1930 reveals how much Gandhi's leadership and power had matured in seventeen years. When he was asked, at the outset of the Dandi march, to compare it with the earlier one in South Africa, he said that here in India would be easier because of its "hospitable environment."[44] He knew that he was swimming in friendly waters and there was power in that knowledge. The Gujarat area had been carefully prepared as Natal and the Transvaal could not have been. The entire force of the movement was now concentrated on that route to Dandi. As events would show, Irwin and the Raj now encountered a much more difficult challenge than faced earlier by the government of South Africa. The difference, therefore, between these two marches is that Gandhi's leadership by 1930 had gained dramatically in self-confidence and political control: satyagraha had acquired a degree of political power that measured favorably against the imperial government of India. Gandhi's whole attitude conveys now—as it did not in South Africa—a mature awareness that he possesses a method of action ripe for use.

Whatever the influence on Gandhi's mind of his South African precedent, it seems that the precise idea of a march to the sea coast at Dandi to "manufacture salt" was not conceived until only days before the march actually began. In late January 1930, Gandhi told the press that he had retreated to Sabarmati ashram because he was "not yet sure of the form it [civil disobedience] will take. I have come here and in my seclusion I hope to evolve a plan of civil resistance. . . ." He said that he was listening intently, to "keep himself in tune with the voice of his followers."[45] By the end of February Gandhi had still not mentioned anything about a "march,"[46] but in his article on the salt tax (cited above), he does show how closely he is listening to "the voice of his followers." He reports on two letters that he has received and the theme of both is that large salt deposits exist on the Bombay Presidency shore from Cambay to Ratnagiri: "If the people had freedom they could pick up salt from the deposits made by the receding tides" and "if a band of volunteers began the work all along the coast, it would be impossible for the whole strength of the police and customs staff to prevent them from collecting natural salt. . . . The poor people on the coast will join in the collection of salt spontaneously in these days of unemployment."[47] Within a week of writing this article, Gandhi had made his decision to undertake a march into the area and along the lines suggested in these letters. He announced his plans at a prayer meeting at Sabarmati ashram in the beginning of March.[48]

Another factor that helped set the stage for the event appeared with Gandhi's choice of those who would accompany him on the march. At Lahore, Gandhi had struggled with those in the Congress like Subhas Bose, who accepted the use of political violence. He managed ultimately to persuade the Congress to adopt nonviolent action not because they believed in it as a creed, but because most admitted its efficacy as a political policy. This was not enough for Gandhi as he planned the march. He wanted a group of followers scrupulously disciplined in his mode of nonviolent conduct and unequivocally committed to *ahimsa* as a creed.[49]

Even for some of Gandhi's own ashramites, a total belief in *ahimsa* did not come easily. D. R. Harkare, another of the eighty-one marchers, related a personal odyssey that began with a youthful involvement in terrorism and contempt for nonviolence. This ended only when he joined Sabarmati ashram and could observe Gandhi closely. He witnessed in Gandhi an absolute fearlessness (initially in the Mahatma's calm handling of poisonous snakes), together with an intense identification with the poor through consistent adoption of their lifestyle.[50] In a manner representative of most ashramites interviewed, Harkare said that only after watching Gandhi's behavior each day did he gain the trust and affection that had made him adopt all aspects of nonviolence, personal and political.

Emphasis on the development of self-discipline in the ashram was met with a range of responses. Some reflecting back on the experience of ashram discipline from a vantage point of forty-five years, stated that it was the most joyful moment of their lives because they felt involved in an exhilarating spiritual quest led by a revered man of action.[51] Madeleine Slade, an English woman who had joined the ashram three years earlier and whom Gandhi named Mira Behn, seemed to welcome the strict code of personal conduct and four months before the march extolled the ashram for having "reached its zenith in physical energy and moral strength."[52] Others, however, noted the difficulty in meeting some of Gandhi's rigorous standards. Youth from high castes or wealthy families found onerous the requirement of daily spinning, cleaning latrines, and other forms of manual labor.[53] Most of the marchers interviewed agreed with Satish Kalelkar (a 19-year-old college student who entered Sabarmati ashram a year before he joined the march) that the training steeled them not only for the trek to Dandi, but perhaps more importantly for the months of rigorous imprisonment that would follow. One invaluable result of the discipline seemed to be a discovery of unexpected personal reserves, and this in turn produced a fearlessness for which satyagraha became renowned in the face of government assaults. When Kalelkar reflected back on his experience, he concluded that Gandhi's genius lay not only in his famed ability to arouse the masses but, even more, to evoke the best from his immediate followers by revealing qualities that they would not have dared believe they possessed.[54]

Gandhi consequently recruited his fellow marchers not from the Congress, but from his own ashram, where he could rely on bonds forged from trust and discipline. No producer or director can ever have lavished more concern and concerted attention on his cast of characters. Men, women and children, Hindus, Muslims and Christians, high-castes and harijans, college-educated poets from the Punjab and musicians from Maharashtra—this diverse community grew united in its unqualified adherence to Gandhian nonviolence and personal devotion to its prophet. V. G. Desai, one of the marchers, recalls that Gandhi repeatedly told members of the ashram that "he was born in order to destroy the British empire in India. He was a man with a mission and just as he was devoted to this cause, so this inspired devotion in us."[55] By the end of February, Gandhi declared his intention to "start the movement only through the inmates of the Ashram and those who have submitted to its discipline and assimilated the spirit of its methods."[56] In this way, Gandhi underscored both his dissatisfaction with the undisciplined politics of the Congress organization, and his own position that among his adherents only one quality really counted, a disciplined belief in the creed of nonviolence.

In the month before the march began Gandhi moved to strengthen the preparation. Timing was a key consideration: a march of only five days was proposed and rejected in favor of the more ambitious period of twenty-four days. The route of the march was decided on the bases of past contact, present recruitment potential, and overall time. Major rest stops were determined and announced in Gandhi's weekly, *Young India* three days before the march began. Advance groups of students from the Gujarat Vidyapith (a national university founded by Gandhi in Ahmedabad) were chosen to scout the area of the march thoroughly. They were to collect data about each of the villages on the route from a questionnaire prepared by Gandhi.[57] This information was then used in the talks that he gave in these villages. Weather was a vital factor because the cool Gujarat mornings yielded to intolerably hot mid-afternoons, so that a marching schedule was devised to make maximum use of the hours between 6:00 and 10:00 each morning and evening.

Publicizing Satyagraha: Gandhi's Letter to the Viceroy and Uses of the Media

Gandhi's next step was to set down, in an open letter to Lord Irwin (dated March 2 and published soon after), the reasons for his decision to begin civil disobedience. This letter, perhaps one of the most extraordinary documents in the history of British rule in India, may be seen as a model of Gandhi's inclusive attitude; its tone suggests Gandhi's acute awareness of his adversary. Gandhi knew Irwin to be an unusual Viceroy, a head of government who was known for his sincere piety and sense of fairness. Gandhi trusted him and from the outset intuited the prospect of a personal accord, however distant or unlikely that seemed under the circumstances of early 1930. He had found that Irwin was capable of deeply humane feelings and a willingness to express them openly. Two years earlier, after Gandhi had suffered a grievous loss with the death of his young nephew, Maganlal Gandhi, Irwin wrote to him a personal note of condolence, sympathizing in markedly unofficial terms, and concluding "I can guess what his loss must mean to you and to his family for all humanity here meets on a common ground of experience, as sorrow and loss come to us all." Gandhi was genuinely affected by Irwin's sympathy.[58]

There is an openness in Gandhi's letter to Irwin, informing the adversary in advance of the plan of battle. It is the antithesis of an exclusivist style, with its core concept of a small secret conspiratorial circle.[59] This is one mark of inclusivity: an open hand extended to the opponent, inviting him to join in an accord. Beginning in Gandhi's classic manner with "Dear friend," it sets the tone of congeniality and trust which befuddled Irwin at first in his dealings with Gandhi. The letter opens with a humble request that the Viceroy help him "find a way out" so that he may somehow avoid undertaking an action he dreads: civil disobedience. The initial tone conveys the peculiar mixture of ultimatum and vulnerability characteristic of Gandhi's approach to the Raj. He seems to be saying, "please help, we both need it," but there is power behind the plea.

Then Gandhi introduces a line of reasoning that lies at the center of his leadership style. While he regards "British rule to be a curse," he does "not intend harm to a single Englishman." How could he, when he has "the privilege of claiming many Englishmen as dearest friends," and when he has learned much about the evil of British rule from "courageous Englishmen" who dared to tell the truth. Thus Gandhi makes one of his favorite points, distinguishing the evils of institutionalized imperialism and racism from the instinctive goodness of individuals who are unwittingly serving these institutions. The implication is clear, that the sins of the system will be visited upon the heads of its servants: but only if they continue to cooperate with it. The nonviolent method is peculiarly suited, Gandhi believes, to promote noncooperation with the system, even among those Englishmen who may most closely identify with it. For, as his friendship with individual Englishmen had shown, there is a higher and more inclusive identity than nationality, and that is humanity.

Gandhi explains next why he sees British rule as a curse and stresses the economic injustice involved. He asks the Viceroy to examine his own salary and to realize that he is earning "much over five thousand times India's average income [whereas] the British Prime Minister is getting only ninety times Britain's average income." Therefore, "a system that provides for such an arrangement deserves to be summarily scrapped." Yet, the system will not die an easy death, for "Great Britain would defend her Indian commerce and interests by all the forces at her command. India must consequently evolve force enough to free herself from that embrace of death." What sort of force? Not of violence. Yet, violence of two kinds is already growing fast in India, the violence of the terrorists and the "organized violence of the British Government." Another kind of force must be applied in order to sterilize violence and liberate India from this cancer. Only "nonviolence . . . expressed through civil disobedience" will achieve not only swaraj for Indians, but also the "conversion" of the British people, making "them see the wrong they have done to India."

If, Gandhi concludes, "my letter makes no appeal to your heart," and the eleven demands,[60] are denied, then civil disobedience is unavoidable, and he provides the date and place that it will begin. The specific issue is the salt tax, for it is "the most iniquitous of all from the poor man's standpoint. As the independence movement is essentially for the poorest in the land, the beginning will be made with this evil." He assures the Viceroy that he has no desire to cause him "unnecessary embarrassment" and asks of Irwin the "favor" not to obstruct his path. The letter ends with an archetypal Gandhian touch: since it is "not in any way intended as a threat," he has chosen "a young English friend," who believes in nonviolence and India's freedom and "whom Providence seems to have sent to me" to hand-deliver the letter to Irwin. The symbolic meaning of this final gesture of a heaven-sent Briton, having seen the truth and charged by Gandhi with the personal task of carrying it to the Viceroy, was not lost on India or on history. As a gesture it perhaps spoke more eloquently for inclusiveness than any words that Gandhi could devise.[61]

The mass media, involving Indian and foreign correspondents from dozens of domestic, European and American newspapers, together with film companies, recognized the drama of the event and participated actively. Perhaps their coverage would not have been so lavish if Gandhi had not provided ample advance publicity and timed the march to their advantage. As one biographer says, on the Dandi march Gandhi "fully entered the world of newsreel and documentary, and three Bombay cinema companies filmed the event."[62] He consistently captured front-page headlines of major Indian newspapers, nationalist and otherwise, throughout the month of March. An American academic, writing for *The Nation*, reported how he had arrived at Sabarmati on the eve of the march and watched as "Thousands flocked to the ashram, filling the four miles of dusty country road from Ahmedabad and camping by the gates of the ashram. The next day Ahmedabad declared a hartal (cessation of activities) and in the evening 60,000 persons gathered on the bank of the river to hear Gandhi's call to arms. This call to arms was perhaps the most remarkable call to war that has ever been made."[63]

This excited tone would be sustained in the coming months by numerous American journalists so that the march was given prominent coverage in major U.S. newspapers and periodicals.[64] The American media appreciated the newsworthy quality of the event, commenting on how the Mahatma "Reversing the 'Boston-tea-party' method of revolt," "like a master showman" "ceremoniously defies the British Government's salt monopoly and its resented tax on salt."[65] It was this kind of drama that led *Time Magazine* to name Gandhi "Man of the Year" for 1930 and conclude that more than Stalin or Hitler, the Mahatma deserved the award, "the little brown man whose 1930 mark on world history will undoubtedly loom largest of all."[66]

Gandhi also sought to prepare for the event through a series of public statements from Sabarmati, issued both at his regular prayer meetings and directly to the press. The general climate of expectation was heightened by his repeated anticipation of arrest in these statements. From the moment of his "letter" of March 2 to the Viceroy announcing plans for civil disobedience, suspense over why and whether the government would or would not arrest him increased, so that on the eve of the march Gandhi could rightly observe, "Everyone is on the tiptoe of expectation, and before anything has happened the thing has attracted world-wide attention."[67] Gandhi helped to produce this atmosphere, too, by using language that became markedly more dramatic and even apocalyptic as the hour approached: "This is a battle to the finish. The Divine Hand is guiding it"; "We shall face the bullets with our backs to the wall . . . there will be no retreat at any cost"; "We are entering upon a life and death struggle, a holy war; we are performing an all-embracing sacrifice in which we wish to offer ourselves as oblation."[68] This was the saint at war, with penance as his weapon, and however somber and sincere their meaning, these words were also theatrical in the extreme.

Gandhi's influence and impact as a mass leader derived in large part from both a professional use of the media and a performer's sense of his audience: he staged and executed his events with an uncanny sensitivity to the mood and temper of those around him. The moment of the march shows Gandhi in possession of his audience through a sure understanding of its expectations, and especially of its trust and devotion. This unusual understanding came not through intuition alone, but also from a cultivated grasp of his tradition, his command of the subtler shades of traditional symbols, and his ability to express these symbolic meanings with an awesome consistency in his daily behavior. The Dandi march demonstrates a masterful awareness and use of symbols that surpasses any other event of Gandhi's career.[69]

Gandhi on the March

On that historic morning of March 12, 1930, the air was indeed heavy with traditional symbolism. After the customary morning prayers, witnessed now by the huge crowds that had stood vigil throughout the night at the ashram, Pandit Khare, the chosen minstrel of the march, offered a series of devotional songs. Gandhi's favorite, "Raghupati Raghava Raja Ram," which told of the legendary glories of Ram and Sita, was followed by two Vaishnava bhajans stressing the courage and valor required of the religious warrior. Not to inflict harm upon another, but to practice self-sacrifice and perform acts of pure renunciation which would ensure liberation: this was the common theme heralded by the Pandit.[70] Then Gandhi spoke, the image of the steadfast leader rising determined and secure in the midst of turmoil. He quietly declared that the struggle could be won only through the awakening of the God within all, for "The Self in us all is one and the same."[71] Kasturba, his wife, then applied the benedictory *tilak* to his forehead and garlanded him, not with flowers but with *khadi*, and handed to him the walking stick that became his trademark on the march. *Tilak, khadi,* and stick, symbols of devotion, simplicity, and strength; given by his wife whom he was now leaving, along with his home, in a spirit of renunciation, searching for truth and liberation. This was the *satyagrahi* on the pilgrimage to swaraj.

One of Gandhi's oldest and closest associates, Mahadev Desai, observed this moment of departure. He guessed that many in the crowd were:

> remembering the Lord Rama on his way to the Ranvati forest bidding farewell to Ayodhyay, the seat of his kingdom. . . . I beheld in Gandhiji an ideal Vaishnav, Lord Rama on his way to conquer Sri Lanka. But more than this I am reminded of Lord Buddha's Great March to attain divine wisdom. Buddha embarked on his march bidding farewell to the world, cutting through the darkness, inspired by the mission of relieving the grief-stricken and downtrodden . . . . What would one say about this march except that it was just like Buddha's great march of renunciation?[72]

Whether the allegorical hero was seen as Rama or Buddha, the symbols Gandhi personified were similar: the renunciation of the saint, the valor of the hero, the superior insight of the guru, all combined to symbolize the perfect leader, one who strove earnestly for self-mastery and so might know how to rule the country.[73] "Swaraj is the only remedy and the way that I have adopted is the only possible way."[74]

Gandhi's symbols were not derived solely from his religious tradition. His dominant concern, articulated often throughout the march, was with serving the "poor dumb millions" in India's villages. The economic burden of the salt tax could have meaning only for them, and his use of this central issue related chiefly to England's expropriation of wealth from the peasant who earned no more than seven pice (four cents) per day.[75] He devoted relentless attention to the problem of reaching the peasantry, and especially to perfecting a style of political leadership that would express his dominant concern for this group. From his viewpoint, successful mobilization of the villages depended chiefly on the consistency of his example. He demanded that simple standards of life must be carefully maintained and he gave scrupulous supervision to all aspects of his own life style and that of his closest followers. Diet, dress, use of commodities, all became means of demonstrating his desire to be at one with his people and to preserve the trust he felt that they had invested in his leadership.

His sensitivity to this issue of maintaining public trust is clear from his personal behavior on the salt march. Throughout it Gandhi became increasingly preoccupied with the maintenance of simple standards of behavior, and with their symbolic expression. Near the end of the march, in the village of Bhatgam, he made what he called "an important" and "introspective" speech. He was concerned, he said, with preserving the "purity" of the march and wanted everyone to "turn the searchlight inward" and examine "lapses" that had occurred. Some volunteers, he discovered, had "ordered milk from Surat to be brought in a motor lorry and they had incurred other expenses which I could not justify. I therefore spoke strongly about them. But that did not allay my grief." How could he criticize the Viceroy's salary, he wondered, when "I myself was taking from the people an unconscionable toll" to finance the march. His action could be justified "only if my living bore some correspondence with the average income of the people. . . . We profess to act on behalf of the hungry, the naked and the unemployed . . . [but] to live above the means befitting a poor country is to live on stolen food. . . . We must become real trustees of the dumb millions." Then, with his usual meticulous attention to detail, Gandhi criticized the marchers' consumption of oranges, grapes, and milk as well as the use of incandescent burners. Discrepancies must be removed, and volunteers will subsist on cereals and water, use candles rather than kerosene, walk for supplies rather than ride on conveyances. "Extravagance has no room in this campaign." He concludes, characteristically, on a personal and tragi-comic note:

> In order to procure goat's milk for me you may not deprive poor women of milk for their children. It would be like poison if you did. Nor may milk

and vegetables be brought from Surat. We can do without them. . . . We may not consider anybody low. I observed that you had provided for the night journey a heavy kerosene burner mounted on a stool which a poor laborer carried on his head. This was a humiliating sight. This man was being goaded to walk fast. I could not bear the sight. I therefore put on speed and outraced the whole company. But it was no use. The man was made to run after me. The humiliation was complete. If the weight had to be carried, I should have loved to see someone among ourselves carrying it. We would then soon dispense both with the stool and the burner. . . . Remember that in *swaraj* we would expect one drawn from the so-called lower class to preside over India's destiny. If then we do not quickly mend our ways, there is no *swaraj* such as you and I have put before the people.[76]

The effect of the speech was stunning. K. M. Dave, then a cub reporter for the local paper, years later conveyed its effect:

As soon as Gandhi started his speech, his inner anguish started flowing. He asked how, when millions and millions of people in this country were not able to feed themselves even once in a day, we *satyagrahis* could indulge in such excesses. How could we attain *swaraj?* Lakhs of huts in lakhs of villages of India were drowned in darkness because no rupees could be found for even a small oil lamp. How could we burn petromax lamps? He asked repeatedly for someone to justify these actions. But everyone was very still on hearing such grief in his voice. His words pierced our hearts. One by one, all the petromax lamps were extinguished, the meeting was in darkness except for a small lantern burning near Gandhi.[77]

No single episode is remembered more vividly by the marchers themselves than this incident at Bhatgam. In one indelible moment it made them all "turn the searchlight inward," and summon greater discipline. One of the marchers could report forty-seven years later that "The lesson [of self-discipline] made such a very strong imprint on my life," that it gave him a calling as a Lok Sevak (servant of the people).[78] Pyarelal Nayar, who was at Gandhi's side in Bhatgam, believed that in his twenty-eight years as his personal secretary, he never witnessed an act of self-criticism to lift a campaign to a higher sense of purpose. The effect on the *satyagrahis*, he recalled, was searing: "If Gandhi made clear anywhere at anytime his meaning of *swaraj* through *satyagraha* then it was that night in Bhatgam." The very next morning Gandhi sensed this impact and said, "we are now on solid moral ground because of this purification."[79]

As Gandhi's arrival at Dandi drew near, he pressed his attack on the Raj with increasing confidence. For it was clear by the beginning of April that the movement had not only caught on, but was also assuming unprecedented proportions in arousing mass sentiment. Enormous crowds were now appearing at Gandhi's major meetings, and the nationalist press rhapsodized over this "tremendous success, to judge only from the swelling lists of volunteers pledged to join his campaign, the impatience even of woman volunteers to be active combatants, and from the steadily increasing number of resignations by Patels and other village officials. . . . Gandhiji's ideas are now spread everywhere and cannot be banished or imprisoned. And if any *Satyagrahi* is imprisoned, the idea of *Satyagraha* becomes ten times more potent and attracts ten times more volunteers."[80]

The government, then, was in a predicament, and another nationalist newspaper expressed succinctly the growing view of the Viceroy's dilemma:

> To arrest Gandhi is to set fire to the whole of India. Not to arrest him is to allow him to set the prairie on fire. To arrest Gandhi is to court a war. Not to arrest him is to confess defeat before the war is begun. . . . In either case, Government stands to lose, and Gandhi stands to gain. . . . That is because Gandhi's cause is righteous and the Government's is not."[81]

Sensitive to both the government's difficulty and the euphoric response of his audience, Gandhi turned on the heat in his speech at Surat on April 1:

> There is no alternative but for us to do something about our trouble and sufferings and hence we have thought of this salt tax. You may say it is a godsend. It is so beastly and inhuman that through salt the Government taxes even little children and young girls. . . . This is an inhuman law, a Satanic law. I have not heard of such justice anywhere in the world; where it prevails, I would call it inhuman, Satanic. To bow to an empire which dispenses such justice is not *dharma* but *adharma* [immorality]. A man who prays to God every morning at dawn cannot, must not, pray for the good of such an empire. On the contrary while praying or saying the *namaaz* he should ask God to encompass the destruction of such a Satanic empire, such an inhuman Government. To do so is *dharma*.[82]

Gandhi now felt the force that the march had summoned and the Government's difficulty. Whereas in the hours before the march he had anticipated his speedy arrest,[83] now he wrote privately to his ashram: "So great is the power of nonviolence that they do not have the courage to arrest me."[84] Publicly he claimed that the movement had become irresistible because

"There is the hand of God in this struggle" and "If Rama dwells in your hearts, it is easy to shake the foundations of not one but twenty empires more powerful than this one."[85]

On April 3, the marchers reached Navsari, railhead for Dandi, and a "royal reception" greeted them; as they walked through the streets a vast procession followed to the place where Gandhi addressed "a mammoth gathering numbering over 50,000. . . . Never before was such a large gathering witnessed by Navsari nor had the enthusiasm of people rose [sic] to such a high pitch." A particular phenomenon, noted by the nationalist press and in government despatches alike, was that "women assembled in thousands" to applaud Gandhi and were taking an uncommon interest in the campaign.[86] Jawaharlal Nehru recalled how at this moment he watched the transformation that occurred as his skepticism melted: "Salt suddenly became a mysterious word, a word of power," "The abounding enthusiasm of the people . . . spreading like a prairie fire," and "we marvelled at the amazing knack of the man to impress the multitude."[87]

Gandhi had set April 6 as the day when the salt law would be broken. He had done this, once again, for symbolic reasons. The day marked the beginning of "National Week," first commemorated in 1919 when Gandhi conceived of a national hartal against the Rowlatt Bills. The symbolism of this day was stressed in the nationalist press:

> On the 6th of April, 1919, India discovered her soul. A grander revelation is not far off. . . . The campaign which Mahatma Gandhi inaugurates on the first day of the National Week is one which has never yet been witnessed in the history of mankind. For the first time a nation is asked by its leader to win freedom by itself accepting all the suffering and sacrifice involved. Mahatma Gandhi's success does not, therefore, merely mean the freedom of India. It will also constitute the most important contribution that any country has yet made towards the elimination of force as an arbiter between one nation and another. It is, therefore, that the eyes of all the world are centered to-day on Dandi.[88]

Gandhi was now nearing Dandi: "my Hardwar" as he called it, for the march had all along been for him a *yatra* or spiritual pilgrimage. His physical energy had amazed all those who witnessed the performance and as he approached Dandi "Gandhiji moved so quickly it seemed he was not walking but flying."[89] And so they flew into Dandi, a full twenty-four hours ahead of schedule, at 8:30 A.M., on April 5. Gandhi used the pause characteristically, to gather suspense. Press correspondents had assembled from all over India and the world and Gandhi directed his words now at a varied audience. He noted, first, that civil disobedience would commence the next morning and underscored the meaning of that timing: "6th April has been to us, since its culmination in the Jallianwala massacre, a day of penance and purification." This year it would be marked by him with a bath in the sea. The nation should observe a day of "prayer and fasting." And this penance would suitably prepare them all for the campaign of civil disobedience immediately following.[90]

But Gandhi was also attuned to his world audience, and he directed an appeal now to the potential force of international opinion. This began by complimenting the Government of India for its commendable "policy of complete non-interference" in the march. Gandhi interpreted this policy, however, as meaning that "the British Government, powerful though it is, is sensitive to world opinion which will not tolerate repression of extreme political agitation which civil disobedience undoubtedly is, so long as disobedience remains civil and, therefore, necessarily nonviolent."[91] Throughout the march, Gandhi had made appeals to world opinion through the media: now, he gave special attention to this audience. In a "message to America" he insisted that sympathy was welcome but not sufficient: "What is wanted is concrete expression of public opinion in favor of India's inherent right to independence. . . . if we attain our end through nonviolent means India will have delivered a message for the world."[92] Finally, Gandhi summed up in a sentence his appeal to the world from Dandi: "I want world sympathy in this battle of Right against Might."[93]

As dusk fell on Dandi on April 5, the tiny village population (460) swelled to more than 12,000, and Gandhi addressed his last prayer meeting of the march. Now he turned back to his Indian audience, and his language again became laden with the familiar symbols. Dandi, he observed, had been his destination for the last twenty-four days, but now "our real destination is no other than the temple of the goddess of *swaraj*. Our minds will not be at peace till we have her *darshan*, nor will we allow the Government any peace." Yet Dandi did mark the place where civil disobedience would commence, and this made it "a sacred ground for us, where we should utter no untruth, commit no sin. . . . Dandi was chosen not by man but by God. . . . This is God's grace; let us remain unmoved and watch his miracles."[94]

Many of those who watched on the shore that early morning of April 6 did indeed believe that they were witnessing a miracle. After prayers, Gandhi walked to the water and declared: "This religious war of civil disobedience should be started only after purifying ourselves by bathing in the salt water." Even this single sentence abounds with symbolism: civil disobedience, clothed in the garb of religious warfare, becomes purified through a special rite, bathing in waters of salt. By one account, as Gandhi and the marchers entered the sea at 6:00 A.M.:

"Thousands of people followed him and so sanctified themselves, an extraordinary sight beyond description." Finally, at 6:30, Gandhi stooped on the shore and picked up the symbolic salt and so offered civil disobedience. The deed was done. "With this," he said, "I am shaking the foundations of the British Empire."[95] A sweeping claim to be sure, but by the end of the year, more than 60,000 Indians (by government estimate) suffered imprisonment for committing an act no more or less than this.

There was a sense now that the movement could never be stopped, and Gandhi acknowledged from Dandi what the march had achieved. "At present," he wrote to Mahadev Desai on April 9, "my very thoughts have grown wings and they seem to have effect even when not expressed in speech or action. That is a fact."[96] On the fact and legend of the march, on the wings of Gandhi's creative imagination, the Indian nationalist movement soared, elevated by symbolic forces, sustained by dramatic impact. During this twenty-four day event, from its opening at Sabarmati to its denouement at Dandi, India and an international audience had been treated to vintage Gandhi, and quintessential satyagraha. As Pyarelal remarked, "After Dandi, the world knew what swaraj was all about."[97]

One could also discover the meanings of swaraj and satyagraha as well as the legend of the salt march through a novel by Raja Rao called *Kanthapura*. Rao wrote the story in 1937 about how Gandhi's movement came to the fictional village of Kanthapura, brought by a young student named Moorthy who conveys to the villagers each day the progress of the salt march:

> "Now," said Moorthy "we are out for action. . . . Do you know, brothers and sisters, the Mahatma has left Sabarmati on a long pilgrimage, the last pilgrimage of his life, he says, with but eighty-two of his followers, who all wear khadi and do not drink, and never tell a lie, and they go with the Mahatma to the Dandi beach to manufacture salt. Day by day we shall await the news of the Mahatma, and from day to day we shall pray

for the success of his pilgrimage, and we shall pray and fast and pour strength into ourselves, so that when the real fight begins we shall follow in the wake of the Master."

"Meanwhile, brothers and sisters, let us get strong. . . . Pray, brothers, pray, for the Mahatma is on the last pilgrimage of his life, and the drums are beating, and the horns are twirling, and the very sea, where he's going to gather and shape and bring back his salt, seems to march forward to give him the waters of Welcome.". . . . Moorthy told us of the pilgrim path of the Mahatma from day to day; for day after day the Congress Committee sent him information, . . . he would tell us of the hundred and seventy Patels [local government officials] that had resigned their jobs—a hundred and seventy mind you—and of the thirty-thousand men and women and children who had gathered at the roadside, pots and beds and all, to have the supreme vision of the Mahatma, and the Britishers will leave India, and we shall be free, . . . And when the Monday evening came, we knew it would be the morrow, it would be at five the next morning that the Mahatma would go out to the sea and manufacture salt and bring it home, and we could not sleep and we could not wake, and all the night we heard the sea conches cry. . . . And the next day the White papers told us the Mahatma had taken a handful of salt after his ablutions, and he had brought it home, and then everybody went to the sea to prepare salt, and cartloads and cartloads of it began to be brought back and distributed from house to house with music and clapping of hands. . . . And so day after day men go out to the sea to make salt, and day after day men are beaten back and put into prison, and yet village after village sends its women and men, and village after village grows empty, for the call of the Mahatma had sung in their hearts, and they were for the Mahatma and not for the Government.[98]

Raja Rao's fiction dramatizes what in fact interviews with dozens of Indians directly involved in the salt satyagraha affirmed: an unprecedented act of mass civil disobedience empowered millions during that Indian spring when "the call of the Mahatma had sung in their hearts."

The March Ends and the Movement Expands, with a View to Inclusiveness

Gandhi attempted, as soon as the march was over, to broaden the movement to include a wider range of groups and interests. His appeal extended to different social strata throughout India during the 1930–31 civil disobedience campaign, and this is evident, first of all, from the testimony of the British officials who struggled to cope with it. In the area of Gujarat touched by the march itself, there was a highly successful mobilization of groups. On April 28, three weeks after the march had concluded and its effects were being felt throughout the Bombay Presidency, Governor Frederick Sykes cabled Irwin:

> Hope entertained in many quarters that movement will be discredited must be abandoned. On the contrary, individuals and bodies of men hitherto regarded as sane and reasonable are day by day joining movement . . . because belief that British connection is morally indefensible and economically intolerable is gaining strength among educated Hindus, Gujaratis mostly, but others also.[99]

On the same day, Sir Purshotamas Thakurdas, a critic of Gandhi and one of the Government of India's confidential advisers, gave the Viceroy this judgment from Bombay:

> So great is the support to Mahatma Gandhi in this movement here, that the masses here, and in fact, anywhere, will not stand anything said against him publicly.[100]

A month later Irwin reported to Wedgwood Benn, Secretary of State for India in London with a summary statement on the movement:

> All thinking Indians passionately want substantial advance which will give them power to manage their own affairs. However much they may deplore the civil disobedience movement, they feel at heart that it is likely to make British opinion more elastic. . . . Student classes are of course ready sympathizers. . . . The movement thus obtains a wider measure of sympathy than many would be willing to accord to it on merits, and in Bombay the commercial classes, largely Gujarati, have openly supported and are said to be financing it.
>
> The masses in the towns are emotional, ignorant, prone to believe any rumors and accept any promises. The influence of Gandhi's name though it varies in different parts is powerful. . . . We think every European and Indian would tell you that he was surprised at the dimensions the movement has assumed, and we should delude ourselves if we sought to underrate it. Appraisement of its constituent factors might be assessed thus:

Communist and Revolutionary: 5 per cent
Gandhi's declared and sincere Congress adherents: 30 per cent

General Nationalist sympathizers, ignorant masses, and hireling volunteers: 50 per cent
Commercial and economic discontent: 15 per cent[101]

The accuracy of Irwin's assessments may of course be questioned. However, these two reports are succinct representations of Government of India
views on the movement's impact in its initial phase. Sykes's alarm at the way
in which the campaign had affected "sane and reasonable" people indicates
the inroads that had been successfully made into moderate opinion. Irwin's
report, in direct contradiction to his estimate of the movement's potential in
early March, indicates the degree of broad-based popular support he is willing to concede the campaign, admitting that "Communist and Revolutionary" elements may constitute only 5 percent of the base, while "general
Nationalist sympathizers, ignorant masses and volunteers" constitute 50
percent.

In the same report, Irwin expresses his special concern over support
gained from women as a "new and serious feature." In his autobiography
Sykes remarks on the salt satyagraha, "Most remarkable of all was the attitude of the women. Many Indian ladies of good family and high intellectual
attainments volunteered to assist in picketing and salt-making. Congress
has no scruples in making use of them, knowing well the embarrassment
which they would cause to the authorities."[102] An official Government of
India report for 1930 affirms that an "unexpected" source of assistance for
the movement came from the women. "Thousands of them many being of
good family and high educational attainments suddenly emerged from the
seclusion of their homes and in some instances actually from *purdah*, in order to join Congress demonstrations and assist in picketing; and their presence on these occasions made the work the police were required to perform
particularly unpleasant."[103]

In fact, as Madhu Kishwar finds in her incisive analysis, *Gandhi on Women*,
"The salt satyagraha marked a new high watermark of women's participation in the movement." The reasons for this, she observes, began with the
issue of the salt tax:

> Gandhi's choice of salt as a symbol of protest had amused many. The
> British had laughed while the Congress intellectuals were bewildered by
> the strange idea. This, once again, proved Gandhi's genius for seizing the
> significance of the seemingly trivial but essential details of daily living
> which are relegated to the woman's sphere. Salt is one of the cheapest of

commodities which every woman buys and uses as a matter of routine, almost without thought. . . .

To manufacture salt in defiance of British laws prohibiting such manufacture, became a way of declaring one's independence in one's own daily life and also of revolutionizing one's perception of the kitchen as linked to the nation, the personal as linked to the political. This was another campaign in which women in large numbers were galvanized into action, precisely because the action, though simple, appealed to the imagination. Its symbolic value was such as to touch the everyday life of women.

On the famous Dandi march through the villages of Gujarat, Gandhi originally started off with 79 *satyagrahis*. People from the villages on route and around spontaneously joined the march. When the procession neared Dandi, there were thousands of people walking with Gandhi. Among them were many women. Some of them were wealthy women from cities but a majority were ordinary village women . . .

Thus, on the one hand, emphasis on women's participation in *satyagraha* sought to ensure that the movement stayed non-violent, while on the other hand, emphasis on non-violence made it possible for larger numbers of women to participate. In fact, Gandhi's non-violence was a powerful revolutionary weapon because it created a favorable atmosphere for participation of very large numbers of people, especially women, giving them all a meaningful place in the struggle.[104]

As Kishwar's conclusion indicates, the politicization of women in the movement carried beyond the salt satyagraha: it was part of Gandhi's program of social reform. Judith Brown believes that a "great social issue with which Gandhi felt bound to grapple in his grass-roots work for swaraj was the place and treatment of women in Indian society." For this reason, she concludes, "it must never be forgotten that in him the women of India found a very considerable champion."[105]

Despite the inclusive approach of the salt satyagraha, Gandhi lost the support of one major group—the Muslims. This was a devastating loss in view of the consequences ahead of civil war. Muslim leaders, who had participated in the noncooperation campaign, were largely estranged by 1930. At the end of 1929 the Muslim Conference Executive Board decided not to follow the Congress lead into civil disobedience and this policy was restated three months later as Gandhi began the salt march.[106] In 1920–21, Gandhi had toured India with the Muslim leader, Shaukat Ali, calling him his "brother." Now Ali denounced civil disobedience and urged a Muslim boycott because the campaign could lead only to the substitution of Hindu for

British rule. Most Muslims followed this advice and, with the exception of those in the North-West Frontier Province, noncooperated with Gandhi throughout the salt satyagraha.[107]

Gandhi's anxiety over this was evident in his writings. On the day that the salt march began, *Young India* carried two articles by him on the same subject, the disaffection of the Muslims. In the first, he denied reports in the Muslim press that certain Muslims had been prevented from joining the march because of a ban on Muslims, noting that two Muslims would be among the marchers.[108] In the second, longer article, Gandhi refuted Shaukat Ali's "grave charge" that this "is a movement not for swaraj but for Hindu raj and against Mussalmans." Gandhi was obviously stung by Ali's charge and took pains to stress his inclusive spirit, expressing his earnest hope that:

Mussalmans, Sikhs, Christians, Parsis, Jews, etc. will join it. Surely all are equally interested in securing repeal of the salt tax. Do not all need and use salt equally? That is the one tax which is no respecter of persons. Civil disobedience is a process of developing internal strength and therefore an organic growth. Resistance to the salt tax can hurt no single communal (religious) interest.

He appealed for united action against the Government in the spirit of the earlier noncooperation campaign and concluded:

I am the same little man that I used to be in 1921. I can never be an enemy of Mussalmans, no matter what any one or more of them may do to me or mine, even as I can never be any enemy of Englishmen, even though they may heap further wrongs upon the Everest of wrongs their representatives have already piled. I am too conscious of the imperfections of the species to which I belong to be irritated against any single member thereof. My remedy is to deal with the wrong wherever I see it, not to hurt the wrong-doer, even as I would not like to be hurt for the wrongs I continually do.[109]

The ideas expressed in this article articulate Gandhi's inclusiveness as well as any that he wrote. They combine his characteristic appeal for Indian unity with his personal credo of perceiving no one as an enemy, opposing the sin and not the sinner. In this case, the sin is clearly separatism. Certain instances of satyagraha, such as the Calcutta fast, which will be examined in chapter 5, did demonstrate Gandhi's ability to reach Muslims, convincing them of his right motives. Yet, in the broad sense, Muslim separatism prevailed with the partition of India and creation of Pakistan. Why did his inclusivism fail to produce the result, which he so ardently desired, of a united India? To the extent that Gandhi's ideas and leadership may be held responsible for the partition of India, it appears with hindsight that the strength of his Hindu symbols, so evident in his ingenious use of language, proved also a weakness when it came to recruiting Muslims. It spoke to them of a Hindu Raj, as Shaukat Ali claimed, that would enforce perpetual domination of Muslims as second-class citizens. Gandhi's passionate reassurances and actions failed to persuade them otherwise. At the end of his life, as India attained independence with civil war, Gandhi saw the national movement as not simply a failure, but as *his* failure, as a verdict on the way that he had misused satyagraha and on India's inability to achieve true swaraj. It was a harsh judgment yet one characteristic of the way he saw his quest.[110]

If one criticism of Gandhi during the salt satyagraha was that the Hindu style of his thought and action alienated Muslims, another is that his class allegiances sold out the poor peasantry to capitalism and thus deprived India of an economic revolution. The origins of this critique have been discussed above in the context of M. N. Roy's theory. During the 1920s and 30s, Roy viewed Gandhi and the Congress as tools of India's bourgeois interests. Recent Marxist analysis is more sophisticated. It describes "the nature of Gandhian leadership" as not a "mere bourgeois tool" but with "a certain coincidence of aims with Indian business interests." These Indian "bourgeois groups" exerted a controlling influence on the salt satyagraha from start to finish. Although "considerable sections of the peasantry" were mobilized in the struggle, the capitalist forces ultimately prevented a full-scale agrarian class revolution. Gandhi served throughout as an agent of capitalism. Because of his restraining influence on the civil disobedience movement, "the bang ended in a whimper." But the Indian bourgeoisie got what it wanted: "unlike China or Vietnam, there was no development in the course of the nationalist movement of an alternative, more radical leadership capable of mobilizing the peasant masses" and so achieving a communist-style revolution.[111] Another historian of this period follows this same line of analysis and in the specific context of the salt satyagraha argues that Gandhi's protection of bourgeois interests is evident in his choice of the salt instead of property tax as the main issue of the campaign because it served as one of those "safely general issues which did mobilize large numbers of poor peasants in some areas but which also inhibited a further broadening and deepening of the movement." Again, this "broadening and deepening" might have led to a Maoist-type class revolution against the zamindars and landed elite.[112]

A major question left unanswered by this criticism of Gandhi is: given the powerful omnipresence of the Raj, how could any leadership have achieved a "broadening and deepening of the movement" that might have produced an agrarian revolution? Lenin's argument against Roy on this point remains valid, that no nationalist movement under those circumstances could have simultaneously mobilized against both the Indian landed elite and the British imperial forces.[113] Gandhi's effectiveness came, first, from the ethical appeal of satyagraha that allowed him to seize the moral high ground from the Raj, and, second, from the precise historical circumstances of India, in stark contrast to China. These circumstances dictated objective constraints imposed by the extent and nature of British power. Gandhi emerged as a leader whose principal asset was a persistent determination to translate ideas into action. He generated a theory and practice of change ideally suited to the particular context of India, a way of action that transformed the apparent limitations of the struggle into its strengths. He caught the Raj badly off guard in a manner that it never anticipated. As Bipan Chandra says, "The dilemma in which it [the Government in 1930] found itself was a dilemma that the Gandhian strategy of non-violent civil disobedience was designed to create. The Government was placed in a classic 'damned if you do, damned if you don't' fix . . ."[114] The dynamics of this strategy as the British perceived them deserve close scrutiny.

The Raj Hesitates: A Study in Ambivalence

What exactly was the effect of Gandhi's method on the power of the Raj as it reacted in 1930 to his civil disobedience? On February 6, the *Times of India*, generally a firm supporter of Government policy, began a series of editorials on the bankruptcy of Gandhi's leadership, condemning especially the "impracticable nature of his demands."[115] The next day, Lord Irwin spoke at Lucknow on the theme of civil disobedience, saying that it "could not fail to involve India in irreparable misfortune and disaster." He stated firmly that "Government would clearly never be justified in permitting the development of any such situation so heavily fraught with danger to the whole body politic and there can, therefore, be no question but that law and order must without reservation be maintained."[116] This public address is in accord with Irwin's views set forth in private correspondence on the eve of

Gandhi's march. On March 11, for example, he wrote to the King of his conviction that:

> Government could not bargain or parley in regard to a considered and announced intention of law-breaking. Meanwhile Mr. Gandhi has announced his intention of starting off on his march tomorrow, and his march is calculated to take him five days.[117] We have considered the whole situation very fully, and I am quite satisfied that, though it will have regrettable repercussions on our Moderate friends, we cannot afford to let the would-be law-breaking forces gather momentum, and that therefore, if and when Gandhi reaches the point of breaking the law, we shall have to arrest him.[118]

Irwin's firm resolve was in accord with that of Governor Frederick Sykes. In January, Sykes put his position on civil disobedience in the sharpest terms, cabling to the Viceroy that it was "essential" that "any overt steps taken in pursuance of the Congress resolution (on civil disobedience) . . . should be met and checked immediately. . . . The Government of India will no doubt agree that what is most important in such circumstances is firm action at the outset of the movement, giving a clear lead and assurance to the loyal population."[119] Yet, Gandhi began his campaign on March 12, exhorted his people to join the movement, himself broke the salt law at Dandi, and then led a national civil disobedience campaign of hundreds of thousands of volunteers until May 5, when he was finally arrested. Why did the Government of India act in such patent contradiction to its public and private pronouncements? It will be suggested here that the Government's response may be explained in part through an examination of Gandhi's method, and the effect it seems to have had on his Government adversaries, by creating an ambivalence in the Government's response which it found difficult to resolve.

During the week before the march, the *Times of India* assumed a hard line on Gandhi similar to that of Irwin and Sykes.[120] Sarder Patel's early arrest on March 5 was applauded, and the *Times of India* quoted favorably from British press statements calling for Gandhi's immediate arrest.[121] It also notes Sir James Crerar's comment in the Legislative Assembly: "I cannot myself believe that breaches of the law, from whatever motive committed, that represent a course of action which is likely to bring contempt for the authority of law can possibly be in the political or economic or any other interest of India."[122]

However, the call for severe action toward Gandhi, including his immediate arrest, was not nearly as affirmative and unanimous as the above accounts might indicate, either in the Government or in the English-language press. In many circles there was ambivalence and confusion. This ambivalence may be appreciated to some extent by focusing on the figure at the apex of British authority in India, Lord Irwin. The shakiness of Irwin's resolve before Gandhi's arrest reflects in a sense the mixed emotions and indecisive attitudes permeating British authority in India at this time. Gandhi's method of satyagraha played on these attitudes in such a manner that it managed to exacerbate Government ambivalence, whereas violence would have resolved it.

Irwin's administration had been badly shaken in 1928 by the Bardoli defeat. Yet it is remarkable that less than two years later, the same sort of hesitation that undercut it there should again bedevil its response to the salt march. This pattern is so significant that it prompts another look at the Government's problem with the Bardoli satyagraha. During the height of the Bardoli resistance, Irwin wrote to his father, the Viscount Halifax, that it posed "a very threatening situation" and hoped that he could "cut the gordian knot."[123] However, this was not easily achieved. As the Government's position in Bardoli worsened, Irwin received increasingly harsh cables from his Secretary of State, Lord Birkenhead, who wrote in July 1928: "It is humiliating to think that the prestige of British rule has sunk so low that any individual or body should dare to deliver to any British Governor an ultimatum" as that given at Bardoli. Then, after a heated session with the Cabinet, Birkenhead asked Irwin if he had any "general plan of campaign to deal with the movement and its possible extension? We simply cannot afford to be supine in the matter or to acquiesce in an insolent assumption of functions of Government. At present only a small part of the prairie has caught fire, but there are other and very inflammable prairies in the vicinity."[124]

This warning, coming twenty months before the salt satyagraha began, was appropriate and Irwin knew it. After the Government's capitulation in Bardoli a month later, Irwin's concern deepened and he pressed his Governor there for advice. Leslie Wilson replied at length, sounding the alarm of another satyagraha on the horizon. He concluded that "the most important lesson" is "that the organisers should themselves be dealt with great promptitude . . . before any such movement had had time to grow, it should be possible for any Provincial Government to make it definitely illegal for anyone to organise a campaign advocating non-payment of taxes."[125]

Irwin seemed to take this lesson to heart. He immediately dispatched that August a general report to all of his Governors that he had "taken counsel with Leslie Wilson" and concluded that the real culprit in Bardoli was the local government's hesitation. He found it essential that "a movement like this must be dealt with . . . as soon as a definite campaign of non-payment of taxes or revenue is launched it would be feasible to declare the organization unlawful . . . the important thing seems to me to be to apply promptly the powers we already possess."[126]

Birkenhead seemed satisfied with this firm resolution, writing soon after to Irwin that "in India directly law-breaking begins the hand of Government should descend on the breakers."[127] Whereupon Irwin reassured him that the problem at Bardoli had surely been delay, that Government power "if vigorously applied in the beginning should suffice," reiterating now to his Secretary of State in London the main lesson just emphasized to his Governors in India, that "The important thing seems that the powers we already possess should be promptly invoked."[128]

As the end of 1929 approached, Irwin stressed, in the manner noted above, the decisive action he must take in the face of civil disobedience.[129] "I propose to take an early opportunity," he wrote to his father, "of making it plain that, if and when the extremists try any policy of what they call Civil Disobedience, we shall lose no time in jumping on their heads."[130] Three months later, as Gandhi was about to march, Irwin wrote again to Halifax:

> We have begun to have our troublesome time, but I feel pretty certain that it is right to jump on Gandhi and other leaders at once as soon as they do anything illegal, and though this will make a great row, I think it would make as big a row later when the conditions might probably be worse. In any case, whether it is right or wrong, it is a great relief to have reached a pretty clear decision in one's own mind.[131]

But Irwin obviously had not made up his mind. He was ambivalent. He did not order Gandhi's arrest until almost two months after this letter. Why did he hesitate? First, because despite all the firm resolve expressed above in his letter to the King, Irwin found unwelcome the consequences of arresting Gandhi. He knew that the Government was in a predicament. Twenty-four hours after Gandhi began the march, Irwin confided his uncertainty in a report to Wedgwood Benn:

> Most of my thought at the moment is concentrated upon Gandhi. I wish that I felt sure what the right way to deal with him is. I think it depends upon the effect produced by his three weeks' march and the probability, or at least possibility, of his going on hunger-strike if we put him in prison. This last is embarrassing, and I have no doubt he knows this as well as we do.[132]

Irwin also hesitated because he was uncertain of moderate opinion. Ten days before the march began, he wrote that "Gandhi and co. must soon show their hand and try some of their folly in action. When they do, the trouble will, I fancy, begin," and he then wonders "how many of our moderate friends will have the courage to stand up, publicly against extreme courses that in private they vigorously condemn."[133] Irwin was right to be concerned about the response of his "moderate friends," for their reaction to the impending struggle was predictably ambivalent. The nature of this feeling may be seen in the press reaction to Gandhi's letter to Irwin.

The *Times of India* and *The Pioneer* both attacked Gandhi's letter strongly, but both also carried its full text and devoted editorials exclusively to it.[134] The impact of its style was felt especially, though, among moderates. *The Leader*, more than most newspapers, was representative of this reaction. At first *The Leader* was dubious, in an editorial on the letter, about the wisdom of Gandhi's policy. However, it offered a full report on the debate over the letter in the Legislative Assembly. Sir Hari Singh Gour argued in this debate that the projected satyagraha could not be effective and would probably degenerate into violence. But Maulvi Mohamad Yakub responded that the letter "placed Lord Irwin in a very difficult position. It has been couched in a friendly tone and written in the form of a friendly letter with . . . a deep touch of sincerity."

Another member, Mian Abdul Haye, said that he most often disagreed with Gandhi, but now he could not say that his action was wrong. "Though today I feel Mahatma Gandhi and his company are taking a leap in the dark, many a time the suspicion comes over me that they are in the right and we on the other side are in the wrong."[135] Then, in a long editorial commenting on this Assembly debate, *The Leader* observed that Mian Abdul Haye's remark was representative of the feelings of many moderates: "There are many others beside him in the legislatures and outside, who do not belong to the Congress, who feel similarly. This section which is unable to make up its mind is likely to take a swing to the left if the Government does not act with severe self-restraint. . . ." The debate in the Assembly, therefore, "demonstrates how morally weak the position of the Government has become and it can easily be made worse by an unnecessary show of strength or by making a fetish of law and order."[136]

Two days later, as Gandhi began the march, *The Leader* moved a step closer to him. In an incisive editorial entitled "The Fateful Letter and After," *The Leader* indicated that it had reconsidered its lukewarm support of Government policy. The piece began with an appropriate quotation attributed to Lord Morley (then Secretary of State for India), writing to Minto (his Viceroy) in May, 1907: "It is an old and painful story. Shortcomings in government lead to outbreaks; outbreaks have to be put down; reformers have to bear the blame, and their reforms are scotched; reaction triumphs; and mischief goes on as before, only worse . . . not only amongst sedition-mongers, but also amongst your law-and-order people, who are responsible for at least as many of the fooleries in history as revolutionists are." The editorial then praised the tone of Gandhi's letter and deplored the Government's stupidity in arresting Sardar Patel. Commenting on the inspiring nature of Gandhi's appeal, it concluded that "Mr. Gandhi is in truth a Mahatma by reason of his moral and spiritual greatness, his soul force . . . a leader and teacher of unique authority."[137]

When Irwin turned from the press to the advice of his Provincial Governors, he found there, too, sentiments on Gandhi that were far from unanimous on any one policy directive. In February, Sir Stanley Jackson, Governor of Bengal, worried that "Civil disobedience must be a very difficult matter to deal with. It is such a direct challenge to authority, and if authority does not assert itself, it will possibly be brought into contempt with dire consequences . . . but I do not think it will last long if the investigators are dealt with firmly."[138] Sir Hugh Stephenson, Governor of Bihar and Orissa, implied that Gandhi's arrest seemed predictable, while Sir Charles Innes, Governor of Burma, urged tough action on the eve of the march: " . . . it seems important to strike hard and quick at the leaders and so to disorganize the whole movement."[139] During the first week of the march, however, Irwin received from other Governors more restrained advice. Sir Geoffrey de Montgomery, Governor of the Punjab, advocated letting Gandhi get to his destination, where he would then make salt and the Government could confiscate it. But arrest was unnecessary. Gandhi, he felt, was "dreadfully anxious to get arrested" and if he were imprisoned, it would only give "a sign for whipping up further activity."[140]

At the same time, Sir George Stanley, Governor of Madras, suggested a wait and see posture, allowing only that "arrests may ultimately be necessary." And before the end of March, a humorous response came from Sir Laurie Hammond, Governor of Assam, who advised that "the best thing to do with Mr. Gandhi (and his followers) is to allow them to manufacture salt and then confiscate it and tell him to increase his output."[141]

But the Governor on the hot spot, Frederick Sykes, was not taking the situation lightly, and Irwin attended closely to his cables. As the campaign intensified in Bombay Province, Sykes in some desperation requested Irwin to meet with him in Delhi to discuss options. They met on March 26 and 27 and were joined by Irwin's trusted advisers, Sir James Crerar and H. G. Haig, the former Home Member of the Viceroy's Executive Council and the latter Home Secretary of the Government of India. It was a somber meeting that began with discussion of Sykes's long "Draft Note." Sykes said that although Gandhi had not yet reached the coast, "the excitement has been great, and the crowds large, even allowing for the importation of a large outside element." In the first ten days of the march, at least 74 village government officers (*patels*) had already resigned, many more resignations had been threatened, and these were only in the areas that Gandhi had so far reached. "Boycott of Government servants" had begun and Gandhi threatened to expand the tax resistance to include land revenue. Even now, in Surat, collection of the latter was difficult. All this showed, Sykes concluded, that the salt march was surely not the "fiasco" that the Government had predicted.[142]

Extraordinary measures were being taken to undermine the march's objectives.[143] Sykes outlined for Irwin and the others several options open to the Government, ranging from arrest and long imprisonment for Gandhi, to indifference toward the whole campaign. Above all, Sykes stressed to them there was an urgent need for a firm statement of Government intentions, and "in the absence of a clear understanding of Government policy" Sykes was convinced that Gandhi's action would soon undermine all British authority in Bombay.

So these four earnest men deliberated, searching for a solution that would do credit to their empire: for decisions that history may later regard as evidence that they wielded power wisely.

O, it is excellent
To have a giant's strength, but it is tyrannous
To use it like a giant.[144]

What leaps from these records of their deliberations is not the sort of wisdom that history finds remarkable, but profound ambivalence and indecision. Sykes yearns for a single stroke of policy that will relieve him from the growing furor, yet he repeatedly acknowledges the undeniable risks of arresting Gandhi. Will an arrest trigger a mass uprising? Uncontrollable violence? Or another fast in prison by the incorrigible Mahatma? All four men recognize the inconsistency of a policy that permits the arrests of other leaders, like Sardar Patel and Jawaharlal Nehru, but leaves Gandhi untouched. And what is to be done about the women resisters? On the one hand, they are increasing in unprecedented numbers. On the other hand, government policy must be "that in no case should women volunteers be handled or searched for salt; different arrangements [are] necessary in their case."[145]

The British would never resolve this dilemma of how to handle female *satyagrahis* but it would be only one of their many problems. The discussion inevitably focused on their lasting preoccupation of how to deal with Gandhi. The Viceroy must decide on whether to arrest the Mahatma. With all the intelligence and insight that has since earned him the reputation as "that most sensitive of Tory Viceroys"[146] Irwin pondered the question. At the end of March, he made his determination—to wait awhile longer. He recognized the urgency of the situation and proclaimed the Government's firm intention was that "the law shall not be openly flouted." But his preference was to postpone Gandhi's arrest until the Legislative Assembly had concluded its session, after which "there would be no objection to arrest him at any time." Irwin then sent Sykes away with rather cryptic instructions: notify him immediately if the situation worsens, but don't arrest Gandhi until he has reached Dandi. In sum, Irwin declared that "the policy in general was not to have more prosecutions than could be helped, but that the situation must in no case be allowed to deteriorate."[147] Shortly after, Sykes returned to Bombay and in an increasingly desperate state wired to Irwin that Gandhi was fast undermining his authority and "he cannot be left at liberty much longer."[148]

In her careful study of this civil disobedience movement, Judith Brown incisively summarizes the Government's dilemma: "If it arrested him [Gandhi] it risked massive public outcry; if it let him remain free it appeared to be frightened of his power and unwilling to back its own supporters."[149] Irwin thus hesitated and would continue in a state of patent ambivalence for almost a month longer. Trying to rationalize his position to Sir George Stanley, he wrote on April 14:

> I am sure that the right policy is to jump on the leaders as quick as possible when you have got decent ground for doing so. I am conscious that our action in not arresting Gandhi is very illogical, but I have little doubt that up to now it has helped us and embarrassed the other side. But we must constantly be on guard against the legend to establish itself that we are afraid of him, or that he is unarrestable.[150]

In his letters to friends abroad, too, Irwin repeatedly seeks to justify his reluctance to arrest Gandhi.[151] In these letters, he occasionally suggests one factor that may have been at the heart of his ambivalence: his perception of Gandhi as a genuine man of God. Irwin was himself devoutly religious and he remarks on Gandhi's reputation of saintliness.[152] Thus, he writes late in April to Sir Samuel Hoare that it has been right not to arrest Gandhi because "Indian opinion distinguished pretty clearly between him, whom they regard as more of a saint than a politician, and others who are more politicians than saints."[153] Had Irwin too in some part of himself come to share this view? In several letters to friends and relatives, he repeats an observation made by a District Magistrate in Ahmedabad which noted the "religious character of Gandhi's movement in popular estimation," and especially how freely the New Testament is drawn on by Gandhians producing an increased sale of Bibles in Ahmedabad.[154] To his father, he tried to explain himself most directly:

> I am anxious to avoid arresting Gandhi if I can do so without letting a 'Gandhi Legend' establish itself that we are afraid to lay hands on him. This we clearly cannot afford. But at present there are no signs of that idea obtaining currency. Apart from this, there is the undoubted fact that he is generally regarded as a great religious leader rather than a politician and that his arrest, while it will certainly not make the world fall in half, would yet offend the sentiment of many who disagree with him and his policy . . .
>
> I saw a letter a day or two ago from the head Government officer in Ahmedabad in which he said that it ought to be recognized that there was a gulf in public estimation separating Gandhi from any of the others concerned and emphasizing how the whole of Gandhi's march had been en-

veloped in a religious atmosphere. According to him, educated Hindus speaking about it drew analogies of, and supported them by quotations from, the New Testament, and this interest had the quaint result of increasing the sale of Bibles in Ahmedabad higher than ever before. A curious side coincidence, isn't it?[155]

Yet Irwin knew that it was not coincidental at all. Direct comparisons of Gandhi with Christ had become a *leitmotif* of popular commentary on the Indian movement, both in Britain and the United States.[156] In November 1929, for example, Fenner Brockway, British Labour M.P., wrote in a publication that was distributed in both London and India that Gandhi, "in living out his creed personally . . . has probably succeeded in doing so more completely than any man since the time of Christ."[157] Such was the image of Gandhi known around the world by 1930 and Irwin was probably sensitive to its implications.

Irwin's ambivalence over Gandhi was finally resolved, it seems, by Sykes's increasing alarm and Sir Malcolm Hailey's intervention. Hailey, Governor of the United Provinces, was perhaps the most trusted adviser in the small group that Irwin liked to call his "wise men." Hailey had himself been ambivalent on the question of Gandhi's arrest, offering, as he later recalled, "a compromise of differing views." Generally, however, Hailey supported Irwin's reluctance to arrest him, and Irwin frequently cited Hailey's support in his correspondence home. But on April 25, with the unrest increasing rapidly, Hailey finally came down hard for Gandhi's arrest, and in a long letter to Irwin advised that they had already waited too long and should act speedily now.[158] It appears that this removed Irwin's ambivalence, and he soon wired a relieved Sykes to prepare conditions for the arrest. Irwin's perception of Gandhi, however, as a religious figure was to return in force, and the Gandhi-Irwin talks a year later were to be marked by the unusual relationship that emerged between these two leaders.[159]

This account of the government's response to the salt march illustrates the sort of ambivalence that Gandhi often managed to create among his adversaries. This ambivalence could occur in very different political and social contexts. Most often, as in the instance of the salt march, the target of his satyagrahas was the British Raj, whose determination to enforce law and order was thrown off balance by the moral thrust of Gandhi's leadership. The peculiar moral force and religious aura of Gandhi's example prompted Irwin to pause and to reflect deeply on his government's purpose, creating an ambivalence in the ruling authority that proved utterly indispensable for the rapid acceleration of the satyagraha movement that followed.

But the British Government's attitude of ambivalance toward Gandhi was fostered not only by Irwin. In London, Wedgwood Benn, who had become Secretary of State for India in 1929, now expressed the position of the Cabinet on the question of Gandhi's arrest. He was as reluctant to arrest Gandhi as his Viceroy. On the day before the march began, Wedgwood Benn cabled to Irwin that the Government "above all" must not be embarrassed by "a lengthy trial with all its opportunities for propaganda," nor should action against Gandhi appear as "vindictive."[160] As the movement gathered momentum, Wedgwood Benn became increasingly disinclined to arrest Gandhi, because "if Gandhi is arrested and disorder followed, it would become merged in the terrorist organization and thereby strengthen it." Then he added significantly that if terrorism should so succeed, at least "it will be a straight fight with the revolver people, which is a much simpler and much more satisfactory job to undertake."[161] The concession is revealing. A "straight fight" meant meeting violence with violence; a "simpler" and "more satisfactory" policy not only because of Government's superior physical force, but also because terrorism, unlike satyagraha, could make no appeal to conscience. British colonial authorities shared this trait throughout their Empire: they evidenced no qualms of guilt in their ruthless execution of terrorists.

Nor was confusion over how to handle the Mahatma confined to high officials. The remarkable memoir of John Court Curry, an English police officer serving in Bombay during Gandhi's campaigns, conveys the extreme emotional distress that British police could experience when dealing with the civil disobedience movement. Curry interviewed Gandhi after his arrest in 1919 and recounts the exchange in detail, recalling the precise effect on him of Gandhi's words and behavior. He concludes:

> He impressed us by his quick, agile and gentle mind, his ready understanding and his great charm of manner. I have always regretted that no opportunity for close personal contact with him came my way after the interview about the Rowlatt Act which I have here described. I am convinced that so far from deserving the adulation which he has received as a Mahatma he has done great harm to the Indian people. The strange mentality which I have here attempted to describe encouraged inherent tendencies of an unhealthy nature just at the time when they required a sane and virile outlook.

Eleven years later, Curry was confronted by mass civil disobedience. When the full force of the salt satyagraha hit, there are many accounts of how civil resisters felt but little is known of police sentiments, so it is impossible to gauge what sort of reaction may be representative. However, Curry's response suggests the ambivalence and confusion that could occur among those charged with direct enforcement of the law. He described his distress in 1930:

> From the beginning I had strongly disliked the necessity of dispersing these non-violent crowds and although the injuries inflicted on the law-breakers were almost invariably very slight the idea of using force against such men was very different from the more cogent need for using it against violent rioters who were endangering other men's lives. At the same time I realized that the law-breakers could not be allowed to continue their deliberate misbehavior without any action by the police. As time went on I found to my dismay that my intense dislike of the whole procedure grew to such an extent that on every occasion when the Congress staged a large demonstration I felt a severe physical nausea which prevented me from taking food until the crisis was over. I knew on each occasion that the crisis would be over in a matter of hours and that the crowd would disperse or be dispersed and the leaders would call off the demonstration. I was at a loss to understand why I should be physically affected by it. I remembered that I had had no such feelings on occasions of serious rioting in Bombay or in my earlier pursuits of frontier raiders. I thought then, and I still think, that I was largely influenced by the feeling that whatever we did the result was to the advantage of the Congress policy and that the policy of our Government in dealing with it was wrong.

Government policy is wrong, that is, not because it is immoral but because it is unenforceable. As a police officer, Curry sees himself as being placed by his superiors in an impossible situation and clearly resents it. He is overcome with physical revulsion as his duties increase with his mounting "nervous tension" and "unable to account for this unless it was due to extreme distaste at the idea of using force against these 'non-violent' people."

These memoirs, written thirty years after the salt satyagraha, do not convey a tone of righteous conviction but rather of lasting uncertainty about what better path the Government might have followed. Curry knows that "the Congress very cleverly put the Government on the horns of a dilemma" because "they virtually compelled the police" to arrest them and so gave the whole world "a completely false idea of the nature of the British raj." What ultimately caused him "extreme exhaustion" and resignation from the police in 1930 was this: "I now think that the most powerful [reason for resigning] probably arose from mixed feelings about the nature of the British raj in India."[162] Gandhi described the Government at this time as "puzzled and perplexed."[163] He was right.[164]

Yet perhaps in a sense the raj was also right. The costs of hesitation can be appreciated without invoking Hamlet, but one wonders whether his immortal lines might have crossed the minds of Irwin and his men:

> Thus conscience does make cowards of us all,
> And thus the native hue of resolution
> Is sicklied o'er with the pale cast of thought,
> And enterprises of great pitch and moment
> With this regard their currents turn awry
> And lose the name of action.[165]

The Strengths and Limitations of Satyagraha

The story of the salt march suggests that Gandhi's ingenious creation of ambivalence through nonviolence constituted a vital step in his exercise of power. However, the necessity of creating ambivalence in the first place may also indicate an inherent limitation of the method. Can Gandhian nonviolence work against totalitarian states, or even petty despots, where power is wielded in a dictatorial manner, without hesitation or restraint? To take an extreme case, could European Jews in the 1930s and 1940s have employed satyagraha against the Nazi regime? Joan Bondurant remarks that Gandhi "believed that [satyagraha] could have been used in such concrete cases as the opposition of Jews in Germany to the Nazis," and then Bondurant supports his belief, arguing that if the Jews had used satyagraha they would have "mobilized world opinion behind them much more rapidly than they did."[166]

Gandhi did indeed believe that satyagraha could succeed against Nazism. He first addressed the issue in November 1938, when readers of his journal *Harijan* pressed him to comment on the plight of Jews in Germany. He began by recognizing that "the German persecution of the Jews seems to have no parallel in history," yet then affirmed his belief in the efficacy of nonviolent resistance. Such resistance to Hitler "may even result in the general massacre of the Jews." But, at worse, this would not wreak greater destruction than nonresistance, and, at best, it might have a result like that of the Indian satyagraha in South Africa. Gandhi insisted, however, that nonviolence could work only if practiced as "an article of faith," that is, not as "passive resistance of the weak" (*duragraha*), but as "active nonviolent resistance of the strong" (satyagraha). If so practiced, then its power would be invincible in any circumstance or situation:

> [Satyagraha] can and does work in the teeth of the fiercest opposition. But it ends in evoking the widest public sympathy. Sufferings of the nonviolent have been known to melt the stoniest hearts. I make bold to say that if the Jews can summon to their aid the soul power that comes only from nonviolence, Herr Hitler will bow before the courage which he has never yet experienced in any large measure.[167]

When *The Statesman* of Calcutta editorialized a week later (in response to Gandhi's views) that Hitler would hardly be impressed by Jewish acts of courage, he reprinted the editorial in *Harijan* and then replied:

> The hardest metal yields to sufficient heat. Even so must the hardest heart melt before sufficiency of the heat of nonviolence. And there is no limit to the capacity of nonviolence to generate heat. . . . Herr Hitler is but one man enjoying no more than the average span of life. He would be a spent force if he had not the backing of his people. I do not despair of his responding to human suffering even though caused by him. But I must refuse to believe that the Germans as a nation have no heart or markedly less than the other nations of the earth. They will some day rebel against their own adored hero, if he does not wake up betimes.[168]

On March 9, 1939, Martin Buber and J. L. Magnes sent directly to Gandhi two lengthy replies to the comments in *Harijan*.[169] Buber's letter especially represents an earnest and thoughtful attempt to reach Gandhi. It begins by refuting Gandhi's assertion that there is "an exact parallel" between the persecution of Jews in Germany and the discrimination against Indians in South Africa. Buber relates in detail the horrors of Nazi oppression and implies that Gandhi's assumption that the two cases are comparable indicates his basic misunderstanding of the German context.[170]

Magnes asks "*how* can Jews in Germany offer civil resistance? The slightest sign of resistance means killing or concentration camps or being done away with otherwise. It is usually in the dead of night that they are spirited away. No one, except their terrified families, is the wiser. It makes not even a ripple on the surface of German life." Magnes implores Gandhi to contrast this with the effect of the salt march, "when the whole world is permitted to hang upon your words and be witness to your acts." Both Buber and Magnes write with sincere respect, but the latter comes gently to the weakness in Gandhi's position when he says: "One of the great things about you and your doctrine has been that you have always emphasized the chance of practical success if Satyagraha be offered. Yet to the German Jews you have not given the practical advice which only your unique experience could offer."[171]

There is unfortunately no record of Gandhi having received these two letters.[172] However, another Jewish correspondent did reach Gandhi. Hayim Greenberg, editor of *The Jewish Frontier* in New York, had knowledge of Indian culture and recent political history as well as a sympathetic understanding of Gandhi's thought and leadership. He responded in 1939 to Gandhi's statement of November 1938, apparently without knowledge of the Buber and Magnes correspondence, but arguing along similar lines. After observing in more detail than the others the differences between the German and Indian situations that made the use of satyagraha impossible for Jews, Greenberg emphasized how Britons appreciated Gandhi's appeal to conscience and so used restraint in their response to civil disobedience. Such consideration could not be expected of the Nazis. Jews in Germany faced the worst circumstances for nonviolent resistance: an overwhelming and largely unsympathetic gentile majority commanded by an unprecedentedly ruthless totalitarian regime.[173]

Gandhi replied directly to Greenberg on May 22, 1939. He began by praising the thoughtfulness of Greenberg's letter and explained that he had commented in the first instance only "at the pressing request of Jewish friends and correspondents." He then continued: "It is highly probable that, as the writer says, 'a Jewish Gandhi in Germany, should one arise, could function for about five minutes and would be promptly taken to the guillotine.' But that will not disprove my case or shake my belief in the efficacy of ahimsa. I can conceive the necessity of the immolation of hundreds, if not thousands, to appease the hunger of dictators who have no belief in ahimsa. Indeed the maxim is that ahimsa is the most efficacious in front of the greatest himsa [violence]. Its quality is really tested only in such cases. Sufferers need not see the result during their lifetime. They must have faith that if their cult survives, the result is a certainty."[174]

As in his previous statements, Gandhi gives no indication of exactly how he thinks Jews might offer satyagraha against Hitler. His next and last published comment on the subject came seven years later, in 1946, when Louis Fischer pressed him for a verdict on the Holocaust: " 'Hitler,' Gandhi said, 'killed five million Jews. It is the greatest crime of our time. But the Jews should have offered themselves to the butcher's knife. They should have thrown themselves into the sea from cliffs. . . . It would have aroused the world and the people of Germany. . . . As it is they succumbed anyway in their millions."[175]

With comments like these, Gandhi discredited his own position.[176] Where is his compassionate understanding for the oppressed or even a hint of a practical program of action? He seemed unable at this time to grasp the enormity of the Holocaust.[177] Yet the differences between Nazi Germany and British India were evident then as now. A government's capacity for ambivalence must matter because it gives a resistance movement license to mobilize or to publicize its cause. Hitler's willingness and ability to use state power in an unrestrained extermination process precluded organized nonviolent action. Jews throughout Europe certainly did resist Nazi persecution but anything like a widespread satyagraha campaign was unthinkable.[178] Whether as small, isolated communities surrounded by hostile gentile majorities or ostensibly assimilated into the latter, the European Jews remained a very vulnerable minority without access to national media or methods of mass politicization.

By contrast Indian *satyagrahis* swam in relatively friendly waters with an immense advantage of media access at all levels, including regional, national, and international press and film agencies. With a leader like Gandhi who could employ mass mobilization techniques to maximum effect, the Indian case provides the premier example of how nonviolent resistance movements may develop. Thus, while the specific political and social context of Nazi Germany exemplifies conditions least favorable to satyagraha, those of the British Raj in India reveal the contrary. Gandhi did not create his historical context but he did show an uncanny intuition for creatively exploiting its political potential. That this intuitive sense was lacking in his advice to Jews only highlights the need for a leader to be intimately familiar with a political situation in order to translate ideas into action effectively.

Most governments do not fall into the category of Nazi Germany, Stalinist Russia, or Communist China: dictatorships prepared to kill a sizable portion of their own civilian population to maintain power. If the difficulty of imagining large-scale civil disobedience against such regimes is conceded, this does not rule out the practicality of nonviolent action in most countries. In fact, political experience since World War II and especially in the last few years has seen a surprising susceptibility of dictatorships to mass nonviolent protest. From the toppling of powerful leaders like Ferdinand Marcos in the Philippines to the overthrow of despotic governments in Eastern Europe, political pundits have failed to predict or later even to acknowledge the extraordinary effectiveness of nonviolent power. We must not miss the import of that elementary axiom of politics, established long before Gandhi but demonstrated by no one better than he, that the very existence of any government depends on the consent of its people.[179]

But every velvet revolution does not make for satyagraha. Most forms of nonviolent action Gandhi criticized as passive resistance or *duragraha*. The crucial distinction lies with the connection between satyagraha and swaraj. The buzzword "people power" often assumes quite wrongly that democracy and freedom follow from any nonviolent expression of the popular will. Such optimism is unwarranted. Even free elections can produce authoritarian regimes, and even democracies may harbor tyrannies of the majority. Gandhi tried to give new meaning to terms like democracy and freedom with his ideas of swaraj and satyagraha. As noted above in chapters 2 and 3, Gandhi's theory of democracy began by rejecting all concentrations of state power. He proposed satyagraha not *duragraha* as a remedy for abuse of power, even within a democracy. Real democracy emerged not from an instant exercise of people power somewhere in the world, but from a process of personal liberation, an attitudinal revolution within each citizen. He insisted that this process could be furthered only through satyagraha: a nonviolent use of power in pursuit of truth, the kind of truth that brings self-knowledge, self-awareness, and self-control. In India, the relationship of satyagraha to swaraj meant that people could engage in nonviolent action in ways that may liberate them from fear or enmity—that their political involvement might nurture a heightened self-esteem, to attain a free India of equality and justice for all. These were the ideals behind the independence movement. The next chapter shows how Gandhi applied them after India's independence, but this time, near the end of his life, to a country mired in civil war.

If ever a person's life may be portrayed as a journey, then it was Gandhi's. The dramatic changes that occurred in his ideas were usually accompanied by differences in dress or facial expression, as illustrated in these photographs.

Mohandas Gandhi, age 7, at his birthplace of Porbandar, Kathiawad, in western India; and at age 17, in nearby Rajkot, where he graduated from high school in 1887.

During his loyalist period, as a staunch admirer of the British Empire: first, age 21, as a law student in London (1890); and then, age 37, at the height of his lucrative career as a barrister in Johannesburg (1906).

A change of dress and countenance that signaled a profound change of thought and action: age 45, at the successful conclusion of a six-year civil disobedience campaign in South Africa (1914); and at age 49, in local dress, after his return to India, in the midst of a tax resistance movement in Gujarat (1918).

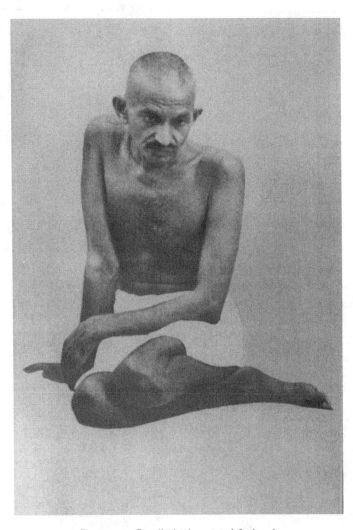

By age 55, Gandhi had so simplified and
reduced his clothing that Winston Churchill
could call him a "half-naked fakir." British
cartoons depicted him thus, but Gandhi saw
this as part of his philosophy of renunciation
and knew that Indian tradition valued
its symbolism.

Gandhi, age 60, beginning
the salt march on March 12,
1930. Pyarelal Nayar (at
right of Gandhi), his
secretary and biographer,
called this moment the most
dramatic in modern Indian
history. At its end, on April
6, at Dandi, Gandhi
picked up natural salt—an
illegal act that inspired a
nation to civil disobedience.

At age 62, on the eve of
his 1932 fast against
untouchability, he joked
that he possessed few
clothes and fewer teeth.
And at age 65, he ranked
among the world's most
prolific writers and
journalists, editor
of a weekly paper
entitled *Harijan*.

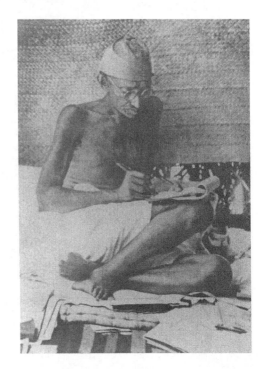

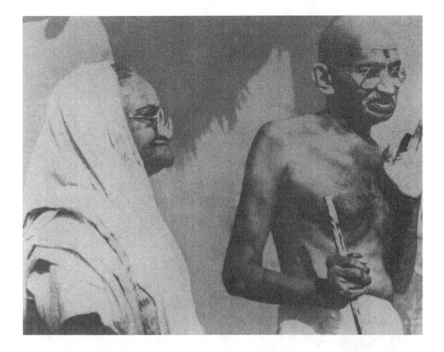

At age 70, in 1940, with Kasturba: their marriage began when they were both 13 and ended with her death 62 years later, when they were in prison together. Also in 1940, with Rabindranath Tagore, his friend and critic and India's poet laureate, at Tagore's home, Santiniketan.

At age 77, in late 1946, Gandhi walked 116
miles through riot-torn Noakhali, Bengal,
visiting 47 villages in a desperate effort at
calming the Hindu-Muslim conflict that raged
there during India's civil war.

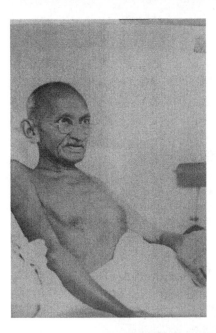

In August-September, 1947, at the peak of religious conflict in northern India, Gandhi fasted in Calcutta with dramatic success and received congratulations from Lord Mountbatten, the last British Viceroy. The letter is a testimony to the power of nonviolent action.

Government House,
~~The Viceroy's House~~
New Delhi

26th August, 1947.

My dear Gandhiji,

    In the Punjab we have 55 thousand soldiers and large scale rioting on our hands. In Bengal our forces consist of one man, and there is no rioting.

    As a serving officer, as well as an administrator, may I be allowed to pay my tribute to the One Man Boundary Force, not forgetting his Second in Command, Mr Suhrawardy.

    You should have heard the enthusiastic applause which greeted the mention of your name in the Constituent Assembly on the 15th of August when all of us were thinking so much of you.

    Edwina has gone off today on a courageous mission to the Punjab with Rajkumari Amrit Kaur, to see what they can do to help relieve the suffering and distress among the refugees.

Yours very sincerely

Mountbatten of Burma

Mr Gandhi.

I will give you a talisman.
Whenever you are in doubt, or when the
self becomes too much with you, apply the
following test. Recall the face of the
poorest and the weakest man whom you may
have seen, and ask yourself, if the step
you contemplate is going to be of any
use to _him_. Will he gain anything by it ?
Will it restore him to a control over his
own life and destiny ? In other words,
will it lead to Swaraj for the hungry and
spiritually starving millions ?

Then you will find your doubtd
and your self melting away.

One of the last notes to be signed and left by Gandhi in 1948 as
a final testament of his deepest belief.

Gangabehn and Ramjibhai Badhia, a harijan (untouchable) couple in Gandhi's
Satyagraha ashram. Gandhi recognized Gangabehn's unique authority in the
community and wrote to her often about ashram matters. He called Ramjibhai
his "guru in khadi weaving" and included him among the Dandi marchers.

Two Britons on opposing sides of India's independence movement: Lord Edward Irwin (1881–1959), as Viceroy of India during the salt satyagraha was Gandhi's chief adversary. Reginald Reynolds (1905–1958) was an English Quaker who joined Gandhi's ashram and then hand-delivered to Lord Irwin Gandhi's letter of March 2, 1930, with its historic proclamation of civil disobedience.

Gandhi's letter of March 11, 1930, to Jawaharlal
Nehru. It was written from his ashram on the eve
of the salt march and begins: "It is nearing 10:00
a.m. now—the air is thick with the rumour that I
shall be arrested during the night." But the British
hesitated and did not arrest him until May 5, thus
giving the movement time to mobilize.

CHAPTER FIVE

The Calcutta Fast

"Let Hindus and Muslims understand
firmly that the cornerstone of *swaraj*, the
cornerstone of the freedom of India is
Hindu and Muslim unity."
                    —*Gandhi, April 7, 1921*[1]

"Lovers and makers of *swaraj* must not be
dismayed by these omens. My advice is
satyagraha first and *satyagraha* last. There
is no other or better road to freedom."
                    —*Gandhi, September 9, 1946*[2]

India attained independence on August 15, 1947. The long
struggle against British imperialism—longer than that of any other colonized country—had ended and the process of decolonization throughout
the world had begun. Gandhi, who was as responsible for this process as
any person on earth, would have had cause to celebrate if India had not been
submerged in mass violence. The religious strife among Hindus, Muslims,
and Sikhs that engulfed northern India from 1946–1948 marked one of the
worst civil wars in history. It demonstrated the grim truth that Indian culture had at least as much capability for civil violence as any other, that this
could occur despite all the emphasis given to nonviolence since 1919, and
that although India had gained independence, it certainly had not achieved
swaraj.

These dark realities with all their implications were not lost on Gandhi.
The civil war and consequent partition of British India into the separate
states of India and Pakistan was the worst period of Gandhi's life. He

took partition as a verdict of failure: not that nonviolence had failed but that he had fallen short in his practice of it. Yet it was then, when this verdict seemed so clear, that he proceeded to demonstrate for one last time the power of satyagraha and the true meaning of swaraj. This chapter tries to tell that story as it happened during those months in Calcutta because at no other time was nonviolent power more effective in action.

Calcutta, 1946–47: In the Crucible of Communal Conflict

In May 1947, after nine months of unprecedented Hindu-Muslim civil war had ravaged Calcutta, Sir Frederick Burrows, Governor of Bengal, observed that this great city had become a tragic microcosm of the nation: "The problem of communal [religious] strife which is vexing the whole of India can be studied in an intensified and concentrated manner in this focal city." Then *The Statesman*, Calcutta's leading newspaper, commented on Burrows's remark. In an editorial of despair more than of indignation, it eloquently voiced the city's agony:

> Calcutta, once the most lively if never the most comfortable city of India, is becoming almost unbearable to its inhabitants. Under the blight of communalism, it is from dusk onwards a city of the dead. Even by day, life is at a low ebb. . . . Shadowed by past calamity, not daring to turn their eyes from the morbid present to a future without hope, [its citizens] drag out meaningless lives, thankful only from day to day that these are still safe from the *goonda* [thug] and the housebreaker. They ask themselves if such terrible conditions are to be permanent and find no answer. If Calcutta passes two "quiet" days in succession, hope revives to fall again as the third day brings news of fresh outrages.[3]

In such an atmosphere of unquiet desperation all of Calcutta had acquiesced by mid-1947. Only six months before, *The Statesman*, long proud of its independent critical stance and crusading spirit, was alive with attacks on the government of Bengal and exhortations to the citizenry. But these had been gradually replaced by the standard front-page entry: "A Government Press Note reports that the number of casualties as a result of yesterday's communal disturbances in Calcutta were. . ." "The Terror," as it was commonly called, lasted more than a year, from August 1946 until September 1947. Two factors determined its character and fostered its growth: religious or "communal" violence and political extremism. Religious conflict, especially between Hindus and Muslims, had long existed in Calcutta as throughout much of India, but now partition was imminent and political extremism gained its head. When these forces coalesced Calcutta's atmosphere was radically transformed; together they wrought "the transference of this dread social phenomenon [of communal violence] into another dimension."[4]

In a thorough analysis of the continuing nature of communal violence in India, Suranjan Das observes: "What, however, most clearly distinguishes the 1946 violence from earlier outbreaks was its highly organized nature and direct links with institutional politics. The leadership for both Hindus and Muslims now came from established political parties: Muslim League for the Muslims and Hindu Mahasabha and sections within the Congress for the Hindus."[5] Hindu political extremism had mixed with religious symbolism in India since the early twentieth century, as noted above in the writings of Aurobindo Ghose. But historical events had now taken a drastically new turn: Britain would soon transfer power not to one but two nations. The plan for Pakistan became at this moment the new factor in the power equation. Hindu-Muslim conflict escalated dramatically as Calcutta plunged into intense party rivalry. As Das observed, both Hindu and Muslim extremists competed in this struggle. The virulent quality of their propaganda is represented in this sample from a Muslim League pamphlet of August 1946:

"The Bombay resolution of the All-India Muslim League has been broadcast. The call to revolt [for the creation of Pakistan] comes to us from the nation of heroes . . . God has granted to the Muslims in the month of Ramzan what they have been clamoring for. The day for an open fight which is the greatest desire of the Muslim nation has arrived. Come, those who want to rise to heaven. Come those who are simple, wanting in peace of mind and who are in distress. Those who are thieves, goondas , those without the strength of character and those who do not say their prayers—all come. The shining gates of heaven have been opened for you. Let us enter in thousands. Let us all cry out victory to Pakistan, victory to the Muslim nation and victory to the army which has declared a *Jehad.*

Another leaflet distributed at this time in Calcutta urged the Muslim minority to "Be ready and take your swords. . . . Your doom is not far and the general massacre will come. We shall show our glory with swords in hands and will have a special victory."[6]

"When the Ganges is in flood," Gandhi remarked in May 1947, "the water is turbid. The dirt comes to the surface."[7] The troubled waters of Calcutta began to swell in November 1945, and nine months later the dirt did indeed come to the surface. The November riots in Calcutta were not communal in nature; rather, they signalled how mob violence had entered political demonstrations, and the subsequent effect that this would have on the city. On Tuesday, November 21, the Indian National Army officers' trial had been resumed in Delhi. A procession of 500 students demonstrated in Calcutta, responding to an appeal from their political leaders, to observe this as "I.N.A. Day." The procession entered a prohibited area, clashed with the police, and a student was killed. Suddenly, without warning, the situation was transformed and that Wednesday "mob violence swept the city." At the same time, another feature of future patterns appeared: a municipal strike "put the city into chaos." *The Statesman* described it as "The Paralyzed City":

> Dazed citizens of Calcutta who up to Wednesday morning were going quietly about their business have lately lived through a fantastic nightmare. . . . They seek to penetrate the cloud of rumor to find out what is happening and why and what prospects there are of an end of this anarchic confusion which has already led to so much tragedy. . . . Lives have been lost, hatred created, business suspended, movement interfered with and discomfort caused to everybody in circumstances which are still largely obscure.[8]

The phrases used here are to recur again and again until finally abandoned the following year as clichés: "paralyzed city," "dazed citizens," "fantastic nightmare," "anarchic confusion," "lives lost," "hatred created," "so much tragedy." Surrounding all this is an air of bewilderment, a search for causes and reasons in the midst of "circumstances which are still obscure." Sir Francis Tuker later wrote that "There was fear about, and fear in India means trouble."[9] The fear was there in November, and its full meaning became clear in the next year. Indeed, this element of fear, beginning with uneasy anxieties over the destructiveness of anarchy, and growing by the following summer into an endemic wave of terror, characterizes above all else the phenomenon of religious conflict in Calcutta. As we shall see, it was precisely the nature and force of this fear that Gandhi understood, confronted, and overcame.

February 1946 set the pattern of disturbances for the new year. Increased Hindu-Muslim tension had been noted by General Tuker, head of the eastern command. Large-scale rioting, though, was not anticipated. On Monday, February 11, students demonstrated as they had in November, in protest against the Indian National Army trials. This time the protest was significantly different: an ex-Muslim officer of the I.N.A. had been court-martialled, and given seven years imprisonment. The demonstrators were therefore mostly Muslim, protesting against the severity of the punishment; Hindu officers, they added, had recently escaped with much lighter sentences.[10] All Muslim shops in Calcutta were closed, and 2,000 Muslims, carrying League flags, demonstrated. Once again, the demonstrations quickly deteriorated into "mob violence," with more casualties and over a longer period than the November riots.[11] "It is an awful warning," *The Statesman* lamented, "but to more than established authority."[12]

Leaders of the Congress and the Muslim League interpreted this warning in different ways. Congressmen like Maulana Azad, Sarat Chandra Bose, and Surendra Mohan Ghosh vied with one another in issuing blanket condemnations of the riots. For them it showed only that "the *goonda* and irresponsible elements of this city have gained the upper hand." H. S. Suhrawardy, however, then a prominent Muslim Leaguer in Bengal and soon to become its chief minister, had taken an active part in the initial demonstrations and enthused over them. Although he criticized the violence, for him the riot "was a warning that, once the Muslim public was aroused, it would need all the forces of Government to restrain it. . . . The reason for our success is the sincerity of purpose behind all this agitation."[13] Suhrawardy's reaction forebode ill for the next of Calcutta's communal riots, when the responsibility was to fall on him, as chief minister, for maintaining law and order.[14]

For Sir Francis Tuker, the February riots had a special significance: they "set a match to the fuse which detonated the charges with such fearful violence months later not only in Calcutta and Eastern Bengal, but far afield in Bihar and into the United Provinces at Garhmukteswar and finally into the Punjab."[15] With hindsight, it is easy to plot such a chain of events. Even without hindsight, though, the ominous aspects of the riots were clear to perceptive observers like R. G. Casey who noted their significance shortly after the expiration of his term of office as Governor of Bengal in February.[16] Casey's successor, Sir Frederick Burrows, arrived in the wake of the February riots to assume an "onerous appointment," (in Tuker's view) "that we would none of us have touched with the proverbial bargepole, and [we] admired the sense of public duty that brought him from gentle England to turbulent Bengal."[17] For a time, it seemed that Burrows had imposed some of this gentleness on the turbulence around him. India, particularly Bombay and Ahmedabad, experienced rioting but Calcutta was relatively calm.

A national political crisis now emerged, though, which was to affect Calcutta directly. At the end of July, the council of the All-India Muslim League met in Bombay and revoked their earlier acceptance of the cabinet mission plan. "The time has now come," the council resolved, "for the Muslim nation to resort to direct action to achieve Pakistan. . . . The Council calls upon the Muslim nation to stand to a man behind their sole representative, the All-India Muslim League, and be ready for every sacrifice."[18] Sacrifices were indeed to be made. August 16 was subsequently fixed by the council for the observance of "Direct Action Day" throughout India. Muslims were urged to stage "a hartal on that day, to hold public meetings and other demonstrations." Another "Day" was thus designated for political demonstrations; but this day India was not soon to forget. It became a defining moment of political extremism.

While the League was making decisions in Bombay that would, in less than three weeks' time, transform Calcutta, Bengal was preoccupied with quite another matter. On the same day (July 29) that the direct action resolution had been passed, a one-day general strike of transport, industrial, and government employees "completely paralyzed" Calcutta. The general strike coincided with the postal strike of 16,000 employees that had been in progress throughout Bengal since July 21. This was in turn followed by still another strike, of the Imperial Bank employees, which further belabored the city.[19] The strike of the previous November had coincided with the riots; now larger strikes preceded far greater rioting. This is not surprising, since the effect of each of these strikes was to quicken the forces of unrest and disorder in the city.

Once the postal strike was resolved, on August 7, Calcutta could turn again to the national scene, which the Congress now dominated. By August 14, Jawaharlal Nehru, leader of the Congress party, had accepted the Viceroy's invitation to form an interim government. Nehru had written to Mohammad Ali Jinnah, head of the Muslim League, asking for his cooperation. The latter replied that "the situation remains as it was and we are where we were." After meeting with Nehru in Bombay on August 15, Jinnah told the press, "There will be no more meetings between me and Pandit Nehru."[20] The stage was thus set for August 16: Jinnah adamantly pledged to direct action, Nehru engrossed in the formation of his interim government, with Lord Wavell, the Viceroy, hoping in vain for a Congress-League reconciliation. And Gandhi, in Sevagram, was pondering, "I have never had the chance to test my nonviolence in the face of communal riots . . . the chance will still come to me."[21]

Gandhi's remark might be thought prophetic, and in a general sense it was because no one was more sensitive than he to the troubles ahead. The remark was not a prophecy, though, of what would happen in Calcutta that August. No Indian political leader foresaw that event. Indeed, most of them do not appear to have had the slightest inkling of the scale on which the Calcutta riots would occur. The Indian press was a shade more foresighted. Among the major English-language papers, mild warnings of the consequences of direct action appeared in *The Times of India* and *The Statesman*; and *The Leader* singled out Calcutta, on the day before the tragedy, as the most likely trouble spot, although it hardly foresaw the scale or intensity of the rioting.[22] One insight into the peculiar context of the political situation in Calcutta occurred in *The Times of India* on August 7. After observing that the Congress had tended to dismiss the very real dangers of direct action, the writer wondered whether the Muslim League ministries, in Bengal and Sind, would resign, since the direct action would be aimed at them. If they did not resign, "quite an interesting situation will have been created by Leaguers breaking the law in Sind and Bengal, where the League may be in charge of the maintenance of law."[23] The remark did anticipate the dilemma the Muslim League ministry in Bengal would face.

H. S. Suhrawardy, as chief minister of Bengal, attempted (like the Muslim League minister in Sind) to overcome this dilemma by declaring August 16 a public holiday. This, Suhrawardy declared, would "minimize chances of conflict," and was preferable to "stopping business by means of stone-throwing, intimidation, and dragging people out of buses and cars and burning the vehicles."[24] The Congress opposition immediately pounced on this remark as a confession of the government's inability to maintain order, or much worse (from the Congress point of view) the use of government to further narrow party ends. It is likely that the chief minister thought that the government could walk the tightrope by having peaceful demonstrations on behalf of the Muslim League which would not degenerate into uncontrollable rioting. This was a major blunder. What is certain, however, is that neither the government nor the opposition nor the press anticipated the magnitude of the tragedy.

While the Congress did attack Suhrawardy and *The Leader* reinforced this censure on the day before the riots, both concentrated their criticism on the chief minister's unwarranted use of government power to achieve party aims. Neither focused its criticism on what was later to form the crux of the indictment, Suhrawardy's failure to take adequate preventive measures. This was simply because neither the opposition nor the press had guessed what "adequate" might involve. The statement issued by the government of Bengal on the riots, six months after their occurrence, cannot be gain-said: "What was not foreseen and what took everybody by surprise including the participants was the intensity of the hatred let loose and the savagery with which both sides killed."[25]

The chief minister, the governor, and the police should have taken stronger precautions at the beginning and then acted with more dispatch as the disturbances gained ground. Suhrawardy in particular was appallingly negligent, perhaps in the early stage of the killing even deliberately provocative. Yet, it is hardly realistic to place all the blame on the government, or on any single party to the conflict. Seen in this light, two points may initially be made on the killing: first, it was precisely the total unexpectedness of the calamity that produced its aftermath of shock, terror, and vengeance. Second, the search for scapegoats that followed only obfuscated (given the political atmosphere of the time) the real lessons that might have been grasped at once. In this connection, one of the most constructive features of Gandhi's approach was his insistence that everyone was in some measure responsible for the continuing violence, and therefore every citizen had it in his power to exercise some degree of control over it. Unfortunately, another year would pass before Calcutta came to appreciate this basic truth.

The Great Calcutta Killing (as it came to be called) began on the morning of August 16, 1946 and lasted until August 20. Approximately 4,000 people were killed and 11,000 injured on a scale of urban violence that was wholly unprecedented. One survivor recalled the tragedy twenty years later: "It was a moment of terror that I never imagined could happen here. I saw the city I loved, the neighbors I trusted, desecrate themselves in a terrible fury unknown before in Calcutta. Those few days of bloodshed proved to me that swaraj had to be much more difficult and distant than we thought."[26] Another observer reported that "For four terrible days this massacre and brutality continued unabated. During this time the life of the city was completely paralysed," including all medical facilities.[27]

The tragedy of the killing continued after the massacre with India's response to it, especially among the politicians. Nehru, consumed with the political demands of forming an interim government, was asked by the press (on early reports of the riots) about how Calcutta's violence would affect his plans. He replied, "Our programme will certainly not be upset because a few persons misbehave in Calcutta."[28] Once the scale of this "misbehavior" struck the Congress, though, no time was lost in placing the responsibility "for all that has happened" on the Muslim League ministry.[29]

Simultaneously, Jinnah was saying, "I cannot believe that any Muslim Leaguer would have taken part in using any violence."[30] No leader or party would accept any responsibility. "There is no indication that the Calcutta riots have induced a calmer frame of mind," wrote *The Times* of London correspondent; rather, "recriminatory and, indeed, vitriolic" comments prevail among all circles in India.[31] Liaqat Ali Khan, then general secretary of the Muslim League, attributed the killing solely to "the Hindu elements whose actions plunged Calcutta into these orgies of violence and slaughter." Liaqat agreed that a "bitterness" now "sweeps India as never before, and the inevitable bloodshed . . . will continue to be caused." But for him the exclusive cause was "the communal arrogance and the spirit of violence fostered by the Congress." The Congress want another "Hindu raj" but "a hundred million Muslims will resist it."[32] *The Statesman* pressed the "leader of the Muslim League" for an "apology." From Mr. Jinnah came word that the main "responsibility" for Calcutta must rest with "the Viceroy, Mr. Gandhi, and the Congress"; for "it was an organized plot to discredit the Muslim League on the part of the Hindus."[33] *The Statesman* did not press further.

In this atmosphere, the question of which side had started the riots on that morning of August 16 could hardly be judged impartially by the parties involved. However, this did not deter the Congress and the League from pursuing their respective "investigations" into the matter. The Congress working committee discovered that first blood was drawn by Muslims carrying "big bamboo sticks, swords, spears, daggers and axes which they brandished" before unarmed Hindus.[34] The working committee of the Bengal Muslim League, however, found that "peaceful Muslim processions almost everywhere had to face a barrage of brickbats, stones, and missiles."[35] The *Modern Review* (Calcutta) replied with "photographic evidence" of the Muslim aggressors on that morning, and concluded that the riots started when "their Fuehrer had declared a Jehad, and thousands of gangsters had been imported to reinforce them."[36] On this hysterical exchange, the most acute comment came from Arthur Moore: "For any given man-made catastrophe, all participating parties bear some responsibility. In party politics the procedure considered correct and honorable is for each component to blame the others and entirely exonerate himself. . . . We have produced a situation in which civil war is an obvious possibility. . . . I have a deep sense of terrible disasters impending."[37]

As early as April 1946, Gandhi had criticized "loose talk of civil war," but by late August such talk was widely accepted. In the press commentary on the killing, no term was more often applied than "civil war." "What befell India's largest city last week," summed up *The Statesman*, "was no mere communal riot. . . . It was three days of concentrated, unprecedented Indian civil war."[38] Ten days after the killing, *The Times* of London correspondent reported: "To put it bluntly, far too many thinking Indians are resigned to the prospect of civil war in the near future. . . . Was Calcutta the first battle of a civil war, and is this country threatened with massacres carried out with ruthless fanaticism by the baser elements of the communities?"[39] Such were the doubts and fears emanating from Calcutta, and Arthur Moore's "deep sense of terrible disasters impending" was widely shared. For Gandhi, the killing was an "ocular demonstration" of the fruits of direct action; for many other Indians, it was an ocular demonstration of the reality of the abyss beyond. "One principal lesson of the tragedy," editorialized *The Times* immediately after the killing, "lies in its illustration of the perilously narrow margin which today divides order from anarchy in India."[40] After August 16, anarchy and civil war of the worst form were no longer abstractions in India; they had become specters that overshadowed all else by the end of the year. It is above all in terms of a "psychosis of fear" that the Great Calcutta Killing marks the watershed of events in a study of India's quest for swaraj. Freedom meant nothing if not freedom from fear. "Would that the violence of Calcutta were sterilized," exclaimed Gandhi, when he heard of the killing, "and did not become a signal for its spread all over."[41] But this was not to be. The grim chain reaction immediately began in which India was soon convulsed: Dacca, Noakhali, Bihar, and the Punjab. Percival Griffiths observed,

> By the end of 1946 India was drifting rapidly to chaos. The real power had passed from British hands; senior officials, anxious about their future, were conscious that they were caretakers under notice and were disheartened; Ministers, paralyzed by the communal situation, seemed unable to come to grips with the problems of administration; and the

unparalleled communal riots in Calcutta, together with serious disorder in many parts of India, made it clear that nobody was in effective control.[42]

Of this situation, Calcutta was an inextricable part, acting from within India upon it, and in turn reacting to the violence from without.

The agony that Calcutta experienced in the year after the Great Killing is indescribable. Fear and violence pervaded the city. Many sought to escape, either fleeing from the city or withdrawing into armed communal camps within it. The first major riot of the year occurred in late March. A series of stray incidents quickly escalated into large-scale mob violence and troops were called in to restore order.[43] After March 1947, rioting became chronic, persisting, in Governor Burrows' words, in "a stream, . . . now ebbing, now flowing, but never completely ceasing for more than a few days."[44] The government had clearly lost control; while Suhrawardy now took maximum precautions,[45] "so far has the position now deteriorated that the public has come to realize that its only protection is, in the last resort, India's armed force."[46] The once effective Calcutta police department had itself become undermined and demoralized by communalism,[47] and the Hindu majority regarded the League ministry with intense suspicion. "We have come to a stage," Suhrawardy admitted, "when nobody, not even the Government, can guarantee that there will not be arson, stabbing or looting."[48]

Gandhi's Response to Communalism: His "Experiment" and Fast

At the national level, Lord Mountbatten, the last Viceroy of India, had induced Gandhi and Jinnah to sign, on April 15, a joint appeal for peace, deploring the recent acts of "lawlessness and violence." All communities were urged "to refrain from violence in any form."[49] This appeal had little affect on India and certainly no influence on Calcutta. Gandhi sensed this, and on a visit to the city in early May, threatened a "fast unto death."[50] On the prospect of Gandhi fasting, *The Statesman* editorialized:

> It is with regret that many will learn that Mr. Gandhi has again spoken of a fast. . . . We think, however, that all those who are close to him should do their best to dissuade him. . . . The contemplated fast could not be expected to influence Muslims generally, whether aggressors or (as both communities tend to believe of themselves when involved) acting on the defensive. In such circumstances, if Mr. Gandhi started a fast, he would presumably continue to the end. As Hindus saw his life ebbing away,

their own bitterness would greatly increase and the outcome would be in every way disastrous.

Like many others, we have never been able fully to understand these Gandhian fasts. The appeal they make is primarily to the emotions, to the heart. But also, perhaps, they are intended to appeal to the head. If one man greatly admired is so strongly convinced of the rightness of the cause he advocates that he is prepared to sacrifice his life for it, then, his opponents may come to think there must be more to be said for it than they concede; and so they start to consider their own position afresh although, we think, under compulsion. But with communal [religious] disputes it is different. That they are primarily emotional is true; but once feelings are aroused to fever-pitch, there is no more possibility of subduing them by appeal to some other nobler emotion than of curing a rabid dog of his madness by talking gently. As for the intellectual factor, that is wholly absent. It should be plain, we think, that fasts, by whoever undertaken, can have little effect in such conditions. We trust that Mr. Gandhi will see that his duty is not to use this last weapon. . . .[51]

Gandhi arrived in Calcutta on August 9. It would be his last and most momentous visit. The previous month had seen the city's worst Hindu-Muslim violence of 1947. The most notable feature of these riots was the flash panic that had instantly consumed the population. "Lurking in the back of most minds is the possibility of a sudden new conflagration on last August's scale. Monday's events started panic which may not be quickly allayed."[52] Many urged the enactment of martial law. No longer, moreover, could Suhrawardy serve as scapegoat: on July 3, a West Bengal cabinet had been formed of which Dr. P. C. Ghosh of the Congress became chief minister. Now he, with Suhrawardy (who would remain de jure chief minister of Bengal until August 14), bore responsibility for the violence. When, therefore, it became obvious that the Congress, like the Muslim League, was unable to curb the riots, the open attacks by the press and others on the Muslim League ministry were superseded by more sweeping indictments of the very process of democratic government itself.[53]

This breakdown in civil authority meant in fact an almost total reliance on the military. In early August, the announcement came that "the military forces in Calcutta will soon be strengthened considerably."[54] This increase of troops was immediately reinforced by the governor's application of the "Disturbed Areas Ordinance" to the whole of Bengal. The ordinance gave utmost powers to magistrates and the police in their enforcement of a prohibition on public assemblies or the carrying of weapons.[55] The civil government, therefore, had gone about as far as it could go, short of acquiescence to martial law. Yet, only a week before independence, severe Hindu-Muslim rioting again broke out, when, on the day before Gandhi arrived in Calcutta, a crowd of more than three hundred had stopped a train, selected twelve of its passengers, and wantonly slaughtered them in full public view. This incident, which ignited many others, is a prime example of the impotence of government when the citizenry, in fear or vengeance, acquiesce before forces of violence.

Gandhi had announced that he would spend independence day in the Noakhali district of Bengal, but after a day spent in Calcutta, "listening to the woes of the city," his departure was postponed. At his prayer meeting, on the evening of August 10, Gandhi told a vast crowd that his "head hung in shame at this recital of man's barbarism" in Calcutta. This was madness, and his aim was to effect a return to sanity. He refused to write off Calcutta's riots as simply a manifestation of *goondaism*. All citizens of Calcutta were responsible for the mob violence, all must "turn the searchlight inwards" and see that "wide open *goondaism* was a reflection of the subtle *goondaism* they were harboring within." He had decided to delay his departure, and work here for peace, because (as he pointedly said) "the argument of his Muslim friends had gone home." Then he promised that he would make an extensive tour of the riot areas, and this brought huge crowds the next day, "Hindus and Muslims, including women, who told him their grievances."[56] Two weeks before, *The Statesman* had commented, "The need now is not so much of political reassurance as of psycho-therapy, could that be practiced on a mass scale."[57] The therapist had arrived, and his genius was such that he, above all Indian leaders, knew intuitively how it could be practiced on a mass scale.

On August 11, Suhrawardy returned to Calcutta from Karachi, and went immediately to see Gandhi at his Sodepur ashram. He implored Gandhi to stay in Calcutta, at least until after independence. Suhrawardy had made a similar plea three months earlier, when Gandhi last visited the city. Gandhi had then replied that he would remain if Suhrawardy would enlist him as "his private secretary"; they could work together as a Hindu-Muslim team against religious conflict, a suggestion the chief minister had then dismissed as "madness."[58] Now, however, Gandhi made an even more extraordinary proposal. He suggested to Suhrawardy that as an "experiment," they both move into a deserted Muslim *bustee*, in one of the worst-affected localities of the city, and live there together, for whatever period was required, until peace was restored to Calcutta. "It would be best," Gandhi thought, "to live unprotected by the police or the military." "In brotherly fashion" they would approach the people, reason with them, and foster a return to sanity. Suhrawardy considered the proposal, and after twenty-four hours gave his unqualified acceptance. "In view of the fact," he told the press, "that an insensate orgy of violence has started and the feeling of revenge, instead of subsiding, is increasing, I have decided to accept Mr. Gandhi's offer."[59]

The year since the killing had humbled Suhrawardy. The irrepressible Calcutta riots had blackened his ministry; and the League itself had partly withdrawn its favor, as suggested by his defeat by Nazimuddin, the week before, in the election for party leader of East Bengal. Gandhi, however, was not concerned with Suhrawardy's political status in the League, but rather with what the chief minister meant to the Muslims and Hindus of Calcutta. When Gandhi wrote to Patel of his Calcutta "experiment," the Sardar, with characteristic humor replied, "So you have got detained in Calcutta and that too in a quarter which is a veritable shambles and a notorious den of gangsters and hooligans. And in what choice company too!"[60] For Gandhi's purpose, Suhrawardy was indeed "choice company." No individual could have better disarmed Muslim suspicion and also attracted the hostilities of the Hindus, drawing them into the "experiment" where they could be neutralized nonviolently.

Hostile Hindu elements were present in full force when Gandhi and Suhrawardy arrived at the deserted "Hydari mansion" in Belliaghatta, the afternoon of August 13. The original crowd of two hundred swelled in size, and eventually broke into the house, hurling stones, smashing doors and windows. Gandhi confronted them. They wanted to know why had he now "come to the rescue of the Muslims" when it was the Hindus who had suffered? How could he, a Hindu, associate himself with Suhrawardy, the Muslim who had been responsible, as chief minister, for the slaughter of countless Hindus a year ago? Gandhi replied with the simple argument that he had used, as a reformer, all his public life: "How can I, who am a Hindu by birth, a Hindu by creed and a Hindu of Hindus in my way of living be an 'enemy' of Hindus?"[61] This reasoning had the desired effect and the crowd eventually dispersed. For almost three weeks after this initial outburst, Calcutta not only remained calm, but on independence day became the scene of unprecedented Hindu-Muslim fraternization. All India was astounded at the sudden transformation.[62]

How far Gandhi's experiment and personal example influenced the independence day metamorphosis in Calcutta is impossible to determine precisely. At the least, Gandhi was "a lightning conductor for unpleasant verbal storms," whose experiment offered "an object lesson in the neighborliness which is the only true answer to communal fury."[63] At most, he was, in the words of the new Governor of West Bengal, C. Rajagopalachari, "the magician" who performed the "Calcutta miracle."[64] Perhaps the truth lies somewhere between these two points. Gandhi's experiment in Belliaghatta did provide, on the eve of independence, "a place of pilgrimage for thousands of Calcutta's citizens. Both Hindus and Muslims came in a constant stream [on August 14] . . . and placed their grievances before Mr. Gandhi and sought his advice."[65] The experiment, therefore, acted as a remarkable catharsis at the critical moment of independence, and its effect continued in the days immediately after. Throughout August, unprecedented crowds gathered at Gandhi's evening prayer meetings, and rejoiced together in an astounding upsurge of Hindu-Muslim harmony. Gandhi did not, it should be noted, suppress or eliminate the atmosphere of extreme tension present in the city since the killing; indeed, he watched as it burst into a form of social hysteria. What Gandhi did was to act, at this point, as one of several forces[66] that served to release desirable social energies, and thereby precipitate an explosion of goodwill rather than of violence. When, however, the city's tensions and anxieties once again sought violent expression, Gandhi abandoned his milder cathartic techniques and applied instead an extreme form of social control. For the fast was the ultimate weapon of satyagraha, employed only when all other means had failed. As it was then used by Gandhi in Calcutta, the fast marked the final and climactic stage of his satyagraha, an intense method of conflict-resolution through nonviolent action. In this sense, the fast may be seen as an "escalation" of nonviolent conflict, the culmination of a process in which power is increasingly applied to achieve swaraj.

As the end of August approached, Calcutta's political leaders and its press enthused over "the miracle of communal harmony in India's largest city."[67] The announcement of the "boundary award," which marked the lines dividing India and Pakistan, had not caused further disturbances; and the *Id* festivities had witnessed still more scenes of "unforgettable communal friendliness."[68] Glowing tributes to Gandhi flowed in from the highest political sources, including India's new governor general, Lord Mountbatten,[69] and the Muslim League.[70] Gandhi's prayer meetings held on the Calcutta maidan (especially the one held for the celebration of *Id*) seemed to demonstrate the complete success of his "experiment." Congress leaders urged him to leave for the Punjab and plans for his departure on September 2 were accordingly made. Nehru had referred to the riots among Hindus, Muslims, and Sikhs in the Punjab, which were now being reported daily in Calcutta, as constituting a "grave crisis," and General Rees warned in Lahore that "the spirit of retaliation is abroad in the land."[71] On September 1, the Calcutta press described the Punjab as being in the throes of "primitive blind vengeance" and torn by a "veritable civil war."[72] Hideous tales of mutual violence caused by Sikhs and Muslims there proliferated throughout Bengal. Reports of restiveness, especially among the Sikhs of Calcutta, now appeared. As the old fears once more emerged in the city, it seemed to many inevitable that, despite the recent "miracle," the urge to retaliate would again prevail.

That the recrudescence of violence in Calcutta actually began at Gandhi's Belliaghatta *bustee* indicates the extent to which his experiment had become the magnet for Hindu-Muslim conflict. Late in the evening of Sunday, August 31, a crowd converged on Hydari mansion, carrying an injured Hindu who had allegedly been knifed by a Muslim. They demanded that Gandhi call for retaliation. His attempts to quiet them failed; he was almost seriously wounded when the crowd attacked his party. The police soon restored order, but Gandhi's detailed statement of the incident to the press indicates the extent to which he himself was severely shaken. The disturbance triggered an outburst of violence the next day throughout the city; by evening fifty people had been killed and more than three hundred injured in uncontrollable rioting. Troops immediately came in, but since the demands of the United Provinces and Punjab had drastically reduced the military resources available to Bengal, the situation, in Tuker's view, was far more critical than it had been in July or August. Major General Ranking, area commander, "acted at once with all the troops at his disposal, calling in Gurkhas" as well; yet even this, the military realized, was inadequate, and Ranking "pressed the government to impose martial law."[73]

Gandhi toured the affected areas, and then wrote to Sardar Patel, "What was regarded as the 'Calcutta Miracle' has proved to be a nine days' wonder. I am pondering what my duty is in the circumstances."[74] When Rajagopalachari came to visit him on the evening of September 1, Gandhi had already made his decision. He proposed a fast. "Can one fast against the *goondas*?" Rajaji asked. "I want to touch the hearts of those who are behind the *goondas*," Rajaji replied. "The hearts of the *goondas* may or may not be touched. It would be enough for my purpose if they realize that society at large has no sympathy with their aims or methods and that the peace-loving element is determined to assert itself or perish in the attempt." Rajaji urged him to "wait and watch a little," but Gandhi was adamant. "The fast has to be now or never. It will be too late afterwards. The minority community cannot be left in a perilous condition. My fast has to be preventative if it is to be of any good. I know I shall be able to tackle the Punjab if I can control Calcutta. But if I falter now, the conflagration may spread."[75]

"The weapon which has hitherto proved infallible for me is fasting," Gandhi announced in his public statement that evening. "To put in an appearance before a yelling crowd does not always work. It certainly did not last night. What my word in person cannot do, my fast may. It may touch the hearts of all the warring elements in the Punjab if it does in Calcutta. I, therefore, begin fasting from 8:15 tonight to end only if and when sanity returns to Calcutta."[76] The focus throughout the country was at once on Gandhi. *The Times of India* commented, "More than his life the peace of India is at stake."[77] Indian political leaders responded with alarm and exhortation. On the first day of the fast, however, it was clear that the city's extremists, inflamed by this latest surge of violence, had not yet felt the impact of Gandhi's move. Looting and rioting persisted as the casualties mounted.

On September 3, the second day of the fast, quiet came to Calcutta. Gandhi cautiously observed that "the leaven has begun to work."[78] The positive effects of his action on the city were plain: a deputation from the Calcutta bar association came to pledge their assistance; and they were followed by a large mixed procession of Hindus and Muslims, who promised to reconcile their differences. Then peace demonstrations of students, political workers, and government officials of both communities paraded through the city to Hydari mansion. Gandhi told them all to "go out together to patrol the troubled areas and relieve the police of its arduous duties." Meanwhile, the police force itself, European and Indian, Christian, Hindu, and Muslim, had commenced a twenty-four hour fast in sympathy while remaining on duty. This show of civic sympathy was precisely what Gandhi wanted; of less interest to him were the public broadcasts with which provincial and national Congress leaders bombarded the city.

By September 4, the third and last day of the fast, the mass therapy had progressed still further. Scores of members of Hindu "resistance groups," formed since direct action day, surrendered to Gandhi a small arsenal of weapons, and admitted to him their complicity in the urban violence. They were followed by a large gang of *goondas* who offered to "submit to whatever penalty you may impose, only that you should now end your fast." To both groups, Gandhi replied, "My penalty for you is that you should go immediately among the Muslims and assure them full protection. The minute I am convinced that real change of heart has taken place, I will give up the fast."[79] "The function of my fast," Gandhi explained, "is not to paralyze us or render us inactive," but "to release our energies."[80] Release them he did: not only was Calcutta without a single incident on this day, it was mobbed with processions to Hydari mansion clamoring for an end to the fast.

Amiya Chakravarty, then a teacher in Calcutta, described the sort of ambivalence that the fast managed to create among skeptics and then how this ambivalent response soon prompted positive action, especially among the students:

> His face and eyes, made luminous by suffering, would show little trace of the agony that his will had mastered, but the nature of his ordeal was unmistakable to the millions. Even while repudiating his method and its efficacy, the one question in peoples' minds would be, "How is Gandhiji?" People would begin to feel uncomfortable; the grocer's boy, the rickshaw-puller, the office clerk, the school and college students would scan the news columns early in the morning and listen to the radio throughout the day and feel more and more personally *involved* in the situation. I remember how University students would come up to us and ask to be excused from attending their classes because they felt disturbed and did not know what to do. But why feel disturbed? They would say that though they did not believe in such methods and in the philosophy behind it all, one thing struck them as curious; after all, if anybody had to suffer for the continued killing and betrayal in the city, it was not Gandhi. He had taken no part in it. So, while others were engaged in crime, it was he who had to suffer like this. They felt awkward and some wanted to stop his suffering, and even gathered together weapons from streets and homes at great personal risk; they wanted to return them to Gandhi.[81]

Earlier *The Statesman* had argued (in the May editorial quoted at length above) against a fast under these circumstances. Its arguments are significant and worth repeating. The editorial had admitted that "we have never been able fully to understand these Gandhian fasts," but this admission did not inhibit its subsequent assumptions: "the contemplated fast could not be expected to influence Muslims generally," and since "Hindu bitterness would greatly increase the outcome would be in every way disastrous." It contended further that the appeal of the fast is "primarily to the emotions, to the heart," although it is also "intended to appeal to the head." It is conceivable, the editorial conceded, that in some instances this appeal might work, "But with communal disputes it is different . . . once feelings are aroused to fever-pitch, there is no more possibility of subduing them by appeal to some other nobler emotion than of curing a rabid dog of his madness by talking gently. As for the intellectual factor, that is wholly absent."

This argument merits reiteration, not only for its suggestion of an almost fatalistic acceptance of the "mad dog" forces of Hindu-Muslim conflict, even among the most intelligent observers, but also because it reflects their confident skepticism of the efficacy of nonviolence. At the crux of this effort was the will of one extraordinary individual, a will he directed at the "rabid dogs" of Calcutta, not merely by talking gently, but through the potent force of satyagraha. This summoned a power so considerable that it persuaded even *The Statesman* to reconsider its position:

> On the ethics of fasting as a political instrument we have over many years failed to concur with India's most renowned practitioner of it, expressing our views frankly. But never in a long career has Mahatma Gandhi,[82] in our eyes, fasted in a simpler, worthier cause than this, nor one more calculated for immediate effective appeal to the public conscience. We cordially wish him unqualified success. . . .[83]

Now, all Calcutta was wishing him "unqualified success." But for Gandhi, the right time to break the fast had still not come. Amiya Chakravarty observed:

> So the fast would continue. Men would come back home from their offices in the evening and find food prepared by their family, ready for them; but soon it would be revealed that the women of the home had not eaten during the whole day. They had not felt hungry. Pressed further, the wife or mother would admit that they could not understand how they could go on when Gandhi was dying for their own crimes. Restaurants and amusement centers did little business; some of them were voluntarily closed by their proprietors.[84]

At 6 P.M. on September 4, what he regarded as a decisive breakthrough occurred. Gandhi was visited by another deputation: they included N. C. Chatterjee and Debendranath Mukherjee, the president and secretary, respectively, of the Bengal Hindu Mahasabha; R. K. Jaidka, a prominent Hindu Punjabi businessman; Sardar N. Singh Talib, the Sikh editor of the influential Sikh daily, *Desh Darpan*; Dr. G. Jilani of the Muslim League; Dr. A. R. Choudhury and M. Rahaman of the Pakistan Seamen's Union, and the everpresent Suhrawardy. As Suhrawardy escorted them in to Gandhi, the deputation joined Rajagopalachari, Acharya Kripalani, and P. C. Ghosh, esteemed Congress leaders, who were already at his bedside. Gandhi, of course, appreciated that among these men were represented the most powerful interests in the city. After listening to their pleas for ending the fast, he demanded of them two promises: first, that communal violence would not recur in Calcutta; second, that if it did recur, they would "not live to report failure," but would lay down their lives to resist it. If these pledges were given and broken then he vowed that he would begin an irrevocable fast until death. The deputation withdrew to another room, conferred, and emerged with a joint agreement: "We the undersigned promise to Gandhiji that now that peace and quiet have been restored in Calcutta once again, we shall never allow communal strife in the city and shall strive unto death to prevent it."[85] Gandhi immediately broke the fast; it had lasted seventy-three hours. Chakravarty concluded that "an immense release filled the atmosphere" at this moment. Then "release turned into rejoicing, the fast actually led up to feasts in which the warring communities joined heartily, while Gandhiji sipped his small glass of orange juice."[86]

On September 7, he left for Delhi. Communal violence, during this critical period surrounding partition, did not return to Calcutta. "Gandhiji has achieved many things," said Rajagopalachari afterwards, "but in my considered opinion, there has been nothing, not even independence, which is so truly wonderful as his victory over evil in Calcutta."[87] Perhaps even more representative of the city's sentiments was the acting mayor's comment on Gandhi's departure that "Calcutta has been spared the horrors of a strife which easily might have been as bad or worse than former disturbances."[88] This was the judgment of the moment, not only by Congressmen, but by the press and political leaders of both communities. But it was not only the judgment of the moment; it has been confirmed by sober reflection as well, nowhere expressed better than by the British historian E. W. R. Lumby in his account of the fast:

> His triumph was complete, and the peace that he brought was destined to
> endure. A Muslim League newspaper, acknowledging the debt Calcutta

Muslims owed him, said, "he was ready to die so that they might live peacefully." He had in fact worked a miracle, perhaps the greatest of modern times.[89]

Analysis of Gandhi's Use of Power in Calcutta

Nicholas Mansergh, in his perceptive account of this period of Indian history, observes that:

> In this, the last year of his life, Gandhi's influence was transcendent. By the people of India he was treated with the awe given to the great prophets and religious teachers of the past. Indeed he was already numbered with them. It was his preaching of the doctrine of nonviolence more than any other single factor that stood between India and bloodshed on a frightful scale.[90]

The aim here is not to proclaim miracles or to canonize Gandhi, but rather to explain the nature of his influence; the sources and dynamics of his power, and the manner in which he used this power in the Calcutta satyagraha.

Mansergh observes further of Gandhi that "As his inclinations seemed to lead him to withdraw more and more from the narrow political issues of the hour and to devote his efforts to the noble work of pacification, so his reputation grew."[91] While it is true that Gandhi's popular influence increased at this time, his withdrawal from politics was accompanied by a sharp decrease in influence within the higher political circles, where the decisions on the partition of India were being made. His decline here had begun at least as early as September 1944, with his failure to reach a compromise in his talks with Jinnah. Deeply aware of this decline, and profoundly discouraged with the political trend of events, he wrote in October 1946, "I know that mine is today a voice in the wilderness."[92] As what he called the "vivisection of India" became imminent, his own sense of impotence increased. This, while, as Mansergh asserts, Gandhi's influence "more than any other single factor stood between India and bloodshed on a frightful scale." This apparent paradox itself illuminates, among other things, the peculiar nature of Gandhi's power, and the extent to which it was, particularly in this last phase, trans-political in character. This is evident especially in the Calcutta satyagraha. In this instance, at least three main dynamics of Gandhi's power emerge: his past experience with Hindu-Muslim conflict, the inclusive method which he developed in dealing with it, and his theory of fasting, which he increasingly applied to its resolution. The last of these is especially noteworthy, since it exemplifies both his leadership achievement as well as elements of his social thought, that is, his ideas on society and on means of social control.

"My South African experiences had convinced me," Gandhi recollected in his *Autobiography* in 1927, "that it would be on the question of Hindu-Muslim unity that my Ahimsa would be put to its severest test, and that the question presented the widest field for my experiments in Ahimsa. The conviction is still there."[93] This conviction had, throughout Gandhi's life, much to sustain it. In September 1924, for example, Hindu-Muslim violence reached a high peak and Gandhi decided to fast, his first major fast on behalf of religious unity. "The recent events," he announced from the home of a Muslim friend in Delhi, "have proved unbearable for me. My helplessness is still more unbearable. My religion teaches me that whenever there is distress which one cannot remove, one must fast and pray. . . . I am therefore imposing on myself a fast of twenty-one days commencing from today."[94] Like the Calcutta fast, undertaken twenty-three years later for the same purpose, this one was begun in a Muslim home and Muslim friends cared for him; these elements of his inclusive method, then, had already taken shape.

The 1924 fast, however, represents only one high point in his consistent concern for religious harmony. Whatever mistakes Gandhi may have made in his later dealings with the Muslim League and Jinnah, no Indian leader gave greater attention, over a longer period, to the fundamental problems of Hindu-Muslim relations. For three decades, during his career in the Congress, he emphasized Hindu-Muslim unity as among "the three pillars of Swaraj"; and, at the end of this long career, when communal violence suddenly gained its head, Gandhi acted intuitively to meet the emergency. He turned first to Bengal. After the Great Calcutta Killing, he realized that an alternate form of "direct action" was necessary; and, when the first report of the Noakhali atrocities reached him in October 1946, he knew that this action demanded, above all, his physical presence in the disturbed areas. With this decision to wage satyagraha against large-scale rioting began developments in method which culminated a year later in the Calcutta "experiment."

While, therefore, the Congress working committee were passing resolutions in Delhi, finding "it hard to express adequately their feelings of horror and pain at the present happenings in East Bengal," Gandhi was heading for the Noakhali villages. Had it not been for the precedent of the Calcutta killing, the early reports of casualties in Noakhali would have seemed incredible (5,000 killed and 50,000 injured). Gandhi arrived there, after a brief stopover in Calcutta, in early November 1946. He was brooding over the power left in his method and in December he wrote: "Is the Satyagraha of my conception a weapon of the weak or really that of the strong? I must either realize the latter or lay down my life in the attempt to attain it. That is my quest."[95]

The next four months were spent in a relentless effort to restore confidence among the Hindu minority. He moved slowly through the area toward his destination of Srirampur, a remote village where he spent six weeks organizing the satyagraha. Then came his renowned "a village a day pilgrimage:" a walking tour of seven weeks in which he covered 116 miles and 47 villages. During this time, Gandhi was receiving reports of the Hindu retaliation in Bihar. This eventually prompted his departure from Bengal, arriving at Patna in early March. Here it was the Muslim minority that he sought out and consoled, while the Hindus now bore the brunt of his censure. The technique, however, was substantially the same in Bengal and Bihar: a tour of the devastated villages, visiting the afflicted homes and families; then the inevitable prayer meeting, with its ingenious admixture of the traditional and the contemporary; and finally the delegation of responsibility to one individual or group in the village that order might be preserved. Occasionally, as at Srirampur, Gandhi would remain for a prolonged period in one of the most remote and ravaged of the villages, until his persuasiveness and sheer courage stabilized the area. Fundamentally, this was the method of conflict resolution that eventually directed the Calcutta satyagraha.

While Gandhi was touring the villages of Bihar, Nehru was preoccupied with running his inter-Asian relations conference in Delhi. Gandhi had been persuaded to attend, so he left Bihar at the end of March to address the closing session. During the summer in Delhi, recurrent reports of disturbances in Bengal and Bihar unnerved Gandhi, and the summer was subsequently broken with visits to Calcutta and Patna. Then, at the end of July, he traveled throughout Kashmir, leaving there in early August for Calcutta en route to Noakhali. Gandhi came to Calcutta, then, as a revered leader who had courageously fought religious violence, first, on behalf of the Hindu minority in Noakhali and then in defense of the Muslim minority in Bihar. His reputation had indeed grown, and for good reason: among India's leaders he was unique in having gone to the villages and struggled there in the interests of both communities. Moreover, as both Hindus and Muslims turned increasingly to him with trust, Gandhi's own confidence in his mission increased. Only days before the Calcutta killing, he had said, "I have never had the chance to test my nonviolence in the face of communal riots." Now, this had been tested. The results were successful—not as dramatic, perhaps, as the Calcutta fast, but the work in Noakhali and Bihar did restore in him confidence in the power of satyagraha to combat communalism.

Gandhi's method of satyagraha and his inclusive mode of leadership, abundantly manifest in his ingenious use of traditional Indian language, images, and symbols, goes further than any other single factor to explain the source and dynamics of his power. His entire style of expression had been cultivated since his early South African experience. It is most evident in his use of words, like *satyagraha*, *swaraj*, *sarvodaya*, *ahimsa* and *harijan*. These were terms which Gandhi either coined or reinterpreted. Language, though, represents only one element of his style: other components, often less obvious, contributed equally to the way in which he communicated with the Indian people. In his last phase, his style had, after a lifetime of public contact, become largely instinctive; and for this reason, his power over the Indian people reached its zenith.

Gandhi's "experiment" at Hydari mansion marks an imaginative use of satyagraha in terms of its inclusiveness. The richness of symbolism here shows everywhere the touch of the master. For at Hydari mansion appeared the microcosm on which the whole should be patterned: Gandhi, the "Hindu of Hindus," moving into a house owned by a Muslim widow, cared for throughout by a volunteer squad of Muslim friends and admirers, and receiving daily an endless stream of Muslim devotees into his "confessional" (men and women, the latter, he always proudly said, never observing purdah in his presence). Then there was his companion, Suhrawardy, the last Muslim for whom any Calcutta Hindu would have felt "brotherly love." Yet, here was Gandhi, saying often and unrepentantly of this notoriously untrustworthy Muslim politician, "I trust him, he is my friend."[96] All this Gandhi could do because he was Gandhi. But there were reasons why this man came to be seen as the Mahatma; and the inclusive spirit of satyagraha, now fully developed, was not the least of the reasons.

Another aspect of satyagraha appears with his use of a device tested in Noakhali and Bihar and further developed in Calcutta: the prayer meeting. In this last phase, almost all Gandhi's major moves and decisions, often of political import, were first announced, not at press conferences, party conventions, or political assemblies, but in prayer meetings. These meetings had two parts: the first consisting of a reading from religious texts followed by hymns and prayers; the second, that of Gandhi's personal "post-prayer message," which he said should "be regarded and listened to as an integral part of the prayer."[97] The first part served to set an example of tolerance: verses from the Koran and the Bible were read along with those from Hindu texts unless, that is, a member of the audience objected. In that case, Gandhi would omit the prayers, and, with consummate skill, take as his text for the "post-prayer message" the very example of intolerance that the objector had shown, discoursing on exclusivity *vs.* inclusivity. The maneuver often resulted in the audience itself castigating the objector and insisting that the prayers be read after all.[98] At the huge gatherings in Calcutta, the emphasis in Gandhi's post-prayer message was often on the need for social discipline; and Gandhi used the meeting itself as a testing ground for the maintenance of discipline, censuring the crowd's restiveness or praising their orderliness. After the meetings, Hindus and Muslims could mingle together in an atmosphere of trust; and although the attendance in Calcutta generally numbered in the hundreds of thousands, no incident of communal violence occurred at Gandhi's prayer meetings. Rather, they provided the opportunity for a needed release of anxiety and display of friendship.

The prayer meeting and its associated psychological effect date far back into the history of organized religion. Gandhi's genius, in this as in other instances, was to adapt a traditional concept and experience to his own use, in this case for the resolution of communal conflict. The most brilliant example of this adaptation appears in his theory and practice of fasting, which is suggestive of some of the main assumptions underlying his conception of satyagraha. "Satyagraha," he said, "has been designed as an effective substitute for violence,"[99] that is, to wage nonviolent conflict in a way that will resolve a conflict situation. When he had been asked about the prospect of fasting in early August 1946, just days before the Calcutta Killing, he responded: "If and when the call comes to fast unto death, I will do so irrespective of others joining it or not. Fasting unto death is the last and the most potent weapon in the armoury of satyagraha. It is a sacred thing. But it must be accepted with all its implications. It is not the fast itself but what it implies that matters."[100] Gandhi repeatedly used the term "weapon" when describing the technique of the fast: "a fiery weapon," "an infallible weapon."[101] The term is employed to convey the idea of waging nonviolent conflict. The course of this conflict should be carefully plotted by the *satyagrahi,* and the fast should come only as "a last resort when all other avenues of redress have been explored and have failed."[102]

Beyond this consideration, two special conditions should be attached to the fast: first, it must be used in a constructive sense, to reform an individual, to gain his repentance for a wrong committed, to awaken his conscience and induce a reexamination of his position. Its general aim, therefore, is "to evoke the best in him [the wrongdoer]. Self-suffering is an appeal to his better nature, as retaliation is to his baser. Fasting under proper circumstances is such an appeal *par excellence*."[103] The second condition attached by Gandhi to the fast reveals his understanding of its dynamics. He says that a *satyagrahi* should always fast against a "lover"; that is, one who shares, however unconsciously, an underlying sympathy and respect for his aim. This condition is significant for at least two reasons. On the one hand, it indicates Gandhi's awareness of the fast's inherent limitation. He concedes that "You cannot fast against a tyrant."[104] On the other hand, with this condition may be seen Gandhi's insight into the real source of the fast's power: in his case the overwhelming sympathy of Indians, manifest in the fact that his fasts worked best when waged against his own people, Hindus and Muslims.[105]

All these requirements and conditions that Gandhi attached to fasting in satyagraha were fulfilled in the Calcutta fast except the last; this was only partially met. The Calcutta criminal elements—goondas—were not tyrants, but even Gandhi did not assume that they were sympathetic to his cause. Rajagopalachari's first objection (noted above) when Gandhi proposed the Calcutta fast came with the question "Can one fast against the *goondas?*" Gandhi replied that the criminals could be overcome by a society determined to keep the peace. It is this emphasis upon social responsibility that lies at the heart of Gandhi's conception of satyagraha: since society, he reasoned, is responsible for the existence of *goondaism* in the first instance, then it both bears the moral responsibility for curing this disease of the body politic as well as the power to do so. Neglect of this responsibility is tantamount to moral cowardice. "*Goondas* do not drop from the sky, nor do they spring from the earth like evil spirits. They are the product of social disorganization, and society is therefore responsible for their existence. In other words, they should be looked upon as a symptom of corruption in our body politic."[106]

This was Gandhi in 1940. When in 1946 he was confronted with the Bihar riots, he again unequivocally placed the responsibility where it belonged by deploring "the habit of procuring a moral alibi for ourselves by blaming it all on the *goondas*. We always put the blame on the *goondas*. But it is we who are responsible for their creation as well as encouragement."[107] Gandhi argued these simple truths because he was intensely involved in the problems posed by communal violence and desperately sought their resolution through satyagraha. For those more removed from the heat of the struggle, it was easier to sidestep the implications of Gandhi's arguments. After Sarvepalli Radhakrishnan had visited Gandhi during the Calcutta fast, he commented to the press: "I have told Mahatmaji not to confuse between *goonda* activities and communal violence. What had happened in Calcutta during the last few days was absolutely the work of *goondas* and nothing else."[108] From Gandhi came a reasoned restatement of earlier views which again steadfastly refused to dodge the crucial question of social responsibility, and the subsequent issue of the right method of social control:

> The conflagration has been caused not by the *goondas* but by those who have *become goondas*. It is we who make *goondas*. Without our sympathy and passive support, the *goondas* would have no legs to stand upon. . . . During one year of past anarchy, it is understandable how these elements in society have gained respectability. But the war between Pakistanis and those for Undivided India has ended. It is time for peace-loving citizens to assert themselves and isolate *goondaism*. Nonviolent non-co-operation is a universal remedy. Good is self-existent, evil is not. It is like a parasite living on and around good. It will die of itself when the support that good gives is withdrawn. The heart of the anti-social elements may or may not be changed; it will be enough if they are made to feel that the better elements of society are asserting themselves in the interests of peace and in the interests of normality.[109]

Gandhi's hopes for communal harmony rested, in the last analysis, not with government or law enforcement agencies, but with the "better elements of society" willing to assert themselves "in the interests of peace and normality." The Calcutta fast, he stressed, was "meant to activize the better, peace-loving and wise elements in society," for only these could forge lasting bonds of communal friendship. In the days immediately after the Calcutta fast, and before his departure for Delhi, Gandhi met with numerous civic groups in an attempt to consolidate, through them, the salutary results of the satyagraha. Private citizens, businessmen, students, volunteer groups, and other social agencies were formed into "Peace Bridges" and assigned to patrol affected areas of the city. These civic forces alone, Gandhi believed, could strengthen the fabric of their society, after a year of incessant violence had left it in shreds. If there was a "miracle" in Calcutta, then it occurred when one man's leadership restored to more than four million people the will and sense of responsibility needed to mend their strife-torn city and ultimately to transform their lives.

The type of ambivalence that Gandhi created in the instance of the Calcutta fast was quite different from the salt satyagraha, yet its key role should be recognized. Here the target of the satyagraha was the Indian population of Calcutta, not the British authority. When Gandhi entered the city he found its inhabitants bitterly divided in their respective Muslim and Hindu communal hatreds but united in their fierce determination to inflict maximum casualties on one another. Gandhi's satyagraha managed to create an ambivalence in that determination. The subsequent pause in the religious violence that followed eventually led to a reexamination of motives that he believed to be essential in the quest for swaraj. Nonviolent power depends on this capacity to pause, evoked now by Gandhi in Calcutta, as earlier from the Raj. In the days following the fast, Gandhi reflected on its lessons and felt both despair and solace in what he had learned. The grim truths that India remained far from real swaraj, that the road ahead appeared so painful, and that the practice of satyagraha had not come more easily were all hard to accept.

Yet there were heartening lessons as well. Calcutta's response to the fast proved again a truth vital for satyagraha, that a common need for peace and security transcends partisan and violent interests even when the latter seem unassailable; that the unusual power of satyagraha can force warring parties to a point where their common interest becomes clear and compelling; and, if India's journey to swaraj was not over, the way to it had proved its worth under the worst circumstances. Gandhi now found a certain glory in how an inclusive act had triumphed over all the exclusivist factions in the city and in how a goal like swaraj still held forth a promise of liberation finer than mere independence, a deeply personal freedom from fear and freedom for peace.[110]

By January 1948, the month of his assassination, Gandhi had determined to fast again, this time in Delhi, once more for communal peace and once again, after six days, the fast ended in success. Yet, northern India was still alive with conflict, so he prepared to leave for the riot-torn Punjab. Only his willingness to perform these heroic acts of self-sacrifice made a difference where civilian or military police could not. Yet, his supreme act of self-sacrifice now lay immediately ahead of him. He must have known this because on January 20 a bomb exploded in one of his prayer meetings. Some Hindus were enraged by his efforts to protect Muslims.

One historian recognizes as Gandhi's "finest hour" these efforts to combat communal violence; but he then concludes: "Unfortunately, Gandhi himself lost his life at the hands of a Hindu fanatic—a tragic commentary on his cherished principles of non-violence and faith in the 'change of heart.' "[111] This judgment does not take into account that Gandhi's assassination, more than any other single event, served to stop the communal violence surrounding partition. It achieved this in the same way as his fasts, by causing people to pause and reflect in the midst of their fear, anger, and enmity: to ask themselves if the cost was worth it. A mixture of motives was probably at work, merciful and rational as well as grief-stricken or guilt-ridden. But somehow a determination came to stop the killing. If Gandhi's assassination had resulted, as so many assassinations have, in an increase of violence and recrimination, then it may be deemed a tragic comment on the futility of nonviolence. As it happened, in the eloquent words of a prominent Muslim politician: "His assassination had a cathartic effect and throughout India men realized with a shock the depth to which hatred and discord had dragged them. The Indian nation turned back from the brink of the abyss and millions blessed the memory of the man who had made redemption possible."[112] There was no higher tribute to his life than the impact of his death, his final statement for swaraj.

CHAPTER SIX

Mohandas, Malcolm, and Martin

My nationalism as my religion is not
exclusive but inclusive and they must
be so consistently with [the] welfare
of all life."   —*Gandhi*[1]

I'm for truth, no matter who tells it.
I'm for justice, no matter who it is for
or against. I'm a human being first
and foremost, and as such I'm for
whoever and whatever benefits
humanity *as a whole*.

—*Malcolm X*[2]

Gandhi and Malcolm X: In Quest of Swaraj

Striking comparisons between the life experiences of Gandhi
and Malcolm X begin with the fact that they (unlike Martin Luther King, Jr.,
or most other political leaders), have produced extraordinarily revealing
autobiographies. These are of such quality that they have become classics
of modern world literature as stories of self-realization that express stages
of personal and political development explicable in terms of their common
responses to racist oppression.

The initial chapters of both autobiographies tell stories of childhoods
marked by terrible fears of inadequacy related to their perceptions of white
superiority.[3] In an important sense, their lives become examples of handling fear and their success is then conveyed to their followers who share

their feelings. The centrality of the emotion of fear in Gandhi's experience is emphasized by Jawaharlal Nehru in the passage cited in chapter 3. Nehru said there about Gandhi that "The essence of his teaching was fearlessness," a teaching sorely needed because "the dominant impulse in India under British rule was that of fear, pervasive, oppressing, strangling fear," that "it was against this all-pervading fear that Gandhi's quiet and determined voice was raised: Be not afraid," and consequently "that black pall of fear was lifted from the people's shoulders, not wholly, of course, but to an amazing degree." Nehru's claim is worth recounting because it explains the dynamics of leadership in a situation fraught with racial oppression and thus suggests parallels between Gandhi and Malcolm X.[4]

Both connect their assumed inferiority to their skin color as a result of fears inspired by white racism. Gandhi is explicit about how tales of "the mighty Englishmen" ruling inferior Indians relate to his childhood fears of personal inadequacy.[5] Malcolm's account of an encounter with his eighth-grade English teacher, Mr. Ostrowski, is unforgettable. Malcolm had been an outstanding student and one afternoon when they were alone together, his teacher asked him if he had thought about a future career. Malcolm replied that he would like to be a lawyer. Mr. Ostrowski "looked surprised" and then responded: "Malcolm, one of life's first needs is for us to be realistic . . . you've got to be realistic about being a nigger. A lawyer—that's no realistic goal for a nigger." Mr. Ostrowski suggested that carpentry was an appropriate career choice. Malcolm said that afterwards the conversation "just kept treading around in my mind," and "It was then that I began to change—inside. I drew away from white people. It became a physical strain simply to sit in Mr. Ostrowski's class. Where 'nigger' had slipped off my back before," now it was different.[6] No other experience that Malcolm recounts exacerbated his fears of personal inadequacy more than this exchange with a white teacher he had respected. The rest of the autobiography may be interpreted as his struggle to overcome these fears by proving himself, striving to gain self-esteem within a racist system. This became his fight for swaraj and, like Gandhi, it developed into a powerful statement of leadership. As Malcolm's biographer, Bruce Perry, observes, "His ability to conquer his fear—and to inspire his followers to conquer theirs . . . was part of his uniqueness" and a major source of his appeal.[7]

Emulation of the colonized by the colonizer is in many cases a response to racist oppression. Both Gandhi and Malcolm conform to this pattern of

behavior as they strive to gain social recognition and self-respect by alter-
ing their appearances in ways that will emulate whites. Gandhi describes
his entry into British society as a young student of law in London in 1888:

> I undertook the all too impossible task of becoming an English gentle-
> man. The clothes after the Bombay cut that I was wearing were, I
> thought, unsuitable for English society, and I got new ones. . . . I wast-
> ed ten pounds on an evening suit made in Bond Street, the center of fash-
> ionable life in London. . . . While in India, the mirror had been a luxury
> permitted on the days when the family barber gave me a shave. Here I
> wasted ten minutes every day before a huge mirror, watching myself ar-
> ranging my tie and parting my hair in the correct fashion. My hair was by
> no means soft, and every day it meant a regular struggle with the brush to
> keep it in position.[8]

Malcolm inflicted on himself more painful measures to imitate whites;
and he is more explicit than Gandhi about their implications. He explains
how he administered his first "conk," a process of lightening and straight-
ening his hair by burning it with a solution of lye:

> My first view in the mirror blotted out the hurting. I'd seen some pretty
> conks, but when it's the first time, on your *own* head, the transformation,
> after the lifetime of kinks, is staggering. . . . on top of my head was this
> thick, smooth sheen of shining red hair—real red—as straight as any
> white man's. How ridiculous I was! Stupid enough to stand there simply
> lost in admiration of my hair now looking "white," . . . I vowed that I'd
> never again be without a conk, and I never was for many years. This was
> my first really big step toward self-degradation: when I endured all that
> pain, literally burning my flesh to have it look like a white man's hair. I
> had joined that multitude of Negro men and women in America who are
> brainwashed into believing that the black people are "inferior" and white
> people "superior" that they will even mutilate their God-created bodies
> to try to look "pretty" by white standards . . . It makes you wonder if the
> Negro has completely lost his sense of identity, lost touch with himself.[9]

Unlike Gandhi, Malcolm in his emulative stage moved from being a "good
Negro" to a "bad Negro," a hustler and pimp. But whether good or bad,
Malcolm was still performing a role or acting out an identity that white cul-
ture had assigned him: a "Negro," doing what whites expected of him, even
as they eventually sent him to prison. When the moment comes for both
Gandhi and Malcolm to reject emulation, they do it from a conscious disillu-

sionment with standards set by white culture: they renounce their assigned roles as false by negating white norms with ideologies of separatism.

In 1905, Gandhi urged his Indian community in South Africa that "We should not envy [Britain], but emulate its example."[10] By 1909, Gandhi had changed drastically: "If India copies England, it is my firm conviction that she will be ruined."[11] The causes of Gandhi's *volte-face* begin with the racist persecution that the British inflicted on Africans during the Zulu Rebellion of 1906. Gandhi, who served as a medic in the British forces, had not anticipated such wholesale butchery of blacks in a conflict that soon appeared outrageously unjust because it was so one-sided. The result was that it changed his view of black-white relations. Erik Erikson observed that "the experience of witnessing [during the Zulu Rebellion] the outrages perpetrated on black bodies by white he-men aroused in Gandhi both a deeper identification with the maltreated, and a stronger aversion against all male sadism," as represented now by British rule in South Africa.[12] A half-century later, racist authority would be conclusively discredited for Malcolm X when he perceived, as Gandhi did, the moral bankruptcy at its base. In 1928, Gandhi wrote in his autobiography how he eventually realized as a result of the Amristar massacre, "to what lengths the British Government is capable of going, and what inhumanities and barbarities it is capable of perpetrating in order to maintain its power."[13] The words might have been Malcolm's, except applied to government in the United States.

After the Zulu Rebellion, Gandhi immediately imposed on himself a strict code of moral discipline including a vow of *brahmacharya* (celibacy) as a personal preparation for the political campaign of civil disobedience that followed only a month later, in September 1906. This radical action of law breaking separated him irrevocably from the law abiding liberal style of politics he had faithfully followed in South Africa: he had become a *satyagrahi*, no longer a practicing English educated lawyer, and his destination was more often prison than the courts. As observed in chapter 1, Gandhi consolidated his separatism with an ideology of exclusiveness set forth in *Hind Swaraj*. The tract rejects the whole of modern Western civilization as fanatically as it defends the entire tradition of India: "I believe that the civilization India has evolved is not to be beaten in the world. Nothing can equal the seeds sown by our ancestors. . . . India, as so many writers have shown, has nothing to learn from anybody else, and this is as it should be."[14]

The stark polarizations between modern Western civilization as irreligious, immoral, and "Satanic" and Indian culture as "unquestionably the best"[15] pervade the book and present a quintessential statement of exclusivist thinking. Toward the end of the work, Gandhi concludes: "In order to restore India to its pristine condition, we have to return to it. . . . one effort is required, and that is to drive out Western civilization. All else will follow. . . . We hold the civilization that you support to be the reverse of civilization. We consider our civilization to be far superior to yours."[16] Gandhi never retracted these assertions. But his later ideas as translated into action make the case for his further journey into inclusivity that became the hallmark of his style.[17] The point here, however, is that *Hind Swaraj* signifies the same sort of ideological leap from imitation to rejection of Western white culture that occurs in Malcolm's autobiography.

Malcolm's *rite de passage* from emulation to exclusiveness occurred in prison. There, after having "sunk to the very bottom of the American white man's society," Malcolm was reborn as a Black Muslim. "I found Allah and the religion of Islam and it completely transformed my life."[18] This story of prison conversion marks a vital moment in his search for self-definition. It signified nothing less than an intense fascination with the world of ideas. His discovery of the Nation of Islam empowered his mind. It whetted an appetite for learning that soon became insatiable. He relates how he devoured the prison library and totally immersed in "my reading books, months passed without my even thinking about being imprisoned. In fact, up to then, I never had been so truly free in life."[19] And so Malcolm joined Thoreau and Gandhi, who had before him experienced as prisoners this certain kind of freedom, born from the power of knowledge. Like them, the empowerment had come directly and distinctly from books: specific books that they used to consolidate a new personal identity. The parallel between the young Mohandas and young Malcolm is especially close because Malcolm's sense of freedom, too, does not at this stage lead to a liberalization of ideas but to exclusivity.

The Black Muslims' Nation of Islam, founded in Detroit in the 1930's by W. D. Fard and Elijah Poole ("The Honorable Elijah Muhammad"), had from its inception preached a racist dogma that branded all whites as "the human beast, the serpent, the dragon, the devil and Satan."[20] Malcolm left prison in 1952 as a convert to this doctrine; by the end of the decade he had organized Harlem and become a national leader of the Black Muslims. His oratorical and organizational skills gained him a place in the movement second only to Elijah Muhammad. For twelve years he crisscrossed America and electrified increasingly larger black audiences with the gospel of separatism:

> My black brothers and sisters, we all have in common the greatest binding tie we could have, we are all *black* people! . . . Our *enemy* is the *white* man! . . . The white man, he has filled you with a fear of him from ever since you were little black babies. So over you is the greatest enemy a man can have and that is fear . . . I am going to preach to you the truth until you are free of that fear. Your slavemaster, he brought you over here, and of your past everything was destroyed . . . You don't know nothing about your true culture. You don't know your family's real name. You are wearing a *white man's* name! The white slavemaster, who *hates* you! . . . So let us, the black people, *separate* ourselves from this white man slavemaster, who despises us so much ! . . . let us *separate* from this white man, and for the same reason he says in time to save ourselves from any more *integration!*[21]

In some respects, Gandhi's separatism never went this far, for his emphasis on nonviolence rescued his ideology from Malcolm's angry, bitter, racist denunciations. When Gandhi developed his inclusive style of leadership after 1919,[22] he could achieve this in a more authentic and credible manner than Malcolm because Gandhi's inclusiveness had been apparent before, especially in his close, easy associations with whites.[23] Yet, in another sense, Gandhi and Malcolm were profoundly alike in their separatism: both emphasized freedom from fear, categorically rejected the assumed moral authority of white culture and its subsequent claims to political legitimacy, adopted strict moral codes of personal discipline enforced by religious vows, and in the course of their rejection of white culture they made the connection for themselves between "self-control and political potency."[24] Malcolm, like Gandhi, gained personal power through vows of abstinence[25] that then empowered him politically. Against dominant, arrogant, white racism, they both consciously sought to restore a spirit of cultural identity to their people through psychological liberation. Gandhi declared that, "As long as there is in us fear of the Europeans and fondness for their institutions, swaraj is unattainable."[26]. If, as Jawaharlal Nehru claimed, Gandhi gave back to India its "identity,"[27] then Malcolm, even more explicitly than Gandhi, defined the purpose of the Black Muslims as "giving us a true identity, and a true position—the first time they have ever been *known* to the American black man!"[28]

In 1963, after almost twelve years of total allegiance to the Nation of Islam, Malcolm's commitment disintegrated. Earlier, when he had discovered corruption in the lower levels of the organization that violated the Muslims' strict moral codes, Malcolm tried to purge it, demanding of others in the movement the firm discipline that he had maintained. Now, however, in April 1963, he "discovered Muslims had been betrayed by Elijah Muhammad himself,"[29] when rumors of Elijah's flagrant sexual indiscretions were confirmed. "I actually had believed," Malcolm said later, "that if Mr. Muhammad was not God, then he surely stood next to God." "I *loved* the Nation, and Mr. Muhammad. I *lived for* the Nation and for Mr. Muhammad." Now, with the revelations of Elijah's hypocrisy, "my faith had been shaken in a way that I can never fully describe." "I felt as though something in *nature* had failed, like the sun, or the stars. It was that incredible a phenomenon to me— something too stupendous to conceive."[30] On March 12, 1964, Malcolm officially broke with the Nation of Islam.

Eleven months later, Malcolm would be killed by the Black Muslims for his heresies but he expressed during these final months immense relief at his freedom from Elijah. "I feel like a man who has been asleep somewhat and under someone else's control. I feel what I'm thinking and saying now is for myself. Before, it was by the guidance of Elijah Muhammad. Now I think with my own mind . . . "[31] Malcolm's friend Maya Angelou expressed the transformation in precise Gandhian terms when she said that after he left the Nation of Islam, "he freed himself from being a totally 'exclusive' person and, instead, became 'inclusive'—aware of and open to differences in the people around him."[32]

Inclusivist perceptions abound in the last three chapters of Malcolm's autobiography. In April, he left on a *hajj* to Mecca and wrote back to friends in America about the effects of the trip:

> That morning [in Jedda] was when I first began to reappraise the 'white man'. It was when I first began to perceive that 'white man' as commonly used, means complexion only secondarily; primarily it described attitudes and actions . . . in the Muslim world, I had seen that men with white complexions were more genuinely brotherly than anyone else had ever been. That morning was the start of a radical alteration in my whole outlook about 'white' men.[33]

> For twelve long years, I lived within the narrow-minded confines of the 'straitjacket world' created by my strong belief that Elijah Muham-

mad was a messenger direct from God Himself and my faith in what I now see to be a pseudo-religious philosophy that he preaches . . . . My religion is Islam as it is believed and practiced by Muslims here in the Holy City of Mecca. This religion recognizes all men as brothers. It accepts all human beings as equals before God, and as equal members in the Human Family of Mankind. I totally reject Elijah Muhammad's racist philosophy.[34]

This inclusive direction formed in Mecca was reinforced by his travels in Africa during July–November 1964. In Kenya, he had a long, searching discussion with William Attwood, the U.S. ambassador—a white man, Malcolm discovered, with an open mind:

We talked for an entire afternoon . . . he told me that as long as he was on the African continent, he never thought in terms of race, that he dealt with human beings, never noticing their color. . . . only when he returned to America would he become aware of color differences. I told him, 'What you are telling me is that it isn't the American white *man* who is a racist, but it's the American political, economic and social *atmosphere* that automatically nourishes a racist psychology in the white man . . . . And we both agreed that if racism could be removed, America could offer a society where rich and poor could truly live like human beings. That discussion with the ambassador gave me a new insight—one which I like: that the white man is *not* inherently evil, but America's racist society influences him to act evilly. The society has produced and nourishes a psychology which brings out the lowest, most base part of human beings.[35]

With this insight, Malcolm had arrived at a tenet of inclusiveness that Gandhi often stressed, to "Hate the sin and not the sinner."[36]

It is important to recognize that the evidence of Malcolm's change to an inclusive attitude is found not only in his autobiography but also in his speeches. In the final year, and especially in the last month of his life, his speeches often carry the same humanist spirit present in his autobiography. Thus in a speech delivered on April 8, 1964, entitled "The Black Revolution," Malcolm declared:

"We have to keep in mind at all times that we are not fighting for integration, nor are we fighting for separation. We are fighting for recognition as human beings. We are fighting for the right to live as free humans in this society. In fact, we are actually fighting for rights that are even greater than civil rights and that is human rights."[37]

In the week before his assassination, he gave two important speeches, the first in Rochester, where he clearly explained his attitude toward whites:

> We don't judge a man because of the color of his skin. We don't judge you because you're white; we don't judge you because you're brown. We judge you because of what you do and what you practice. And as long as you practice evil, we're against you. And for us, the most—the worst form of evil is the evil that's based upon judging a man because of the color of his skin . . . So we're not against people because they're white. But we're against those who practice racism.[38]

Finally, in his last public speech, given on February 18, 1965 at Barnard College in New York, Malcolm reiterated a theme that he had first expressed at Harvard University two months earlier:

> It is incorrect to classify the revolt of the Negro as simply a radical conflict of black against white, or as a purely American problem. Rather, we are today seeing a global rebellion of the oppressed against the oppressor, the exploited against the exploiter. The Negro revolution is not a racial revolt. We are interested in practicing brotherhood with anyone really interested in living according to it.[39]

This inclusive global vision had not been conceived before Malcolm's travels abroad. It recalls Gandhi's frequent indictments of imperialist exploitation. Yet, there does remain a substantial difference, even in Malcolm's final phase, between his position on the one hand and Gandhi's or King's on the other. This is over the issue of violence.

Gandhi's unequivocal advocacy of nonviolence and particularly of the necessary relationship between nonviolent means and ends has been discussed at length above. Martin Luther King's views on this are identical to Gandhi's. King believed that "Constructive ends can never give absolute moral justification to destructive means, because in the final analysis the end is preexistent in the means."[40] Malcolm remained unimpressed by this argument to the end. In the final chapter of his autobiography, which represents the last stage of his thought, he wrote: "Well, I believe it's a crime for anyone who is being brutalized to continue to accept that brutality without doing something to defend himself. If that's how 'Christian' philosophy is interpreted, if that's what Gandhian philosophy teaches, well, then, I will call them criminal philosophies."[41] He could hardly have put it more forcefully and he argued this position consistently in his speeches:

When it comes time for you and me to protect ourselves against lynch-ings, they tell us to be nonviolent . . . I have never advocated any vio-lence. I have only said that black people who are the victims of organized violence perpetrated upon us by the Klan, the Citizens Councils, and many other forms, should defend ourselves. . . . I wouldn't call on any-body to be violent without a cause. But I think that the black man . . . will be justified when he stands up and starts to protect himself, no matter how many necks he has to break and heads he has to crack. . . . So we only mean vigorous action in self-defense, and that vigorous action we feel we're justified in initiating by any means necessary.[42]

This last phrase, "by any means necessary," was one of Malcolm's favor-ites,[43] and its frequent use indicated what he thought of Gandhi's and King's conception of the necessity of nonviolent means. Further, when King, fol-lowing Gandhi, argued against Malcolm that "nonviolent resistance is not a method for cowards," that it resists with the "principle of love,"[44] Malcolm countered in his old sardonic tones: "Don't you give me that you love me and make me do the same thinking when there's nothing in our back-grounds nor anything around us which in any way gives either of us reason to love each other. Let's be real!"[45]

Malcolm never appreciated the power of nonviolent political action. Martin Luther King, Jr. actively demonstrated in America, as Gandhi had in India, that there is nothing "unreal" about nonviolence. Their capacity for expressing in action theories of nonviolence was not the only feature they shared. Another evident similarity was that although both Gandhi and King would be deeply traumatized by racism, their family backgrounds were sta-ble, and, in particular, economically secure. Unlike Malcolm X, whose fam-ily, especially after his father's murder when he was a child, was chronically poor, the fathers of Gandhi and King were strong and ample providers who exercised considerable influence within their respective communities.[46] Their relatively privileged status was accompanied by privileged educa-tion, at least when compared to many others of their communities. Whereas Malcolm went without a formal education after elementary school, educat-ing himself in prison, the families of Gandhi and King ensured graduation from institutions of higher education, in law and theology respectively, that were expensive and empowering. Each employed his elite education to maximum effect in his personal advancement. Malcolm enjoyed none of these advantages. Perhaps it follows from this sort of class analysis of Gandhi and King that they should have remained comfortable with capitalists albeit critical of capitalism. They handled money well themselves and profited from contacts with the wealthy.[47]

King's Use of Satyagraha: The Montgomery Bus Boycott

The conception of King as "America's Gandhi," however, did not come from such similarities. It sprang from a signal event that will live long in the lore and legend of nonviolent action, the Montgomery bus boycott of 1955–56, when 50,000 blacks of that city in Alabama gave the American civil rights movement its prototype for the future.[48] In the decade 1955–65, Malcolm and King remained rivals in the arena of black movement politics, but the contest was always uneven. King constantly eclipsed Malcolm's leadership because he could implement his ideas in action. Even in Harlem, Malcolm's base of power, his most sympathetic critics would say, "All he's ever done was talk. CORE and SNCC [Congress on Racial Equality and Students Non-violent Coordinating Committee] and some of them people of Dr. King's are out getting beat over the head."[49] King had shown a capacity for mobilizing blacks and getting them on the streets in campaigns of dramatic defiance; he had mastered a method of action that Malcolm seemed unable to grasp, even though the method was initiated entirely by black leaders and practiced *en masse* by blacks as oppressed and deprived as any among Malcolm's urban proletariat. The proof of this came from Montgomery, Alabama.

The Montgomery story began on the evening of December 1, 1955, when Rosa Parks, a black seamstress on her way home from work, refused to yield her seat on a crowded bus to a white man. By doing so she was defying the city segregation ordinance.[50] It is significant that the protest began on a bus, where the daily humiliation of blacks was most prominent and predictable, and by a woman, for black women used buses for their transportation to work and suffered persecution the most. From the moment of Rosa Parks's defiance, women played a prominent role in the boycott and in this respect she "merely exemplified the spirit, commitment and determination of black women in the city . . . black women were very much the backbone of this movement."[51]

The first week of that December was an especially good one for the his-

tory of nonviolent action in America. Rosa Parks's momentous "No"—
"the accumulated *NO* of Negro history in America"[52]—was immediately
reinforced by a ringing affirmation of justice in her black community, for its
instantaneous response to the news of her arrest was compliance by nearly
all its members with the call for a bus boycott.[53] During that week also, the
black community of Montgomery discovered that it had an authentic leader
in its midst, the twenty-six-year-old minister of its Dexter Avenue Baptist
Church.

On the evening of December 5, Martin Luther King, Jr. addressed a mass
meeting called to endorse the proposed bus boycott. For King to have assumed a role of leadership at that moment and place seemed most improbable, given his youth and inexperience. He had been in Montgomery for
only a year. His main professional qualification was a Ph.D. in systematic
theology from Boston University, not an obvious asset for leadership of a
civil disobedience campaign in Montgomery. His first year at the Baptist
Church had been successful, but there was no indication from this that he
was inclined toward political activism. King had been educated at a good
"colored elementary school," where he was taught that "a good nigger was
a black who minded his own business and accepted the way things were
without dissent."[54] One might have predicted on the basis of this record
that his speech that December evening would fall flat. But the opposite happened: King delivered a "masterpiece"[55] that "shook the church to its foundations."[56]

Later, King called this "the most decisive speech of my life," while his
biographers recognize it as a prototype for the many that followed.[57] It began by introducing one of the major themes of the civil rights movement to
come: "We are here because of the bus situation in Montgomery. We are
here also because of our love for democracy, because of our deep-seated
belief that democracy transformed from thin paper to thick action is the
greatest form of government on earth. We are here because we are American citizens, and we are determined to apply our citizenship to the fullness
of its means."

If the good news for America was that its black citizens love democracy,
its *de jure* system of rights, then the bad news was that the *de facto* situation
in Montgomery fell far short of the democratic ideal. This gap must be
closed by direct action so that blacks may realize the "fullness" of their citizenship. King dwelt on the de facto, the humiliation and fear that pervaded

the black community because of racism and how the persecution of Rosa Parks personified this. Then he reinforced his statement of allegiance to democracy with an appeal to Christian values as well: "I want it to be known throughout Montgomery and throughout this nation that we are a Christian people. We believe in the Christian religion. We believe in the teachings of Jesus. We only assemble here because of our desire to see right exist. This is the glory of democracy. The great glory of American democracy is the right to protest for the right."

Democracy and Christianity: these two ideas constitute the core of the American value system and King weaves them together to use them well. Blacks want only to embrace this system; they protest, but only "for the right."

King proceeds now, in the latter part of the speech, to the method of protest, and how its commitment to nonviolence embraces rather than rejects the ideals of democracy and Christianity:

> Don't let anybody make us feel that we are to be compared in our actions with the Ku Klux Klan or the White Citizens Council. These organizations are protesting for the perpetuation of injustice in our community. We are protesting for the birth of justice. Their methods lead to violence and lawlessness. We will be guided by the highest principles of law and order. We are not here advocating violence. There will be no crosses burned at any bus stops in Montgomery. There will be no white persons pulled out of their homes and taken on some distant road and murdered. There will be nobody among us who will stand up and defy the Constitution of this nation. Our method will be that of persuasion, not coercion. Our actions must be guided by the deepest principles of our Christian faith. Love must be our regulating ideal. Once again we must hear the words of Jesus echoing across the centuries: 'Love your enemies'. . . we must not become bitter, and end up by hating our white brothers. As Booker T. Washington said, 'Let no man pull you so low as to make you hate him.'
>
> And we are not wrong; we are not wrong in what we are doing. If we are wrong, the Supreme Court of this nation is wrong. If we are wrong, the Constitution of the United States is wrong. If we are wrong, God Almighty is wrong. If we are wrong, justice is a lie.

This is probably, together with King's incomparable "I have a dream" speech of August 1963, his finest piece of oratory. It shows his rare skill at presenting protest as a glorious part of the American experience. "Our method," he declares, represents "the highest principles of law and order"; "our actions" constitute the "deepest principles" of Christianity. The message is as conservative in essence as it is radical: as citizens we must strive to obtain the best in our national tradition.

King concludes the speech with a statement of ethnic identity:

"We are going to work together. Right here in Montgomery, when the history books are written in the future, somebody will have to say, 'There lived a race of people, of black people, of people who had the moral courage to stand up for their rights. And thereby they injected a new meaning into the veins of history and of civilization.' "[58]

Malcolm might have made such an appeal to black pride, but King's speech is significant more for its cogent statement of themes that Malcolm could not have expressed, even in his last stage. Like Malcolm, King discovered in the 1950s that he had extraordinary oratorical powers, and he used them to condemn the hypocrisy of white racists. Yet, unlike Malcolm, King appealed directly to America's value system of constitutionalism and Christianity.[59] In this speech, it is clear how King came across as a strong preacher and patriot, a man of God and nation. Malcolm, conversely, projected himself until the end as a staunch Muslim, insisting that "I don't even consider myself an American," and emphasizing an ideology of Black Nationalism which he persistently opposed to Christian/American patriotism.[60] King sought to reform a system so that it would keep its promises. When the Montgomery bus boycott was ultimately won, the triumph was due to a favorable Supreme Court decision[61] and King rejoiced that "God Almighty has spoken from Washington, D.C."[62] At least for the federal system, then, there was hope: the Constitution expressed it, and sometimes the courts.

Malcolm, in contrast, saw the entire American system as rotten and never ceased to say that it must be scrapped. In this respect, Malcolm and Gandhi had more in common than Gandhi and King; for Gandhi's opposition to the British system in India was total. Yet, Malcolm, unlike Gandhi and King, devised no method to attain his radical end. This was not only his fatal flaw but it was the major weakness as well of Black Power leaders who followed him. They tended to miss the main point of Montgomery even though King had argued it incisively. This was that nonviolent action by blacks in America proved tactically superior to methods of violence.[63]

For this reason, King found Gandhi's ideas useful. Whereas Malcolm, as noted above, scorned both Christianity and Gandhism as "criminal philosophies," King declared that at Montgomery, "Christ furnished the spirit and motivation, while Gandhi furnished the method."[64] It was indeed the method of satyagraha that appealed to King. Relatively early in his intellectual development, while a theology student at Crozer Seminary, he heard Mordecai Johnson, President of Howard University, lecture on Gandhi. This was the fall of 1950 when King had a psychology of religion course taught by George Davis, a pacifist and strong admirer of Gandhi.[65] In fact, King could have heard about Gandhi from many sources within his community because black Americans had developed a strong interest in Gandhi since the early 1920s. His achievements in India had inspired abundant notice in the black American churches and press.[66] Delegations of black leaders had traveled to India to seek his advice as early as 1936. Gandhi was so impressed with their earnestness that he remarked in 1936 that "it may be through the Negroes that the unadulterated message of non-violence will be delivered to the world."[67]

In that lecture by Mordecai Johnson, King might have heard Gandhi's prophecy repeated because he recalled that Johnson's "message was so profound and electrifying that I left the meeting and bought a half-dozen books on Gandhi's life and works." So began what King calls a serious study of Gandhi:

> As I read I became deeply fascinated by his campaigns of nonviolent resistance. I was particularly moved by the Salt March to the Sea and his numerous fasts. The whole concept of 'Satyagraha', (*Satya* is truth which equals love, and *graha* is force; '*Satyagraha*' therefore, means truth-force or love force) was profoundly significant to me. As I delved deeper into the philosophy of Gandhi my skepticism concerning the power of love gradually diminished, and I came to see for the first time its potency in the area of social reform. Prior to reading Gandhi, I had about concluded that the ethics of Jesus were only effective in individual relationships. . . . But after reading Gandhi, I saw how utterly mistaken I was.
>
> Gandhi was probably the first person in history to lift the love ethic of Jesus above mere interaction between individuals to a powerful and effective social force on a large scale. For Gandhi, love was a potent instrument for social and collective transformation. It was in this Gandhian emphasis on love and nonviolence that I discovered the method for social reform that I had been seeking for so many months. . . . I came to feel that this was the only morally and practically sound method open to oppressed people in their struggle for freedom.[68]

Once again, it is Gandhi's method that appeals most to King and not the twists and turns of Gandhi's journey to swaraj that parallel so strikingly the

life of Malcolm X. *Stride Toward Freedom* attempts to systematize key principles of nonviolent resistance. The analysis is strictly faithful to the theory of
satyagraha. Its tenets range from a Gandhian insistence that this "is not a
method for cowards" because it demands courageous resistance, to its humane attitude toward adversaries. It concentrates on King's distinctive contribution of the Christian concept of *agape* or "disinterested love," "redeem-
ing good will for all men."[69] This idea of *agape* brings Gandhi's spirit of
inclusiveness into an American context more than any other aspect of
King's philosophy. Yet it is clear that the achievements of both men lie not
in the realm of theory but of an exceptional ability to express their ideas in
action.[70] King did have a firm understanding of satyagraha but the sublime
element in the story of Montgomery is of how he and his people found a
way to practice it.

Unfinished Journeys: Martin and Malcolm from the Perspectives of Swaraj and Satyagraha

In his biography of Malcolm X, Peter Goldman comments that "The grand-
est dream of all is the *entente noire* that might have been between Malcolm
and Martin Luther King—the confluence of two great currents in contemporary black history in a single, irresistible revolutionary tide."[71] Advocates of King or of Malcolm will suggest many reasons why this dream was
doomed, but from a Gandhian perspective at least one set of causes might
be found in those qualities that each leader lacked, or perhaps was not given
time to develop further.

Malcolm's failing is the more obvious because his lack of a credible method of political action found him, in the end, without any movement at all. At
the basis of his failure was an apparent inability to face an issue that King
had resolved in Montgomery. This was the problem of means, and specifically of the use of violent means for attaining social and economic justice for
black Americans. King was able to gain the moral high ground in the civil
rights struggle by unambiguously advocating an unconditional adherence
to nonviolence. Malcolm was denied this moral advantage by his persistent
approval of violent action. As Peter Goldman has observed, "The distance
between. . . Malcolm's proposition that ends justify means and King's that
means and ends are one was a vast one."[72] This distance not only separated
Malcolm from King, it also removed him from the realities of movement
politics in the United States. King saw, as Malcolm did not, that for blacks in

America the appropriation of morality to politics was sound strategy. None of Gandhi's insights helped King more than that into the centrality of means.[73]

King's shortcomings are less apparent than Malcolm's because, like Gandhi, he has been canonized since his assassination.[74] Yet, when King's life is compared with Malcolm's, one must be impressed with how far the latter came in terms of personal growth. The distance, as compared with King, is dramatic from the viewpoint of class origins, but to make the contrast in class terms alone tells only a fraction of the story. The depth of Malcolm's achievement is expressed eloquently in his autobiography. This is, above all, an account of "Malcolm's emancipation as a man—a victory of soul so complete that, having achieved it, he didn't even need to hate whitey any more."[75]

It is Malcolm's journey to personal emancipation that connects him with Gandhi and the idea of swaraj. Malcolm has come to personify a certain kind of freedom that signifies much more than civil liberty or political independence. His life manifests a tortuous quest for inner freedom that does imply, as Gandhi insisted, the achievement of self-discipline and self-restraint with self-realization. Malcolm would have understood Gandhi's meaning that "The pilgrimage to swaraj is a painful climb." Ossie Davis conveyed Malcolm's achievement of swaraj as well as it can be described in the eulogy that he gave to his friend:

"But in explaining Malcolm, let me take care not to explain him away. He had been a criminal, an addict, a pimp, and a prisoner; a racist, and a hater, he had really believed the white man was devil. But all this had changed. Two days before his death, in commenting to Gordon Parks about his past life he said: 'That was a mad scene. The sickness and madness of those days! I'm glad to be free of them.' And Malcolm was free. No one who knew him before and after this trip to Mecca could doubt that he had completely abandoned racism, separatism, and hatred."[76]

Such a transcendence of exclusivist attitudes cannot be easily explained but fortunately Malcolm's brilliant autobiography is up to the task. A comparison with King's autobiographical *Stride Toward Freedom* is instructive: the latter relates in impersonal tones the success of a method but without any journey of the self. Its discovery of satyagraha seems relatively uninvolved in a pilgrimage to swaraj. Only a few pages convey a sense of inner struggle. After its publication in 1958, King produced a vast amount of words, speeches and sermons, essays and articles, but little that conveys swaraj. In contrast, Malcolm's autobiography was written (with Alex Haley) at the end of his life, and it exudes intellectual energy, personal dynamism, above all, a desire for more growth. Malcolm reports that when a government agent accused him of being a "Communist," he replied that the only thing that he could be found guilty of "was being open-minded. I said that I was seeking for the truth, and I was trying to weigh objectively everything on its merit. I said that what I was against was strait-jacketed thinking, and strait-jacketed societies."[77]

The point is not that King's thought or action became "strait-jacketed," but rather that, as compared with Malcolm's, it seems relatively static after Montgomery. If King's early writings are compared with his later, then it is remarkable how little his ideas developed in the 1960s. In his final book, *Trumpet of Conscience* (published posthumously in 1968), King's lasting concern with the means-ends relationship is evident, and he courageously applies it to the Vietnam war. He argues that "if we are to have peace in the world, men and nations must embrace the nonviolent affirmation that ends and means must cohere." This idea had been ignored in American foreign policy, for "every time we drop our bombs in Vietnam, President Johnson talks eloquently about peace," overlooking the basic truth that "we must pursue peaceful ends through peaceful means."[78] Toward the end of his life, then, King, winner of the Nobel Peace Prize in 1964, an international figure, spoke out bravely and independently on global affairs: the "conscience of the world." Yet, as King's star appeared high in the heavens, so, too, it seemed, did the Montgomery experience become increasingly remote.

Did world acclaim stifle King's inner struggle? In one sense, it seemed only to increase it, for King was tormented with feelings of guilt and doubt over his real personal worth, and toward the end he suffered severe bouts of depression and agonized preoccupations with death.[79] Whereas earlier he had discovered through Gandhi "a means not only of harnessing his anger, but of channeling it into a positive and creative force,"[80] now his psychic turmoil blocked creative energy. As the Black Power movement grew around him, he feared that history had overtaken him. Gandhi had those anxieties, too, especially in the late 1920s, before his decisive breakthrough in the salt satyagraha. Might King have achieved in his forties or fifties another leap of consciousness comparable to Montgomery? Racism in America did not give him that chance. We only know that at the end of his life, King repeatedly asked his audiences, "Where do we go from here?" and radical young blacks like Stokely Carmichael would respond, "Martin, baby, you got a long way to go."[81] The most that King could offer was satyagraha. This was hardly enough to satisfy Carmichael or the Black Panthers but it did show King's persistent attempt to apply Gandhian techniques.

In a lecture delivered only five months before his death, King decried the "impasse" in the movement. He focused on economic issues, especially the relentless poverty among blacks, and proposed this method of attack:

> Nonviolent protest must now mature to a new level to correspond to heightened black impatience and stiffened white resistance. This higher level is mass civil disobedience. There must be more than a statement to the larger society; there must be a force that interrupts its functioning at some key point. That interruption must not, however, be clandestine or surreptitious. It is not necessary to invest it with guerrilla romanticism. It must be open and, above all, conducted by large masses without violence. If the jails are filled to thwart it, its meaning will become even clearer. The Negro will be saying, 'I am not avoiding penalties for breaking the law—I am willing to endure all your punishment.' . . . Mass civil disobedience as a new stage of struggle can transmute the deep rage of the ghetto into a constructive and creative force.[82]

This is a succinct evocation of satyagraha with echoes of Gandhi's statements during the salt march. There are even lines in this lecture that recall those in a sermon that King gave to his Montgomery congregation in 1959, after his return from India, on Gandhi.[83] But unlike Gandhi's campaigns of mass civil disobedience, this remained a promise unfulfilled, an idea never translated into action.

Malcolm X embodied the idea of swaraj but not of satyagraha and King the converse, with no American leader managing to combine the two ideas, in theory and practice, as Gandhi did. Perhaps if both Malcolm and Martin had not been assassinated at age thirty-nine, their leadership might have carried the freedom struggle much further. Certainly if Gandhi had been killed at that age, he would be unknown today. Yet time alone is not enough to provide greater effectiveness for most leaders of political movements. In the United States, many such leaders faded into political obscurity. What should not be obscured is the common purpose of liberation that these three remarkable leaders shared. Differences that must persist between Malcolm and Martin are transcended by their unity.[84] James H. Cone captures their complementary nature in his comparative analysis. In his eloquent conclusion to the book he uses language that could have come from Gandhi:

Martin and Malcolm are important because they symbolize two necessary ingredients in the African American struggle for justice in the United States. We should never pit them against each other. Anyone, therefore, who claims to be for one and not the other does not understand their significance for the black community, for America, or for the world. We need both of them and we need them together. . . . . We must break the cycle of violence in America and around the world. Human beings are meant for life and not death. They are meant for freedom and not slavery. They were created for each other and not against each other. We must, therefore, break down the barriers that separate people from one another. For Malcolm and Martin, for America and the world, and for all who have given their lives in the struggle for justice, let us direct our fight toward one goal—the beloved community of humankind.[85]

Malcolm said at the end that his "ultimate objective was to help create a society in which there could exist honest white-black brotherhood."[86] King, in his final "Mountaintop" speech, concluded that "I have a dream this afternoon that the brotherhood of man will become a reality."[87] Few American leaders have illuminated the way to this goal of human brotherhood more brilliantly than they, and their heroic struggles against the awesome tide of racism in their country continue to inspire whites and blacks alike with a vision of humanity that transcends both race and nation, a vision that is vitally and inclusively Gandhian.

Gandhi's Contribution from Various Angles

"I may be taunted with the retort
that this is all Utopian and, therefore, not worth a single thought. If
Euclid's line, though incapable of
being drawn by human agency, has
an imperishable value, my picture
has its own for mankind to live.
Let India live for this true picture,
though never realizable in its
completeness. We must have a
proper picture of what we want,
before we can have something
approaching it.
—*Gandhi, 1946, when asked about
his conception of an independent India*[1]

To best appreciate Gandhi, we should view his experience from
several angles. While we have focused on how Gandhi practiced swaraj and
satyagraha, especially during the salt march and the Calcutta fast, these two
ideas may also be viewed from a philosophical perspective. They are prod-
ucts of Gandhi's vision: although he was decidedly an activist, he was also
very much a visionary, an idealist, as the above epigraph shows.

The Idealist Perspective: Plato and Gandhi on Freedom and Power

Gandhi was hardly the first idealist in politics. Plato was among the first to argue the importance of ideals for politics, even though they might be unrealizable. When Socrates, in *Plato's Republic*, defends idealism, he asserts:

> When we set out to discover the essential nature of justice and injustice and what a perfectly just and a perfectly unjust man would be like, supposing them to exist, our purpose was to use them as ideal patterns . . . We did not set out to show that these ideals could exist in fact.
> That is true.
> Then suppose a painter had drawn an ideally beautiful figure complete to the last touch, would you think any the worse of him, if he could not show that a person as beautiful as that could exist?
> No, I should not.
> Well, we have been constructing in discourse the pattern of an ideal state. Is our theory any the worse, if we cannot prove it possible that a state so organized should be actually founded?"[2]

Of course, Gandhi was primarily an activist and Plato, a philosopher. But Gandhi, who invoked the metaphor of Euclid's line, would have accepted the spirit of Plato's idealism[3] and would have agreed with him that "An ideal has an indispensable value for practice, in that thought thereby gives to action its right aim."[4] For Gandhi, an ideal standard of nonviolence does exist and all action must be guided by it. Both thinkers not only put ideas first, but cherish certain ideals as essential in politics.

When a philosophical perspective on Gandhi is taken further, strong similarities are found with Plato's idea of freedom. Plato views freedom in the same dual sense as liberation of both self and system and he also identifies freedom with both self-restraint and self-realization. He has Socrates argue that "Genuine freedom" cannot exist in a state where "anyone is allowed to do what he likes," "subject to no order or restraint,"[5] and then invoke a logical relationship between the genuinely free individual and community that also occurs in Gandhi's thought. Socrates says:

> Bearing in mind, then, the analogy between state and individual, you shall tell me what you think of the condition of each in turn. To begin with the state: is it free under a despot or enslaved?

Utterly enslaved.

And yet you see it contains some who are masters and free men.

Yes, a few; but almost the whole of it, including the most respectable part, is degraded to a miserable slavery.

If the individual, then, is analogous to the state, we shall find the same order of things in him: a soul laboring under the meanest servitude, the best elements in it being enslaved, while a small part, which is also the most frenzied and corrupt, plays the master. Would you call such a condition of the soul freedom or slavery?

Slavery of course.

And just as a state enslaved to a tyrant cannot do what it really wishes, so neither can a soul under a similar tyranny do what it wishes as a whole. Goaded on against its will by the sting of desire, it will be filled with confusion and remorse. Like the corresponding state, it must always be poverty-stricken, unsatisfied, and haunted by fear. Nowhere else will there be so much lamentation, groaning and anguish as in a country under a despotism, and in a soul maddened by 'the tyranny of passion and lust.'[6]

Socrates then concludes that:

. . . the happiest [and freest] man is he who is first in goodness and justice, namely the true king who is also king over himself; and the most miserable is that lowest example of injustice and vice, the born despot whose tyranny prevails in his own soul and also over his country.[7]

This idea of freedom and its nexus of conceptual connections is not unique to Plato: it occurs in religious theories of East and West. However, from a philosophical perspective, Plato develops with systematic logic the organic relationship between the individual and the community and the respects in which freedom (and happiness) for both demand liberation from fear and ignorance.

Plato's ideal state is in many ways the opposite of Gandhi's democracy because *The Republic* presents an aristocratic vision of a polity ruled by a philosophical elite. Plato and Gandhi share a love for moral authority but the latter would not allow a concentration of power in the hands of a few Platonic Guardians. As discussed in chapter 3, Gandhi wanted a decentralized democratic system and "True democracy cannot be worked by twenty men sitting at the centre. It has to be worked from below by the people of every village."[8] Yet Plato's conception of power does parallel Gandhi's in one sense: they agree that since use of power is unavoidable, it can and should be wielded wisely by leaders who are capable because they are liberated from illusion and selfish interest. Plato claims that as a result of his system of education, the enlightened leaders of his Republic will not practice politics as "in most existing states, where men live fighting one another about shadows and quarrelling for power, as if that were a great prize." They will rather

> think of holding power as an unavoidable necessity . . . then only will power be in the hands of those who are rich, not in gold, but in the wealth that brings happiness, a good and wise life. All goes wrong when, starved for lack of anything good in their own lives, men turn to public affairs hoping to snatch from thence the happiness they hunger for. They set about fighting for power, and this internecine conflict ruins them and their country. The life of true philosophy is the only one that looks down upon offices of state; and access to power must be confined to men who are not in love with it.[9]

If Plato's theory of freedom is close to Gandhi's because of the common connections drawn between individual and community, then his idea of power, despite its elitism, connects with a conception of leadership that believes power can be wielded in a disinterested way. Political leaders may know and employ the power of truth because they are engaged in a Socratic quest for wisdom. In Gandhian terms, the *satyagrahi* must "wrestle with the snake" of political power yet not be bitten by a lust for it. From their mutual perspective, the "internecine conflict" or civil war that they both witnessed and abhorred came from a failure of leadership. Leaders are driven by a love of power because they lack swaraj or any concern for it: they have not found freedom, so they corrupt themselves and their country. Plato and Gandhi shared an optimistic, idealistic vision of the purpose of leadership: to shape a community according to a right set of moral values "that brings happiness, a good and wise life."

Political Movements: Gandhi as "Transforming Leader"

This discussion of leadership suggests another perspective on Gandhi—from the point of view of political movements. James Burns in his study of leadership distinguishes between two types of leaders, the "transactional" and the "transforming." The former is the typical sort of power broker or wheeler-dealer common to most political situations, whether at the national or local levels. The latter is rare, a leader who tries to create fundamental change through a transformation of public attitudes and values. Burns concentrates on defining and explaining the idea of transforming leadership, citing the example of Gandhi in particular. The theory applies both to the ideas of satyagraha and of swaraj. Burns writes:

> Transforming leadership ultimately becomes *moral* in that it raises the level of human conduct and ethical aspiration of both leader and led, and thus it has a transforming effect on both. Perhaps the best modern example is Gandhi, who aroused and elevated the hopes and demands of millions of Indians and whose life and personality were enhanced in the process. Transcending leadership is dynamic leadership in the sense that the leaders throw themselves into a relationship with followers who will feel "elevated" by it and often become more active themselves, thereby creating new cadres of leaders. . . . The search for wholeness—that is, for this kind of *full, sharing feeling* relationship— between "teachers" and "students," between leaders and followers, must be more than merely a personal or self-regarding quest. Fully sharing leaders perceive their roles as shaping the future to the advantage of groups with which they identify, an advantage they define in terms of the broadest possible goals and the highest possible levels of morality. Leaders are taskmasters and goal setters, but they and their followers share a particular space and time, a particular set of motivations and values. If they are to be effective in helping to mobilize and elevate their constituencies, leaders must be whole persons, persons with fully functioning capacities for thinking and feeling. The problem for them as educators, as leaders, is not to promote narrow, egocentric self-actualization but to extend awareness of human needs and the means of gratifying them, to improve the larger social situation for which educators or leaders have responsibility and over which they have power. Is it too much to believe that it is "the grand goal of all leadership—to help create or maintain the social harbors for these personal islands?" Gandhi almost perfectly exemplifies this . . . . The transforming leader taps the needs and raises the aspirations and helps shape the values—and hence mobilizes the potential--of followers.
> Transforming leadership is elevating. It is moral but not moralistic. Leaders engage with followers, but from higher levels of morality; in the enmeshing of goals and values both leaders and followers are raised to more principled levels of judgment. Leaders most effectively "connect with" followers from a level of morality only one stage higher than that of the followers, but moral leaders who act at much higher levels—

Gandhi, for example—relate to followers at all levels either heroically or through the founding of mass movements that provide linkages between persons at various levels of morality and sharply increase the moral impact of the transforming leader. Much of this kind of elevating leadership asks sacrifices *from* followers rather than merely promising them goods.[10]

Burns gives to the conception of leadership a normative dimension that Plato stressed but that is often missing in contemporary political science analysis. Burns views the leader as essentially an educator engaged in a creative relationship with followers. Gandhi saw satyagraha as heuristic because it employed a kind of power that encouraged reflection and reexamination of motives, needs and interests. He believed, as Burns suggests, that this educative procedure depended on the development of an engagement of all those involved in a situation "to extend awareness of human needs and the means of gratifying them." The leader "raises the expectations and helps shape the values" of others while also requiring sacrifices. This is an exact description of the purposes of satyagraha, and when Burns recognizes that there is "a transforming effect on both" leader and led, he states Gandhi's point that each act of satyagraha sought to move him and the country further on the path to swaraj.

When the concept of swaraj relates to Burns's theory of transforming leadership, then ideal leaders "must be whole persons, persons with fully functioning capacities for thinking and feeling." Their sensitivity to the needs of their following enables them to exercise a therapeutic influence of the sort that Nehru identified in Gandhi, as cited in chapter 3: "It was a psychological change, almost as if some expert in psychoanalytical methods had probed deep into the patient's past, found out the origins of his complexes, exposed them to his view, and thus rid him of that burden." The passage bears repeating because it relates closely to a description of Malcolm X's achievement as a leader: "The niche he ultimately carved for himself in history was largely the result of his unique ability to transform his own personal struggle for identity into a universal one, and to liberate his ardent followers from the kind of conflict about skin color that had afflicted him all his life."[11]

But more than Malcolm, Gandhi's particular accomplishment as a political leader was to relate both the power of satyagraha and the purpose of swaraj to the ideal of inclusivity. Erik Erikson comments in this context that

Gandhi tried to revive "the more inclusive identity promised in the world religions," and that the "best leader" is one who can reaffirm these "more inclusive identities" through the techniques of nonviolence.[12]

Gandhi saw the task of leadership as educative in another sense, that satyagraha must be used to gain the empowerment of those who had never been politicized. Rajagopalachari observed that the purpose of the Dandi march was to manufacture not salt but civil disobedience. Gandhi responded that more precisely it was to use satyagraha to produce swaraj.[13] The function of a leader, in this case, was to instruct en masse in the art of nonviolent action for the purpose of personal and political autonomy "by demonstrating that real swaraj will come not by the acquisition of authority by a few but by the acquisition of the capacity by all to resist authority when abused. In other words, swaraj is to be attained by educating the masses to a sense of their capacity to regulate and control authority."[14]

A month before the salt march began, Gandhi stressed this purpose of swaraj: "Mere withdrawal of the English is not swaraj. It means the consciousness in the average villager that he is the maker of his own destiny."[15] Satyagraha alone could develop this consciousness and self-confidence because it empowered people. As Nehru had witnessed from the first use of it in 1919, it worked to overcome the pervasive fear of British authority in India by politicizing the apolitical, including them in a mass movement that demanded assumption of collective responsibility through direct action. From the perspective of political science, this was Gandhi's success as a leader and as a case study of the dynamics of political movements, it remains a very substantial accomplishment.

Gandhi in Fiction: "Waiting for the Mahatma"

Dramatic reconstructions of Gandhi's life in film and fiction range from Richard Attenborough's academy award winner in 1982 to Indian novels like Raja Rao's *Kanthapura* and Mulk Raj Anand's *Untouchable* that are noted in chapters 2 and 4. R. K. Narayan's novel, *Waiting for the Mahatma* is still another classic of Indian literature about Gandhi. It tells the story of Sriram, a twenty-year-old student in search of swaraj. Gandhi becomes central to Sriam's *rite de passage* through his service to India. At their first meeting he is intimidated and Gandhi, sensing this, "looked up at Sriram and said, 'Sit down, young man. Come and sit as near me as you like.' There was so much unaffected graciousness in his tone that Sriram lost all fear and hesitation."

But Sriram is so afraid of making a fool of himself that he cannot communicate. Gandhi tried to reassure him saying, " 'By the time we meet again next, you must give me a very good account of yourself.' He laughed in a kindly manner, and Sriram said, 'Yes, Bapuji [father], I will be a different man.' 'Why do you say "different"? You will be all right if you are fully yourself.' "[16]

From numerous fictional and nonfictional accounts of first-time meetings with Gandhi,[17] R. K. Narayan's depiction of Sriram's encounter would seem representative. Gandhi's message to millions, in one form or another, was that "You will be all right if you are fully yourself." Self-realization became both the means and end. In the novel, Gandhi always seems to be fully himself. Sriram follows him through countless villages, and observes: "He met the local village men and women, spoke to them about God, comforted the ailing, advised those who sought his guidance. He spoke to them about spinning, the war, Britain and religion. . . . He trudged his way through ploughed fields, he climbed hard rocky places, through mud and slush, but always with the happiest look, and no place seemed too small for his attention."

Gandhi arrives at a tiny train station, unexpected by the stationmaster, "a small man with a Kaiser-like moustache," who becomes excited over the Mahatma's sudden appearance: "The stationmaster panted for breath, and constantly nudged and instructed his children to behave themselves although they were all the time standing stiffly as if on a drill parade. Mahatmaji said: 'Station Masterji, why don't you let them run about and play as they like? Why do you constrain them?' 'I'm not constraining them, master. It's their habit,' he said with the hope of impressing the visitor with the training of his children. The Mahatma said: 'Friend, I fear you are trying to put them on good behavior before me, I would love it better if they ran about and played normally, and picked up those flowers dropping on the ground, which they want to do. I'm very keen that children should be free and happy.'"[18]

So this is Gandhi as a great novelist portrays him: urging those he meets to be fully themselves, confident that with a gentle lead, individuals will learn the self-discipline and self-awareness necessary for swaraj. This was his method and purpose on the Dandi march, to bring India into its own. This was also his aim with the Calcutta fast except by that time he knew how far India was from swaraj. The irony of the civil war was that while it proved Gandhi right in his warning that independence may not bring swaraj, that proof led him to despair. By the time of the fast, his optimism had been tested beyond its limits. From November 1946, when he began his arduous trek through the riot-torn villages of East Bengal, until January 30, 1948, when he was assassinated in Delhi by a Hindu fanatic, he appeared to exist for one purpose, to lessen the suffering of the civil war. The dream of swaraj seemed distant. Then the result of the Calcutta fast restored his vision. It led him to Delhi and inspired him to undertake still another fast, for the same cause of Hindu-Muslim harmony just before his death. The success of this Delhi fast reassured him that the method of satyagraha was still intact and it appears that at the very end he faced the future again, at age seventy-eight, with renewed commitment and confidence. Swaraj beckoned him.

The Judgment of History: What Verdict on Gandhi's Vision?

Did Gandhi fail? He thought he had, by the standards he set for himself. But what of the historical perspective, the judgment of history? Chapter 3 reported some of his severest critics and among recent historical assessments are those who now judge him harshly as one who "far from being infallible, committed serious blunders, one after another, in pursuit of some Utopian ideals and methods which had no basis in reality."[19] Compare with this the work of Judith Brown, historian of Gandhi, whose three volumes on him constitute perhaps the most scrupulous and fair study of his life and leadership available. Brown concludes her recent biography with this judgment: "Gandhi was no plaster saint. Nor did he find lasting and real solutions to many of the problems he encountered. . . . He was also deeply human, capable of heights and depths of sensation and vision, of great enlightenment and dire doubt. . . . But fundamentally he was a man of vision and action, who asked many of the profoundest questions that face humankind as it struggles to live in community."[20]

It is the way that Gandhi combined vision and action that gives him, as Brown says, "enduring significance," a person "for all times and all places."[21] Some historians object that a proper assessment of Gandhi's significance must rest not with his role and relevance "for all times and all places," but with what he did in a specific time and place, that is, India in the twentieth century, and that the scope of his contribution there was much less than claimed. This is because the Raj would certainly have left India anyway regardless of Gandhi, perhaps even sooner without him. In any case, the decisive causes of the demise of the British Empire were the two world wars, especially the second and its immediate aftermath, which quickly persuaded the Labour government in England to transfer power. This is a compelling argument but it hardly does justice to the role of the Indian nationalist movement. It misses the point that the movement's achievement was not merely the attainment of an independent government, but more than that, the method that was developed and steadfastly employed of a nonviolent struggle without parallel in world events. Susanne Rudolph is right that the question of "whether Gandhi did or did not speed Britain's exit from India" is a "distraction" that overlooks the main point about the way that the movement managed to translate ideas like swaraj and satyagraha into action: "Gandhi's leadership, regardless of its objective success or failure, had important subjective consequences, repairing wounds in self-esteem, inflicted by generations of imperial subjection, restoring courage and potency, recruiting and mobilizing new constituencies and leaders, helping India to acquire national coherence."[22]

India has emerged since Gandhi's death as a democracy—indeed it remains the world's largest—and Gandhi's vision was of a democratic India. However India may differ today from that vision, it does survive unlike most other nations of comparable economic development or colonial legacy as a country with working democratic institutions that have served intact since its independence. Gandhi's theory of democracy has been discussed in chapter 3, but we return to it because it remained one of the major ideas that he strove to express in action. "Democracy," he wrote in 1939, "must in essence mean the art and science of mobilizing the entire physical, economic and spiritual resources of all the various sections of the people in the service of the common good of all."[23] When he was asked in 1940 about the practice of democracy in America, he replied:

> My notion of democracy is that under it the weakest should have the same opportunity as the strongest. That can never happen except through non-violence. No country in the world today shows any but patronizing regard for the weak. The weakest, you say, go to the wall. Take your own case. Your land is owned by a few capitalist owners. The same is true of South Africa. These large holdings cannot be sustained except by violence, veiled if not open. . . . The way you have treated the Negro presents a discreditable record . . . Your wars will never ensure safety for democracy.[24]

Gandhi's critique of his contemporary democratic systems has relevance today. His central argument was that exploitation of the weak or poor is a form of "veiled violence," that this and any other form of violence is incompatible with the democratic ideal. The abiding promise of democracy is for freedom with equality which means freedom from fear and insecurity.

"I value individual freedom," Gandhi remarked, "but you must not forget that man is essentially a social being," and "unrestricted individualism" must be curtailed by social conscience "to strike the mean between individual freedom and social restraint." The task in any democracy is to realize the value of swaraj, "social restraint for the sake of the well-being of the whole society [that] enriches both the individual and the society of which one is a member."[25] This was the vision of swaraj and also of *sarvodaya* or social equality that Gandhi sought to express in action. It was an ideal that pitted inclusivity against exclusivity, arguing that the former meant placing the category of humanity above those of caste or class, race or religion because the latter necessarily bred attitudes of domination or dehumanization:

"A variety of incidents in my life," Gandhi wrote in his Autobiography, "have conspired to bring me in close contact with people of many creeds and many communities, and my experience with all of them warrants the statement that I have known no distinction between relatives and strangers, countrymen and foreigners, white and colored, Hindus and Indians of other faiths, whether Muslims, Parsis, Christians or Jews. I may say that my heart has been incapable of making any such distinctions."[26]

This is the vision that other inclusivists like Albert Einstein would recognize as Gandhi's gift to posterity because, as he would remark shortly after Gandhi's assassination, "in our age of moral decay he was the only statesman who represented that higher conception of human relations in the political sphere."[27] The vision held power because it grew out of a personal and political experience in which ideas were tested in action. Gandhi's distinctive quality was not merely his inclusivism, but that plus his statesmanship, his persistent attempts to apply vision to the arena of politics. If it is true that without a vision people will perish, Gandhi's example shows that an inclusivist vision is not incompatible with political practice, that it may be forged in its crucible, that political leadership and a lifelong career in national politics can permit personal reexamination and refinement of ideas, even when these ideas challenge powerful social or political institutions.

Careers of legions of political leaders in this century suggest that politics is not the place for serious or original thought, that Socrates's maxim "The unexamined life is not worth living" excludes the lives of politicians. Gandhi's three decades of national leadership suggest otherwise, that political experience may serve as precisely the right place for testing or perfecting ideals because that is where vision is most needed and ideas most wanted in a field of nonviolent conflict. This is perhaps why George Orwell, in 1949, after writing an essay sharply critical of Gandhi, could nevertheless conclude it on this note: "regarded simply as a politician, and compared with the other leading political figures of our time, how clean a smell he has managed to leave behind!"[28]

The clean smell endures today, decades after Einstein's and Orwell's judgments. It comes not only from Gandhi's imaginative use of nonviolence but even more because of his identification of nonviolence with truth, and with the practice of truthfulness. A thorough reading of Gandhi's voluminous writings uncovers no duplicity: this from a political career that spanned the first half of the twentieth century. Just as Gandhi's theory of satyagraha insisted on both pursuit of truth and the actual conduct of truthfulness, so it also related truthfulness to trust. Lying brings distrust and this in turn breeds suspicion and fear. When Gandhi insisted that for the *satyagrahi*, "an implicit trust in human nature is the very essence of his creed," so "he will repose his trust in the adversary," he saw this conduct as a form of empowerment because "Distrust is a sign of weakness and satyagraha implies the banishment of all weakness" as we become liberated from fear.[29] Gandhi's letter to Lord Irwin announcing the plan of the salt march is a classic example of trusting the adversary, denial of secrecy, and consequent empowerment.

Sissela Bok has captured this idea in her analysis of lying in politics and the way that deceit corrodes the value of social trust.[30] She aptly subtitles her book "Moral Choice in Public and Private Life," implying a connection between the personal and the political that Gandhi argued in his theory of swaraj. It was because Gandhi understood and practiced the relationship between truthfulness and trust in both his public and private life that he received abundant trust from his people in return. Bok evaluates Gandhi's achievement as a political leader in these terms:

> Along with nonviolence, the most important observance for Gandhi was a concern for truthfulness and truth. And fidelity—to his vows in their own right, to his ideals and thus to himself, to his obligations to others— was for him what held all the observances together and bound him to them in turn. Through making and holding such vows, he trained himself

to become someone who could trust himself and who could be trusted by others. Finally, Gandhi rejected secrecy in his dealings with supporters as with those who opposed him.[31]

This was Gandhi's nexus of values: nonviolence and tolerance, truth and truthfulness, trust and openness, all connected to both personal and political experience. The attempt in this book is to explain these values in the context of the relationship that Gandhi developed between swaraj and satyagraha: that we become liberated from fear and distrust as we are empowered by truthfulness and nonviolent action; that freedom is not merely license because it must also mean a social awareness and responsibility that comes with a sense of human connectedness. It was King who wrote about freedom and justice from a jail in Birmingham: "Injustice anywhere is a threat to justice everywhere. We are caught in an inescapable network of mutuality, tied in a single garment of destiny. Whatever affects one directly, affects all indirectly."[32] Gandhi's thought and action rest on this same premise of inclusivity, that we are all part of one another and violence retards that realization. This is a truth, as King would say, with the power to set us free.

Gandhi understood something important
about political struggle: that it is always,
in the last instance, a struggle within the
self. . . . The real 'clash of civilizations'
is not 'out there' between admirable
Westerners and Muslim zealots. It is
here, within each person, as we oscillate
uneasily between self-protective aggression and the ability to live in the world
with others.

—*Martha C. Nussbaum,* The Clash Within

The initial publication of my book in 1993 happened to coincide
with the appearance of an extraordinary article by Samuel P. Huntington
entitled "The Clash of Civilizations?"[1] One purpose of this afterword is to
examine those aspects of Gandhi's theory that give him a place in the vigorous debate initiated by Huntington.

From my perspective, Huntington's central thesis throws Gandhi's
thought into sharper relief because the two theories stand in such stark opposition. Huntington views contemporary history in terms of violent conflicts. He contends that these are fomented especially by religious traditions
of not merely nations but civilizations, such as the Islamic and Hindu. He
poses his central question of why clashes must occur in the future along the
"cultural fault lines" that separate them as follows:

First, differences among civilizations are not only real; they are basic. Civilizations are differentiated from each other by history, culture, tradition, and, most
important, religion.

> The people of different civilizations have different views on the relations between God and man, the individual and the group, the citizen and the state, parents and children, husband and wife, as well as differing views of the relative importance of rights and responsibilities, liberty and authority, equality and hierarchy. These differences are the product of centuries. They will not soon disappear. They are far more fundamental than differences among political ideologies and political regimes. Differences do not necessarily mean violence. Over the centuries, however, differences among civilizations have generated the most prolonged and the most violent conflicts.[2]

Huntington, like Gandhi, gives primacy to religion, but he views it as problematic, provoking violence, and does not acknowledge its traditional values of nonviolence. Their ideas of what is "real" and "basic," as Huntington uses these words, differ dramatically. Unlike Bernard Lewis, the prominent historian of Islam who introduced the "clash" metaphor in 1990,[3] Huntington, a political scientist, conceives the world from a realist's lens, warning that since the end of the Cold War a stark shift of power has occurred around clashing civilizations. Both Lewis and Huntington agree that America is now dangerously vulnerable to non-Western cultures, especially Islamic systems of belief. Profound, ominous differences exist not merely between transient political regimes but as vast gulfs separating the deepest cultural values of entire civilizations. Whereas Gandhi emphasizes a universal harmony infusing such values, Huntington sees non-Western religions as largely malign with lethal capacities for metastasis. He predicted in the 1990s that power struggles will occur along the civilizational "fault lines" that divide us. Especially since September 11, the religious force behind terrorism has made his argument even more compelling.

The fact that neither Lewis, Huntington, nor anyone else in the ongoing debates published in *Foreign Affairs* makes any mention of Gandhi or aspects of the Gandhian tradition in India is noteworthy. India is referred to dozens of times in Huntington's book but not Gandhi. Is this because notions of nonviolence are irrelevant to the main arguments as they frame them? If one considers his historical record as a world-class political leader who was dramatically and for decades involved in religious conflict and efforts at resolution, Gandhi deserves a place in this debate. Gandhi, who identified himself as a "Hindu of Hindus," inspired Buddhists such as Aung San Suu Kyi and the Dalai Lama and Christians like Bishop Tutu and Martin Luther King Jr. If the world is fractured mainly by religious conflict, the influence of renowned religious leaders like these, to mention only a few, who are committed to nonviolent conflict resolution demands acknowledgment at least, or, at best, inclusion in an expanded dialogue that illustrates the varieties of religious experience. The question is, why should the basic and real forces of history be restricted to religious leaders and political movements characterized by violence?

We do not need to be reminded by Hobbes or Machiavelli of the power of fear behind threats of violence. This certainly is an undeniable aspect of our reality, once again painfully evident in America since September 11. But thankfully this is not our sole reality. Not only Gandhi and King, but religious prophets and writers for millennia have demonstrated that nonviolence can be as consequential as war. In many universities, bastions of civilization, the disciplines of history, religion, and philosophy offer peace studies in the hope that we might better manage conflict so that the terrible carnage of the last century might not be repeated—even though this one is off to a poor start. When only sounds of dissonance are heard, we easily become tone deaf to consonance. Real rhythms of harmony do resound in any civilization. The great ideas of God and society that Huntington lists include a capacity to resolve conflict peacefully as well as to exacerbate it through violence.

Gandhi drew on most of the world's major religions to shape his thought. During his lifetime of evolving perspectives, he shaped a mature synthesis of ideas that guided his personal and political conduct. His value system may be expressed in terms of dual contesting forces that exist within each self and civilization as well as in the world. One way to see this opposition is through the conceptual prisms of what he termed "exclusivism" and "inclusivism," and in the manner that analysts of Gandhi like Erik Erikson (*Gandhi's Truth*, 1969) and Martha Nussbaum explain his inclusiveness. Gandhi wrote characteristically that "my nationalism as my religion is not exclusive but inclusive."[4] He opposed a xenophobic world view held by many religious extremists that assigns people abstract identities or character traits derived arbitrarily from stereotypes of class, caste, gender, ethnicity, or nationality. And his political and social campaigns spoke more loudly than his words.

The vital element of Gandhi's inclusivism that is distinctive to his experience is his invention of satyagraha. This is the central concern of my book, especially chapters 4 and 5 on the Dandi march and the Calcutta fast. The book's subtitle suggests the opposition of Gandhian nonviolence to "passive resistance." Gandhi denounced this idea as the opposite of satyagraha. Martin Luther King Jr., while professing his own pacifist inclusivism, discovered Gandhi's significance for the civil rights struggle in the realization that satyagraha was not passive but "spiritually active."[5] Gandhi's inclusivism, therefore, was consequential to India and America because it gave a dynamic and undeniable demonstration of nonviolent power in action.

Edward Said contended in his critique of Huntington's thesis that a major flaw in its approach was to "build a conceptual framework around the notion of us-versus-them" rather than to "emphasize and maximize the spirit of cooperation and humanistic exchange." The former mindset winds up "superficially and stridently banging the drum for 'our' culture in opposition to all others."[6] Nussbaum cogently presents Gandhi as a vigorous opponent of the "fault lines" in his own Hindu culture, and as waging a constant struggle against "a 'clash of civilizations' in India" rather than "the one depicted by Samuel Huntington, between a democratic West and an antidemocratic Islam." Gandhi's transcendent leadership is defined by his "richness in inclusiveness."[7]

Nussbaum is concerned with the religious violence from today's Hindu right, the progeny of those who assassinated Gandhi. In direct opposition to this violent separatism, Gandhi constructed his program for India's liberation around "three pillars of swaraj." Through satyagraha he vigorously attacked a tripartite structure of exclusivity: not only Hindu-Muslim enmity but also the dehumanization of the untouchables and the alienation of the upper-class intelligentsia from the poor peasantry. In each case, the evil was in turning another into the Other.

Gandhi's inclusivism was born of pride in Hinduism, especially of its capacities for synthesis and tolerance, civility and humility. He understood the syncretic spirit of Indian civilization, its constant appeal to "unity in diversity" articulated eloquently by modern Hindu reformers whom he respected like Vivekananda and Rabindranath Tagore. The point that Huntington overlooks or ignores is how history's largest mass movement for independence was dynamized by a call for religious inclusivism, mobilized around a creed of nonviolence. Here was a political leader who began his autobiography insisting that only from "my experiments in the spiritual field . . . I derived such power as I possess for working in the political field."[8] As Margaret Chatterjee concludes in her incisive analysis of the centrality of religion in his experience, "Gandhi certainly stood for the spiritualizing of politics."[9]

If journals like *Foreign Affairs* omitted any mention of Gandhi in the clash of civilizations debate, his relevance was not missed by the *New York*

Times. A. M. Rosenthal, writing three months before Huntington's article appeared, deplored in Gandhian terms Hindu-Muslim violence in India, and editorialized that "Gandhi, founder of Indian freedom, used religion to combat bigotry, not promote it."[10]

Four years later, Anthony J. Parel contributed significantly to our understanding of how Gandhi's religious thought reinforced his political philosophy. In a cogent introduction to his new edition and translation of *Hind Swaraj,* Parel analyzed the theoretical context of Gandhi's first major treatise, calling it "the seed from which the tree of Gandhian thought has grown to its full stature."[11] Gandhi's project was "to free religion of the evil of sectarianism. . . . *Hind Swaraj* teaches that there are good *religious* reasons for practicing toleration" (Gandhi, liv; italics in original).

Parel's interpretations of Gandhi's philosophy may be construed within the context of the clash of civilizations debate, although he makes no reference to it. He shows, for example, how Gandhi, laying claim to the essential ethical and spiritual core of his religion, employs Tolstoy's similar claim as an advocate of pure Christianity to oppose Hindu terrorists like V. D. Savarkar, the intellectual leader of a young group of Indian expatriates in London. Gandhi debated Savarkar personally on his visit in 1909. One might imagine their exchange as a microcosmic political-cum-religious clash within Hindu civilization, as well as an ominous forecast of Gandhi's assassination almost forty years later by one of Savarkar's followers.

This moment in London, as Parel conveys it, constitutes an ideological time capsule of Savarkar's exclusivist Hinduism, his "terrorism legitimized by nationalism," versus "all the essential ingredients of [Gandhi's] political philosophy" (Gandhi, xxvii, 1). Their two positions at that time and henceforth proved to be irreconcilable, despite Gandhi's earnest efforts. When Gandhi demanded, through satyagraha, that human lives must never be treated as means but cherished for their sanctity and dignity, he was asserting a principle that stood at the magnetic center of his theory and practice.

Parel notes a root of satyagraha in Gandhi's theory of means and ends, his affirmation of "an inviolable connection between ends *(sadhya)* and means *(sadhan)*" (Gandhi, 81). This idea was born with *Hind Swaraj* and flowed abundantly through Gandhi's writings henceforth. In 1924, when Stalin's state terror was becoming evident and Indian Communists accepted Bolshevism on faith, Gandhi declared emphatically against it: "I am an uncompromising opponent of violent methods even to serve the noblest of causes. There is, therefore, really no meeting ground between the school of violence and myself."[12] From the perspective of political theory, the fulcrum of Gandhi's thought is his insistence on the logical and necessary relationship of means and ends (see pages 9–10, 204 of this book). This is the theme of my article, "Gandhi's Originality."[13]

The renewed focus on *Hind Swaraj* has been sharpened further by the remarkable work of S. R. Mehrotra, a longtime distinguished historian of the Indian nationalist movement. His lengthy introduction to the century edition of *Hind Swaraj* begins with the discovery that Dr. Pranjivandas J. Mehta (1864–1932), Gandhi's "oldest and closest friend," and a staunch proponent of religious tolerance, had a decisive intellectual and material influence on the development and promulgation of Gandhi's ideas at this time, especially on *Hind Swaraj*.[14] As late as 1940, "Gandhi made a startling disclosure about the genesis of *Hind Swaraj*," revealing for the first time that "I wrote the entire *Hind Swaraj* for my dear friend Dr. Pranjivan Mehta."[15]

During Gandhi's decades in South Africa, a crucial time in his ideological development, he engaged in vigorous dialogues with Mehta, whom he regarded as "an intellectual giant." Mehta, the first to refer to Gandhi as "Mahatma" and the first Indian to write a biography of him, played a key role in Gandhi's connection with Tolstoy. Martin Green wrote in-depth about *Tolstoy and Gandhi*, but he barely mentions P. J. Mehta. Yet it was their joint discovery of Tolstoy that prompted Gandhi to send him a copy of *Hind Swaraj*. Tolstoy's response exceeded Mehta's or Gandhi's expectations: *Hind Swaraj* addressed the question that "is important not only for Indians, but for the whole of mankind."[16] Gandhi, inspired by Tolstoy's writing and example, regarded himself as an "ardent disciple" and "humble follower" and soon established Tolstoy Farm, an ashram, or settlement, near Johannesburg. The early and enthusiastic affirmations of Gandhi's work by two pacifists whom he held in the highest esteem were decisive as he moved ahead.

Mehrotra, after emphasizing Mehta's crucial role, then joined Parel in examining Gandhi's key correspondents at this time. Whether he was writing in intimate terms to Mehta or H. S. L. Polak (his "closest political associate in South Africa" and a "fellow seeker") or Lord Ampthill (governor of Madras, 1900–1906, and acting viceroy of India in 1904, who wrote an admiring introduction in August 1909 to Joseph Doke's biography of Gandhi), or Tolstoy,[17] he emphasized ideas about violence and nonviolence, grounded in the theoretical connection of means and ends. Gandhi's brief correspondence with Tolstoy is remarkable for their mutual preoccupation with these ideas, as evidenced in a collection of their correspondence entitled *Letter to a Hindoo.*[18]

In Gandhi's letters to Polak and Ampthill, written in the month before the composition of *Hind Swaraj*, he frames his arguments in terms clearly expressive of a clash of ideas within India's independence struggle. To his British benefactor he writes:

> I have made it a point to see Indians here [in London] of every shade of opinion. Opposed as I am to violence in any shape or form, I have endeavoured especially to come into contact with the so-called extremists who may be better described as the party of violence. This I have done in order if possible to convince them of the error of their ways. . . . They wield an undoubted influence on the young Indians here. They are certainly unsparing in their efforts to impress upon the latter their convictions. One of them came to me with a view to convince me that I was wrong in my methods and that nothing but the use of violence, covert or open or both, was likely to bring about redress of the wrongs they consider they suffer. . . . I share the national spirit but I totally dissent from the methods whether of the extremists or of the moderates. For either party relies ultimately on violence.[19]

To Polak he reiterated the "true spirit" of his method and concluded: "If you agree with me, it will be your duty to tell the revolutionaries and everybody else that the freedom they want, or they think they want, is not to be obtained by killing people or doing violence, but by setting themselves right and by becoming and remaining truly Indian."[20]

These two original essays by Mehrotra and Parel on the philosophical meanings and historical context of *Hind Swaraj* capture Gandhi as a creative synthesizer, contending first and foremost that "violence is an evil and must be avoided at all costs. Satyagraha is not merely a means of aborting violence, it is an infallible remedy. . . . It blesses him who practices it and also him against whom it is practiced."[21] The relationship of means and ends is crucial here. Martin Luther King Jr. clearly recognized and expressed it when he wrote that this idea set Gandhi apart from other revolutionaries: "Constructive ends can never give absolute moral justification to destructive means, because in the final analysis the end is preexistent in the means."[22] King also goes mostly unmentioned in the clash of civilizations debate, yet no American deserves a greater place in it today.

Faisal Devji, a contemporary historian of South Asia, is concerned, like Nussbaum, with religious violence. However, he offers a very different interpretation of Gandhi's meaning in *The Terrorist in Search of Humanity*.[23] He begins by citing Karl Jaspers' view of Gandhi "as the chief and indeed only global example of modernity's sacrificial logic," as seen in his "practices of sacrifice, which ran the gamut from fasting and celibacy to non-cooperation and passive resistance." Devji acknowledges that Gandhi "was of course the very antithesis of a terrorist in his espousal of nonviolence," yet he nonetheless "resembles Al-Qaeda's militants by his suprapolitical deployment of sacrifice, which like them he glorified in the form of a willingness to die for principles. So Gandhi, like Bin Laden, very regularly used the Islamic word for martyrdom, *shahadat*, to describe this sacrifice," even as he spoke of his willingness to give innocent lives in the cause of India's freedom (Devji, 18–19). Devji further explains that his reason for invoking Gandhi's humanitarian and nonviolent example is "not only to offer a new perspective on militant Islam, but also to point out how important South Asia in fact is to this phenomenon, comprising as it does the world's largest Muslim population together with some of the chief sites of Islamic militancy today" (Ibid., 21).

Gandhi is invoked throughout Devji's book, from his militant tone in *Hind Swaraj* to his opinions on how the Jews should martyr themselves in the Holocaust.[24] Devji argues that Muslim terrorists mimic Gandhi in their martyrdom, and so they might, but it is not clear why they should choose a prophet of nonviolence, since Gandhi emphasized that the force of satyagraha depends on love of one's enemies and for this reason is "a thousand times more effective . . . it excludes every form of violence, direct and indirect, and whether in thought, word or deed. . . . Satyagraha is gentle, it never wounds. It must not be the result of anger or malice. It was conceived as a complete substitute for violence."[25] This should hardly appeal to a terrorist of any faith. James Rowell grasps this as an obvious point of difference between satyagraha and terrorism in his study *Gandhi and Bin Laden: Religion at the Extremes* (2009). In this short book Rowell manages to include an acute analysis of Gandhi's varied legacies to King and Abdul Ghaffar Khan (the Muslim "Frontier Gandhi"), as well as a succinct criticism of Huntington.

Terrorists cannot adopt a Gandhian theory of power because it would transform completely their use of it. King had an excellent grasp of the meaning and use of satyagraha, martyrdom and all, and like Gandhi stressed self-sacrifice as among the major elements in his philosophy of nonviolence, "a willingness to accept suffering without retaliation, to accept blows from the opponent without striking back. 'Rivers of blood may have to flow before we gain our freedom, but it must be our blood,' Gandhi told his countrymen. The nonviolent resister is willing to accept violence if necessary, but never to inflict it."[26] This comes from an American Baptist minister recommending an extreme sacrificial course of action to a primarily Christian audience. However, as suggested above, there is plenty of the martyr's spirit to go around: King did not share many of Malcolm X's doctrines, but there is an eerie similarity between the former's famous "mountaintop speech" that seems to anticipate his death on the eve of his assassination, and Malcolm's declaration forty-eight hours before his murder that "it's a time for martyrs now."[27]

In Gandhian terms, the essential difference is between the use of *duragraha* (passive resistance) and *satyagraha*. As discussed in this book, Aurobindo Ghose, a Hindu terrorist, advocated the former at the same time that Gandhi developed the latter (see pages 37–40). Gandhi's theory of power, as excluding every form of violence, physical and psychological, would seem to disqualify him and King as models for terrorists (in King's words, satyagraha must act never in anger or hatred "to defeat or humiliate the opponent"). If Muslim extremists want a philosopher of terrorism in South Asia, complete with a full dose of religious martyrdom, then Aurobindo might be their man. After all, Aurobindo, an exquisite writer, excelled Gandhi in his eloquent espousal of humanitarianism in the cause of Indian liberation, and no Hindu theorist formulated a loftier spiritual vision of global unity. His powerful advocacy for violence invoked the *Bhagavad Gita*, and was arguably more faithful to that sacred text than Gandhi's unorthodox interpretation of it. Aurobindo's main argument with Gandhi was over the superiority of nonviolent power and, consequently, the logical and integral relationship of means and ends, but terrorism never pauses to consider these latter ideas.

Among recent American studies of Gandhi and his legacy, a cogent case for the power of self-sacrifice in a nonviolent cause is made by Joseph Kip Kosek in *Acts of Conscience*, a thorough new exploration of Gandhi's impact on Christian pacifists like Richard Gregg, John Haynes Holmes, A. J. Muste, and the Fellowship of Reconciliation from World War I to the Montgomery bus boycott.[28] Kosek does not mention Huntington and offers no original analysis of Gandhi, but he certainly demonstrates a complete command of how leading American pacifists transformed their personal acts of suffering into the Age of Conscience from 1945 to 1956 (see chapter 6). We may infer from this that an authentically Gandhian response to "sacrificial logic" came with the culmination of this quality in King's civil rights movement, as

Kosek relates the story with meticulous scholarship, scrupulously unearthing documents about the sacrifices of individual pacifists that are not usually regarded as among America's heroes.

We have focused so far on theories of clashes or conflicts and their resolution. This leaves the concept of civilization, Huntington's other major concern. He concluded his first essay, in accordance with his realist philosophy, on a cautious note, following his thesis about the power and tenacity of cultural fault lines: "For the relevant future, there will be no universal civilization, but instead a world of different civilizations, each of which will have to coexist with the others."[29] Four years later, after expanding a short article into a long book, his last paragraph acknowledges the positive features of "the world's great civilizations, with their rich accomplishments in religion, art, literature, philosophy, science, technology and compassion" as "the surest safeguard against world war." Peace depends on forming an "international order based on civilizations" to stand against the threat of terrorism. We must choose between civilization and barbarism if humanity is to survive,[30] and Huntington leaves no doubt about the dominant role that the West must play in this momentous struggle.

Most of the responses in the two collections from *Foreign Affairs* are favorable, offering relatively moderate criticisms. A genuine critique of Huntington's thesis comes in Wendy Brown's piercing assault on the contemporary value of tolerance in *Regulating Aversion*. Brown makes no mention of Gandhi in her discussion, but she sharply indicts both American liberals and conservatives who assert "the superiority of the West and of liberalism by valorizing (and even ontologizing) individual autonomy."[31] It would have been useful here to introduce Gandhi's idea of autonomy into the discourse, especially as it is interpreted by Ronald Terchek, the prominent Gandhi theorist. Wendy Brown succinctly states the case against Huntington's advocacy of "a civilizational discourse that codifies the superiority and legitimates the superordination of the West."[32]

If only in terms of elegance of style, though, the better assault is by Edward Said, who condemns Huntington for encouraging us to be

> ostrich-like to maintain our civilization by holding all the others at bay, increasing the rifts between peoples in order to prolong our dominance. That is, in effect, what Huntington is arguing, and one can quite easily understand why it is that his essay was published in *Foreign Affairs*, and why so many policy-makers have drifted toward it as allowing the United States to extend the mind-set of

the Cold War into a different time and for a new audience. Much more productive and useful is a new global mentality that sees the dangers we face from the standpoint of the whole human race.[33]

The imperative, Said urges, is for civilizations to define themselves and others in such a way that they will work toward harmony and not hegemony.

Although Said was no pacifist, much of his cosmopolitan humanism was akin to Gandhi's conception of inclusive nationalism. Both were strident critics of Western imperialism, especially its arrogance of power. Both were born into and championed oppressed peoples yet also enthusiastically embraced selective elements of European and American culture. Although these shared qualities are impressive, their differences are most dramatic. Said was an authentic renaissance man and prestigious professor, whereas Gandhi rightly said, "I am not built for academic writings. Action is my domain" (page 1).

Gandhi's original if nonacademic philosophy emerged from a decade of activism in South Africa, synthesizing ideas that produced *Hind Swaraj*. His concept of civilization announced here is the most controversial part of the tract. When bloggers connect Huntington with Gandhi on the Internet, it is invariably over Gandhi's quip that Western civilization would be a "good idea."

Whereas Huntington and his sympathizers clearly see the West as best, Gandhi identified its colonialism and consequent harm with barbarism. Both viewed the idea of a civilization in terms of shared values, but—contrary to Huntington's characterization of his culture—Gandhi contrasted the spirit of Indian civilization as "good conduct" (*sudharo*), diametrically opposed to *kudharo* (uncivil behavior) found in the West's endemic violence, its brutal subjugation and dehumanization of every country it colonized. Gandhi asks in *Hind Swaraj*, "what is civilization?" and then answers that it was correctly conceived in ancient India as "that mode of conduct which points out to man the path of duty."[34] Gandhi affirms not the primacy of individual rights of which the West is so proud but the conviction that rights must be derived from duties properly performed, thus switching the imperative to the fulfillment of social responsibility (pages xi–xiii).

Gandhi formulated his critique of Western civilization while in South Africa, during a period of thirteen years leading up to the publication of *Hind Swaraj*. He read strong American and British critics of their own countries like Thoreau and Edward Carpenter (whose *Civilization: Its Cause and Cure* is listed in the appendices of *Hind Swaraj*), and tested his ideas about Western versus Indian civilizations on close European friends such as Polak and Hermann Kallenbach, who also condemned aspects of their own societies, England and Germany, respectively. When he sent a copy of *Hind Swaraj* to Tolstoy, he knew that he had found a sympathetic ear. Tolstoy wrote in his diary on April 10, 1910, "Read Gandhi about civilization, wonderful."[35]

As R. N. Iyer observed, in this context, although Gandhi did not mention them, Marx and Rousseau were also obvious critics of the West who played a vital role in providing authority and a sense of validity to Gandhi's position. The extent to which he used a prestigious array of other Western writers to criticize the West is clear from the list of those cited or quoted in the appendix to *Hind Swaraj*, beginning with Plato's Socrates and extending to contemporary "eminent men" of Germany and England. Iyer drew numerous parallels between Gandhi and Western philosophers who entered into this spirit of self-criticism, developing Gandhi's critique of Western civilization into a penetrating indictment of the industrial age. Gandhi's notorious opposition to machinery, for example, was cogently interpreted by Iyer in the context of his whole thought—and especially the evolution of his ideas after *Hind Swaraj*—into an indictment of the craze for acquisitions that resonates throughout contemporary critiques of consumerism and "luxury fever." As a political theorist, Iyer's intention was not to defend Gandhi, because he freely acknowledged his excesses, but rather to clarify his mature concept of civilization and its enduring relevance.

Overview Of Gandhi Scholarship

Social and political theory comes from a historical context. A study of the Indian independence movement, and Gandhi's example in particular, provides a classic case of ideas emerging from action. To understand his multiple meanings, we turn to a study of Gandhi's voluminous writings and then to his more prominent and recent biographers; Judith Brown (1989), Yogesh Chadha (1997), and Rajmohan Gandhi (2006) have worked through a vast corpus of materials connected with their subject. There is certainly a plethora of primary sources by or about him to study. Mountains of records relating to the Indian nationalist movement as it was from the beginning of his career can be found in the Indian Office Library and various archives, public and private, throughout India that have been a staple for my research.

Regarding the last decade of Gandhi's life alone, *The Transfer of Power,* *1942–1947,* edited by Nicholas Mansergh, served as an indispensable reservoir of documents relating to the partition of India. It has fortunately been much expanded and enhanced by Sabyasachi Bhattacharya, the general editor (and successor of Sarvepalli Gopal) of *Towards Freedom, 1937–1947* (2009). With a formidable team of Indian scholars, including Gandhi experts like Sumit Sarkar and Bimal Prasad, he has, like Mansergh, skillfully collected and edited a mass of official records, private papers, newspapers and heretofore unpublished documents relating to India's freedom struggle. These are filled with Gandhi's writings published alongside correspondence to him by other key figures including Jawaharlal Nehru.[36]

All of these historians mined the archives and abundant Gandhiana in India and abroad to provide a more comprehensive and deeper grasp of his leadership. Subaltern historians like Shahid Amin (1984) and David Hardiman added still another dimension by interpreting his appeal through village and local peasant studies. As if this were not enough, individual collections of the writings of prominent actors in the movement, led by Gandhi's *Collected Works* in 100 volumes (1958–1964) and accompanied by the *Selected Works of Jawaharlal Nehru* (2006 and in progress), are followed by similar collections from the writings of a host of other participants in the independence struggle that feature important interactions with Gandhi. The initial point, therefore, is that the raw data for a study of the Indian nationalist movement, and Gandhi's central role in it, are formidable, arguably greater than for any of the major mass movements of the last century.

What is especially striking though, beyond this treasure trove of sources, is the distinct pattern of interaction between political theorists and historians dealing with the Gandhi phenomenon. The task of understanding this individual has not been undertaken by historians alone: political thinkers have recognized the originality of his methods from the outset and analyzed the meaning of his power. In my experience, this pattern was exemplified by the Gandhi studies of my two mentors: Hugh Tinker (1965, 1967) and W. H. Morris-Jones (1960, 1971). The first biography of Gandhi was published during his lifetime by J. J. Doke (1909), followed by theorists of satyagraha who tried to formulate a systematic construct of satyagraha: C. M. Case (1923), Richard Gregg (1938) and Krishnalal Shridharani (1939). This first flush of political theory flowed into the early biographies of Louis Fischer (1950) and B. R. Nanda (1958), which were in turn enlarged by the multivolume Mahatma tomes compiled by D. G. Tendulkar (1960), Pyarelal and Sushila Nayar

(10 vols., 1958–1989), and Narayan Desai. Sometimes these biographies are hagiographical and fail to convey the harsh yet eloquent and theoretically sophisticated critiques of the Mahatma from his adversaries. They demand a brief comment here, in addition to the analysis offered in chapter 3.

It was inevitable that as Gandhi gained control of the nationalist movement in 1920 (founded with the India National Congress in 1885), he would face immediate ideological challenges from well-established leaders like B. G. Tilak (see pages 35–38), as well as from prominent political theorists, including M. N. Roy, B. R. Ambedkar, Rabindranath Tagore (see chapter 3), and an array of others such as C. R. Das and Subhas Bose, who are hardly mentioned in my book. Even so, this is just a short list of his critics. More are discussed in the new third edition of *Sources of Indian Tradition* (see chapter 6). Altogether they comprise a formidable series of critiques from vociferous contemporaries, some of whom, like V. D. Savakar and Palme Dutt, carried on a relentless barrage of attacks on all aspects of Gandhi's personal life and his social and political programs. An early assault by an Indian in South Africa was both physical and ideological, while the last by Nathuram Godse killed him. The premise that Gandhi was anointed as the Mahatma by his nation and subsequently swam in friendly waters of *ahimsa* natural to India is false. In reality, Indian adversaries were omnipresent and harder on him than the British colonizers, including Churchill and Lord Wavell. After all, there is no evidence that the Raj ever proposed shooting him; that task was left to one of his own religion, who offered a defense at trial that is stunning for its eloquent evocation of orthodox Hindu views. Godse's remarkable testimony alone demonstrates well the depth of the "clash within."

By the late 1950s a substantial body of literature about Gandhi's thought and practice had been completed or was well underway. At this moment a systematic study of his theory of conflict resolution appeared. Joan Bondurant's *Conquest of Violence: The Gandhian Philosophy of Conflict* (1958) was distinguished especially by its exploration of the centrality and implications in satyagraha of the means-end relationship, Bondurant's formulation of "The Gandhian Dialectic and Political Theory" (see chapter 6). Twenty-five years later Howard Gardner, in *Creating Minds* (1993), would reflect on the intellectual revolution that Gandhi represented and, comparing him with other geniuses of the twentieth century like Einstein, Freud, and Picasso, concluded that "Gandhi was a thinker of the highest order. The conception of satyagraha was worked out as carefully as a philosophical system, with every step and its possible consequences carefully calibrated."[37]

The 1960s brought another fresh theoretical perspective on Gandhi with the original psychological insights of Lloyd and Susanne Rudoph and of Erik Erikson (1969), as well as a more conventional but solid theoretical analysis by J. Bandyopadhyaya (1969). The 1970s spawned two more substantial yet sharply contrasting theoretical approaches: R. N. Iyer's rigorous, unsurpassed theoretical analysis in *The Moral and Political Thought of Mahatma Gandhi* (1973) and Gene Sharp, an early and illustrious theorist of nonviolent power (1973) who published *Gandhi as a Political Strategist* (1979). Iyer reinforced his earlier book with what Judith Brown called "an immensely valuable three volume selection of Gandhi's Works" (1986–87). Coterminous with these came the historians, with the scrupulous research in 1970 of Stephen Hay (exploring the profound Jain influence on Gandhi), Judith Brown on Gandhi's power (1972, 1977), and James Hunt on Gandhi's experiences in London (1978). Once again came the juncture of history and theory with Arne Naess's *Gandhi and Group Conflict* (1974). This was followed by a return to psychological analysis by Ashis Nandy in *At the Edge of Psychology* (1980) and *The Intimate Enemy: Loss and Recovery of Self Under Colonialism* (1983). Nandy's imaginative approach was nicely complemented by Partha Chatterjee, whose *Nationalist Thought and the Colonial World* (1986) offered its powerful interpretation of *Hind Swaraj* as "the most crucial theoretical foundation" of Gandhi's method for attaining swaraj (87). Later came two important systematic philosophical works on Gandhi by Bhikhu Parekh (1989, 2001), the first in the same year as Brown's biography.[38] Thomas Weber produced a unique work of historical research on the salt march as well as a theory of Gandhian conflict resolution.[39] He has become a noteworthy unifier of historical and theoretical analysis of Gandhi with recent works like *Gandhi as Disciple and Mentor* (2010) and *Gandhi, Gandhism and the Gandhians* (2011).

In the 1990s came first, and at long last, the definitive biography of Subhas and Sarat Bose (1990) by Leonard Gordon, who has devoted over half a century of intense scholarship to the intellectual history of India and published incisive comparisons between Bengali nationalists and Gandhi in *Brothers Against the Raj*. Gordon's grasp of Subhas Bose's life set a gold standard for understanding a biographical subject's complex motives and ideas as well as the precise political context of nationalist India, especially during Bose's feud with Gandhi throughout the 1930s. In 1993 I offered additional theoretical analysis about ideas of freedom and power in the first edition of this book, and Anthony Parel provided a trenchant examination of *Hind Swaraj*.

Gandhi scholars feed on continuously updated references to writings about him, especially bibliographical volumes, of which there are many. The best is by Ananda Pandiri, a remarkably dedicated researcher who published in 1995 and 2011 a two-volume annotated bibliography that is as rich in sources cited as it is thoroughly reliable in its commentary.

The pattern of interdisciplinary studies of Gandhi noted here continued in the new century with a second enlarged edition of this book (2000) and a substantial biography by Rajmohan Gandhi, together with the intricate historical analysis of S. R. Mehrotra and an overview of Gandhi's meaning and relevance by David Hardiman entitled *Gandhi in His Time and Ours* (2003). Hardiman sought to "understand the reasons why Gandhi's ideas continue to resonate in the world today" and presented a perfect definition, in his preface and introduction, of Gandhi's theory and practice of inclusiveness. His analysis of *Hind Swaraj* disagrees at one point with my interpretation of the text (pages 20–21). He comments that I view *Hind Swaraj* as an "immature" representation of Gandhi's thought. He is correct; I do hold that this early treatise contains, to reiterate Parel's metaphor, "the seed from which the tree of Gandhian thought has grown to its full stature." An understanding of *Hind Swaraj* is unquestionably indispensable for any study of Gandhi, and Hardiman is right that it presents a dramatic, compelling critique of Western civilization. Yet even after the renewed attention that scholars like Parel and Mehrotra have recently given it, let us not overstate its place in the whole corpus of Gandhi's thought and practice. This tract is still no more than the seed that needed nearly forty more years of Gandhi's experience as a political leader and inspirational figure in India to fully ripen.

The main thrust of my book, regarding its assessment of Gandhi's theory and practice, is that two principal ideas are introduced in *Hind Swaraj* that gradually came to fruition in Gandhi's mature system. These are the concepts of freedom (swaraj) and power (satyagraha), ingeniously enforced by his emphasis on the relationship of means and ends. Gandhi's experimentation with the theory and practice of nonviolence ultimately produced original contributions to political thought. A long lifetime of intense engagement was utterly essential to this result. His evolving views on the institution of caste (pages 49–58), for example, show how greatly his mind changed during the decades after writing *Hind Swaraj*. This is only one instance. In terms of his essential ideas and their antinomies such as *purna swaraj* versus mere political independence, or of satyagraha versus *duragraha,* an exciting story unfolds of the intellectual transformation of a revolutionary thinker who could firmly declare that "it is the whole of Hinduism that has to be purified and purged" (see page 49). This is Gandhi writing about politics and religion in 1933. He had called satyagraha "a banyan tree with innumerable branches,"[40] and after 1917 the seed sown in South Africa did indeed blossom.

An excellent example of history well informed by theory is Mithi Mukherjee's "Transcending Identity: Gandhi, Nonviolence, and the Pursuit of a 'Different' Freedom in Modern India."[41] Mukherjee examines not only the distinctiveness of the Gandhian concept of freedom but also differences between Western ideas about freedom and those of several prominent modern Indian theorists. As this overview of the literature indicates, there is now a staunch company of Gandhi theorists from India, Britain, Australia, and the United States. Many of these join in the method of comparative theory with Bondurant and Iyer, albeit developing with their own distinctive variations by comparing Gandhi's thought with a range of Western political philosophers. Thomas Pantham, for example, wrote a resounding critique of liberal democracy and secularism in India that drew from Habermas and other Western philosophers, while Fred Dallmayr, in one of his articles on Gandhi, sought a definition of swaraj in part through Kant and Arendt. This philosophical analysis of Gandhi often profits from a fruitful exchange of ideas between historians and political and social theorists because the context of his activism is so crucial.

In 2006 a superb collection entitled *Debating Gandhi*, edited by A. Raghuramaraju, presented in one volume the extraordinary range of Gandhi analysis over the last four decades. It begins with A. L. Basham, historian of ancient India, who wrote in 1971 about Gandhi's debt to classical Hindu texts that he read and admired. There follows an array of wisdom on Gandhi in splendid articles by Ashis Nandy, Partha Chatterjee, and a pro and con exchange by Madhu Kishwar and Sujata Patel on the question of Gandhi's empowerment of women. Kishwar's contribution to the subject of Gandhi and feminism came in 1985 (see pages 118–119). Its superiority to the relatively superficial commentary by most American feminists came from her intimate knowledge of the historical context of Gandhi's India. It established her work as the standard against which all other writing on the subject should be measured. Hers is only one of the thirteen vital voices heard in this valuable selection.

This edition is followed by a prestigious collection, *The Cambridge Companion to Gandhi* (2011), appropriately edited by Brown and Parel—one the leading British historian of Gandhi, the other an outstanding political theorist. Their edition confirms the pattern noted earlier by offering a blend of philosophers and historians, including first-rate Gandhi theorists like Ronald Terchek—who excelled, like Raghavan Iyer and Bhikhu Parekh, in comparing Gandhi's thought with major Western political philosophers, focusing on the idea of autonomy—and Akeel Bilgrami, also included in Raghuramaraju's collection, who in 2002 published a challenging essay contrasting Gandhi and John Stuart Mill on the idea of truth. The assembly of historians is equally formidable: in addition to Thomas Weber and David Hardiman, the collection includes Yasmin Khan, who wrote a riveting study of partition, and Tanika Sarkar, author of the acclaimed *Hindu Wife, Hindu Nation* (2001).

A classic complement to the Cambridge companion is chapter 6 in the third edition of *Sources of Indian Tradition*, vol. II, which is on Gandhi (Columbia University Press, 2012). This is edited chiefly by Rachel McDermott, whose profound understanding of Hinduism is matched by her stellar teaching, with a team of experienced South Asia specialists: Leonard Gordon, Ainslie Embree, Frances Pritchett (Columbia's treasured Hindi and Urdu authority), and me. Suffice it to say that, as a member of this group for the last several years, it has been a genuine pleasure to learn from the expertise of these renowned scholars; just to witness Embree's intellectual range and vast personal reservoir of recollections from his long career as America's preeminent historian of India is an education on South Asia in itself.

All of these distinguished books on Gandhi, and many more too numerous to mention, attest to the phenomenal significance of this man, his thought and role as a leader. When the vast collection of works about him is joined to those relating to leaders that he inspired, especially Martin Luther King Jr., one realizes that the depth and range of material on nonviolent theory and practice rivals that of any other subject in the political history of the last century. Since the first edition of my book, there has been an explosion of literature by and about King. It is odd, though, that relatively little has been published comparing the ideas and leadership of Gandhi and King. Now a monumental project is underway with the publication of *The Papers of Martin Luther King Jr.*, edited by Clayborne Carson.[42] This source alone makes a higher-quality Gandhi-King comparison more feasible than before.

In addition, the subject of the so-called Americanization of Gandhi, or the preparation in the United States for a nonviolent movement before the emergence of King, must include journalists who descended on Gandhi, especially those from the United States, beginning with his civil disobedience campaign in 1930. They came mainly because they saw a good story.

Gandhi himself still ranks among history's most prolific and widely read print journalists. So he not only welcomed his kind but also gave them what they wanted.[43] Until recently, the best biography by a journalist had been Louis Fischer's in 1950. Now another distinguished American journalist, Joseph Lelyveld, a Pulitzer prize–winning *New York Times* correspondent who started covering India in the late 1960s, has published *Great Soul* (2011). This is a predictably fluent and fair story of the Mahatma's life, warts and all—hardly a hagiography—but like Fischer's book, it skillfully connects personal with political experience.

Serious scholarship on the Americanization of Gandhi began with Sudharshan Kapur's *Raising Up A Prophet: The African American Encounter with Gandhi* (1992). A decade later Leonard Gordon published "Mahatma Gandhi's Dialogues with Americans" in *Economic and Political Weekly* (January 2002). Although Gordon is known mainly for his intellectual history of modern Bengali thought (1974), once he turned his mind to Gandhian studies, he again provided valuable insights, especially into the significance of Gandhi's relationships with American missionaries and journalists. Joseph K. Kosek's *Acts of Conscience* (2009) has already been examined here. An excellent complement to Kosek is Sean Scalmer's *Gandhi in the West: The Mahatma and the Rise of Radical Protest* (2010) . It details with scrupulous documentation the rise of nonviolent activists from the aftermath of World War I to the early 1960s, in both the civil rights movement and the anti-nuclear campaign. It is a testimony to the reservoir of material on this period and subject that the works of Gordon, Scalmer, and Kosek are complementary, each valuable for understanding the theory and practice of nonviolent power in America before King. The philosopher Kwame Appiah's *The Honor Code: How Moral Revolutions Happen* (2010) evokes the idealist spirit of satyagraha without mentioning Gandhi, King, or nonviolence, but his argument still reinforces an optimistic theory of change that offers a persuasive counterbalance to the realism prominent in the discipline of international relations.

Another large category to be distinguished in Gandhi studies is what Thomas Weber calls the relationship between his "thought/praxis and conflict resolution."[44] The theoretical roots of the discipline of peace and conflict studies are found in the writings of Johan Galtung, a Norwegian sociologist who published with Arne Naess an analysis of Gandhi's "political ethics" in 1995. As noted above, Naess proceeded with *Gandhi and Group Conflict* (1974), but Galtung has been the more influential theorist by focusing on the means-end relationship and continues to dominate the field among Europeans.

By far the most prominent American theorist of conflict resolution is Gene Sharp, whose early work on Gandhi (1960), followed in 1973 by an encyclopedic examination of nonviolent tactics (noted earlier), has become legendary for his direct influence on revolts around the world. *From Dictatorship to Democracy*, which has been translated into thirty languages and is now in its fourth edition, has inspired dissent in Myanmar, Bosnia, Tunisia, and Egypt.[45]

Contemporary theorists-cum-activists in nonviolent conflict resolution include George Lakey, whose ideas of "waging nonviolence" have, like those of Phil and Daniel Berrigan in the 1960s, been consistently translated into praxis. Other inspired and committed efforts in this field are by Glenn Paige, an admirably unorthodox political scientist who, with Sharp, set forth a program of nonviolent conflict resolution called *Nonkilling Global Political Science*.[46] Paige, whose contributions to political theory predate even Gene Sharp's, established the Center for Global Nonkilling in 2009.

Michael Nagler, founder of the Peace and Conflict Studies Program at the University of California, Berkeley, wrote *The Search for a Nonviolent Future* (2004). This work is grounded in a long career of Gandhian activism and intimate knowledge of Gandhi's relevance for movement politics in America. Nagler's online Webinar on October 21, 2010, which explored Gandhi's significance for the environmental movement, is also pertinent (www.nonviolent-conflict.org). Another prominent scholar of peace studies who has written about Gandhi's legacy is David Cortright at the University of Notre Dame's Institute for Peace Studies. His *Gandhi and Beyond: Nonviolence for a New Age* (2009) offers constructive appraisals of the roles taken by leading American Gandhi activists such as Dorothy Day and Barbara Deming. In three cogent chapters of the book Cortright presents balanced judgments of the role of women in nonviolent movements, an often controversial topic (pages 203–204, 223–224). This topic has been addressed, too, by Weber in *Going Native: Gandhi's Relationship with Western Women* (2011), which features his characteristic in-depth and original mode of research.

I conclude this essay on a brief personal note. When I first arrived in India in 1960, Gandhi had been gone only twelve years. Many of his associates were alive and eager to discuss their reasons for joining the nationalist movement and choosing him as their leader. First and foremost among them were

Pyarelal and Sushila Nayar, his personal secretary and physician, respectively. For over four decades I lived in their homes and corresponded with them, commenting on their publications, regularly until their deaths. They not only inspired and read what I wrote about Gandhi, but through them, I was able to enter a network of Gandhiwallahs. What vivid memories I have of interviewing Vinoba Bhave, C. Rajagopalachari, and Maurice Frydman, as well as many of the Dandi marchers and former Congress leaders like Archarya Kripalani. This extraordinary group had dozens of unforgettable stories about the Mahatma, and it extended throughout the cities and villages of India and beyond, from Abdul Ghaffar Khan in Kabul to Mira Behn in Vienna, Horace Alexander in England, and Haridas Muzumdar in America. Everyone I interviewed had worked personally with Gandhi—some, like Frydman, Mirabehn, and the Dandi heroes having lived with him in his ashrams, joined him on the salt march, or like Nirmal Kumar Bose, observed his Calcutta and Delhi fasts, central dramas in his career.

It was my good fortune to be able to meet them, yet it saddens me to think that all of these participants in India's glorious freedom movement are now gone. Because of them, as much as any archival material or other literature that I have consulted, a strong affection for Gandhi runs through this volume. This sentiment was expressed eloquently by one of my informants, William Shirer, an American journalist who joined Gandhi in 1930 and wrote a memoir (see page 8). As he told me, Gandhi's thought and significance chiefly surrounded two vital human experiences: the power of love and the passion for liberation. This is one reason why I have made satyagraha and swaraj the twin themes of my book.

Notes

1. Originally published in *Foreign Affairs* in 1993, it has been frequently reprinted, first with a collection of seven critical assessments followed by a response by Huntington (1996), and most recently in James Hoge, ed., *The Clash of Civilizations? The Debate*, 2nd ed. (New York: Council on Foreign Relations, 2010), 1–32. This single article provoked a fierce and enduring debate both in and outside the field of political science and international relations, so that by 2010 two volumes devoted to the debate, including Huntington's reply, were published by *Foreign Affairs*. Hoge notes that the tide of commentary has not subsided, with Huntington's article remaining the most requested reprint from *Foreign Affairs*. Even these two anthologies on the debate do not include such exceedingly sharp critiques as, for example, Edward W. Said's "The Clash of Definitions" in *Reflections on Exile*

(Cambridge, Mass.: Harvard University Press, 2000), pages 569–589. Three years after his initial article, Huntington developed his thesis at length in a book with the same title but without the question mark: *The Clash of Civilizations and Remaking of World Order* (New York: Simon and Schuster, 1996). His argument engaged a wide range of political thinkers. Gandhian thought was missing from the debate until Martha Nussbaum's *The Clash Within: Democracy, Religious Violence, and India's Future* (Cambridge, Mass.: The Belknap Press of Harvard University Press, 2007). Although Nussbaum astutely employs Gandhi's example, her focus, as the subtitle indicates, is on the threat of Hindu extremism in India after his death.

In the case of two other notable theoretical analyses of democracy, Huntington and Gandhi are mentioned but their focus is not on the clash of civilizations debate: Ashutosh Varshney, "Why Democracy Survives," *Journal of Democracy* 9, no. 3 (1998): 36–50; and Amartya Sen, "Democracy as a Universal Value," *Journal of Democracy* 10, no. 3 (1999): 3–17. Likewise, Mark Juergensmeyer, in *Global Rebellion: Religious Challenges to the Secular State, from Christian Militias to al Qaeda* (Berkeley: University of California Press, 2008), a longtime Gandhi scholar, refers once to Huntington's position and only briefly to how Gandhi "applied religious [Hindu] concepts to political tactics" (Ibid., 105, 261), thus choosing not to engage him significantly in the debate or to emphasize that religious toleration was a main pillar of Gandhi's value system.

If a single article by Samuel Huntington, an international relations specialist who applied political theory to history, could prompt one of the most vigorous and sustained debates within the academy, then can scholars of conflict resolution, drawing especially from literature by and about Gandhi, enter this debate from the perspective of peace studies? The difficulty of this prospect is underscored by Adam Roberts and Timothy Ash, eds., *Civil Resistance and Power Politics. The Experience of Non-violent Action from Gandhi to the Present* (Oxford: Oxford University Press, 2009). In this book, no fewer than twenty-two often distinguished writers from various disciplines address the subject as part of the Oxford University Project on Civil Resistance and Power Politics. Gandhi is invoked throughout the collection and an entire chapter is devoted to him. The book, however, lacks an integrated or unified theoretical analysis of nonviolent power relating to "power politics." Evidently, a better marriage of theory and history will be needed to gather greater coherence and force if this subject is to be taken to a higher level of credibility in the rough field of international relations and political realism.

2. Samuel P. Huntington, "The Clash of Civilizations?" in *The Clash of Civilizations? The Debate*, ed. James Hoge (Foreign Affairs, 2010), 4–5.

3. Ibid., 13.

4. *CWMG* 51:129.

5. Martin Luther King Jr., *Stride Toward Freedom: The Montgomery Story* (New York: Harper, 1958), 102.

6. Said, "The Clash of Definitions," 577, 584.

7. Nussbaum, *The Clash Within*, 332.

8. *Gandhi: An Autobiography*, trans. Mahadev Desai (Boston: Beacon Press, 1993), xxvi.

9. Margaret Chatterjee, *Gandhi's Religious Thought* (Notre Dame: University of Notre Dame Press, 1983), 163.

10. A. M. Rosenthal, "On My Mind: Hindus Against Hindus," *New York Times*, March 5, 1993, A29.

11. M. K. Gandhi, *Hind Swaraj*, trans. Anthony J. Parel (Cambridge University Press, 1997), xiii. Hereafter cited in text.

12. *CWMG* 25:424.

13. Dennis Dalton, "Gandhi's Originality," in *Gandhi, Freedom, and Self-Rule*, ed. A. J. Parel (Lanham, M.D.: Lexington Books, 2000).

14. M. K. Gandhi, *Hind Swaraj*, ed. S. R. Mehrotra (New Delhi: Promilla Publishers, 2010).

15. Ibid., 9.

16. Tolstoy quoted in S. R. Mehrotra, *Towards India's Freedom and Partition* (New Delhi: Vikas, 1979), 39; and Gandhi, *Hind Swaraj*, trans. Parel, 139.

17. Mehrotra, *Towards India's Freedom and Partition*, 11, 28–29, 82.

18. *Letter to a Hindoo: Taraknath Das, Leo Tolstoi and Mahatma Gandhi*, ed. Christian Bartolf (Berlin: Gandhi Information-Zentrum, 1997).

19. Gandhi to Ampthill, October 30, 1909, quoted in Mehrotra, *Towards India's Freedom and Partition*, 33, 35; and in Gandhi, *Hind Swaraj*, trans. Parel, 133–135.

20. Gandhi to Polak, October 14, 1909, quoted in Mehrotra, *Towards India's Freedom and Partition*, 27; and in Gandhi, *Hind Swaraj*, trans. Parel, 132.

21. Mehrotra, *Towards India's Freedom and Partition*, 70.

22. Martin Luther King Jr., *Stride Toward Freedom* (New York: Harper, 1958), 176.

23. Faisal Devji, *The Terrorist in Search of Humanity: Militant Islam and Global Politics* (Columbia University Press, 2008). Hereafter cited in text.

24. See, for a more extensive discussion in this book, pages 134–139 and 228–230.

25. *CWMG* 25:563, 54:416–17.

26. King, *Stride Toward Freedom*, 103.

27. Malcolm X, *Autobiography* (New York: Ballantine Books, 1999), 436.

28. Joseph Kip Kosek, *Acts of Conscience: Christian Nonviolence and Modern American Democracy* (Columbia University Press, 2009).

29. Samuel P. Huntington, "The Clash of Civilizations?" *Foreign Affairs* 72, no. 3 (Summer 1993): 49.

30. Samuel P. Huntington, *The Clash of Civilizations and the Remaking of World Order* (New York: Simon and Schuster, 1998), 321.

31. Wendy Brown, *Regulating Aversion: Tolerance in the Age of Identity and Empire* (Princeton University Press, 2006), 202.

32. Ibid., 7.

33. Said, "The Clash of Definitions," 589.

34. Gandhi, *Hind Swaraj*, trans. Parel, 66–67.

35. Tolstoy quoted in R. N. Iyer, *The Moral and Political Thought of Mahatma Gandhi* (New York: Oxford University Press, 1973), 24. See also *The Moral and Political Writings of Mahatma Gandhi* (Oxford: Clarendon Press of Oxford University Press, 1986), especially vol. 1, chapter 4, "Hind Swaraj, Modern Civilization and Moral Progress," pages 199–369.

36. For one instance of the remarkably candid exchange between Gandhi and Nehru, see the 1945 volume of *Towards Freedom, 1937–1947*, ed. Bimal Prasad (New York: Oxford University Press, 2009). Gandhi's unchanging commitment to *Hind Swaraj* was met with Nehru's brusque dismissal that its views were "completely unreal" (Ibid., xxiii).

37. Howard Gardner, *Creating Minds* (New York: Basic Books, 1993), 355.

38. The second work is Bhikhu Parekh, *Gandhi: A Very Short Introduction* (New York: Oxford University Press, 2001).

39. Thomas Weber, *On the Salt March* (New Delhi: HarperCollins, 1997), and "Gandhian Philosophy, Conflict Resolution Theory and Practical Approaches to Negotiation," *Journal of Peace Studies* 38, no. 4 (2001): 493–513.

40. *CWMG* 15:244.

41. Mithi Mukherjee, "Transcending Identity: Gandhi, Nonviolence, and the Pursuit of a 'Different' Freedom in Modern India," *American Historical Review* 115, no. 2 (April 2010): 453–473.

42. *The Papers of Martin Luther King, Jr.*, ed. Clayborne Carson, vols. 1–6 (1929–1963) (Berkeley: University of California Press, 1992, ongoing).

43. See pages 107–108 and 221, note 66, in this book.

44. Thomas Weber, "Gandhian Philosophy, Conflict Resolution Theory and Practical Approaches to Negotiation," *Journal of Peace Research* 38, no. 4 (2001): 493–513.

45. Gene Sharp, "Shy U.S. Intellectual Created Playbook Used in a Revolution" *New York Times*, Feb 16, 2011. See also Sharp's Web site, www.aeinstein.org.

46. Glenn Paige's *Nonkilling Global Political Science* (Xlibris, 2009) has been translated into over thirty languages. See also www.nonkilling.org.

1869: Mohandas Karamchand Gandhi, son of Karamchand and Putlibai Gandhi, was born on October 2, the youngest of three sons, in Porbandar (population 72,000) on the western coast of India, now in the state of Gujarat. The family was of the Vaisya caste, meaning that it was on a lower rung of the caste hierarchy, usually associated with commerce. But his family did not lack prestige or income: his father served as prime minister in Porbandar and the region of Rajkot. His mother was his father's fourth wife.

1876–1887: Gandhi was educated at primary school and Alfred High School in Rajkot until twelfth year. He was betrothed to Kasturbai Makanji in 1876 and married in 1882, when they were both thirteen. In 1884 he experimented with eating meat and then severely regretted it, becoming a lifelong vegetarian.

1888: Harilal, the first of his four children (all sons), was born. The others were Manilal (1892), Ramdas (1897), and Devadas (1900). On September 8 Gandhi sailed for England to study law, with the support of his family but in the face of strong disapproval from his caste elders, who forbade travel abroad.

1888–1891: On November 6 he enrolled as a law student at the Inner Temple in London, and in June 1891 he was called to the bar and enrolled in the High Court of Justice in London. During this period he met H. P. Blavatsky and Annie Besant of the Theosophical Society and became a member. Although he had previously read the *Bhagavad Gita*, he now gained a deeper understanding of this supreme sacred text of Hinduism. Later he gained inspiration from the Sermon on the Mount. On June 12 he sailed for India.

1892–1893: He failed to practice law successfully at home, so he left India for South Africa to be a legal adviser to Dada Abdullah & Company, where he would represent members of the Indian community there. But in June 1893 he experienced brutal racial prejudice when he was thrown off a train from Durban to Pretoria. He later recalled this event as a moment of truth that motivated him to combat racial discrimination through the South African courts and in the press.

1894: He studied religious literature, including the Koran and the Bible, as well as the writings of Leo Tolstoy. The latter's *Kingdom of God Is Within You* "overwhelmed" him, as he put it in his autobiography, by strongly confirming his faith in nonviolence. On August 22 he organized the Natal Indian Congress (on the model of the Indian National Congress founded in 1885), to oppose discriminatory legislation against South African Indians. He began his twenty-year career in law there by enrolling as a barrister in the high courts of Natal and the Transvaal against the disapproval of European lawyers.

1896–1897: Gandhi sailed to India to mobilize support for Indians in South Africa, but on his return he was attacked by a mob in Durban and barely escaped serious injury.

1899: He organized the Indian Ambulance Corps to provide medical support in the Boer War with the English colonial government.

1904: After establishing a successful law practice in Johannesburg and launching *Indian Opinion*, he was influenced by reading John Ruskin's *Unto This Last* and founded the Phoenix Settlement, his first ashram, near Durban to begin experiments in simple living.

1906: He again supported the English South African government by organizing an ambulance corps to support the suppression of the so-called Zulu Rebellion in June. After he witnessed British brutality toward the Zulus, he deemed the event not a revolt but a massacre. Bitterly disillusioned, he became deeply introspective. Erik Erikson, in his psychobiography of Gandhi, analyzed the profound personal impact of this moment (see page 171). In July he took a vow of chastity *(brahmacharya)* to gain greater self-discipline. On September 11 he addressed a mass meeting of Indians at the Empire Theater in Johannesburg to urge civil disobedience against repressive government legislation that required registration of Indians. Later he recalled this date as the "advent of *satyagraha*," or direct nonviolent action.

1907: Not until a year after this first act of resistance in South Africa did Gandhi read Henry David Thoreau's famous treatise "On the Duty of Civil Disobedience," but once he discovered it, Gandhi acknowledged Thoreau, often later, as the inventor of civil disobedience and among "the greatest and most moral men America has produced" (*CWMG* 7:279).

1908: Imprisoned in January and again from October to December for civil resistance. He now adopted the term *satyagraha*, or "truth-force" (as he often defined it), signifying the power of nonviolence when employed in the cause of truth and love. On February 10 he was assaulted and nearly killed by a member of his own Indian community, an ominous foreshadowing of his assassination 40 years later by a Hindu. In the 1908 case, though, Gandhi lived to ask that his assailants be forgiven and to witness their repentance.

1909: After being arrested again and released, he sailed for a five month visit to London, where he carried on a sustained dialogue with Indian terrorists, led by V. D. Savarkar, and English friends like Lord Ampthill who were sympathetic to his cause of Indian freedom. From these exchanges, and inspired by close friends such as P. J. Mehta (see my afterword), he wrote his classic treatise *Hind Swaraj*, an ideological proclamation of Indian independence, while sailing back to South Africa in November.

1910: In April he sent Tolstoy a copy of *Hind Swaraj* (translated as *Indian Home Rule)*, and Tolstoy replied in May that Gandhi was addressing "a question of the greatest importance not only for India but for the whole [of] humanity." Gandhi then established near Johannesburg his second ashram, called Tolstoy Farm, to train and accommodate civil resisters.

1913: Civil disobedience was revived in South Africa, first by Kasturbai, Gandhi's wife, who was imprisoned for three months of hard labor, and then by Gandhi, who led a march of over 2,000 Indian coal miners and workers on sugar plantations—men, women and children—to protest discriminatory legislation and abusive work conditions. The march lasted from November 6 to 10, after which Gandhi was sentenced to nine months imprisonment with hard labor for inducing a mass strike. He was released, however, in December in order to negotiate with his main adversary, General J. C. Smuts, leader of the South African government.

1914: On January 22 Gandhi negotiated with Smuts favorable terms for the Indian community, so civil disobedience was suspended, and on July 18 Gandhi sailed for London en route to India, leaving South Africa for the last time. He arrived in England on August 6, two days after World War I began, and he stayed in London.

1915: He arrived in Bombay on January 9, and by May 20 had established his third ashram, called the Satyagraha Ashram, located in Sabarmati, near Ahmedabad in Gujarat. He resumed his campaign for the abolition of untouchability, admitting an untouchable family to Satyagraha Ashram.

1917: After touring India and Burma in 1916 to familiarize himself with the political situation in South Asia, he began in April 1917 to work on the problems of indigo farmers in Champaran, a district in a remote northern part of India. By October he had concluded his first satyagraha campaign in India, mobilizing sharecroppers to protest unjust labor conditions, and a settlement favorable to the poor peasantry was reached with the indigo planters.

1918: In February he presided over the annual gathering of Bhagini Samaj in Bombay to promote women's education and empowerment, a prominent cause especially in the civil disobedience campaign of 1930 (see pages 118–119). From February to March he launched a satyagraha in Ahmedabad on behalf of mill workers, and resorted to a fast to reach a settlement with employers. After these sustained uses of satyagraha, he uncharacteristically decided to support the British war effort by trying to raise Indian recruits for the British armed forces. His expectation that this would prompt a sympathetic response from the English, who might make concessions toward India's independence, was disappointed and led to his disillusionment with the empire the next year.

1919: Oppressive legislation by the British government in India (the Raj) prompted Gandhi to announce on February 24 his intention to lead the first nation-wide satyagraha campaign. In March he issued his "Satyagraha Leaflet," in which he quoted Henry David Thoreau, and on April 6 he inaugurated the all-India Satyagraha movement with a general strike, or *hartal*. The government reacted immediately by arresting Gandhi on April 10. Outbreaks of violence ensued, and the Raj now used maximum force. On April 13, in the city of Amritsar, a crowd of 10,000 gathered in the town square to celebrate a religious holiday. General Reginald Dyer, who had earlier imposed martial law, interpreted this as defiance and, marching his troops into the square, fired on the assembly without warning, killing 400 and wounding 1,500. He followed up this attack with acts of public humiliation that were intended to compel Indian repentance. C. F. Andrews, Gandhi's close friend, wrote that the "Amritsar massacre" turned Gandhi into a revolutionary, though one still firmly committed to nonviolence. On April 18 Gandhi suspended satyagraha to prevent further violence.

1920: Gandhi led meetings of the Indian National Congress to adopt programs of noncooperation to redress the wrongs inflicted on India by the Raj and to declare its objective to be the attainment of independence, or swaraj, by peaceful means.

1921: The mass campaign of satyagraha began in December after a year of extensive mobilization through the Indian National Congress, which Gandhi had transformed into a full-scale grassroots organization throughout the country. Many Congress leaders were arrested in the campaign.

1922: After a mob of Indians killed twenty-two police officers on February 5 in the town of Chauri Chaura, Gandhi fasted for five days in protest against the violence. Against the advice of Congress leaders, he stopped the entire satyagraha campaign, having determined that the participants were not sufficiently disciplined to sustain the movement nonviolently. The government responded by arresting him for sedition on March 10 and then, after a dramatic trial, sentencing him to six years' imprisonment. He was released, however, in 1924, after having surgery in prison for appendicitis.

1924: Gandhi advocated for the cause of Hindu-Muslim unity, culminating in a twenty-one day fast to improve relations between these communities, which ended on October 8.

1925: He began writing his autobiography, entitled *The Story of My Experiments with Truth*, and published serial entries in his newspaper, *Young India*. The installments—written in Gujarati, his native language—were completed in February 1929.

1927: He advocated the wearing of homespun cloth, or *khadi*, and made this a vital part of swaraj, because it represented freedom from British manufactured clothing and a simple way of life in solidarity with the poor. He regarded this as part of his "Constructive Program" for social reform, which also included his promotion of the spinning wheel (*charka*) as a symbol of welfare for all. He toured the country extensively from January to November. See the glossary for definitions of terms like *charka, khadi, sarvodaya,* and *swadeshi* and their association with swaraj.

1928–1929: Vallabhbhai (Sardar) Patel led a campaign against the payment of property taxes in the region of Bardoli, in Gujarat, with Gandhi's support. Its success inspired Gandhi to plan a nation-wide tax resistance movement. On December 27, 1929, at the annual meeting of the Indian Congress in Lahore, Gandhi was fully empowered to inaugurate the next national civil disobedience campaign in 1930.

1930: At age 61, Gandhi began the most energetic political movement of his life. First, a declaration of independence prepared by him was proclaimed throughout India on January 26. Then in mid-February, in opposition to skeptical members of the Working Committee of the Indian Congress, he alone decided on his plan of action. He unexpectedly selected the government tax on salt rather than property to be the campaign issue, and a march to the seacoast, over a distance of over 240 miles and taking about twenty-four days, as the method of protest. On March 2 he wrote an eloquent letter to the Viceroy, Lord Edward Irwin, giving the precise details of his plan. As the government, torn by ambivalence, hesitated to arrest him, Gandhi commenced his civil disobedience campaign by leaving his ashram at Sabarmati on March 12 and marching with eighty members of his ashram to the village of Dandi on the coast of western India. There, on April 6, he defied the government tax on salt by collecting natural salt deposits from the sea. Although the action was heavily symbolic, it inspired millions of Indians to break the law by following his example. Finally, on May 5, the government belatedly arrested and imprisoned Gandhi without trial, along with over one hundred thousand other satyagrahis, both men and women. The movement had been launched and was now surging toward swaraj (see chapter 4).

1931: Gandhi was released together with other Congress leaders on January 26. Direct negotiations between Gandhi and Lord Irwin followed and a pact was signed that enabled Gandhi to attend a round table conference in London from September 12 to December 5. The conference failed to reach an agreement on Gandhi's demand for India's complete independence.

1932: When Gandhi returned to India, he was immediately arrested in Bombay on January 4. While in prison, he fasted from September 20 to 26 to protest the government policy of "separate electorates" for untouchables. Gandhi interpreted this plan as being potentially divisive, invidiously institutionalizing untouchability instead of breaking down its barriers. He was opposed by B. R. Ambedkar, leader of the untouchable community. (Gandhi referred to untouchables as "harijans," or children of God, the Raj called them "scheduled castes," and today they are known as "dalits," or downtrodden). In the face of

Gandhi's weakening condition, Ambedkar and caste Hindus alike signed the Poona Pact, a compromise that granted all sides some satisfaction.

1933–1934: Released from prison unconditionally on August 23, Gandhi plunged into his campaign against the institution of untouchability with renewed vigor throughout 1934, announcing his decision on September 17, 1934, to retire from politics to devote himself to Harijan service and basic education. On October 30 he resigned from the Indian National Congress.

1936–1939: On April 30 he settled in his last ashram, called Sevagram (village of service), near Wardha in central India's Maharashtra state. He made it his headquarters and the prime example of his commitment to social reforms. An educational conference was held there in October, 1937, and he constantly appealed for social change in the form of his "three pillars of swaraj": abolition of untouchability, Hindu-Muslim unity, and economic equality. He emphasized his commitment to the revival of cottage industries through khadi production and made Sevagram a demonstration of the simplicity that Thoreau had exemplified.

1940: As a pacifist, Gandhi opposed World War II and India's forced participation in it as a colony without representation. On October 17 he launched a limited civil disobedience campaign to register his opposition, now assuming again an active role in the Indian Congress.

1941: Gandhi divided his efforts between social reform and political independence. On the one hand, he intensified his work on swadeshi, khadi, caste, and untouchability; on the other, as the relations between the Raj and the Congress deteriorated over the war, he was drawn into the politics of negotiating with Britain. Regarding the former, he published *Constructive Programme* in December 1941, his comprehensive statement of social reform.

1942–1944: It was politics that ultimately consumed him, especially as the prospect loomed of a divided British India, a "vivisection," as he called it, of his country into separate nations for Hindus and Muslims. After negotiations over independence with Sir Stafford Cripps broke down in March 1942, he launched his last national civil disobedience movement, proposing his "Quit India" resolution to the Indian Congress on August 8. Millions responded to this call for the British to leave India, and the Raj's repression was harsh. Gandhi, along with Congress leaders, were arrested and imprisoned from August 9, 1942, until May 6, 1944. During this time in prison, Kasturbai remained with him, but she contracted pneumonia and died, ending their sixty years of marriage on February 22, 1944.

1945–1946: After Gandhi's release from prison, the political scene surrounding independence—especially the idea of partitioning India advanced by M. A. Jinnah, leader of the Muslim League—preoccupied him. With Congress leaders in prison, the whole organization had been immobilized, while the Muslim League had mobilized the Muslim-majority areas of northern India behind its demand for a separate nation of Pakistan. Gandhi's direct talks with Jinnah in September 1944 had failed, nor could there be any resolution of the conflict at conferences of the Raj and Congress and Muslim League leaders in Simla in June 1945 and May 1946. Negotiations continued without success until August 16, 1946, when suddenly the national situation was cruelly crystallized. With the

Great Calcutta Killing, when mass violence consumed that city for four days, the threat of civil war became a reality. Four thousand Hindus and Muslims were slaughtered and eleven thousand injured. Religious (or "communal") violence spread through Bengal, and Gandhi responded by trying to calm its villages, walking 116 miles through the remote area of Noakhali in November and December. Later, he turned to Bihar with the same purpose.

1947: India attained independence on August 15, but it was not the swaraj that Gandhi envisaged. Instead, British India was divided into two nations, with Pakistan the country of Islam. As the civil war metastasized from Bengal and Bihar to Delhi and the Punjab, Gandhi focused on Calcutta, where for an entire year acute urban violence had been endemic. In desperation he fasted from September 1 to 4 for Hindu-Muslim unity. His success was dramatic, and "the miracle of Calcutta" was proclaimed as one of his greatest feats of nonviolent action (see chapter 5).

1948: Gandhi fasted in New Delhi from January 13 to 18 to overcome communal violence there. He declared, "I do not wish to live if peace is not established in India and Pakistan." On January 30, on the way to prayers, he was assassinated by a Hindu fanatic, Nathuram Vinayak Godse. The sole motive, as Godse declared unrepentantly in his trial testimony, was Gandhi's tolerance of Muslims. Yet the consequence of this murder was that at a stroke, the civil war came to a halt. Indian Hindus could not bear the shame that Gandhi had been killed by one of their own.

Introduction

1. M. K. Gandhi, *The Collected Works of Mahatma Gandhi* [hereafter, *CWMG*], Publications Division, Ministry of Information and Broadcasting, Government of India, 1961, 10, p. 64; and M. K. Gandhi, *Hind Swarajya* (Ahmedabad, Navijivan, Prakashan Mandir Publishing House), 1979, p. 269–271. The latter is a photostatic copy of Gandhi's original handwritten text in Gujarati. The present author is indebted to Pyarelal Nayar, D. G. Dave, and Sita N. Kapadia for their assistance in translating and interpreting the Gujarati text, and for the former's interpretation of satyagraha as "power." Although Gandhi himself translated satyagraha as "truth-force," it is suggested here that "power" is a preferable translation because "force" is often associated with violence. The specific identification of satyagraha as a form of power accords with the valuable analysis of power in Gene Sharp, *The Politics of Nonviolent Action* (Boston: Porter Sargent, 1973), pp. 3-48. See Gandhi's discussion of power in Pyarelal, *Mahatma Gandhi: The Last Phase*, vol. 2 (Ahmedabad: Navajivan, 1958), pp. 630–633.

2. *CWMG* 83: 180

3. *CWMG* 45: 263–264.

4. The Sanskrit pronoun *sva* means "own, one's own, my own, or self." (Sir M. Monier-Williams, *A Sanskrit-English Dictionary*, New Edition, Oxford, Clarendon, 1899, pp. 1275- 1276). Thus *sva-raj* स्वराज् as used in Vedic texts signified "self-ruling," "self-

ruling," "self-ruler," one's own rule. *Sva* becomes *swa* with most modern Indian writers, with *svarajya* (self-rule) as the Sanskrit substantive. The *Rig Veda* and *Atharvaveda* used *svaraj* in the political sense of "self-ruler" and usually "king." This kingship could be either divine or terrestrial, applying to Indra, "king" of the gods, or occasionally to earthly kings of western India. (A. A. MacDonell and A. B. Keith, *Vedic Index of Names and Subjects* (London, John Murray, 1912), 2: 494; *Aitareya Brahmana* VIII. 14. in Mac-Donell and Keith, ibid., p. 494. For complete reference see *Rigveda Brahmanas, The Aitareya and Kausitaki Brahmanas of the Rig-Veda*, translated by A. B. Keith, Harvard Oriental Series, 30 volumes (Cambridge: Harvard University Press, 1920), 25: 330.

5. *The Bhagavad-Gita*, 2: 71–72, translated by Barbara Stoler Miller (New York: Bantam, 1986), p. 39. The meaning of freedom in this sense need not exclude kings or political leaders because they may possess also the spiritual qualities of self-rule. Barbara Miller examines the idea of the "royal sage," a leader of spiritual power and knowledge in *Theater of Memory* (New York: Columbia University Press, 1984), pp, 8–9.

6. *Chandogya Upanishad*, VII, 25, 2, in *The Principal Upanishads*, edited by S. Radhakrishnan (London: George Allen and Unwin, 1969), p. 488. Those who do not possess knowledge of self and of the universal Self "have no freedom" and are "subject to others (*anya-raj*)." This concept of spiritual freedom may be compared and contrasted with the idea expressed in Christ's maxim, "And ye shall know the truth and the truth shall make you free." St. John. 8:32.

7. *Bhagavad-Gita*, VI, 29, p. 66, and XIII, 30, p. 119.

8. Dadabhai Naoroji, *Speeches and Writings* (Madras: G.A. Natesan, 1910), p. 76. Bal Gangadhar Tilak, *Writings and Speeches* (Madras: Ganesh & Co., 1918), pp. 97–115, 152–53.

9. Aurobindo Ghose, "Ideals Face to Face," in *Bande Mataram*, May 3, 1908, as contained in Haridas and Uma Mukherjee, *Bande Mataram and Indian Nationalism* (1906–1908) (Calcutta: Firma K. L. Mukhopadhyay, 1957), pp. 84–85.

10. B. C. Pal, *Writings and Speeches* (Calcutta: Vugayatri Prakashak Ltd., 1958), pp. 75–77. And Madan Gopal Sinha, *The Political Ideas of Bipin Chandra Pal* (Delhi, Commonwealth Publishers, 1989), pp. 35–36.

11. *CWMG* 89: 356.

12. Isaiah Berlin, "Two Concepts of Liberty" in *Four Essays on Liberty* (New York, Oxford University Press, 1984), pp. 131–166. For comparison of these Europeans with Gandhi, see: Joan Bondurant, *Conquest of Violence* (Princeton: Princeton University Press, 1988), pp. 161–164, 211–214; Raghavan N. Iyer, *The Moral and Political Thought of Mahatma Gandhi* (New York: Oxford University Press, 1973), pp. 115–118, 236, 346–357; W. H. Morris-Jones, "Mahatma Gandhi—Political Philosopher?" in *Political Studies*, 7 (1) (1960): 16–36; Bhikhu Parekh, *Gandhi's Political Philosophy* (Notre Dame, Indiana: University of Notre Dame Press, 1989), pp. 33–34.

13. Sri Aurobindo Ghose, *The Ideal of Human Unity* In *The Human Cycle, The Ideal of Human Unity and War and Self-Determination* (Pondicherry, India: Sri Aurobindo Ashram), 1962, pp. 564–566. These volumes first appeared serially in the journal *Arya* in 1915–1920. Revised editions appeared in 1950.

14. The ideas of Aurobindo Ghose are examined further in the author's *Indian Idea of Freedom* (Gurgaon, India: The Academic Press, 1982), pp. 85–126; and also "The Idea of

Freedom in the Political Thought of Vivekananda and Aurobindo," *South Asian Affairs. The Movement for National Freedom in India.* St. Anthony's Papers No. 18, S. N. Mukherjee, ed. (London: Oxford University Press, 1966), pp. 34–45. These two writings emphasize what has not been discussed here, the critical influence of Swami Vivekananda, who wrote a decade before either Aurobindo Ghose or B. C. Pal formulated their ideas on freedom: "That ideal of freedom that you perceived was correct, but you projected it outside yourself, and that was your mistake. Bring it nearer and nearer, until you find that it was all the time within you, it was the Self of your own self." *The Complete Works of Swami Vivekananda,* 8 volumes (Calcutta: Advaita Vedanta Ashram, 1952) 2: 128. Vivekananda had a direct and profound influence on Ghose especially.

   15. *CWMG* 69: 52.
   16. *CWMG* 35: 294.
   17. *CWMG* 38: 1–2
   18. *CWMG* 38: 18.
   19. Iyer, *The Moral and Political Thought of Mahatma Gandhi,* p. 354. In another place, Iyer offers an incisive explanation of Gandhi's ideas of freedom and *swaraj:* "Freedom for Gandhi was neither a condition granted by some social contract nor a gratuitous privilege; freedom was grounded in the moral autonomy of the individual and was thus inalienable. Furthermore, he saw freedom as a social necessity which cannot be severed from its roots in the individual psyche; only a society based on some minimal degree of awakened individual conscience can sustain itself for long. Freedom as an inherent characteristic of human nature is true *swaraj* or self-rule. The social and institutional dimensions of *swaraj* are enormously dependent upon the individual dimension. Thus, while *swaraj* is open equally to individuals and to groups, its first step lies in individual consciousness. National self-rule has the same exacting requirements for its nurture and sustenance as individual self-rule. . . . *Swaraj* in its fullest sense is perfect freedom from all bondage and, for Gandhi, it could be equated with *moksha* or liberation. But, like that knowledge which can be gained even as one becomes increasingly aware of the scope of one's ignorance, *swaraj* is attainable by degrees so long as its achievements are measured honestly against ideals. This is possible because *swaraj* on the individual level involves perforce self-awareness and conscious choice." *The Moral and Political Writings of Mahatma Gandhi,* Raghavan Iyer, ed. (Oxford, Clarendon Press, 1987), 3 ("Introduction"): 8–9.
   20. *CWMG* 27: 134.
   21. Gloria Steinem's discussion of Gandhi's life suggests that his personal journey offers parallels with a woman's struggle for freedom and self-esteem when faced with sexual oppression. She conveys the meaning of Gandhi's call for "reform from within" in her *Revolution From Within* (Boston: Little, Brown, 1992), pp. 49–53. Not all American feminists have shared Steinem's enthusiasm for Gandhi. Carol Gilligan argues that Gandhi was led "in the guise of love, to impose his truth on others without awareness of or regard for the extent to which he thereby did violence to their integrity." Citing Gandhi's own autobiographical confessions of his mistreatment of his wife, Gilligan concludes that "Gandhi compromised in his everyday life the ethic of nonviolence to which, in principle and in public, he steadfastly adhered." *In a Different Voice* (Cambridge: Harvard University Press, 1982), pp. 103–105, 155). This negative appraisal of Gandhi is rein-

forced by Judy Costello, "Beyond Gandhi: An American Feminist's Approach to Nonviolence" but countered by the more careful reading of Gandhi by Lynne Shivers, "An Open Letter to Gandhi," both essays in *Reweaving the Web of Life*, edited by Pam McAllister (Philadelphia: New Society Publishers, 1982), pp. 175–194. Steinem's application of Gandhi's ideas to the concerns and values of feminists today is shared in large part by Shivers and also by Sara Ruddick, *Maternal Thinking: Toward a Politics of Peace* (New York: Ballantine Books, 1989), especially ch. 7, pp. 160–174 and Pam McAllister, *You Can't Kill the Spirit* (Philadelphia: New Society Publishers, 1988), pp. 1–5. An American feminist who expressed Gandhi's ideas in action is Barbara Deming, *We Are All Part of One Another: A Barbara Deming Reader*, Jane Meyerding, ed. (Philadelphia: New Society Publishers, 1984). Her essay "On Anger" has become a classic of its kind, especially the use of Gandhi on pp. 210–213. A deficiency in the writing of American feminists about Gandhi is that they often do not assess his ideas or experience within their historical context; that is, the precise ways that he tried to apply his ideas about the role of women in India. This study has been done by Indian feminists who have related their concerns about women in their society to a thorough analysis of Gandhi's contribution. The work of Madhu Kishwar (noted below in chapter 4, pp. 118–19) is exemplary in this regard.

22. *CWMG* 24: 227.
23. *CWMG* 75: 158.
24. *CWMG* 36: 470.
25. *CWMG* 31: 46.
26. *CWMG* 75: 158.
27. William Shirer, *Gandhi: A Memoir.* (New York: Simon and Schuster, 1979) p. 245.
28. *CWMG* 29: 92.
29. Bhikhu Parekh argues that *agraha* was used by Gandhi "in its ordinary Gujarati and not the classical Sanskrit sense, [that] means insisting on something without becoming obstinate or uncompromising" which then denotes "both insistence on and for truth." *Gandhi's Political Philosophy* (Indiana: University of Notre Dame Press, 1989), p. 143. These two connotations from Gujarati and Sanskrit are complementary and Parekh's point highlights the distinction that Gandhi made between passive resistance (or *duragraha*) and *satyagraha*: the former in Gandhi's view was "obstinate or uncompromising."
30. *CWMG* 54: 416.
31. *CWMG* 10: 431. Analysts of Gandhi's thought have focused on the centrality of his theory of means. Joan Bondurant devotes careful attention to this in *Conquest of Violence* (Princeton: Princeton University Press, 1988), especially chapter 7, pp. 189–233, which begins "The challenge of Gandhian *satyagraha* centers upon the necessity of reconciling ends and means through a philosophy of action." Raghavan Iyer offers a cogent analysis of the subject in *The Moral and Political Thought of Mahatma Gandhi*, chapter 13, arguing that "Gandhi seems to stand almost alone among social and political thinkers in his firm rejection of the rigid dichotomy between ends and means and in his extreme preoccupation with the means to the extent that they, rather than the ends, provide the standard of reference" (p. 361).
32. *CWMG* 25: 480.
33. *CWMG* 25: 424.

34. *CWMG* 37: 250–251.
35. *CWMG* 15: 244.
36. *CWMG* 21: 457.
37. *CWMG* 33: 247.
38. *CWMG* 19: 466.
39. *CWMG* 16: 409.
40. *CWMG* 46: 216.

Chapter 1

1. *CWMG* 29: 92.
2. *CWMG* 7: 43.
3. *CWMG* 7: 108.
4. *CWMG* 6: 336, 385. 7: 65, 73–74, 130, 453.
5. *CWMG* 5: 27, 50, 84, 111.
6. *CWMG* 5: 419–420.
7. *CWMG* 7: 67.
8. *CWMG*, 39: 254–255.
9. Stephen N. Hay examines this point in depth: "Jain Influences on Gandhi's Early Thought," in Sibnaryan Ray, ed. *Gandhi, India and the Word* (Melbourne: The Hawthorn Press, 1970), pp. 29–37. Hay stresses Gandhi's concern for the "Jain ideal of *moksha*," or liberation (34, 36).
10. *CWMG* 7: 455.
11. *CWMG*, 29: 92. Gandhi relates the result of this contest in his Autobiography: "As a result Maganlal Gandhi coined the word 'Sadagraha' (Sat-truth, Agraha-firmness) and won the prize. But in order to make it clearer I changed the word to 'Satyagraha'." *CWMG*, 39: 255.
12. B. R. Nanda, *Mahatma Gandhi* (Bombay: Allied, 1958), p. 121.
13. *CWMG*, 29: 27–28, 32–34.
14. Ibid., p. 60.
15. Ibid., p. 61.
16. *CWMG* 33: 165.
17. The chief influences on Gandhi's thought during his South African experience, aside from the Sermon on the Mount and the *Gita*, came from Tolstoy's *The Kingdom of God is Within You*, Ruskin's *Unto This Last*, and Thoreau's essay *On Civil Disobedience*. The two main personal influences were both Indian: Rajchandbhai, a Jain religious teacher, and G. K. Gokhale. Gandhi also read Vivekananda, and was sufficiently impressed to have tried (unsuccessfully) to see him while in Calcutta. The actual extent of any of these influences on Gandhi's thought is difficult to determine for he gave to each a personal twist, using it as he saw fit.
18. *Hind Swaraj or Indian Home Rule* is published in various editions and appears in *CWMG*, 10: 6–68. It has inspired copious commentary. Among the most incisive analyses are: James D. Hunt, *Gandhi in London* (New Delhi: Promilla and Company, 1978), pp. 155–172. Hunt calls it "the most imaginative, intense and idiosyncratic" of Gandhi's

writings. From another perspective, Erik Erikson, *Gandhi's Truth* (New York: Norton, 1969), pp. 217–226 says "that the whole imagery evoked here harbors a fantasy of the kind which usually breaks through in a dream, and one wonders whether the sea-voyage did create a special state of consciousness in the writer." P. van den Dungen, *Essays on Gandhian Politics* R. Kumar, ed. (Oxford: Clarendon Press, 1971) examines the decisive nature of the 1905 to 1909 period in Gandhi's intellectual development and asserts that the ideas in *Hind Swaraj* represent "the culmination of four and a half years of thought" that marked the basis of his revolutionary attitude toward the British empire and his willingness to use *satyagraha* (pp. 54–63). Partha Chatterjee presents an original analysis of *Hind Swaraj* in *Nationalist Thought in the Colonial World*, London, Zed Books, 1986. He argues that Gandhi saw "the source of modern imperialism" in its "system of social production," and "spirit of ruthless competitiveness." This was "the most crucial theoretical foundation of his entire strategy of winning swaraj for India." (p. 87) A wide range of critical commentary by western writers on *Hind Swaraj* was published by *The Aryan Path* 9 (9) (September 1938): 421–456. For example, Claude Haughton wrote: "We must take responsibility for ourselves. There are no short cuts—there are no scapegoats. If we find ourselves in chains, *we* have forged them—link by link. And we must break them—link by link." (p. 449) Another author, Hugh I. A. Fausset called the book "a revolutionary message," "one of the best modern handbooks of that real revolution which must happen in us all, if we are to fulfill the creative purpose of life." (p. 446) The most extensive analysis of *Hind Swaraj* is by Pyarelal and Sushila Nayar, *Mahatma Gandhi* (Ahmedabad: Navajivan, 1965–1989) 4 Volumes. The last of these volumes analyzes *Hind Swaraj*, pp. 489–516. It emphasizes how this tract signified a radical change in his thinking. It also presents a summary of some of the critical commentary that followed its publication.

    19. *CWMG* 19: 277.

    20. *CWMG* 6: 269.

    21. This sentence from Thoreau which Gandhi noted is found in *Civil Disobedience*: J. W. Krutch ed. *Walden and Other Writings* (New York: Bantam, 1989), p. 97. It is representative of Thoreau's insight into the meaning of freedom. Its similarity to Gandhi's concept of freedom forms part of a nexus of ideas that they share: perceptions of truth, the authority of the State, and, of course, civil disobedience. Louis Fischer, in his classic biography of Gandhi, *The Life of Mahatma Gandhi* (New York: Collier Books, 1966), p. 93, quotes the sentence cited above from Thoreau's *Civil Disobedience* and says that "Gandhi cherished this excerpt from Thoreau." The theme of freedom and this particular passage from *Civil Disobedience* in terms of its influence on Gandhi is also discussed by the Thoreau scholar George Hendrick, who asserts that Gandhi's acceptance of the idea that "the soul was left free," despite imprisonment, signified "Gandhi's transformation from a respectable lawyer to a radical political leader." ("The Influence of Thoreau's 'Civil Disobedience' on Gandhi's Satyagraha," in Thoreau, *Walden and Civil Disobedience* Owen Thomas ed., [New York: Norton, 1966], p. 370). Broader aspects of Thoreau's appeal for Gandhi because of the former's understanding of Hinduism are related in M. Yamumnacharya, "Thoreau and Indian Thought," in *Gandhi, His Relevance for Our Times*, G. Ramachandran and T. K. Mahadevan, eds. (Bombay: Bharatiya Bhavan, 1964), pp. 344–353, and in Barbara Miller's Afterword to her translation of *The*

Bhagavad Gita (New York: Bantam, 1986), pp. 155–161, entitled "Why Did Henry David Thoreau Take the Bhagavad-Gita to Walden Pond?"

22. *CWMG* 75: 159.

23. Gandhi in D.G. Tendulkar, *Mahatma*, 1, Delhi, Government of India Publications Division, 1960, p. 100. Also *CWMG* 9: 182 and 10: 189.

24. Gandhi describes *Hind Swaraj* as "a faithful record of conversations I had with workers, one of whom was an avowed anarchist." *Hind Swaraj*, Ahmedabad: Navajivan, 1939, p. 18.

25. Ibid., p. 18.

26. *CWMG* 10: 8.

27. Ibid., p. 10.

28. Ibid., p. 11.

29. Ibid., p. 13.

30. Ibid., pp. 15–16.

31. Ibid.

32. Ibid., pp. 35–36.

33. Ibid., p. 20.

34. Ibid., pp. 36–38.

35. Ibid., p. 38.

36. *CWMG* 22: 18.

37. *CWMG* 25: 251.

38. *CWMG* 85: 33, 79.

39. *CWMG* 10: 37.

40. Ibid., p. 39.

41. *CWMG* 22: 500.

42. *CWMG* 25: 451.

43. *CWMG* 69: 52.

44. *CWMG* 73: 93–94.

45. *CWMG* 69: 356.

46. *CWMG* 73: 24.

47. *CWMG* 85: 351.

48. *CWMG* 64: 191–92.

49. *CWMG* 35: 294.

50. *CWMG* 10: 48.

51. Ibid., pp. 50–51.

52. Ibid., p. 43.

53. Ibid., pp. 46, 64.

54. *CWMG* 12: 461.

55. *CWMG* 14: 56.

56. Ibid., pp. 49–66.

57. Ibid., p. 60.

58. *CWMG* 13: 385–394, 435–440, 569–604; Judith Brown, *Gandhi's Rise to Power* (Cambridge: Cambridge University Press, 1972), pp. 64–83

59. *CWMG* 39: 321–338; Tendulkar 1: 201.

60. Ibid., p. 338.

61. Ibid., p. 330.
62. *CWMG* 14: 64–65.
63. *CWMG* 32: 553.

Chapter 2

1. *CWMG* 22: 27.

2. Gandhi wrote in 1921, that Lord Reading, the Viceroy, "must know that sedition has become the creed of the Congress. . . . Non-cooperation, though a religious and strictly moral movement, deliberately aims at the overthrow of the Government." *CWMG* 21: 222. Ranajit Guha argues that despite Gandhi's self-proclaimed position of rebellion, he in fact remained attached to an "idiom of Obedience," that is, he was a moderate and liberal to the end. The argument is representative of the particular inter-pretation of Gandhi as a representative of bourgeois interests that occurs consistently through the Subaltern Studies. See R. Guha, "Dominance Without Hegemony and its Historiography," in R. Guha ed., *Subaltern Studies* 6 (Delhi, Oxford University Press, 1989), pp. 253–256.

3. *CWMG* 23: 245.

4. Ibid., p. 246.

5. Leslie Calman offers a perceptive analysis of the theory and practice of move-ment politics with a focus on India in her two books: *Protest in Democratic India: Authority's Response to Challenge*, Colorado, Westview Press, 1985; and *Toward Empowerment. Women and Politics in India*, Westview Press, 1992.

6. *CWMG* 23: 271.

7. *CWMG* 23: 242.

8. Gopal Krishna," The Development of the Indian National Congress as a Mass Organization, 1918–1923," *Journal of Asian Studies* 25 (3) (May 1966): 419–430.

9. Judith Brown, *Gandhi's Rise to Power*, pp. 322, 343–346.

10. Shahid Amin, "Gandhi as Mahatma: Gorakhpur District, Eastern UP, 1921–22," Ranajit Guha, ed., *Subaltern Studies II* (Delhi: Oxford University Press, 1984), pp. 38, 60, 19.

11. Ibid., Rajat Kanta Ray also analyzes how "Gandhi's charismatic approach" gave rise to a "millennial hope of *Swaraj* [that] stirred the lowest elements in Indian Society." *Social Conflict and Political Unrest in Bengal: 1875–1927* (Delhi: Oxford University Press, 1984), p. 307.

12. *CWMG* 63: 339.

13. *CWMG* 35: 456.

14. *CWMG* 35: 456.

15. *CWMG* 19: 80.

16. Gandhi, *Harijan*, July 27, 1947, p. 253; in Pyarelal, *Mahatma Gandhi: The Last Phase* (Ahmedabad: Navajivan, 1958), 2: 315.

17. *CWMG* 16: 484.

18. *Akkodhena jine kodham*. In the *Dhammapada*, trans. Narada Maha Tera (Calcutta: Maha Bodhi Society of India, 1952), p. 165.

19. *Yeyatha mam prapadyamte tams tathaiva bhajamy aham.* In the *Bhagavad Gita,* (IV, 11) trans. by F. Edgerton (New York: Harper, 1964) p. 24.

20. *CWMG* 16: 490–491.

21. Or: "An eye for an eye"; "wickedness unto the wicked"

22. Or: "Do only that which is truthful"; "Truth even unto the wicked," Ibid., pp. 490–491.

23. *CWMG* 20: 369.

24. Jawaharlal Nehru, *Autobiography,* Bombay, Allied Publishers, 1962, p. 76.

25. *CWMG* 19: 383–385.

26. *CWMG* 54: 416–417.

27. *CWMG* 19: 466.

28. *CWMG.* 16: 368–369.

29. Aurobindo Ghose, *The Doctrine of Passive Resistance* (Pondicherry, 1952), p. 36. Leonard Gordon has perceptively analyzed Ghose's thought, including the doctrine of passive resistance, in *Bengal: The Nationalist Movement 1876–1940* (New York: Columbia University Press, 1974), pp. 101–134.

30. Ibid., pp. 40–44.

31. Ibid., p. 46

32. Ibid., pp. 53–60.

33. Ibid., pp. 62–66.

34. Susanne and Lloyd Rudolph, *Gandhi* (Chicago: University of Chicago Press, 1983), pp. 37–38, 60–62.

35. *CWMG* 14: 63–65.

36. *CWMG* 19: 166–167.

37. M.K. Gandhi, *Harijan. A Journal of Applied Gandhism* (New York: Garland pub. Inc.: 1973), XI: 251 (July 27, 1947). Gandhi's admission here is startling. For another, slightly different version, see *CWMG* 88: 336–337.

38. *CWMG* 29: 166–67.

39. M. K. Gandhi, *Delhi Diary* (Ahmedabad: Navajivan, 1948), pp. 56–57, and *CWMG* 89: 279.

40. Joan Bondurant. "Satyagraha vs. Duragraha," in G. Ramachandra, ed. *Gandhi. His Relevance for our Times* (Bombay: Bharatiya Vidya Bhavan, 1964), p. 70.

41. Ibid., p. 71.

42. Ibid., p. 71–72. See also Bondurant's analysis of *duragraha* in *Conquest of Violence* (Princeton: Princeton University Press, 1988), pp. 42–45, 236–238; Raghavan N. Iyer, *The Moral and Political Thought of Mahatma Gandhi* (New York: Oxford University Press, 1973), has written a trenchant analysis of *duragraha* and *satyagraha,* especially pp. 310–323.

43. *CWMG* 21: 457.

44. *CWMG* 59: 42.

45. Iyer, *Moral and Political Thought,* p. 181.

46. *CWMG* 59: 401.

47. *CWMG* 84: 47.

48. Ibid.

49. Iyer, *Moral and Political Thought,* pp. 195–96.

50. Ibid., p. 209. Iyer notes, *"Ahimsa* is intended and expected to convert rather than coerce the wrongdoer." Ibid., p. 183.

51. Ibid., p. 215.

52. *CWMG* 21: 458.

53. B. R. Nanda, *Mahatma Gandhi* (Bombay: Allied Publishers, 1966), p. 229.

54. *CWMG* 22: 143.

55. Nanda, *Mahatma Gandhi,* p. 230.

56. Tendulkar, *Mahatma* (Delhi: 1963) 2: 82.

57. *CWMG* 22: 418.

58. Ibid.

59. *CWMG* 47:246.

60. *CWMG* 50: 352.

61. *CWMG* 9: 180–181.

62. Gandhi as quoted in C. F. Andrews, *Mahatma Gandhi's Ideas,* London, Allen and Unwin, 1931, p. 123.

63. *CWMG* 13: 301–303.

64. The ideal social order was set forth, in ancient Indian thought, in the theory of *varnashramadharma* (often shortened by Gandhi to *varnashrama* or *varnadharma*). The system of the four *varnas* or social orders ensured, in theory, the harmonious interrelationship of four social functions: those of the *brahman* (spiritual authority and instruction), *kshatriya* (temporal power), *vaishya* (wealth), and *sudra* (labour). The working of society depended upon the political fulfillment by each of these *varnas* of its social role as prescribed by *dharma* or the sacred law. For a statement on the meaning of this theory see, especially, A.L. Basham, "Some Fundamental Ideas of Ancient India," in C. H. Philips ed., *Politics and Society in India* (London: Allen and Unwin), 1963.

65. Gandhi also defended caste at this time in *CWMG* 19: 83–85, 174–176.

66. *CWMG* 15: 122–3.

67. Gandhi, *Young India,* January 5, 1921, in N. K. Bose ed., *Selections from Gandhi* (Ahmedabad, Navajivan, 1948), pp. 232–233.

68. *CWMG* 19: 83–84.

69. *CWMG* 21: 247.

70. *CWMG* 35: 519.

71. *CWMG* 19: 410–411.

72. *CWMG* 62: 291.

73. *CWMG* 34: 511–512.

74. *CWMG* 35: 2.

75. *CWMG* 55: 60.

76. *CWMG* 62: 121.

77. *CWMG* 82: 326.

78. *CWMG* 84: 389.

79. *CWMG* 64: 402.

80. *CWMG* 59: 65–66.

81. B. R. Nanda, *Gandhi and His Critics* (Delhi, Oxford University Press, 1985), pp. 18–26.

82. *CWMG* 4: 430 and 6: 470.

83. *CWMG* 13: 232–233.
84. Jugatram, Dave. "Shri Ramjibhai Gopalji Badhia" in *Vattavriksha*, May 1972 (in Gujarati); and interview with Arjubhai Badhia, son of Ramjibhai, July 1975, Ahmedabad.
85. *CWMG* 24: 227.
86. Ibid.
87. *CWMG* 19: 20.
88. *CWMG* 36: 153–154.
89. *Congress Presidential Addresses, 1911–1934*, 2nd series (Madras: G.A. Natesan, 1937) pp. 800–801.
90. Ibid., pp. 804–807.
91. *CWMG* 33: 147.
92. Tendulkar, *Mahatma*, 4: 2.
93. *Harijan*, February 10, 1946.
94. *CWMG* 57:147.
95. B. R. Ambedkar, *What Congress and Gandhi Have Done to the Untouchables* (Bombay: Thacker, 1946), pp. 270–271.
96. Mulk Raj Anand, *Untouchable* (New Delhi: Orient, 1970), pp. 149–165.
97. *CWMG* 75: 149.
98. *CWMG* 25: 121–122.
99. Tendulkar, *Mahatma*, 5: 58.
100. *CWMG* 40, p. 118.
101. *CWMG* 24: 396.
102. C. R. Das, *Freedom Through Disobedience*, Presidential Address at 37th Indian National Congress (Madras: Arka, 1922), p. 40.
103. Bhagavan Das, *Ancient versus Modern Scientific Socialism* (Madras: Theosophical Pub. House, 1934) p. 135.
104. C. R. Das, *Outline Scheme of Swaraj*, National Convention Memoranda, No. 2 (Madras: Besant Press, 1923), p. 3.
105. Ibid., p. 4.
106. Ibid., p. 27.
107. *CWMG* 21: 308.
108. Tendulkar, *Mahatma* 6: 25.
109. *CWMG* 26: 538.
110. *CWMG* 28: 188.
111. *CWMG* 26: 538.
112. *CWMG* 39: 122.
113. Ibid., p. 401.
114. *CWMG* 26: 568.

Chapter 3

1. Nirad Chaudhuri, *Thy Hand, Great Anarch! India 1921–1952*. New York, Addison-Wesley Publishing Co., 1987, p. 28.

2. B. R. Ambedkar, *What Congress and Gandhi Have Done to the Untouchables*, pp. 39, 308, 284, 295; and *Gandhi and Gandhism*, Jullundar, Punjab, Bheem Patrika Publications, 1970, pp. 3–23, 35–41, 119–145. Gandhi responded indirectly to Ambedkar in his *Harijan* column: "Let not Dr. Ambedkar's just wrath deject the reformer, let it spur him to greater effort. For whilst it is true that the number of workers against untouchability has greatly increased, there can be no doubt that the number is yet too small to overtake the prejudice of ages." *CWMG* 62: 65.

3. Churchill proclaimed this on February 23, 1931, as his verdict on Gandhi during the latter's talks with Lord Irwin, Viceroy of India, following the salt *satyagraha* discussed in the next chapter. *India. Speeches* (London: Thornton Butterworth, 1931), pp. 94–95. Churchill's criticism of Gandhi in public was relentlessly scathing. However, he wrote privately to Madeleine Slade, Gandhi's English associate, "Although I am strongly opposed to Mr. Gandhi's politics, I am a sincere admirer of the heroic efforts he is making to improve the position of the depressed classes [i.e., the untouchables] in India." Churchill to Slade, September 21, 1934. Gandhi Papers. Gandhi Memorial Library and Museum, Rajghat, Delhi. (S.N. 9096).

4. *Wavell: The Viceroy's Journal*, Penderel Moon, ed. (London: Oxford University Press, 1973), pp. 353, 314, 185, 236, 413, 439.

5. Edwin S. Montagu, *An India Diary*, ed., Venitra Montagu (London:Heinemann, 1930), p. 58.

6. Gokhale quoted in Tendulkar, *Mahatma*, 1: 112.

7. J. Nehru, *Discovery of India*, (New York: Doubleday, 1959), pp. 274–275. Nehru emphasizes the connection between overcoming fear and "a new sense of freedom" in his *Autobiography*, p. 69.

8. Leonard Gordon has examined the ideas of Rabindranath Tagore and M. N. Roy as related to Gandhi in "Bengal's Gandhi," in David Kopf, ed., *Bengal Regional Identity* (Michigan, 1969), pp. 104–112.

9. *CWMG* 21: 288.

10. R. Tagore, *Nationalism*, p. 111.

11. Tagore, "The Sunset of the Century" in *Nationalism*, p. 133.

12. Ibid., p. 135.

13. R. Tagore, *Gitanjali* (Song Offerings) London: Macmillan 1920), p. 27.

14. Tagore, *Nationalism*, p. 16.

15. Tagore, *Nationalism*, pp. 26–27.

16. Ibid., p. 26.

17. C.R. Das, *India for Indians* (Madras: Ganesh, 1918) p. 9.

18. Tagore, *Nationalism*, p. 97.

19. Ibid., p. 12.

20. Ibid., p. 113.

21. Ibid., pp. 113–114.

22. Ibid., p. 120.

23. Ibid., pp. 120–123.

24. *CWMG* 21: 291.

25. Tagore quoted in R. K. Prabhu and Ravindra Kelekav, eds., *Truth Called*

Them Differently (Tagore-Gandhi Controversy) (Ahmedabad: Navajivan, 1961), pp. 14–17.

26. R. Tagore, *Letters to A Friend*, C. F. Andrews, ed. (London: Allen & Unwin, 1928), p. 132.

27. R. Tagore, *Towards Universal Man*, (London: Asia Publishing House, 1961), p. 253.

28. Ibid., p. 254.

29. Ibid., p. 259–260.

30. Ibid., p. 262.

31. Ibid., pp. 262–263.

32. Ibid., p. 270.

33. Ibid., p. 268.

34. Ibid.

35. Ibid.

36. Ibid., p. 272.

37. Ibid., p. 271.

38. *CWMG* 28: 427.

39. Ibid.

40. *CWMG* 20: 159.

41. *CWMG* 23: 340.

42. *CWMG* 22: 462.

43. Tendulkar, *Mahatma* 3: 273.

44. Charles Andrews quoted in *CWMG* 21: 41.

45. Ibid., p. 42.

46. Ibid.

47. R. Tagore, *Reminiscences* (London: Macmillan, 1920), p. 128.

48. Krishna Kripalani examines the differences between Tagore and Gandhi in *Rabindranath Tagore. A Biography* (London: Oxford University Press, 1962). He observes that "What Tagore, however, feared was not the Mahatma's spirit of exclusion—he knew the latter was above it—but that of his followers who would not scruple to appeal to any prejudice or passion to work up the fever of nationalism" (p. 295) Also see Kripalani's informative comparisons of Gandhi and Tagore on, pp. 296–301, 320–323, 366–369, 374–389. In a rich comparative study of Tagore's thought, Stephen N. Hay analyzes the clash between Tagore and Gandhi in these terms: "Essentially they differed because one was a reformer bent on changing the world, the other a poet listening for harmonies inaudible to less finely tuned ears. Beyond these basic differences in vocation and temperament, each man looked at India and the world through the lenses of his own regional, caste, and family traditions." *Asian Ideas of East and West: Tagore and His Critics in Japan, China and India* (Cambridge: Harvard University Press, 1970), p. 284.

49. *CWMG* 39: 319.

50. M. K. Gandhi, *Harijan*, January 18, 1942.

51. J. Bandyopadhyaya, *Social and Political Thought of Gandhi* (Bombay: Allied Publishers, 1969), 89.

52. M. K. Gandhi, *Democracy: Real and Deceptive*, Ahmedabad, Navijivan, 1961, p. 6.

53. *Young India*, July 30, 1931.

54. *Young India*, December 1, 1927.

55. *CWMG* 75: 148.

56. *Young India*, July 28, 1920.

57. *Harijan*, May 27, 1939.

58. Leonard A. Gordon, offers an excellent analysis of Roy's background as a leader in "Portrait of a Bengal Revolutionary," *Journal of Asian Studies* 27 (2) (February 1968): 197–216.

59. Roy acknowledges the brahmanical influence in his *Memoirs* (Bombay, 1964), pp. 163–64.

60. Roy, *New Orientation* (Calcutta, 1946), p. 27.

61. Edward Shils, "Ideology" in *The International Encyclopedia of the Social Sciences*, 7: 69.

62. Robert C. North and X. J. Eudin, *M. N. Roy's Mission to China* (Berkeley and Los Angeles: University of California Press, 1963) p. 1.

63. *Ibid.* North believes that "Roy ranks with Lenin and Mao Tse-tung in the development of fundamental Communist policy for the underdeveloped . . . areas of the globe."

64. One reference to Roy by Gandhi occurs in *Young India*, January 1, 1925, a criticism of Roy's account of Bolshevism.

65. See the comment on Roy's relation to his tradition by Edward Shils in "The Culture of the Indian Intellectual," University of Chicago Reprint Series, pp. 15–16. (Reprinted from *Sewanee Review*, April and July 1959).

66. Roy, *Memoirs*, p. 379.

67. Ibid., p. 543.

68. Ibid., p. 413.

69. G. D. Overstreet and Marshall Windmiller, *Communism in India* (Berkeley and Los Angeles: University of California Press, 1959), p. 40.

70. Roy, *India in Transition* (Geneva, 1922), p. 205.

71. Ibid., p. 207.

72. Ibid., p. 235.

73. Ibid., p. 208.

74. Ibid., p. 209.

75. M. N. Roy and Evelyn Roy, *One Year of Non-Cooperation* (Calcutta, 1923), pp. 56–58.

76. See especially: M. N. Roy, *Crime and Karma, Cats and Women: Fragments of a Prisoner's Diary*, 1 (Calcutta, 1957): 112–119; *India's Message: Fragments, etc.* 2 (Calcutta, 1950).

77. Roy, *India's Message*, p. 307.

78. Ibid., p. 189.

79. Ibid., pp. 237–307.

80. Ibid., pp. 210–211.

81. Ibid., pp. 214, 215, 216, 222, 228, 236.

82. *Independent India*, October 16, 1938, p. 453.

83. At precisely the time when Roy says he was expressing his "appreciation" of

Gandhi to one of the Mahatma's colleagues, we find him writing to a Marxist comrade abroad: "Our real fight is against the right wing which is still very powerful thanks to the popularity of Gandhi. . . . I am striking at the very root. Gandhist ideology must go before the nationalist movement can develop its enormous revolutionary potentialities. And Gandhi has recognized in us his mortal enemy. As a matter of fact, in his inner circle I am branded as the enemy No. 1." (Roy to Jay Lovestone, October 19, 1937, Bombay.) Exactly one year after writing his appreciation, Roy wrote to an Indian associate for help in the great effort "to destroy this curse of Gandhism." (Roy to Makhan Lal Sen, September 12, 1939.) The quotations are from Roy's correspondence examined in the M. N. Roy Archives of the Indian Renaissance Institute then at Dehradun, U.P., India.

84. P. Spratt, Foreword to Roy, *New Orientation* (Calcutta, 1946), p. xv.

85. Roy, *New Orientation*, p. 56.

86. Roy, *Reason, Romanticism and Revolution* (Calcutta, 1952), 1:v.

87. Philip Spratt, 'Gandhi and Roy,' unpublished article and interview with Philip Spratt in Madras, May, 1967.

88. *Independent India*, February 22, 1948, p. 67.

89. *Independent India*, April 18, 1948, p. 176.

90. John Haithcox examines Roy's changing attitudes toward Gandhi and concludes that "After Gandhi's death a new respect for him emerged in Roy's thinking . . . Roy came closer to Gandhi in his emphasis on human solidarity, the relation of means to ends, the necessity of some form of economic and political decentralization, and the rejection of party politics." *Communism and Nationalism in India. M. N. Roy and Comintern Policy 1920–1939* (Princeton: Princeton University Press), 1971, p. 256.

91. *Independent India*, January 30, 1949, p. 37.

92. *Independent India*, February 22, 1948, p. 67.

93. Roy, *Politics, Politics, Power and Parties* (Calcutta, 1960), p. 121.

94. Ibid., pp. 81–82. Compare this view with Gandhi's address to the Hindustani Talimi Sangh Group in December, 1947, recorded in Tendulkar, *Mahatma* 8: 227–232.

95. Leonard Gordon, *Brothers Against the Raj* (New York: Columbia University Press, 1990) offers a study of the Boses outstanding for its scholarship and originality.

Chapter 4

1. *Young India*, March 27, 1930, *CWMG* 42: 135.

2. This meant that 55% of a maund of salt, priced at Rs. 2-4-7 (82 cents), went for revenue. Of the total revenue collected by the Raj (Rs. 800,443,369 or $292,161,830), 8.4% came from the salt tax (Rs. 67,646,354 or $24,690,919) in 1929–1930. By Gandhi's calculation, the tax could represent as much as three days' income per year of an average villager, or as much as Rs 720 per year from an average village's consumption of salt. See *CWMG* 43: 51–2, 62.

3. Details relating to the Dandi march are given in *CWMG* 43: 59–188; Gandhi's periodical, *Young India* (Ahmedabad), March-April, 1930; Home Poll. File #122. 1930 and File #247/II/1930; *Mahatma Gandhi: Source Material for a History of the Freedom Move-*

ment in India. 3, Part III, 1930–1931 (Bombay: Directorate of Printing and Stationery, 1969), pp. 8–114; Indian newspapers, especially *Bombay Chronicle* and *Times of India* (both published in Bombay); *Mahadev Desai's Diary (Mahadevabhaini Dayari,* in Gujarati), N. D. Parkh, ed. (Ahmedabad: Navajivan Prakasan Mandir, 1948–1949) 13 (1929–1931): 224–333; Kalyanji Vithalbhai Mehta and Ishwari Desai, *Dandi Kutch* [March] (in Gujarati) (Ahmedabad: Gujarat Rajya Samiti, 1969); S. R. Bakshi, *Gandhi and Salt Satyagraha* (Kerala: Vishwavidya Publishers, 1981); and Thomas Weber, "Historiography and the Dandi March: The Other Myths of Gandhi's Salt March," *Gandhi Marg* 8 (8) (November 1986): 457–476; Weber, "Kharag Bahadur Singh: The Eighth [sic] Marcher," *Gandhi Marg* 6 (9) (December 1984): 661–673. The two articles by Thomas Weber are particularly useful because he tries to correct inaccuracies in previous accounts of the Dandi march. Thus he shows that while Gandhi began the march at Sabarmati with 78 followers, two more joined him at the village of Matar on March 14 to accompany the chosen group for most of the distance, raising the total number of official marchers to 81. Moreover, many accounts of the march report that the distance traveled was 241 miles. Weber walked the entire route of the march, interviewed those who witnessed it, and calculates that the distance covered was "somewhere between" 241 and 200 miles. Finally, he observes that what Gandhi collected on the beach of Dandi that early morning, April 6, was not really salt but "a handful of saline mud"; the pure salt crystals were not picked up by him until three days later near the village of Bhimrad, 15 miles from Dandi. Weber's book on the salt march is forthcoming. But his comment on the purpose of the salt *satyagraha* in his article on "Historiogaphy and the Dandi March" states well the meaning of *swaraj*: "The revolution Gandhi sought to achieve was not merely political, it was also social. The independence he fought for was not only national but also personal. The Salt March was about empowerment. It told people that they were stronger than they thought and that the rulers were weaker than they imagined. It was about reforming society and about the self-reformation of the individual. For Gandhi the two were inextricably linked—reform yourself and you have started to reform the world, reform the world nonviolently and you will have reformed the self" (p. 460).

4. *CWMG* 42: 480.

5. The most informative single volume on the Bardoli *satyagraha* is Mahadev Desai, *The Story of Bardoli: Being a History of the Bardoli Satyagraha of 1928 and its Sequel* (Ahmedabad: Navajivan, 1929). Desai (Gandhi's personal secretary at this time) offers no criticism of the *satyagraha,* but his facts, when checked against the press and other critical sources seem substantially accurate. Also *CWMG* 36, pp. 35–36, 79–81, 88–90, 319–322, 353–354, 368–370, 384–386, 419–421, reflect Gandhi's unusually strong response to the Bardoli resistance. Additional analysis of the significance of Bardoli is in, Ghanshyam Shah, "Traditional Society and Political Mobilization: The Experience of Bardoli *Satyagraha* (1920–1928)" in *Contributions to Indian Sociology.* No. 8, 1974 (Delhi): 89–107; Ishwarlal I. Desai ed., *Bardoli Satyagraha* (Surat, 1970) (in Gujarati); Joan Bondurant, *Conquest of Violence,* 1988, gives a short account of Bardoli pp. 53–64, and a concise historical analysis is in Judith M. Brown, *Gandhi and Civil Disobedience* (Cambridge: Cambridge University Press, 1977), pp. 28–33.

6. *Times of India,* Bombay, July 3, 1928, p. 7.

7. Ibid., 4, July 1928, p. 11.

8. July 2, 1928, Wilson wrote to Irwin. "I also must let you fully realize the strength of feeling which there is in the Presidency on this Bardoli question. This inflamed feeling has been worked up by the Gujaratis, but unfortunately most of the Indian businessmen come from Gujarat. If no settlement is arrived at, we are certainly in for a very great deal of trouble. I am, however, perfectly willing to face this, but, with Gandhi and Vallabhbhai Patel working together, it is no use my minimizing to you the difficulties which probably will arise, and eventually we may have to ask for full support, even of troops, to carry out a policy of insisting firmly on the rights of Government." On July 6 Irwin wired Wilson in reply that it was "imperative" to "demonstrate unmistakably that Government can and will govern," and that he will support fully any firm Government action in Bardoli including arrest of leaders and use of troops. IOR/MSS. Eur. C. 152/22, Lord Irwin's Correspondence with Persons in India, Jan.–Dec. 1928. Nos. 462, 415, pp. 599, 279–280.

9. *CWMG* 36: 22–23, 79–81.

10. Ibid., pp. 169–170. for a comment on "Dyerism" see chapter 6, note 13.

11. Ibid., p. 353.

12. *CWMG* 37: 179.

13. Ibid., p. 200.

14. *CWMG*, 41: 164.

15. Ibid., pp. 208–209.

16. Ibid., 42: 194.

17. Ibid., p. 454.

18. When the final "report" on Bardoli appeared, written by an impartial investigative committee, and unfavorable to the Government position, Irwin asked Frederick Sykes (who had now replaced Wilson as Governor) "that you should confine yourself to saying the absolute minimum" about the report for publicity would inevitably be "embarrassing to your authority and . . . evoke strong criticism from home." IOR/MSS. Eur. C. 152/23. Irwin Correspondence with Persons in India, 1929, No. 240. April 29, 1929, Telegram to Sykes, p. 183. Moreover, during the height of the Bardoli agitation, Irwin realized the weakness of the Government's position and wrote to his father that "I am afraid we are in for very considerable trouble." IOR/MSS. Eur. C. 152/27, Irwin Correspondence with Viscount Halifax, Apr. 1926–1931. No. 117, July 17, 1928, p. 186.

19. Judith Brown's analysis confirms this judgement: "In Bardoli," she concludes, "he [Gandhi] thought he had found the answer," for his preparation of the salt *satyagraha*. *Gandhi and Civil Disobedience*, pp. 32–33.

20. See the succinct statement of Patel's position on partition as opposed to Gandhi's in C. S. Venktachar, "1937–1947 in Retrospect: A Civil Servant's View,"C.H. Philips and M.D. Wainwright eds., *The Partition of India* (London: Allen and Unwin, 1970), pp. 474–476. Also, Pyarelal, *Mahatma Gandhi: The Last Phase*, II (Ahmedabad: Navajivan, 1958), pp. 254–255, 694–695.

21. Fenner Brockway to M. K. Gandhi, Oct. 31, 1929, Gandhi Papers, Gandhi Memorial Library, Rajghat, Delhi, (S.N. 15730).

22. Horace Alexander to M. K. Gandhi, Oct. 12, 1929, Gandhi Papers (S.N. 16278).

23. Henry S.L. Polak to M. K. Gandhi, December 13, 1929, Gandhi Papers (S.N. 16211). Also Polak to Gandhi, December 5, 1929 (S.N. 16286) and cable of December

19, 1929 (S.N. 16205). All correspondence from Polak begins, "Dear Bhai" [Brother] and concludes "Love, Henry."

24. Dr. M.A. Ansari to M. K. Gandhi, March 5, 1930, Gandhi Papers (S.N. 16598). Ansari would later retract this diagnosis by writing to Gandhi on July 5, 1933 that the civil disobedience movement "has definitely succeeded. . . . It has revolutionized the mentality of the people and it has moreover consolidated that revolution." (S.N. 21514).

25. Asaf Ali to Gandhi, February 25, 1930. Gandhi Papers (S.N. 16528).

26. The Gandhi Papers in Delhi has on file copies of 30 letters from students that Gandhi received during the week before the march began, asking him to enroll them as volunteers (S.N. 16594–16675).

27. Miss J. Kabraj to M. K. Gandhi, Feb. 26, 1930. Gandhi Papers, (S.N. 16537).

28. D. V. Ranga Rao and Asankaran, Students in Youth League, Kalahasti, Chittore District, Madras, To M. K. Gandhi, March 3, 1930, Gandhi Papers, (S.N. 16735).

29. Bhupendra Marayen Sen Gupta to M. R. Gandhi, February 24, 1930, from Bairampur, Bengal, Gandhi Papers (S.N. 16527).

30. Interview with Satish Kalelkar, Ahmedabad, March 13, 1975.

31. Sir Chiminlal Setalvad. Quoted in B. D. Shukla, *A History of the Indian Liberal Party* (Allahabad: Inidan Press Publications, 1960), p 306.

32. The question has intrigued writers on Gandhi, and explanations range from the plausible to the absurd. At one extreme, E. Victor Wolfenstein observes that one of "the basic symbolic significances of salt is human semen. If it had this unconscious meaning for Gandhi, then we may understand his depriving himself of condiments, including salt, as a form of sexual abstinence. . . . In the context of the Salt March, Gandhi's taking of salt from the British can thus be seen as reclaiming for the Indian people the manhood and potency which was properly theirs." *The Revolutionary Personality: Lenin, Trotsky, Gandhi* (Princeton: Princeton University Press, 1967); p. 221. To his credit, Erikson is critical of this psychological reductionism, saying that except in cases of demonstrable "irrationality . . . one should take any interpretation that explains a human act by recourse to sexual symbolism with a grain of salt." "On the Nature of Psycho-Historical Evidence: In Search of Gandhi," *Daedalus* (Summer 1968): 722. See also Robert Coles, *Erik H. Erikson* (Boston: Little Brown, 1970), p. 292. Perhaps the clearest explanation for the choice of the salt tax is given by Mira Behn (Madeleine Slade). She was with Gandhi in early 1930 as a close associate and later recalled: "Gradually it became clear that he was searching in his mind for some sort of all-India *Satyagraha* which would rouse the spirit of the masses down to the poorest in the land. Everyone was expecting an obvious choice, such as refusal to pay revenue, boycott of law courts or something of that sort, but Bapu ["father," honorific term of endearment often given to Gandhi] saw snags for the masses in all these things. It must be something that touched each villager, and his mind fixed on salt. Salt was a necessity of life for all, both man and beast, and could be garnered from the sea as well as from so many soils. And yet salt was taxed, and man was forbidden to collect it for himself. The more Bapu thought about it the more convinced he became that to break the salt laws was *the* thing to decide on." *The Spirit's Pilgrimage* (London: Longmans, 1960), p. 109; and interview with Mira Behn in Vienna, August 1975. This subject was also discussed at length with other members of the ashram who were in daily contact with Gandhi in February, 1930, especially Pyarelal Nayar, and with

a member of the Working Committee of the Congress, present at the meeting of February 14–15, C. Rajagopalachari, the latter in an interview in Madras, May 1967. They
agreed with the interpretation of Mira Behn. From another perspective, however, salt
may be seen as limiting rather than enlarging the campaign because it did not appeal
sufficiently to the urban poor, or to those where salt production was unfeasible. These
and related issues are analyzed in Sumit Sarkar, "The Logic of Gandhian Nationalism:
Civil Disobedience and the Gandhi-Irwin Pact" *The Indian Historical Review* 3 (1) (July
1976): 114–146. Yet what has become the historical consensus was expressed only
months after the salt march when Professor L. F. Rushbrook Williams, British scholar
of India, declared that "It was nothing less than a stroke of genius on his [Gandhi's] part
to seize upon the salt tax as the centre point of his campaign.""Indian Unrest and American Opinion," in *The Asiatic Review* 26 (87) (July 1930): 491.

33. Gopal Krishna Gokhale, *Speeches and Writings*, vol 1, R. P. Patwardhan and D. V.
Ambeker, eds. (Bombay: Asia Publishing House, 1962), p. 8.

34. *CWMG* 5: 101.

35. *CWMG* 10: 12.

36. Ibid., 42: 434.

37. *Times of India*, February 5, 1930, p. 11.

38. Interviews with Archarya Kripalani in Ahmedabad, July 1975, and Pyarelal
Nayar in New Delhi, October and November, 1966; and with C. Rajagopalachari in
Madras, May 1967; and account by Mira Behn, *Spirit's Pilgrimage*, pp. 109–110 and B. R.
Nanda, *Mahatma Gandhi* (Bombay: Allied Publishers, 1968), pp. 290–291. Jawaharlal
Nehru admitted later that once the campaign caught on, "we felt a little ashamed for
having questioned the efficacy of this method [of resisting the salt tax] when it was first
proposed by Gandhiji." *Mahatma Gandhi*, Bombay, Asia Publishing House, 1965, p. 63.

39. *CWMG* 42: 501.

40. Gene Sharp, *Gandhi Wields the Weapon of Moral Power*, (Ahmedabad: Navajivan,
1960), p. 56. In his case history of the 1930–1931, satyagraha, Sharp comments that
Gandhi "could hardly have picked an issue which touched directly the lives of more
people."

41. Note that these symbolic arguments are not particularly Indian in form, but are
familiar to Western political thought as well, especially the ideas of anarchist thinkers,
P.J. Proudhon and Peter Kropotkin.

42. *CWMG* 29: 240–243. "The Great March," Ibid., 12: 258–269. R. A. Huttenback,
Gandhi in South Africa, 1971, Cornell University Press, pp. 316–319. D. G. Tendulkar,
Mahatma, rev. ed. (Delhi: Government Publications Division, 1960) 1: 139–145, "The
Epic March." Sushila Nayar *Mahatma Gandhi* (Ahmedabad: Navajivan, 1989), 4: 643–
667. Maureen Swan offers another perspective on the South African march by placing it
in the context of the labor strike and the economic issues involved in 1913: *Gandhi: The
South African Experience*, (Johannesburg: Ravan Press, 1985), pp. 243–256.

43. *Rand Daily Mail*, November 11, 1913, p. 6 and *Natal Witness*, November 15, 1913,
p. 3. The march received extensive reporting and editorial comment from these papers
as well as from the *Natal Mercury*, *Cape Times*, *Evening Chronicle*, and *Sunday Post*. Dr.
A.D. Lazarus, a South African Indian who was fifteen at the time of the march and later
became a prominent leader of his Indian community there, recalled that the press and

government initially ridiculed the protest as ludicrous, in contrast to the pro-Gandhi nationalist press later in India, especially the *Bombay Chronicle* and local Gujarati papers that glorified the Dandi march from the outset. (Interview with A. D. Lazarus in Durban, South Africa, August 1975) A notable exception was the *Cape Times*, whose sympathetic reporter called it "The Great Indian Trek," praised the patience and discipline of the marchers, and remarked on the enthusiasm of the women and the devotion of all to Gandhi.

44. *CWMG* 43: 61.

45. *CWMG* 42: 419–420. Joan Bondurant (following Louis Renou) goes so far as to describe Gandhi's "inner voice" "In terms more familiar to the West, as a feeling of what the masses expected of him." "The Non-conventional Political Leader in India" in Richard Park and Irene Tinker eds., *Leadership and Political Institutions in India* (Princeton: Princeton University Press, 1959), p. 280. Gandhi's thinking at this crucial period would seem to confirm Bondurant's suggestion. W. H. Morris Jones has also noted the significance of this input in Gandhi's decision-making.

46. In Gandhi's Congress resolution, adopted by the Working Committee meeting in Ahmedabad on February 15, the language is quite vague, authorizing Gandhi and his followers to "start civil disobedience as and when they desire and in the manner and to the extent they decide." *CWMG* 42: 480.

47. Ibid., p. 500.

48. *CWMG* 43: 12..

49. *CWMG* 42: 481–82.

50. Interview with Dwarkanath Harkare, Bombay, July 31, 1975.

51. Interview with Pannalal Balabhai Zaveri, one of 79 marchers, July 28, 1975, Ahmedabad, India.

52. Bapu's Letters to Mira. 1924–1928. Ahmedabad 1949, p. 98, Note to Gandhi's letter of Nov. 26, 1929.

53. Haridas T. Muzumdar, who had just received his Ph.D. in Social Science from the University of Wisconsin, confessed to being "torn by conflicting desires, pulled by different ideas" before he volunteered to join Gandhi. But he was persuaded that "The greatest battle of human history is being fought," and so he became one of the marchers. Haridas T. Muzumdar, statement in Gandhi Papers (S. N. 16557, 44, #586) and interview in New York City, Oct. 11, 1976. Another marcher, Harilal Mahimtura, concurred. Interview in Bombay, July 30, 1975.

54. Interview with Satish Kalelkar, Ahmedabad, March 13, 1975.

55. Personal communication to author from Valji Govindji Desai, Vododara, Gujarat, October 1, 1975.

56. *CWMG* 42: 497.

57. *CWMG* 43: 33–35.

58. Irwin to Gandhi, from Viceroyal Lodge, Simla, May 13, 1928, *Gandhi Papers* (S.N. 13385) and interview with Pyarelal Nayar, February 13, 1967 in Delhi. Pyarelal, who was at Gandhi's side throughout the march, was the principal informant for the present accounts of the salt satyagraha; he read earlier drafts of this chapter and made extensive comments on them. The account of the salt march was also discussed with Dr. Haridas T. Muzumdar. His own chronicle of the march is presented in his book *India's Non-Violent Revolution* (New York: India Today and Tomorrow Series, 1930).

59. Gandhi's approach may be compared with V. I. Lenin's model of a political movement depicted in *What Is To Be Done?*: "We are surrounded on all sides by enemies, and we have to advance almost constantly under their fire." This is an "exclusive group": "A small, compact core of the most reliable, experienced, and hardened workers . . . connected by all the rules of strict secrecy. . . . such an organization must have the utmost secrecy. Secrecy is such a necessary condition for this kind of organization that all the other conditions (number and selection of members, functions, etc.) must be made to conform to it" (New York: International Publishers, 1973), pp. 11, 116, 133. It may be argued with much validity that Lenin's model of politics was suitable to Czarist Russia as was Gandhi's to British India. However, M. N. Roy and other Indian revolutionaries, Communist and terrorist, preferred Lenin's model, but applied it without success to India, thus not accepting Gandhi's emphasis on openness and inclusivity in the Indian context. See John P. Haithcox, *Communism and Nationalism in India: M. N. Roy and Comintern Policy, 1920–1939*, (Princeton: Princeton University Press, 1971), pp. 27–30.

60. Cited above, and listed in *CWMG* 42: 434–435, Gandhi cites these as "pressing," "very simple but vital needs of India." They include, in addition to abolition of the salt tax, reduction of the land revenue, of the military expenditure, of salaries of higher grade civil servants; discharge of political prisoners; tariff on foreign cloth; and abolition of the secret intelligence service.

61. The English friend, a young Quaker, Reginald Reynolds, wrote "My taking of this letter was, in fact, intended to be symbolic of the fact that this was not merely a struggle between the Indians and the British . . . ." *To Live in Mankind*, quoted in *MGCW*, 43: 8. Gandhi's letter to Irwin appears in *CWMG* 43: 2–8.

62. Geoffrey Ashe, *Gandhi:. A Study in Revolution*, (London: Heinemann, 1968), p. 286 The Bombay companies were the Sharda, Krishna, and Ranjit.

63. Herbert A. Miller, "Gandhi's Campaign Begins," *The Nation*, April 23, 1930, p. 501

64. Harnam Singh, *The Indian National Movement and American Opinion* (New Delhi: Rama Krishna & Sons, 1962), p. 277. *The New York Times* published regular, almost daily, reports of the salt march from March 12 to April 5th and with Gandhi's completion of the march printed two front page articles about it on April 6 and 7. Unfortunately, these reports contain numerous factual errors and also reflect the confusion of British policy, especially about the likelihood of Gandhi's arrest.

65. *The Literary Digest*, April 19, 1930, p. 12.

66. *Time Magazine*, January 5, 1931, pp. 14–15. Gandhi's picture appeared on the cover and the article featured the reporting of the British journalist Henry Noel Brailsford who stressed the revolutionary nature of Gandhi's movement. He claimed that the British government now had the allegiance of only the military, the Princes, and the older Muslims. The vast majority of Indians followed Gandhi. Both American and British journalists who met Gandhi during this time and then covered his movement have written extraordinarily vivid and favorable assessments. Among the most striking are: William L. Shirer, *Gandhi. A Memoir* (New York: Simon and Schuster, 1979); Webb Miller, *I Found No Peace* (New York: Simon and Schuster, 1936), pp. 238–241; Negley Farson, *The Way of a Transgressor* (New York: Harcourt Brace, 1936), pp. 558–560; Robert Bernays, *"Naked Fakir"* (London: Victor Gollancz, 1931); and Malcolm Muggeridge, *Chronicles of Wasted Time*. I: *The Green Stick* (New York: Morrow, 1973), pp. 108–113. All

are fascinated by the mass allegiance to Gandhi and ponder its causes. Muggeridge considers several reasons for Gandhi's appeal to the average Indian and then concludes: "He drew them to him, I decided, because he gave them a feeling that they mattered; that they, too, existed in the scheme of things, and were not just helots, extras in a drama which did not concern them. This was why they saw him as a Mahatma, and took the dust of his feet." (110) Finally, one must mention the outstanding contribution of the American journalist Louis Fischer. Although he met Gandhi later than the others, in 1942, his remarkable biography, *The Life of Mahatma Gandhi* (New York: Harper, 1950), is foremost among those journalists who were informed by their personal acquaintance with Gandhi.

67. *CWMG* 43: 37.

68. Ibid., pp. 38 and 60.

69. Gandhi explained the purpose of the march to the ashramites as a "symbolic action," undertaken at first by a few, and then the force of the example would ignite the whole nation. Interview with C. K. Nair, one of the initial 78 marchers, in Delhi, July, 1975.

70. Mehta and Desai, *Dandi Kutch*, pp. 52–53; Desai, *The Story of Bardoli*, p. 13.

71. *CWMG* 42: 60.

72. Mahadev Desai, "The Great March," *Navajivan*, March 16, 1930 (in Gujarati).

73. The relationship of the modern Indian conception of the political leader to the traditional ideals of the "hero, saint, and teacher" is drawn by Karl H. Potter, *Presuppositions of India's Philosophies* (New Delhi 1965), p. 5.

74. "Speeches delivered by Gandhi on course of march to sea to break the salt laws" in Home Poll. File #122, 1930. There are two primary sources of Gandhi's speeches during the salt march: *CWMG* 43: 62–185; and the Government file cited here, which contains the complete translations of the speeches from the notes of a stenographer employed by the Government to follow Gandhi on the march. The Government official also comments on the degree of enthusiasm and size of the audience. When the transcript of the speeches in this file is compared with that in the *Collected Works* there are many differences, one being that the former retains Gandhi's frequent usage of words like *swaraj*. For example, the translation in the *Collected Works* of the sentence just cited reads: "Your reply can only be winning complete freedom. How could you do that? Only by following my path." (p. 80).

75. *CWMG* 43: 62. A paisa = 1/64 of a rupee. The exchange rate in 1930 was one rupee = .365 cents.

76. *CWMG* 43: 146–149.

77. Kapilprasad M. Dave, "My Reminiscences of Dandi March," personal communication to author, from Ahmedabad, Jan. 1976.

78. Communication to the author from N. P. Raghava Poduval, Kerala, March 7 and May 6, 1977.

79. Interview with Pyarelal in Delhi, February 20, 1967. Careful attention was given to the diet of the marchers: for breakfast, gram and groundnuts; for lunch, rice, dal, chapati and vegetables; for supper, khichdi (mixture of rice and dal), chapati and vegetables, and milk.

80. *Bombay Chronicle*, 25 March 1930, p. 6.

81. *Jamnabhumi*, quoted in *Bombay Chronicle*, 28 March 1930, p. 6.

82. *CWMG* 43: 162.

83. Ibid., pp. 44, 49.

84. Ibid., p. 166.

85. Ibid., p. 167.

86. *Bombay Chronicle*, 5 April 1930, p. 1.

87. Jawaharlal Nehru, *Mahatma Gandhi* (Bombay: Asia Publishing House, 1965), pp. 61, 63.

88. *Bombay Chronicle* 5 April 1930, p. 8.

89. Mehta and Desai, *Dandi Kutch*, p. 286. K. M. Dave, correspondent for two Gujarati newspapers, *Bombay Samachar* and *Prajabandhu* (Ahmedabad), covering the Dandi march, recalled that Gandhi "used to walk so fast during the march that those with him were actually forced to run to keep pace with him." Some of the journalists arranged for horses or cars to stay with the march. (K. M. Dave, "My Reminiscences of the March," personal communication to the author, Ahmedabad, January, 1976). Newton Phelps Stokes, recently graduated from Yale University, joined the march for a short distance and reported that Gandhi walked "at an amazingly fast pace." He was struck by the vast crowds that joined or observed the marchers as they passed through villages. "Marching with Gandhi," *The Review of Reviews* 81 (6) (June 1930): 38.

90. *CWMG* 43: 179.

91. Ibid.

92. Ibid., p. 180.

93. Ibid.

94. Ibid., pp. 182–84.

95. Mehta and Desai, *Dandi Kutch*, pp. 291–93.

96. *CWMG* 43: 216. S. R. Bakshi calculates that as Gandhi did his deed at Dandi on April 6, the salt laws were broken "throughout India by at least five million people at over 5,000 meetings," (*Gandhi and Salt Satyagraha*, p. 58).

97. Interview with Pyarelal, Delhi, February 20, 1967

98. Raja Rao, *Kanthapura* (London: Oxford University Press, 1963), pp. 169–174.

99. IOR/L/PJ/6/1983. Viceroy to Secretary of State, April 28, 1930. (Irwin reproduces Sykes's telegram from Bombay, which is quoted above).

100. IOR/MSS. Eur. C. 15²/24. Sir Purshotandas Thakurdas to Irwin, April 28, 1930.

101. IOR/L/PJ/6/1983 Viceroy to Secretary of State, June 2, 1930.

102. Sir Frederick Sykes, *From Many Angles: An Autobiography* (London: 1942, George Harrap), p. 392.

103. *India in 1930–31: A Statement Prepared for Presentation to Parliament* (Calcutta: Government of India Central Publishing Branch, , 1932), p. 73. Jawarharlal Nehru wrote in these same terms, recalling the salt *satyagraha*: "Many strange things happened in those days, but undoubtedly the most striking was the part of the women in the national struggle. They came out in large numbers from the seclusion of their homes, and, though unused to public activity, threw themselves into the heart of the struggle." *Mahatma Gandhi*, p. 63. Judith Brown documents the extensive mobilization of women in *Gandhi and Civil Disobedience*, pp. 136, 146, 291–92. S. R. Bakshi uses interviews with

women participants in the struggle to show the depth of their resistance across the nation, *Gandhi and Salt Satyagraha*, pp. 98–105.

104. Madhu Kishwar, "Gandhi on Women," *Economic and Political Weekly*, 20, No. 40, October 5, and No. 41, October 12, 1985, pp. 1696, 1757–1758. H. N. Brailsford, a British journalist who observed the civil disobedience movement in 1930, wrote that "nothing in this astonishing movement was so surprising" as the participation of women. *Rebel India* (New York: New Republic, 1931), p. 2.

105. Judith Brown, *Gandhi: Prisoner of Hope*, pp. 208–209. Insight on Gandhi's approach to the recruitment of women may be gained from M. K. Gandhi, *The Women in Gandhi's Life* (New York: Dodd, Mead, 1953); Eleanor Morton, *Women Behind Gandhi*, New Delhi, 1961; and *CWMG* 75: 155; and Susanne Rudolph, *Gandhi* (Chicago: University of Chicago Press, 1983), pp. 60–62.

106. Judith Brown, *Gandhi and Civil Disobedience*, p. 86.

107. Ibid., pp. 90–91, 104–106; Bipan Chandra, *India's Struggle for Independence, 1857–1947* (Delhi: Viking, 1988), pp. 282–283.

108. *CWMG* 43: 54–55.

109. *CWMG* 43: 55–57.

110. The profound extent of Gandhi's despair over the civil war was related in a personal interview with his associate, Nirmal Kumar Bose, who was with him in Calcutta at the time of India's independence. Interview in Calcutta, November, 1966.

111. Sumit Sarkar, "The Logic of Gandhian Nationalism: Civil Disobedience and the Gandhi-Irwin Pact (1930–1931)" *The Indian Historical Review* 3 (1) (July 1976): 117, 146; Sumit Sarkar, *Modern India*, 1885–1947 (Delhi: Macmillan India Ltd., 1983), pp. 281–308.

112. Tanikar Sarkar, "The First Phase of Civil Disobedience in Bengal, 1930–1931," *The Indian Historical Review*, 4 (1) (July 1977): 83.

113. Heman Ray, "Changing Soviet Views on Mahatma Gandhi," *Journal of Asian Studies* 29 (1) (November 1969); "To Lenin, Gandhi as the leader of the mass movement like the Indian National Congress was a revolutionary," p. 87.

114. Bipan Chandra, *India's Struggle for Independence*, p. 273.

115. *Times of India*, 6 Feb. 1930, p. 10.

116. Quoted in *Times of India*, 8 Feb. 1930, p. 13.

117. It is not clear from where Irwin could have derived this estimate of only five days, but it does indicate how poor was his understanding of the pattern of Gandhi's forthcoming campaign on the very eve of the march.

118. IOR/MSS. Eur. C. 15²/1, Irwin Correspondence with the King, 1926–1931, No. 71, March 11, 1930, p. 109b.

119. IOR/MSS. Eur. F. 15⁰/2. Sir Frederick Sykes Collection. Correspondence to and from Viceroy, Jan. 1, 1930–Dec. 1, 1930. Telegram No. S.D. 82., Jan. 17, 1930.

120. *Times of India*, March 7, 1930, p. 8.

121. *Ibid*, March 10, 1930, pp. 10, 15. (The quotes are from the *Daily Telegraph, Daily News* and *Daily Chronicle*).

122. Ibid. March 11, 1930, p. 11.

123. IOR/MSS. Eur. C. 15²/27. Irwin to Halifax, No. 116, 10 July 1928.

124. IOR/MSS. Eur.C. 15²/9, Secretary of State to Irwin, July 10 and July 12, 1928.

125. Leslie Wilson to Irwin, August 16, 1928, Home Poll. File #197, 1928.

126. Irwin to All Governors, August, 1928. Home Poll. File #197. 1928.

127. Secretary of State to Irwin, September 13, 1928, Home Poll. File # 197. 1928.

128. Irwin to Secretary of State, October 11, 1928, Home Poll. File #197. 1928.

129. Irwin should have felt reinforced in his determination to deal firmly with the nationalist movement by a "Minute on the present political situation" from Sir David Petrie, dated June 19, 1929. Petrie had served as Head of the Civil Intelligence Department in India from 1925–1929 and in a less senior capacity for 15 years before that. From this seasoned perspective, he concluded that the political situation in 1929 was "the gravest I have known," because among a large number of Indians "disaffection has given place to undisguised hostility, and a determination to end the present system of Government as soon as may be. The whole Congress movement . . . stands for nothing else. I have seen it said that when Mahatma Gandhi will raise the banner of Independence, 33 crore [one crore - 10 million] Indians will take a vow to prefer death to slavery." Petrie concluded: "The only safe, guiding principle I can see is that violence must be *at all costs* repressed and prevented from getting anything like a general hold. . . . manifestations of it as take place must be dealt with exemplary severity. But they must also be dealt with promptly . . . If the Congress leaders at the beginning of next year should institute a widespread movement for the attainment of Complete Independence—that is, for the deprivation His Majesty of the sovereignty of His Indian dominions, such a step must obviously have far-reaching effects in stimulating violence on a wide scale. If such a contingency should arise, the Government of India should be in no two minds as to the lines on which they should meet it." Home Poll. File #133. 1930. Petrie's memo is noteworthy in two respects: first, it associates civil disobedience with terrorist violence in a way that hardliners were wont to do, arguing that once *satyagraha* challenged government authority, the system of law and order was undermined and, especially in India, likely to dissolve into anarchy. In 1930, the validity of this assumption became Irwin's burden to prove. This was difficult in the face of Gandhi's insistence that *satyagraha* released forces of nonviolence to counter the violence of both Government and the terrorist movement. Second, Petrie perceives the Government's weakness, by insisting that it must not be in "two minds" about how to act against Gandhi. Hesitation would be Irwin's downfall.

130. Irwin to Halifax, December 31, 1929, p. 271.

131. Ibid., March 10, 1930, p. 282.

132. IOR/MSS Eur. C. 15²/6. Irwin to Wedgwood Benn, March 13, 1930.

133. Irwin to Halifax, March 2, 1930, p. 281.

134. *The Pioneer*, Allahabad, found in the letter "blind and fanatical prejudice," "amazing egotism" with a "ridiculous" plan of action, March 9, 1930, p. 12.

135. *The Leader*, March 9, 1930, p. 9.

136. Ibid., March 10, 1930, p. 8.

137. Ibid., March 12, 1930, p. 8.

138. IOR/MSS. Eur. C. 15²/24, Irwin Correspondence with Persons in India, 1930, No. 63d February 16, 1930, p. 124.

139. Ibid., No. 71b, February 24, p. 143a; No. 86a, March 10, p. 164e.

140. Ibid., No. 89f, March 17, p. 164r.

141. Ibid., No. 99a, March 22, p. 177; No. 107, March 26, p. 187.

142. Home Poll. File # 257/IV. 1930.

143. In an apparent lapse of reason, Sykes actually deployed a large police force around Dandi to destroy all the natural salt before Gandhi arrived. But he nevertheless feared that "there will still be opportunities for manufacturing it unless a force is kept constantly at the work of destroying it." However, at the moment Gandhi broke the law at Dandi, "Not a single police or excise officer was present." (S. R. Bakshi, *Gandhi and Salt Satyagraha*, p. 57).

144. William Shakespeare, *Measure for Measure*, II, ii, *The Complete Works* (New York: Viking, 1986), p. 41.

145. Home Poll. File # 257/IV. 1930.

146. Judith Brown, *Modern India, The Origins of An Asian Democracy* (Delhi: Oxford University Press, 1985), p. 260.

147. IOR/MSS. Eur. F. 15⁰/₂, Sykes Collection, Correspondence to and from Viceroy, 1 Jan. 1-Dec. 1930, "Draft Note for Discussion at Delhi," March 27, 1930. R. J. Moore offers this rationalization of Irwin's policy at the end of March and early April: "The Government recognized that the purpose of the campaign was to educate Indians in civil disobedience, and that Gandhi planned to use his arrest for breaking the salt laws as the signal for a mass response on a wide range of issues. They unobligingly determined not to arrest him so long as he seemed likely to provoke less excitement by being free than he would by being arrested. They would deny him the mass sympathy that his arrest would arouse. However, they would not ignore the transgression of the salt laws by any other leader if a clear case could be proved against him." *The Crisis of Indian Unity 1917–1940*, (Delhi: Oxford University Press, 1974), pp. 170–71. By the end of April, this policy and its rationale would become untenable.

148. IOR/MSS. Eur. C. 15²/24, Irwin Correspondence with Persons in India, 1930, No. 124, April 9, 1930, Telegram from Sykes to Irwin, p. 216.

149. *Gandhi and Civil Disobedience*, p. 108.

150. IOR/MSS. Eur. C. 15²/24. Irwin Correspondence with Persons in India, 1930, No. 111, April 14, 1930, p. 71.

151. IOR/MSS. Eur. C. 15²/19. Irwin to Persons Abroad. Jan–Dec. 1930, No. 41, March 31 (to Bray); No. 43, March 31 (to Lane-Fox); No. 45 (April 7) to G. Dawson.

152. Irwin relates his Christian heritage in his autobiography, *Fulness of Days* (London: Collins, 1957), pp. 18–25. Historians have remarked that he was "a man of deep religious conviction." Hugh Tinker, *South Asia* (London: Pall Mall, 1966), p. 214; and Percival Spear, *India* (Ann Arbor: The University of Michigan Press, 1961), comments that "Irwin was a deeply religious man, and Gandhi's moral approach to politics made a deep impression upon him." (p. 374) Also, R. P. Masani, *Britain in India* (London: Oxford University Press, 1960), p. 126.

153. IOR/MSS. Eur. C. 15²/19. Irwin to Persons Abroad. Jan.–Dec. 1930, No. 58, April 24, 1930, p. 55.

154. Ibid., No. 45, April 7, to G. Dawson, pp. 43–44.

155. IOR/MSS. Eur. C. 15²/27. Irwin to Halifax, No. 187, April 7, 1939, p. 286.

156. In New York, *The Literary Digest* in an editorial on the salt march titled "A Saint in Politics," wrote that Gandhi "is marching to the sea to further his campaign. The Sermon on the Mount is his book of etiquette." Moreover, an editorial in *The Nation*, 104,

No. 13, March 29, 1930, p. 24, entitled "The Terrible Meek," remarked that Gandhi had always acted "in the name of Christ Jesus and the Holy Word," and that "whether he is alive or dead, Gandhi's soul will go marching on." 130, No. 3385, May 21, 1930, p. 588. *The Christian Century* (Chicago) called its commentary on the salt march "Gandhi Before Pilate" and drew a series of parallels with Christ and termed the event "a gigantic success" because of the spiritual force it had generated. 47, No. 16, April 16, 1930, p. 488. In a letter to the editor that followed this editorial, written by Blanche Watson, the salt march was called "the greatest manifestation of spiritual power ever recorded in history. Jesus *is* 'winning India' through Gandhi—and by that I mean the spirit of Jesus, the spirit of truth and love." 47, No. 30, July 23, 1930, p. 919. The American characterization of Gandhi as a modern Christ began as early as April, 1921, when the New York theologian, Rev. John Haynes Holmes preached a sermon on Gandhi entitled "Who is the Greatest Man in the World?" and proclaimed: "When I think of Gandhi, I think of Jesus." J. H. Holmes, *My Gandhi* (London: George Allen and Unwin, 1954), p. 31. The remarkable extent to which this image of Gandhi caught on in the American press by as early as 1922 is suggested in *Gandhi and Non-Violent Resistance. The Non-Cooperation Movement of India, Gleanings from the American Press,* Compiled by Miss Blanche Watson (Madras: Ganesh and Co., 1923), pp. 280–544. But it was the British who first came forth with biographies that stressed Gandhi's spiritual qualities: the earliest biography by Rev. Joseph J. Doke, *M. K. Gandhi: an Indian Patriot in South Africa* (London: The London Chronicle, 1909), contained a glowing introduction by Lord Ampthill. Thus began a prolific commentary on Gandhi by Britons who identified with Gandhi because of his moral stature. Many were Quakers like Horace Alexander, Agatha Harrison, and Reginald Reynolds. The last is noteworthy here because of the circumstances of his delivery of Gandhi's letter of March 2, 1930, to Lord Irwin, recounted in *A Quest for Gandhi* (New York: Doubleday, 1952), pp. 51–52. Perhaps most important is the contribution of Charles Freer Andrews, who began as an Anglican priest and eventually became Gandhi's intimate friend. Andrews published a series of books on Gandhi: in 1930 appeared, *Mahatma Gandhi—His Own Story*, edited by Andrews (New York: Macmillan) and with an introduction by John Haynes Holmes. The latter claims that with the salt *satyagraha*, Gandhi "has at last become, like Jesus, one of the 'terrible meek'—the meek who 'inherit the earth' . . . Long before the War the Mahatma was compared with the Christ for the sheer beauty and sanctity of his inner life. Now this comparison is immeasurably clarified and strengthened by the spectacle of what Gandhi is seeking to do for India and for the world. If we would know what Jesus was as a saint, and also what he did, or tried to do, as a savior, we have only to look across the seas to this greatest man in the world today" (pp. 30–31). Unlike Holmes or Reynolds, however, Andrews was involved in correspondence with Lord Irwin during the salt march. The seriousness of this exchange is succinctly stated in the outstanding biography of Andrews by Hugh Tinker, *The Ordeal of Love. C. F. Andrews and India* (Oxford: Oxford University Press), 1979, pp. 237–240. Irwin's high regard for Andrews's views on Gandhi is suggested in his biography, The Earl of Halifax, *Fulness of Days*, pp. 147–148. Finally, parallels between Gandhi and Christ were stressed before 1930 in Romain Rolland's influential and widely read biography, *Mahatma Gandhi. The Man Who Became One With the Universal Being*, in French and translated into English both published in 1924.

157. In Preface to *Mahatma Gandhi, His Mission and Message* (London: G. S. Dara, November, 1929), p. 6.

158. IOR/MSS. Eur. C. 15²/24, Irwin Correspondence to Persons in India, Hailey to Irwin, No. 157, 25 April 1930, pp. 262–265.

159. Judith Brown, *Gandhi and Civil Disobedience*, pp. 174–191 offers a thorough examination of the Gandhi-Irwin talks and the resulting pact. S. R. Bakshi, *Gandhi and Salt Satyagraha*, pp. 60–66, emphasizes the central aspect of Irwin's ambivalence; an emphasis first given by the present author in 1974: Dennis Dalton, "Gandhi's Style of Leadership" in B. N. Pandey, ed., *Leadership in South Asia* (New (Delhi: Vikas Publishers, 1977), pp. 598–623.

160. IOR/MSS. Eur. C. 15²/11. Wedgwood Benn to Irwin, March 11, 1930.

161. IOR/MSS. Eur. C. 15²/6. Wedgwood Benn to Irwin, April 22, 1930.

162. John Court Curry, The Joy of the Working. Memoirs of an Indian Policeman. 2, pp. 76, 202–203, 209–210, 216–217. IOR/MSS. EUR.C. 21½.

163. *CWMG* 43: 37

164. Gandhi also realized the discomfort that Government violence was causing many Indians who felt loyal to the Raj. Representative of this ambivalence is a letter from Sir A. K. Ghuznavi to Irwin. Ghuznavi was a Member of the Legislative Assembly and a Muslim supporter of the Government. He wrote to Irwin: "It is impossible and it is impolitic to overlook the bitter psychological effect this method [of police dispersing crowds with violence, using *lathis* or steel-tipped clubs] is having on people who are pro-government and are anxious to support it. Every time one of these *lathi* charges takes place some supporters of Government are alienated and the Congress are enabled to strengthen the impression that they are non-violent while Government is meeting non-violence with violence." Home Poll. File #190. 1930.

165. Shakespeare, *Hamlet*, III, i, *Complete Works*, p. 951.

166. Bondurant, pp. 226–227.

167. *Harijan*, Nov. 26, 1938 and Dec. 17, 1938, in *CWMG* 68: 137–141, 191–193.

168. *Harijan*, Jan. 7, 1939 in *CWMG* 68: 276–278, 381–382.

169. A thorough and illuminating analysis of the entire subject of this and related correspondence occurs in Gideon Shimoni, *Gandhi, Satyagraha and the Jews: A Formative Factor in India's Policy Towards Israel* (Jerusalem: The Hebrew University, 1977), pp. 37–60.

170. Martin Buber and J. L. Magnes, *Two Letters to Gandhi* (Jerusalem: Rubin Mass, April, 1939) pp. 2–7. Martin Buber (1878–1965), Israeli theologian and philosopher, born in Austria, had an intimate knowledge of Nazism through his residence in Germany from 1933–1935. Judah Magnes (1877–1948) was an American rabbi and like Hayim Greenberg, a pacifist with a sympathetic grasp of Gandhi's thought and experience. He was Chancellor and President of the Hebrew University in Jerusalem. The present writer is indebted to Dr. Daniel Argov, for his assistance in researching the Buber-Gandhi correspondence in Jerusalem, August 1966.

171. Ibid., pp. 23–25. Magnes's letter is dated two days later than Buber's, February 26, 1939; both are written in Jerusalem.

172. Shimoni concludes "that the letters may have gone astray in this period, or that Gandhi never actually read them" and cites a communication from Gandhi's secretary, Pyarelal Nayar, *Gandhi, Satyagraha and the Jews*, p. 47. When the present author dis-

cussed this with Pyarelal he was certain that Gandhi had never received or read the letters. (Interview in Delhi, March, 1975).

173. Greenberg, "An Answer to Gandhi," in *The Inner Eye. Selected Essays* (New York: Jewish Frontier Association, 1953), pp. 230–238. Hayim Greenberg (1889–1953), a Labor Zionist, was editor of *The Jewish Frontier* from 1934–1953. The profound influence that Gandhi had on his thought is evident in his public exchanges as well as in his eulogy to Gandhi on February 1, 1948 (pp. 157–161). Also see Marie Syrkin, ed., *Hayim Greenberg: Anthology* (Detroit: Wayne State University Press), 1968.

174. *CWMG* 69: 290.

175. Louis Fischer, *The Life of Mahatma Gandhi* (New York: Harper, 1950), p. 348.

176. Gandhi's advice to Hitler was no more persuasive than to the Jews. He wrote two letters to Hitler dated July 23, 1939 and December 24, 1940. Both open with his customary salutation, "Dear Friend," but unlike his classic letter to Lord Irwin, they have no concrete or practical implications. The first appealed to Hitler as "the one person in the world who can prevent a war," and so implicitly assigns the sole responsibility for the impending conflict to him. (*CWMG* 70: 21) The second letter is much longer and substantive. It condemns Hitler's action as "monstrous and unbecoming of human dignity," "degrading humanity," but again implores him, this time "in the name of humanity to stop the war." Most of this letter tries to present a case for nonviolence as "a force which, if organized, can without doubt match itself against a combination of all the most violent forces in the world." (*CWMG* 73: 253–255) When Gandhi put this same argument to Irwin it carried weight because it was backed by the real prospect of mass civil disobedience. It could have no such meaning for the Nazis. There is no evidence that either of these two letters was received. Both were suppressed by the British (*CWMG* 73, Editor's introduction, p. vi) and there was no acknowledgement from Germany. However, the Fuehrer did remark ominously in January, 1942 that "If we took India, the Indians would certainly not be enthusiastic, and they'd not be slow to regret the good old days of English rule!" *Hitler's Secret Conversations. 1941–1944* (New York: Farrar, Straus, 1953), p. 163. Joseph Goebbels commented particularly on Gandhi, derisively and contemptuously, calling him "a fool whose policies [of 'passive resistance'] seem merely calculated to drag India further and further into misfortune." He believed that India needed "an energetic nationalist," presumably like Subhas Chandra Bose, to combat British imperialism, and characterized Gandhi's fasting as "a great comedy for the world." *The Goebbels Diaries. 1942–1943*, edited and translated by Louis P. Lochner (New York: Doubleday, 1948), pp. 162, 177, 273. There was no evident ambivalence among the Nazis about Gandhi and his method. But Gandhi was not ambivalent about Hitler. He wrote that "it almost seems as if Herr Hitler knows no God but brute force," (*CWMG* 70: 162) and pitted his method against Hitler's in these stark terms: "If we wish to win *swaraj* through *ahimsa*, this is the only way. If, however, we wish to use force, then Hitler would point the way. There are only two courses open—either Hitler's, that is, the way of violence, or mine, that is, the way of non-violence." (*CWMG* 75: 10) Such comments may only underscore the importance of Gandhi's activism, without which his testaments of faith could come as hollow homilies.

177. Gandhi was unusually well informed during the 1930s and 1940s about the plight of Jews in Europe in the face of Nazi persecution. In South Africa, from 1904–1914, he had formed a close relationship with Hermann Kallenbach, a German Jew, who

served as the manager of the protest march of 1913. Kallenbach visited Gandhi at the Sevagram ashram in 1937 and 1939. He was an ideal source for presenting to Gandhi an informed and sympathetic account because he came as an old and trusted friend, who shared with Gandhi abundant literature on this subject as well as on Zionism and Palestine. Gideon Shimoni examines Kallenbach's role in detail, *Gandhi, Satyagraha and the Jews*, pp. 22–37. While Kallenbach was at Sevagram, a Captain Strunk, representative of an official newspaper in Germany and member of Hitler's staff, visited Gandhi, and the latter asked him "why the Jews are being persecuted in Germany," as he introduced him to Kallenbach, "a German Jew sitting there bare-bodied and in a *khadi dhoti*." Strunk replied "I personally think we have just overdone it. That's the mistake revolutions always do." *Harijan*, July 3, 1937. Maurice Frydman, a Polish Jew who fled Europe in 1935 to join Gandhi, lived at Sevagram continuously from 1938–1941. He affirmed Kallenbach's key role in educating Gandhi on issues relating to European Jews at that time. Frydman judged Gandhi exceptionally knowledgeable on the subject and also claimed that he "never observed a trace of anti-Semitism in Gandhi." (Interview with Maurice Frydman in Bombay, November, 1966).

178. Ample evidence exists of Jewish resistance during the 1930s and 1940s in Europe. See the extensive discussion in *Jewish Resistance During the Holocaust. Proceedings of the Conference on Manifestations of Jewish Resistance*, Jerusalem, April 7–11, 1968 (Jerusalem: Yad Vashem, 1971). Blair B. Kling, "Gandhi, Nonviolence, and the Holocaust," *Peace and Change*, 16 (2) (April 1991): 176–196, analyzes thoroughly Gandhi's position on the Jews and examines problems of Jewish nonviolent resistance. He concludes that no evidence of *satyagraha* exists because "Although in their resistance Jews did often make use of the techniques of nonviolent action, the spirit in which these were used was non-Gandhian." He also makes the important point that because the Jews were invariably a small minority, "In general, studies of Jewish resistance show that the success with which Jews, particularly in Eastern Europe, were able to survive and resist, violently or nonviolently, depended primarily on the non-Jews among whom they lived." This fact underscores the difference between the Indian and German situations. Gene Sharp documents numerous instances of what Kling calls "techniques of nonviolent action" used by Jews and non-Jews alike in his classic and encyclopedic work, *The Politics of Nonviolent Action*.

179. Sharp, Ibid., p. 28.

Chapter 5

1. *CWMG* 19: 541.
2. *CWMG* 75: 282.
3. *The Statesman* (Calcutta), May 20, 1947, p. 4.
4. Ibid. August 21, 1946, p. 4.
5. Suranjan Das, *Communal Riots in Bengal 1905–1947* (Delhi: Oxford University Press, 1991), p. 176. Also his article "Towards an Understanding of Communal Violence in Twentieth Century Bengal," *Economic and Political Weekly*, August 27, 1988, pp. 1804–1808.

6. G. D. Khosla, *Stern Reckoning: A Survey of the Events Leading Up To and Following the Partition of India* (Bombay: Claridge and Co., 1952), pp. 52–53; and Richard D. Lambert, "Hindu-Muslim Riots," Ph.D. Dissertation in Sociology, University of Pennsylvania, 1951, pp. 169–170.

7. Gandhi, as quoted in D.G. Tendulkar, *Mahatma* (1953), vii, p. 475.

8. *The Statesman*, November 24, 1945, p. 4.

9. Sir Francis Tuker, *While Memory Serves* (1950), p. 102.

10. Ibid., p. 100.

11. *The Statesman*, February 13–15, 1946. The rioting lasted four days; 42 killed and 380 injured.

12. Ibid. February 15, 1946, p. 4.

13. Ibid. February 13, 1946, p. 7.

14. It may be noted that the largest riots of February occurred not in Calcutta, but in Bombay (*The Times of India*, February 22–24, 1946). Indeed, during the months of late 1945 and early 1946, Bombay's incidence of large-scale rioting became the highest in India. Significantly, these riots were noncommunal in nature, and therefore the situation in Bombay did not deteriorate on the Calcutta model. These riots did, however, drive home the realization of the terrifying scale that could be reached. Thus, when Gandhi commented on them he struck precisely the note of anxiety that was in the air, and the press throughout India commented on his words: "A combination between Hindus and Muslims and others for the purpose of violent action [as had happened in Bombay] is unholy and will lead and probably is a preparation for mutual violence bad for India and the world." (Gandhi quoted in *The Times of India*, February 25, 1946, p. 7).

15. Tuker, *While Memory Serves*, p. 108.

16. R.G. Casey, *An Australian in India* (1947), p. 38.

17. Tuker, *While Memory Serves*, p. 114.

18. *The Statesman*, July 31, 1946, p. 1.

19. Ibid. July 31-August 2, 1946.

20. Ibid. August 13–16, 1946.

21. Gandhi, quoted in *The Times of India*, August 5, 1946, p. 5.

22. *The Leader* (Allahabad), August 16, 1946, p. 4.

23. *The Times of India*, August 7, 1946, p. 6. ("Candidus").

24. *The Statesman*, August 15, 1946, p. 6.

25. Ibid. February 23, 1947, p. 11.

26. Interview with Nirmal Kumar Bose, Calcutta, November 16, 1966. Suranjan Das in his focused study of communal riots observes that "The survivors of the Great Calcutta Killing, for example, still talk about their experience in the same way the second world war provides a framework for Europeans who lived through it." "Towards an Understanding of Communal Violence in Twentieth Century Bengal," *Economic Political Weekly*, August 27, 1988, p. 1808. The casualty figures are from official reports, also cited in Das, *Communal Riots in Bengal*, pp. 171, 269. These figures are often higher in other accounts. G. D. Khosla, *Stern Reckoning* gives an estimate of 5,000 killed and 15,000 injured, commenting that "the Muslims fared almost as badly as the Hindus." (p. 66). R. D. Lambert,'Hindu-Muslim Riots." says that "the deaths are generally put well over 5,000 and the number of injuries about five times that number." (p. 173).

27. G.D. Khosla, ibid., p. 64.

28. Nehru, quoted in *The Statesman*, August 18, 1946, p. 1.

29. Maulana Azad quoted in *The Statesman*, August 20, 1946, p. 1. The indictment was repeated by Sarat Chandra Bose, leader of the opposition in the central assembly of Bengal.

30. Jinnah, quoted in *The Statesman*, August 18, 1946, p. 1.

31. *The Times* of London: August 26, 1946, p. 5.

32. Liaqat Ali Khan, quoted in *The Statesman*, August 28, 1946, pp. 1, 5.

33. Jinnah, quoted in *The Statesman*, September, 5, 1946, p. 1.

34. *The Statesman*, September 1, 1946, p. 1.

35. Ibid. September 7, 1946, p. 5.

36. *The Modern Review*, edited by K. Chatterji (Calcutta), September, 1946, p. 171.

37. Arthur Moore, in a letter to the editor from Delhi, dated August 22, 1946. *The Statesman*, August 27, 1946, p. 4.

38. *The Statesman*, August 23, 1946, p. 2. Suranjan Das, comparing riots in Bengal from 1905–1947, argues that the Great Calcutta Killing was unprecedented in character: "For the first time, Bengali Hindus and Muslims joined their coreligionists of up-country origin on a large scale in the Great Calcutta Killing of 1946. While the earlier riots were mostly characterized by looting and other forms of violence committed by a large crowd, those in the 1940s also saw the killing of individuals by small groups. The emphasis now was not on economic gain but on revenge and humiliation of the members of the rival community. This rite of violence displayed communal animosity at its peak, thereby completing the process of dehumanisation," p. 1806.

39. *The Times* of London, August 26, 1946, p. 5.

40. Ibid. August 20, 1946, p. 5.

41. Gandhi, quoted in *The Statesman*, August 27, 1946, p. 5.

42. Percival Griffiths, *Modern India* (1957), p. 85.

43. The riots lasted from March 26 to April 1; 73 were killed and 481 injured. See *The Statesman*.

44. Governor Burrows, quoted in *The Statesman*, May 28, 1947, p. 7.

45. For example, on "Pakistan Day," March 23, 1947, Suhrawardy banned all processions, demonstrations, and public meetings in Bengal, and enforced this ban stringently with troops. *The Statesman*, March 21 and 22, 1947.

46. *The Statesman*, April 10, 1947, p. 4.

47. See Tuker on this point, *While Memory Serves*, pp. 234, 412.

48. *The Statesman*, April 9, 1947, p.1.

49. Ibid., April 16, 1947, p.1.

50. Ibid., May 10, 1947, p. 1.

51. Ibid., May 12, 1947, p. 6.

52. Ibid., July 9, 1947, p. 4.

53. Ibid., August 4, 1947, p. 4.

54. Ibid., August 5, 1947, p. 1. This followed the Viceroy Lord Mountbatten's visit to Calcutta at the end of July during which he expressed his "grave concern at the disturbed conditions in the city." Lord Spens remarked that he had himself urged the central government to increase military forces in Calcutta at this time.

55. Ibid. August 7, 1947, p. 1.

56. Ibid. August 11–12, 1947, p. 1.
57. Ibid. July 31, 1947, p. 6.
58. The incident is related in N. K. Bose, *My Days with Gandhi*, p. 232.
59. *The Statesman*, August 13, 1947, p. 1.
60. Sardar Patel quoted in Pyarelal, *Mahatma Gandhi, The Last Phase* (Ahmedabad: Navajivan, (1958), ii, p. 365.
61. Ibid. p. 367.
62. Khosla offers this assessment of this critical moment: "In the beginning of August 1947, when the partition of the province was imminent and the Government of the future East Bengal was ready to leave Calcutta, attacks on Muslims increased. Calcutta appeared to be on the verge of another catastrophe similar to the one in which it had been plunged a year previously. Mahatma Gandhi then came to the rescue and decided to live in Calcutta until peace was restored. Accompanied by Mr. Suhrawardy, he took up residence in the house of a Muslim and braving the anger of the Hindus, began to preach his gospel of non-violence. On one occasion a Hindu mob attacked the house in which he was living and a *lathi* was actually thrown at him. He stood his ground undaunted and his courage worked a veritable miracle in Calcutta." (*Stern Reckoning*, p. 67) Richard D. Lambert observes that "At the time of partition the country looked to Calcutta for a replica of the Punjab disorders, but . . . the quieting effect of the joint efforts of Gandhi and Suhrawardy forestalled large-scale violence. And with Calcutta quiet, Bengal was divided with only minor disturbances." ("Hindu-Muslim Riots," p. 163) Suranjan Das, *Communal Riots in Bengal,* says that Gandhi "persuaded Suhrawardy to stay with him in the riot-torn areas which caused a rapid improvement of the situation. Largely as a result of this, the Hindus and Muslims jointly celebrated the end of the Raj on August 15—a scene which contrasted sharply with the continuous fratricidal warfare which had plagued the city for the last year" (p. 205). These assessments of Gandhi's influence in Calcutta during Independence are accurate as far as they go, but they do not proceed with accounts of his September fast. In fact, as the analysis here suggests, Gandhi's use of nonviolence in Calcutta had two stages, the first an essential preparation for the second. His "experiment" with Suhrawardy was a necessary but not sufficient condition for meeting the violence in Calcutta. His fast proved decisive mainly because of the high degree of self-sacrifice that it represented. The force of self-suffering is called *tapas* and Gandhi regarded it as a central idea in his tradition, felt by Hindus and Muslims alike.
63. Comment in *The Statesman*, August 15, 1947, p. 6 (Leader).
64. Rajagoplachari in *The Statesman*, August 19, 1947, p. 5.
65. *The Statesman*, August 15, 1947, p. 1.
66. Sir Francis Tuker gives several other reasons for the explosion of communal goodwill at the moment of independence. He terms Gandhi's influence "considerable." *While Memory Serves*, pp. 415, 421–2.
67. Comment by *The Statesman*, August 28, 1947, p. 4.
68. Ibid. August 19, 1947, p. 1.
69. On August 26th, Mountbatten wired Gandhi in Calcutta: "My Dear Gandhiji, In the Punjab we have 55 thousand soldiers and large scale rioting. In Bengal our forces consist of one man, and there is no rioting. As a serving officer, as well as an administra-

tor, may I be allowed to pay my tribute to the One Man Boundary Force, not forgetting his Second in Command, Mr. Suhrawardy." Gandhi, *Correspondence with the Government, 1944–47* (1959), p. 277.

70. On August 24, 1947, The Muslim League party in the Indian constituent assembly passed a resolution expressing its "deep sense of appreciation of the services rendered by Mr. Gandhi to the cause of restoration of peace and goodwill between the communities in Calcutta" (*The Statesman*, August 25, 1947, p. 1). The press throughout India acclaimed Gandhi's achievement in exalted terms: see, *The Mail* (Madras), August 20, 1947, p. 4; *The Leader* (Allahabad) August 20, 1947, p. 4; and *The Times of India*, September 3, 1947, p. 4.

71. Nehru and Rees reported in *The Statesman*, August 29, 1947, pp. 1, 5–6.

72. *The Statesman*, September 1, 1947, p. 5.

73. Tuker, *While Memory Serves*, p. 426.

74. Gandhi to Patel, Calcutta, September 1, 1947, in M. K. Gandhi, *Letters to Sardar Patel* (1957), pp. 225–6. Also, Pyarelal, *Mahatma Gandhi*, p. 406.

75. Pyarelal, ibid., p. 407.

76. Gandhi in *The Statesman*, September 2, 1947, p. 10; and *CWMG*89: 132.

77. *The Times of India*, September 3, 1947, p. 4.

78. Pyarelal, *Mahatma Gandhi*, p. 412.

79. Ibid. p. 421.

80. Ibid. p. 420.

81. Amiya Chakravarty, *A Saint at Work*. William Penn Lecture, 1950, Philadelphia, The Young Friends Movement of the Philadelphia Yearly Meetings, 1950, pp. 23–24.

82. The shift, in this *The Statesman* leader, from the use of "Mr." to "Mahatma" is not coincidental; an editorial of September 1 had announced it as part of the paper's future policy. The change was made in response to numerous requests from readers, one of whom wrote (letter to editor, September 1, 1947, p. 4): "I have always had great respect for Mr. Gandhi, but could not make up my mind to speak of him as Mahatma. However, seeing the wonders he has done in Calcutta I have no hesitation now in doing so. I hope that you will take the same view and in future write Mahatma Gandhi and not Mr. Gandhi."

83. *The Statesman*, September 3, 1947, p. 4.

84. Chakravarty, p. 25.

85. Quoted in Pyarelal, *Mahatma Gandhi*, p. 423.

86. Chakravarty, p. 25.

87. Quoted in *The Statesman*, September 6, 1947, p. 1.

88. Ibid. September 7, 1947, p. 1.

89. E. W. R. Lumby, *The Transfer of Power in India*, 1945–1947 (London: Allen and Unwin, 1954), p. 193. For further specific comment on Gandhi's achievement in the Calcutta *satyagraha*, and especially the September fast, see V. P. Menon, *The Transfer of Power in India* (1957), p. 434; also, Lord Pethwick-Lawrence et al. *Mahatma Gandhi* (London: Odhams Press, 1949), pp. 297–98; Tuker, *While Memory Serves*, p. 426. Extensive accounts of the fast itself are in Pyarelal, *Mahatma Gandhi*, N. K. Bose, *My Days with Gandhi*, D.G. Tendulkar, *Mahatma*, vols. 7 and 8, and Manubehn Gandhi, *The Miracle of Cal-*

cutta (Navajivan: 1959). A dramatic relation of Gandhi's achievement in Calcutta occurs in Larry Collins and Pierre Lapierre, *Freedom at Midnight* (New York: Avon, 1983), pp. 338–360. These authors conclude: "This time the 'miracle of Calcutta' was real and it would endure. On the tortured plains of the Punjab, in the Frontier Province, in Karachi, Lucknow and Delhi, the worst was yet to come, but the city of Dreadful Night would keep faith with the old man who had risked death to give it peace. Never again during Gandhi's lifetime would the blood of a communal riot soil the pavements of Calcutta" (p. 360). General comment on the extent of Gandhi's influence during the partition period occurs in Nicholas Mansergh, *Survey of British Commonwealth Affairs, 1939–1952* (1958), p. 222, and his *The Commonwealth and The Nations* (1958), p. 142; Penderel Moon, *Divide and Quit* (1961), p. 249; Wilfred Russel, *Indian Summer* (1951), p. 26; and Percival Spear, *India, A Modern History*, p. 142. My account of the Calcutta satyagraha is indebted especially to personal interviews with Pyarelal (Jan., 1967, Delhi), Archarya Kripalani (Oct., 1966, Ahmedabad) C. Rajagopalachari (May, 1967, Madras), and Nirmal Kumar Bose (Nov., 1966, Calcutta).

90. Nicholas Mansergh, *The Commonwealth and The Nations*, p. 142.

91. Ibid., p. 142.

92. *CWMG* 75: 366.

93. *CWMG* 39: 350.

94. *CWMG* 25: 171.

95. *CWMG* 86: 143.

96. Suhrawardy, moreover, not only behaved like Gandhi's trusted comrade during the experiment, but, to the astonishment of his Hindu antagonists, he admitted what he had heretofore denied vehemently: that he should bear the largest responsibility for the Calcutta Killing.

97. Gandhi, *Delhi Diary* (1948), p. 302.

98. The technique of the prayer meeting, developed in Calcutta, was perfected by Gandhi in Delhi (September 1947–January 1948). For his use of the "objector" in the audience see, for example, *Delhi Diary*, pp. 27, 29–32, 38, 45–48.

99. *CWMG* 55: 412.

100. *CWMG* 75: 147.

101. *CWMG* 63: 91 and *CWMG* 83: 401.

102. *CWMG* 83: 401.

103. *CWMG* 86: 318.

104. *Young India*, May 1, 1924. Gandhi's theory and practice of fasting may be compared and contrasted with the Irish employment of the technique against the British government from 1917–1973. On the one hand, Terence McSwiney, who died in a hunger strike in 1920, stated his philosophy in Gandhian terms: "It is not those who inflict the most but those who suffer the most who will conquer." Yet, the Irish did not regard their adversaries as "lovers" nor did they adhere to creedal nonviolence. From a Gandhian perspective, the Irish hunger strike seems more *duragraha* than *satyagraha*. See Padraig O'Malley, *Biting at the Grave. The Irish Hunger Strikes and the Politics of Despair* (Boston: Beacon Press, 1990), pp. 26–27; and Tim Pat Coogan, *Michael Collins: A Biography* (New York: Arrow Books, 1991), pp. 154–155. Julie Boyer contributed these references.

105. The analysis of Gandhi's use of the fast in Calcutta in Collins and Lapierre, *Freedom At Midnight*, emphasizes this point. It also notes that "a fast gave a problem a vital dimension of time. Its dramatic message forced people's thoughts out of the ruts in which they were accustomed to run and made them face new concepts." (p. 356).

106. *CWMG* 72: 456.

107. *Harijan*, November 17, 1946; and *CWMG* 76: 76.

108. Radhakrishanan, quoted in *The Statesman*, September 5, 1947, p. 8.

109. *CWMG* 89: 132, 149.

110. This concluding summary and analysis is indebted to interviews with Pyarelal Nayar and Nirmal Kumar Bose, as noted above, and particularly to the insights of Mirabehn (Madeline Slade), interviewed in Vienna, Austria, August, 1975.

111. Suranjan Das, *Communal Riots in Bengal*, p. 205.

112. Humayun Kabir, "Muslim Politics, 1942–47," *The Partition of India*, C. H. Philips and M.D . Wainwright eds. (London: Allen and Unwin,1970), p. 405. This point is also made in Richard Lambert 'Hindu-Muslim Riots." "Communal violence continued at a peak until the assassination of Gandhi in January 1948, and after that it tapered off and almost disappeared altogether." (p. 227) Percival Spear, *Modern India* (Ann Arbor: University of Michigan Press, 1961) comments: "The manner and circumstances of his [Gandhi's] death transformed the situation. The Mahatma was even more powerful in death than in life. The policy oi revenge was abandoned. The Hindu extremists were discredited . . . The danger of bitterness boiling over into anti-Muslim pogroms was averted." (p. 424).

Chapter 6

1. Gandhi's cable to William Shirer, September, 1932, in *CWMG* 51: 129. Gandhi repeatedly condemned "exclusiveness" in a variety of contexts. See Gandhi, *All Men Are Brothers*, K. Kripalani, ed. (New York: Columbia University Press, 1972), pp. 108–110. The concept of inclusiveness and the way that Gandhi understood and exemplified it has been explained especially by Erik Erikson, *Gandhi's Truth* (New York: Norton, 1969), pp. 432–33; *Identity Youth and Crisis* (New York: Norton, 1968), pp. 314–316; and *Dialogue With Erik Erikson* by Richard I. Evans (New York: Dutton, 1969). In the last book, Erikson says: "the best leader is the one who realizes what potentials can be activated in those led, and most of all, what more inclusive identities can be realized . . . Gandhi's nonviolent technique . . . was not only tied to the political realities of his day, but also revived the more inclusive identity promised in the world religions" (pp. 70–71). An essential difference that Gandhi found between an exclusive and inclusive attitude is that the former connoted a kind of separatist thinking which tended to dehumanize or demonize the "other," turning one's adversary into the *enemy*. He insisted that in satyagraha there could be no enemies.

2. Malcolm X, *The Autobiography of Malcolm X* (hereafter referred to as *AMX*) (New York: Ballantine Books, 1973), p. 366.

3. *CWMG* 39 (*Autobiography*), pp. 21–22; *AMX*, pp. 1–38.

4. S. R. Mehrotra also quotes this passage from Nehru. He then concludes that

among Gandhi's major contributions to the nationalist movement was that "Gandhi broke the hypnotic spell of the British Raj in India. He tried to rid the Indian people of the pervasive, perpetual and paralysing fear with which they were seized. He taught them to say 'no' to their oppressors, both foreign and indigenous. He uplifted the spirit and exalted the dignity of a vast people by teaching them to straighten their backs, to raise their eyes, and to face circumstances with a steady gaze." *Towards India's Freedom and Partition* (New Delhi: Vikas, 1979, p. 154. This sounds remarkably like the purpose of both Malcolm X and Martin Luther King, Jr. in the United States.

5. *CWMG* 39: 22. *AMX*, pp. 1–22. Beginning with the odd double message that Malcolm received from his father and his mother over the fact that he was lighter than his siblings (pp 4, 7–8), and traumatized by his father's murder by whites, Malcolm's fears of inadequacy because of his color were ruthlessly confirmed by his eighth-grade English teacher, as the subsequent account here indicates. Bruce Perry has analyzed Malcolm's early intense fears about his own masculinity and how these were related to his later violent attitudes and behavior in "Opposition to Nonviolence: A Revealing Case Study," *Gandhi Marg*, #59, February, 1984, pp. 751–758. The present author is grateful to Mr. Perry for his communications on this subject.

6. *AMX*, pp. 36–37.

7. Bruce Perry, *Malcolm: The Life of a Man Who Changed Black America*. Station Hill Press, Barrytown (New York: 1991), p. 380.

8. *CWMG* Ibid., pp. 46–47.

9. *AMX*, p. 54.

10. *CWMG* 5: 117.

11. *CWMG* 10 ("Hind Swaraj"), p. 18. This sense of a lost identity among blacks who emulate whites is expressed well in Malcolm's classic contrast between the "two kinds of slaves, the house Negro and the field Negro." The former, ancestor of "modern Uncle Toms," "loved his master," and identified with him so closely that rebellion for him was impossible. *Malcolm X Speaks: Selected Speeches and Statements*, George Breitman, ed. (New York: Grove Press, 1966), pp. 10–12.

12. Erik Erikson, *Gandhi's Truth*, p. 194.

13. *CWMG* 39: 380. On April 13, 1919 in the city of Amritsar, an event occurred that contributed substantially to Gandhi's determination to resist British rule in India. Approximately 10,000 Indians gathered in the town square were fired upon by troops under the command of Gen. Reginald Dyer, about 400 were killed and 1500 wounded. Charles Andrews wrote: "No one can understand Mahatma Gandhi's attitude towards Great Britain and the British empire unless he has come to realize that 'Amritsar' was the critical event which changed Mahatma Gandhi from a wholehearted supporter into a pronounced opponent" C. F. Andrews, *Mahatma Gandhi's Ideas* (London: Allen and Unwin, 1930), p. 230.

14. *CWMG* 10: 36–38.

15. Ibid., pp. 21, 35, 39.

16. Ibid., pp. 57, 61.

17. J.D. Sethi remarks on this transformation in his thought: "Gandhi's concepts of *Swaraj* and *Swadeshi* began as expressions of fierce nationalism. But even in his lifetime he had already transformed his national concepts into universal concepts." *Gandhi Today* (Durham, North Carolina: Carolina Academic Press, 1978) p. 195.

18. *AMX*, p. 150.

19. *AMX*, p. 173.

20. Elijah Muhamad in *When The Word Is Given* by Louis E. Lomax (New York: Signet Books, 1963), p. 56. The historical context of the Black Muslim movement, its ideology of vehement separatism and its organizational structure is examined in Louis E. Lomax, *The Negro Revolt* (New York: Harper, 1962), ch. 13, pp. 164–177; E.U. Essien-Udom, *Black Nationalism: The Rise of the Black Muslims in the U.S.A.* (New York: Penguin, 1966), Ch. 10, pp. 206–238; Theodore Draper, *The Rediscovery of Black Nationalism* (New York: Viking, 1970), pp. 69–96; Harold Cruise, *The Crisis of the Negro Intellectual* (New York: Morrow, 1971), pp. 420–448; and C. Eric Lincoln, *The Black Muslims in America* (Boston: Beacon, 1961). The term "Black Muslim" was coined by C. Eric Lincoln in his doctoral dissertation; members of the movement call themselves Muslims.

21. *AMX*, pp. 251–255.

22. Whereas in 1916 Gandhi said, "My patriotism is both exclusive and inclusive," (*CWMG* 13: 224), his later uses of the term "exclusive" are all negative, as noted above, and he becomes after 1919, when he assumes leadership of the Indian Congress, an inclusive figure in his ideology and organization of the national movement. In 1924, he said, "As my patriotism is inclusive and admits of no enmity or ill will, I do not hesitate . . . to take from the West what is beneficial for me." *CWMG* 25: 461. See my analysis of "the inclusive style of Gandhi" in "Gandhi's Styles of Leadership," in *Leadership in South Asia*, pp. 598–623.

23. Gandhi not only developed close personal friendships with whites from early in his South African experience, he also placed them in positions of considerable responsibility after having converted them to his cause. In his autobiography, he discusses key white Europeans who joined his movement: Henry and Millie Polak, Hermann Kallenbach, A. H. West, Sonja Schlesin, L. W. Ritch, and the Rev. Joseph Doke, who wrote the first biography of Gandhi in South Africa. Martin Luther King, Jr. also managed to establish such relationships.

24. This phrase is from Susanne and Lloyd Rudolph, *Gandhi*, pp. 38–62. The Rudolphs write about Gandhi's renunciations: "to control his outer environment he must control the inner" (p. 58).

25. Malcolm relates how, when he was in prison but before he had been converted fully to the Nation of Islam, the initial instructions that he abstain from pork and stop smoking cigarettes affected him. When he first turned down pork on the food line, he discovered that "It was mentioned all over the cell block. . . . It made me very proud, in some odd way. One of the universal images of the Negro, in prison and out, was that he couldn't do without pork. It made me feel good to see that my not eating it had especially startled the white convicts" (*AMX*, p. 156). Adherence to strict codes of moral discipline became singularly important to Malcolm. As noted below, when he discovered that his leader, Elijah Muhammad had transgressed the code of sexual discipline he was sufficiently shocked to leave the Nation of Islam. Elijah's authority and power had disintegrated in his eyes because of this personal indiscipline and immorality. This suggests again close parallels with Gandhi's morality.

26. *CWMG* 40: 297.

27. Erik Erikson mentions this with comment on its significance in "Identity, Psy-

chosocial," *International Encyclopedia of the Social Sciences,* Volume 7 (New York: Macmillan, 1968), p. 65.

28. *AMX*, p. 252.

29. Ibid., p. 294.

30. Ibid., pp. 292, 304.

31. Malcolm, quoted in Archie Epps ed., *The Speeches of Malcolm X At Harvard* (New York: Morrow, 1968), pp. 40–41. Epps offers perceptive analysis of Malcolm's ideas throughout this volume. He observes that "The third, and final, Harvard Speech [pp. 161–182] was an intensely personal speech . . . it conveyed an intense search by Malcolm X for a humane view toward whites." (p. 95)

32. Maya Angelou in Peter Goldman, *The Death and Life of Malcolm X* (New York: Harper, 1973), p. 136.

33. *AMX*, pp. 333–334.

34. Malcolm X quoted in Goldman, *Death and Life of Malcolm X*, p. 210.

35. *AMX*, p. 371. Malcolm explains immediately after this account in his autobiography how he returned to the United States with this "new insight," but that in trying to communicate it, "my earlier public image, my so-called 'Black Muslim' image, kept blocking me. I was trying to turn a corner, into a new regard by the public, especially Negroes; I was no less angry than I had been, but at the same time the true brotherhood I had seen in the Holy World had influenced me to recognize that anger can blind human vision" (375). Malcolm said that although he welcomed the help of "sincere white people," he did not trust white liberals (376–77); and white liberals in turn often distrusted Malcolm, refusing to believe that he had changed. This abiding suspicion was eloquently expressed by the radical American songwriter Phil Ochs in his song, "Love Me, I'm a Liberal," written in 1965, shortly after Malcolm's assassination:

> "I cried when they shot Medgar Evers,
> Tears ran down my spine
> I cried when they shot Mr. Kennedy
> As though I'd lost a father of mine
> But Malcolm X got what was coming
> He got what he asked for this time
> So love me, love me, love me, I'm a Liberal"
> *"Love Me, I'm a Liberal" Lyrics and music*
> *by Phil Ochs. Copyright 1965. Barricade Music*
> *Inc. All rights administered by Almo Music Corp.*
> *(ASCAP). All rights reserved-international*
> *copyright secured. Song interpreted*
> *by Leslie J. Calman.*

36. Gandhi argued that "It is quite proper to resist and attack a system," that is, what Malcolm called the "political, economic and social *atmosphere*," but wrong to condemn any individual solely because of the color of his/her skin, or the individual's sex, nationality, race or religion. It was in this context that Gandhi said that "Man and his deed are two distinct things . . . . Hate the sin and not the sinner" (*CWMG* 39: 220).

37. *Malcolm X Speaks*, p. 51.

38. *Malcolm X. The Last Speeches*, edited by Bruce Perry (New York: Pathfinder Press, 1989), pp. 158–159; and *Malcolm X: The Final Speeches, February 1965* (New York: Pathfinder, 1992), pp. 149–150.

39. *Malcolm X Speaks*, p. 217. Malcolm's change of attitude toward whites after March 1964, was expressed in his praise of white civil rights workers who were killed that summer in Mississippi and in his support of interracial marriage. This change is discussed in George Breitman, *The Last Year of Malcolm X* (New York: Pathfinder Press, 1970), pp. 23–24. Also this change is noted in *AMX*, p. 424 and *Malcolm X Speaks*, pp. 212–214. In his Epilogue to *AMX* Alex Haley wrote: "Recalling the incident of the young white college girl who had come to the Black Muslim restaurant and asked 'What can I *do?*' and he told her 'Nothing,' and she left in tears, Malcolm X told Gordon Parks, "Well, I've lived to regret that incident. In many parts of the African continent I saw white students helping black people. Something like this kills a lot of argument. I did many things as a Muslim that I'm sorry for now. I was a zombie then—like all Muslims—I was hypnotized, pointed in a certain direction and told to march. Well, I guess a man's entitled to make a fool of himself if he's ready to pay the cost. It cost me twelve years" (p. 429). This is also reported in *Malcolm X: The Final Speeches*, p. 231. This volume is remarkable because it contains the speeches of only the last three weeks of his life. This change in Malcolm's attitude toward whites should be placed in the context of his overall quest for truth. Spike Lee, director of the film of Malcolm X's life, commented that "Malcolm was always in search of truth. He was in that one percent able to repudiate their past life because of what was no longer true" (Quoted in *New York Magazine*, September 14, 1992, p. 50). Malcolm X and Gandhi have both been subjects of three and a half hour films of their lives, the latter directed by Sir Richard Attenborough. Each film depicts their meaning in terms of their life journeys—or struggles for *swaraj*.

40. Martin Luther King, Jr., *Stride Toward Freedom* (New York: Harper, 1958), p. 92.

41. *AMX*, pp. 366–367.

42. *Malcolm X Speaks*, pp. 164–165. Speech of February 14, 1965.

43. Malcolm says, in *By Any Means Necessary*, edited by George Breitman (New York: Pathfinder Press, 1970): "I don't go along with anyone who wants to teach our people nonviolence until someone at the same time is teaching our enemy to be nonviolent. I believe that we should protect ourselves by any means necessary when we are attacked by racists." January 18, 1965, p. 160.

44. Martin Luther King, Jr., *Stride Toward Freedom: The Montgomery Story* (New York: Harper, 1958), p. 85.

45. *The Speeches of Malcolm X at Harvard*, p. 160.

46. Judith Brown, *Gandhi* (New Haven: Yale University Press, 1989), p. 17; Taylor Branch, *Parting the Waters* (New York: Simon and Schuster, 1988), pp. 41–43; Stephen Oates, *Let the Trumpet Sound* (New York: Harper, 1982), p. 7; and David J. Garrow, *Bearing the Cross*, New York: Morrow, 1986), p. 33.

47. Branch, pp. 116–118; Brown, pp. 204–205. Comparative analysis of Gandhi and King may be made from several angles. A study of their respective movements, examining each "leader's style and personality as revealed through language," is presented by Mittie Jo Ann Nimocks in her Ph.D. dissertation, "The Indian Independence Movement Under the Leadership of Mahatma Gandhi and the U.S.A. Civil Rights

Movement Under the Leadership of Dr. Martin Luther King, Jr.: A Comparison of Two Social Movements to Assess the Utility of Nonviolence as a Rhetorical Strategy," University of Florida, 1986. The contrasts of speaking styles, rhetoric, and interaction of speaker with audience are analyzed with a view to the efficacy of nonviolence in chapters 3 and 4, pp. 117–227.

48. Lamont H. Yeakey, "The Montgomery, Alabama Bus Boycott," Ph.D. Dissertation, Columbia University, 1979, pp. 663–664. Yeakey argues that "it was the black bus boycott in Montgomery, Alabama that spawned the ideas, tactics, leadership, and most of all the spirit that constituted so much of what came later what has been termed the recent civil rights movement."

49. Alex Haley reports this as a representative criticism from Harlem in 1964 in his "Epilogue" to *AMX*, p. 420. For a brilliant study of the activities of the Student Nonviolent Coordinating Committee (SNCC), see Clayborne Carson, *In Struggle* (Cambridge: Harvard University Press, 1981).

50. See Yeakey, "Bus Boycott," pp. 249–255; Louis E. Lomax *The Negro Revolt* (New York: Harper, 1962), pp. 3–4, 81–93; Oates, *Let the Trumpet Sound*, pp. 64–65; *Martin Luther King, Jr.*, edited by C. Eric Lincoln (New York: Hill and Wang, 1970), pp. 7–39; and Rosa Parks herself in *My Soul is Rested*, Howell Raines, ed. (New York: Penguin Books, 1983), pp. 40–41. "The Montgomery Story" that follows has been told so often and eloquently that, beginning with Martin Luther King's authoritative account in *Stride Toward Freedom*, it has become the stuff of American folklore. In the 1980s several studies have appeared that relate the story again with uncommon style and mastery of detail: David J. Garrow, *Bearing the Cross*, pp. 11–82; Taylor Branch, *Parting the Waters* pp. 120–205; Stephen Oates, *Let The Trumpet Sound*, pp. 46–112; and Harvard Sitkoff, *The Struggle for Black Equality* 1954–1980 (New York: Hill and Wang, 1981), pp. 41–68. Sitkoff's analysis is particularly incisive in its comparisons between King and Gandhi.

51. Yeakey, "Bus Boycott," p. 656. For a powerful and incisive statement on the role of black women in the American civil rights movement, their achievements as well as the tensions and difficulties emerging from their interaction with black and white male counterparts see the documentary film, "FUNDI: The Story of Ella Baker," produced and directed by Joanne Grant, 1983, distributed by New Day Films. For a compelling narrative of the remarkable leadership of Jo Ann Gibson Robinson, see her memoir, *The Montgomery Bus Boycott and the Women Who Started It*, edited by David J. Garrow (The University of Tennessee Press, 1987).

52. Josephine Carson, quoted in Yeakey, "Bus Boycott," p. 248A.

53. King, *Stride Toward Freedom*, p. 40.

54. Oates, *Let the Trumpet Sound*, p. 11.

55. E. D. Nixon, one of the key leaders of the Montgomery boycott, as quoted in Raines, p. 49.

56. Yeakey, "Bus Boycott," p. 338.

57. King, *Stride Toward Freedom*, p. 45. Yeakey comments on the speech: "To be sure, whatever else King would say in the future, not only in Montgomery but over the short duration of his magnificent career, all other speeches would be but a variation of the theme presented the night of December 5, 1955" (p. 339).

58. The above paragraphs from King's speech represent a composite drawn from

several different accounts of what he said on this evening: Martin Luther King, Jr., "Address" dated December 5, 1955, Holt St. Baptist Church, Montgomery, Alabama, in The Martin Luther King, Jr. Center for Nonviolent Social Change Library and Archives, Atlanta, Georgia; Yeakey, "Bus Boycott," Appendix A, pp. 666–669; King's own account in *Stride Toward Freedom*, pp. 47–48; and Oates, *Let the Trumpet Sound* pp. 70–72, who calls the speech "sixteen minutes of inspired extemporizing."

59. James H. Cone characterizes King as a powerful "Internal Critic" of American Christianity, influential with his attack from within on racism in the religion. *Martin and Malcolm and America* (New York: Orbis Books, 1991), p. 295.

60. *The Speeches of Malcolm X at Harvard*, pp. 134, 140–143.

61. On November 13, 1956, the U.S. Supreme Court "affirmed a decision of a special three-judge U.S. District Court in declaring Alabama's state and local laws requiring segregation on buses unconstitutional" (Oates, *Let the Trumpet Sound*, pp. 102–103).

62. King, reporting the comment of a "joyful bystander," in *Stride Toward Freedom*, p. 140.

63. Black Power leaders such as Eldridge Cleaver, advocate for the Black Panthers, had by 1967 made a cult of revolutionary violence. See his *Post Prison Writings* (New York: Vintage Books, 1969), pp. 20, 72–78. The thesis that nonviolent tactics are superior to violent ones within the context of contemporary movement politics has been argued by many scholars from a strictly pragmatic viewpoint. Why and how this should be is presented in a cogent manner by Leslie J. Calman in her study, *Protest in Democratic India: Authority's Response to Challenge* (Boulder, Colorado: Westview Press, 1985). Calman contrasts the effectiveness of violent and nonviolent movements in post-independent India.

64. *Stride Toward Freedom*, p. 67.

65. David J. Garrow, *Bearing the Cross* (New York: William Morrow and Co., 1986), p. 43; and Taylor Branch, *Parting the Waters* (New York: Simon and Schuster, 1988), p. 74.

66. In an admirably thorough analysis of the perceptions of Gandhi by black Americans, Sudharshan Kapur carefully documents how extensively Gandhi's life and message were publicized by black leaders such as Marcus Garvey and W. E. B. DuBois. George Hancock, black clergyman and educator, wrote in one representative article of March, 1931: "The sooner some black Gandhi comes with a reform program dedicated to revising our standards to conform to our economic opportunity, the better it is going to be for the Negro race." Quoted in Kapur, *Raising Up a Prophet: The African American Encounter With Gandhi* (Boston: Beacon Press, 1992), p. 50.

67. *CWMG* 62: 202. This comment was in response to the first delegation of Howard Thurman, Sue Baily Thurman and Edward Carroll in February, 1936. That December Gandhi met with Benjamin E. Mays and Channing H. Tobias. *CWMG* 64: 221–225. These interviews were unusually extensive and it is clear how seriously Gandhi took the situation of black Americans and their prospects for nonviolent protest. Sudharshan Kapur concludes that "long before the rise of Martin Luther King, Jr., a growing number of African-Americans not only grasped the relevance of the doctrine of nonviolence to their own situation in this country, but also sought to experiment with its uses. . . .

Thus, the soil which had been prepared and nurtured for a generation and more by some of the key African-American leaders was ready not only to receive the seed of non-violence, but also to bear fruit as never before" (*Raising Up a Prophet*, pp. 161–163). This may be seen in direct contrast to the situation in Germany where no such development occurred among the Jews. Gandhi's advice to black Americans was perhaps more appropriate and relevant for this reason because the situations in the United States and Germany during the 1930s and early 1940s were so markedly different.

68. *Stride Toward Freedom*, p. 78–79. Taylor Branch expresses doubt about the extent of King's commitment to Gandhi's ideas, claiming that "King mentioned buying a half-dozen books about Gandhi in a single evening, but he never bothered to name or describe any of them. He almost never spoke of Gandhi personally, and his comments about Gandhism were never different than his thoughts about nonviolence in general." *Parting the Waters*, p. 87. These generalizations seem unfounded. While it is true that even during the Montgomery boycott, King's understanding of Gandhi was elementary, it developed and deepened especially during and after his visit to India in February-March, 1959 (Garrow, *Bearing the Cross*, pp. 72–73, 113–114). King did emphasize his indebtedness to and respect for Gandhi after his return from India ("Sermon on Gandhi," March 22, 1959, noted below; "My Trip to the Land of Gandhi," *Ebony* (July 1959), pp. 84–92; "More Than Any Other Person in History," Peace News, January 1, 1958, p. 2). In interviews with Gandhians that King met in India, the present author noted their uniform high regard not only for King's achievements in the United States but also for his grasp of Gandhi (Interviews with Jayaprakash Narayan, Delhi, May, 1967; Vinoba Bhave, Wardha, February, 1975; Pyarelal and Sushila Nayar, Delhi, February and March, 1975).

69. *Stride Toward Freedom*, pp. 83–88. The influence of Gandhi's thought on King, and the latter's concept of nonviolent action, including the idea of *agape* are cogently examined by John J. Ansbro, *Martin Luther King, Jr. the Making of a Mind* (New York: Orbis Books, 1984). Ansbro focuses on the similarities and differences in their uses of nonviolence and concludes that "Some of these differences in method stemmed from the fact that while Gandhi was seeking independence from an alien system, King's goal was the transformation of the structure of the existing system so that all citizens could experience integration within the system" (p. 134).

70. In a comparison of the attitudes of Gandhi and King, a marked similarity appears in their relationships to those of other races and faiths. For example, Gandhi, a Hindu, and King, a Christian, both men of color, worked easily and well in their political campaigns with those of the Jewish faith. Gandhi observed that he "lived with Jews many years in South Africa," (*Harijan*, May 18, 1947) and several served as valued leaders of his *satyagrahas* there: Hermann Kallenbach, noted above; Millie and Henry Polak (the former became Gandhi's early biographer, the latter, a key source of his intellectual development); and Sonia Schlesin, whose courage and intellect Gandhi praised in his autobiography. (*CWMG* 39: 227). King's relationship to Jews and his sympathetic understanding of their historical experience as a minority is a much appreciated aspect of his leadership. Among those who were trusted, intimate, and contributed most to the civil rights movement were Stanley Levison, whom Branch calls "King's closest white friend and the most reliable colleague of his life," (*Parting the Waters*, p. 208) and Harry

Wachtel, who met King in 1962 as a Wall Street lawyer seeking to lend his ability to the struggle. Branch remarks that Wachtel and Levison "were destined to be paired for years as King's twin Jewish lawyers . . . Whereas Levinson knew a host of union officials, ideologues and activists from the American Jewish Congress, Wachtel knew how to get high government officials on the phone and how to touch corporate officers" (p. 582). People of all faiths contributed to these movements; that Jews found them worthwhile and appealing, sensing no strains of anti-Semitism, is one indication of the quality of inclusiveness both Gandhi and King shared.

71. Goldman, *Death and Life of Malcolm X*, p. 389. Goldman's comparisons and contrasts between King and Malcolm are drawn incisively in this book, pp. 383–392. See also Amiya Chakravarty, "Satyagraha and the Race Problem in America," in S. N. Ray, ed., *Gandhi, India and the World*, pp. 300–318 for a consideration of this and also several of the other themes examined here.

72. Goldman, *Death and Life of Malcolm X*, p. 391.

73. Gandhi's influence on King's thought in this regard has been indicated by King in *Stride Toward Freedom*, pp. 78–80; *Strength to Love* (New York: Pocket Books, 1968), p. 169; and *Where Do We Go From Here* (New York: Bantam Books, 1968), pp. 51–52; and in Oates, *Let the Trumpet Sound*, pp. 31–33. Norman W. Walton has commented on Gandhi's importance in his detailed analysis of the Montgomery bus boycott in "The Walking City, A History of the Montgomery Boycott," in *The Negro History Bulletin* 20 (1 pt. 1) (October, 1956): 17. Contributors to Raines, *My Soul Is Rested*, have stressed the particular effect that the example of Gandhi's salt march had on the imagination of blacks, pp. 28, 53, 110, 361.

74. The consensus that has formed across the political spectrum in the U.S. in praise of King was indicated on October, 19, 1983, when the U.S. Senate voted to make the third Monday in January a national holiday to commemorate the birth of King. The *New York Times*, October 20, 1983, pp. 1, 27.

75. Goldman, *Death and Life of Malcolm X*, p. 381.

76. Ossie Davis, "On Malcolm X" in *AMX*, pp. 458–459.

77. *AMX*, p. 372.

78. King, *The Trumpet of Conscience* (New York: Harper and Row, 1968), pp. 70–71.

79. King's psychological state in the last days of his life has been described as markedly depressed, anxious, or fatigued by several sources: David Garrow, *Bearing the Cross*, p. 622; Ralph D. Abernathy, *And the Walls Came Tumbling Down* (New York: Harper, 1989), p. 42; and Stephen Oates, *Let the Trumpet Sound*, pp. 459, 472–73.

80. Ibid., p. 32. King expressed his fears about loss of creative force in a wry manner: "I'm worried to death . . . A man who hits the peak at 27 has a tough job ahead. People will be expecting me to pull rabbits out of the hat for the rest of my life." *New York Times*, October 30, 1983, p. B9.

81. Oates, p. 420.

82. King, *The Trumpet of Conscience*, p. 15.

83. "Sermon on Gandhi," March 22, 1959, Delivered at Dexter Ave. Baptist Church, Montgomery, in Papers of MLK, III/5, The Martin Luther King, Jr. Center for Nonviolent Social Change Library and Archives, Atlanta, Georgia.

84. Alex Haley and James Baldwin both emphasize the basic similarities between

Martin Luther King, Jr. and Malcolm X in *Malcolm X. As they Knew Him*, edited by David Gallen (New York: Carroll and Graf, 1992), pp. 247–249, 276–279. Baldwin believes that "By the time each met his death there was practically no difference between them." (p. 257).

85. James H. Cone, *Martin and Malcolm*, pp. 315–316, 318.

86. *AMX*, p. 375.

87. Oates, *Let the Trumpet Sound*, p. 486. It is interesting to note that in an interview with a delegation of American blacks in February, 1936, Gandhi remarked of this "dream" that "it may be through the Negroes [of the United States] that the unadulterated message of non-violence will be delivered to the world." *CWMG* 62: 202.

Conclusion

1. *CWMG* 85: 33.

2. *The Republic of Plato*, translated by F.M. Cornford (New York: Oxford University Press, 1945), pp. 177–178.

3. Nor was Plato, who devoted his life to education and proposes in his Republic education as a method of change, indifferent to practice. Socrates does pledge after stating the above that "I am to do my best to show under what conditions our ideal would have the best chance of being realized." Ibid., 178.

4. F.M. Cornford's explication in Ibid., p. 176.

5. Ibid., pp. 301, 282, 286.

6. Ibid., pp. 303–304.

7. Ibid., p. 306.

8. *Harijan*, Jan. 18, 1948.

9. *Republic*, pp. 234–235.

10. James MacGregor Burns, *Leadership* (New York: Harper, 1978), pp. 4, 20, 448, 455. R. C. Zaehner captures the transforming purpose of Gandhi's leadership in his study, *Hinduism* (London: Oxford University Press, 1962, ch. 8). He describes Gandhi not primarily as "the architect of Indian independence from British rule but as the liberator of the Indian spirit from the fetters of greed and anger, hatred and despair." (p. 224)

11. Bruce Perry, *Malcolm*, p. 199.

12. Erik Erikson quoted in *Dialogue with Erik Erikson*, pp. 70–71. This is also conveyed in Robert Jay Lifton, *The Genocidal Mentality* (New York: Basic Books, 1990), p. 263 on Gandhi and King.

13. Interview with C. Rajagopalachari in Madras, May 24, 1967.

14. *CWMG* 26: 52.

15. *CWMG* 42: 469.

16. R. K. Narayan, *Waiting for the Mahatma* (Mysore: Indian Thought Publications, 1964), pp. 44–45.

17. Interviews with Maurice Frydman, one of Gandhi's associates in the 1930s and 1940s, a Polish Jew and civil engineer who lived at Gandhi's Sevagram ashram, in discussions with author in Bombay and Delhi, 1966–1967, related his own experience and those of others whom he observed in these terms.

18. R. K. Narayan, pp. 60–61.

19. R. C. Majumdar, *History of the Freedom Movement in India*, 3, 2nd Revised Edition (Calcutta: Firma KLM Private, Ltd., 1977), p. xviii. This is part of an extended severe criticism of Gandhi's role in the Indian independence movement, the importance of which Majumdar believes to be vastly exaggerated. Majumdar emphasizes the influence of Subhas Chandra Bose against that of Gandhi. (pp. 609–610)

20. Judith Brown, *Gandhi*, p. 394.

21. Ibid.

22. Susanne and Lloyd Rudolph, *Gandhi*, p. 3.

23. *Harijan*, May 27, 1939.

24. *Harijan*, May 18, 1940.

25. *Harijan*, May 27, 1939.

26. *CWMG*, Autobiography, 39: 221.

27. Albert Einstein's statement for the memorial service in Washington on February 11, 1948, quoted in *Einstein on Peace*, edited by Otto Nathan and Heinz Norden (New York: Avenel Books, 1981), pp. 467–468.

28. George Orwell, "Reflections on Gandhi" in *A Collection of Essays* (New York: Harcourt, 1953), p. 180.

29. *CWMG* 29: 130, 264–265.

30. Sissela Bok, *Lying. Moral Choice in Public and Private Life* (New York: Vintage, 1979), pp. 28,33.

31. Sissela Bok, *A Strategy for Peace* (New York: Pantheon Books, 1989), p. 47.

32. Martin Luther King, Jr., "Letter from Birmingham Jail," in *Why We Can't Wait* (New York: Mentor Books, 1964), p. 77.

Abhaya: Fearlessness. A vital component of Gandhi's thought because he stressed courage as an indispensable element of satyagraha.

Ahimsa: Nonviolence, conceived as both a personal and a political value as an active agent of change.

Ashram: Spiritual community. Gandhi established ashrams in Sabarmati (near Ahmedabad) in Gujarat and in Sevagram (near Wardha) in Maharashtra.

Atman: The Universal self.

Bania: Subcaste to which Gandhi belonged, within the *vaishya* social order in the system of four *varnas*.

Bapu: "Father," a general term of affection and respect often applied to Gandhi.

Bhagavad-Gita (often shortened to Gita): A philosophical dialogue and sacred text of Hinduism that had a profound influence on Gandhi.

Brahmacharya: Vow of celibacy. Taken by Gandhi in 1906 to signify devotion to God, self-discipline, and commitment to public service.

Charka: Spinning wheel, promoted by Gandhi in his effort to spread the use of *khadi*.

Communalism: Conflict and intolerance among religious communities of Hindus, Muslims, and Sikhs.

Dandi: Village on the shores of Gujarat on the coast of western India. Here, Gandhi's "march to the sea," or salt march, ended.

Glossary

Daridranarayan: "Divinity of the poor," a term used by Gandhi and others to support social change.

Darshan: A sight or view of holiness that conveys a blessing, adapted by Gandhi to mean that Indians must have the *darshan* of the "goddess of swaraj."

Dharma: Righteousness, adherence to the Hindu code of morality. Its opposite is adharma or immorality.

Duragraha: Biased action by an individual or group to attain a selfish goal. Although an act of duragraha may not commit physical violence, it will still harbor "violence of the spirit" in the form of anger and enmity. Gandhi also called this "passive resistance," and distinguished it from satyagraha.

Dyerism: Signifies the brutal abuse of power seen in British imperialism, derived from Gen. Reginald Dyer, commander of troops responsible for the massacre of 400 Indians at Amritsar in 1919.

Goonda (and goondaism): Thug or street criminal. In Calcutta, during partition, *goondas* terrorized both Hindus and Muslims, thus contributing to an epidemic of urban and communal violence. "Goondaism" signified a kind of social disease sanctioned by a city consumed with fear and conflict.

Harijan: "Child of God," Gandhi's term for a member of the untouchable community. Also the title of his weekly journal after 1933.

Hartal: Mass strike by labor and business as an act of satyagraha and nonviolent noncooperation against British rule.

Hind swaraj: "Indian Home Rule," the title of Gandhi's first book, published in 1909 in South Africa and setting forth the basis of his political thought, especially the connection between swaraj and satyagraha.

Karmayoga: "Discipline (yoga) of action" set forth in the Bhagavad Gita. Gandhi interpreted it as a gospel of political and social action, performed in a selfless manner, without desire for personal rewards.

Khadi (or khaddar): Homespun cotton cloth. Gandhi urged its production (by the spinning wheel) and use as the dress of the nationalist movement to symbolize identification with the masses and practice of swadeshi.

Mahatma: "Great [Maha] Soul [Atma]." An honorific title bestowed on Gandhi by Rabindranath Tagore.

Moksha: Spiritual liberation. Gandhi sometimes interpreted this as synonymous with swaraj but moksha usually did not connote political independence.

Panchayat: Village council; local organ of political administration advocated by Gandhi to form the basic unit of a decentralized system of democracy in an independent India.

Partition: Political division of British India into two independent nations, India and Pakistan, in August, 1947. Gandhi opposed the plan of partition but ultimately yielded to it in the face of civil war.

Raj: Government, denoting in Gandhi's period the administrative system of British rule over its colony, India. The Viceroy was at the apex of this system, under him were various governors, civil servants, and the army. It was a formidable force but never numbered more than 100,000 Britons in India.

Ram Raj: "Rule of Ram," the Hindu ideal of ancient India's golden age, evoked by Gandhi to mean an ideal society of harmony and justice for all religious communities, consistent with his advocacy of a secular state for independent India.

Sadhu (or Sannyasin): A Hindu holy person, ideally with saintly qualities that Gandhi saw (in contrast to B. G. Tilak) as consonant with political action and leadership.

Sarvodaya: "Welfare of all," Gandhi's term for an ideal system of social and economic equality produced by social reforms.

Satya: Truth. A fundamental concept of Hindu philosophy. Gandhi combined the word with "agraha," thus coining his key word, "satyagraha," to mean literally "Clinging to the truth," and so producing a form of moral power.

Satyagraha: Power (or force) of truth, love and nonviolence. The word has a broad meaning to include various forms of social and political action: individual or mass civil disobedience, as in the "salt satyagraha," or fasting for communal harmony, or campaigns for social reform, such as for the abolition of untouchability.

Satyagrahi: One who practices the method or employs the power of satyagraha.

Swadeshi: "One's own country, "meaning the principle of relying on the products of India rather than foreign goods. This often demanded boycott of British produce specifically.

Swaraj: Freedom. Gandhi interpreted the word to mean freedom in two distinct senses: the "external freedom" of political independence and "internal freedom." The latter meaning evoked the ancient Hindu (and Buddhist) idea of spiritual liberation, denoting a psychological freedom from illusion, fear, and ignorance. Swaraj in these two senses thus implied knowledge of self and consequent self-mastery. The idea of "freedom as self-rule," conceived by the Indian nationalist movement, originally meant only political independence. Gandhi enlarged its meaning to emphasize personal as well as political liberation. Both together became necessary conditions of India's freedom, with satyagraha as the only way to achieve it.

Taluka: District, e.g., Bardoli, designated for purposes of land revenue collection.

Tapasya: Self-sacrifice, as in Gandhi's practice of fasting. As a form of personal renunciation, *tapasya (or tapas)*, if practiced with purity of intent, evoked respect among Hindus. In the instance of Gandhi's Calcutta fast, he gained trust and power from his self-sacrifice.

Upanishads: Ancient philosophical discourses of India, regarded as main sources of Hindu metaphysics.

Varna: Social order or group, of which there were four in traditional Hindu social theory. Each varna had a specific social function: the *brahmin*, spiritual authority and instruction; *kshatriya*, temporal power; *vaishya*, wealth and commercial activity; and *sudra*, manual labor and service of the others. The theory of the duties and relationships of these four varnas was variously called *varnashrama, varnadharma*, or *varnashramadharma. Varna* is sometimes translated as "caste," but Gandhi tried to distinguish them, arguing ultimately that while caste should be abolished, the system of *varna* was in theory consistent with democratic values of freedom and equality and should be preserved as a model of social harmony and cooperation.

Glossary

Yajna: Sacrifice. Gandhi used this in a political sense, as *satyagraha* should be offered as a *yajna* in a spirit of sacrifice.

Yatra: Spiritual or religious pilgrimage, used by Gandhi to describe the salt march.

Zamindar: Landholder, Hindu or Muslim, paying revenue to British.

The Bibliography is arranged under the following main headings:

I. Primary Sources
    A. Manuscript Collections
    B. Official Records and Reports
    C. Newspapers and Periodicals
    D. Interviews
II. Collections of Source Material and Secondary Works: Published and Unpublished

I. Primary Sources

A. Manuscript Collections

All-India Congress Committee Files, 1927–1947. Jawaharlal Nehru Memorial Museum and Library, New Delhi
Gandhi Papers, Gandhi Memorial Library and Museum, Rajghat, New Delhi
Gandhi Papers, Sabermati Ashram Preservation and Memorial Trust, Ahmedabad
M. N. Roy Papers, Personal Correspondence and Documents, 1930–1953, Indian Renaissance Institute, Dehra Dun, U.P.

Bibliography

Pyarelal Nayar Papers, Correspondence and Documents, New Delhi
Papers of Sir George Cunningham, Mss. EUR.D.670, India Office Library, London
Papers of the Earl of Halifax, Lord Irwin, Mss. EUR. C.152
Papers of Sir Frederick Sykes, Mss. EUR. F.150, India Office Library, London
King Library and Archives, The Martin Luther King, Jr., Center for Nonviolent Social
    Change, Inc., Atlanta, Georgia
Papers of Reginald Reynolds, Peace Collection, Swarthmore College, Pennsylvania

B. Official Records and Reports

Government of India, Home Department. *Political Proceedings and Files*, 1919–1946, Na-
    tional Archives of India, New Delhi
Government of India, Public and Judicial Department, India Office Library, London

C. Newspapers and Periodicals

Aryan Path (India)
Amrita Bazar Patrika (India)
Bombay Chronicle (India)
Cape Times (South Africa)
Chicago Daily Tribune (U.S.)
Christian Century (U.S.)
Harijan (India)
Hindu (India)
Hindustan Times (India)
Independent India (India)
Lahore Tribune (India)
Leader (India)
Literary Digest (United States)
Manchester Guardian (U.K.)
Mail (South Africa)
Modern Review (India)
Montgomery Advertiser (U.S.)
Natal Mercury (South Africa)
Natal Witness (South Africa)
New Republic (U.K.)
New York Times (U.S.)
Nation (U.S.)
Pioneer (India)
Radical Humanist (India)
Rand Daily Mail (South Africa)
Statesman (India)
Sunday Post (South Africa)

Times of India (India)
The Times (London, U.K.)
Time Magazine (U.S.)
Washington Post (U.S.)
Young India (India)

Interviews

1. Among the eighty Indians who marched with Gandhi to Dandi, personal interviews were conducted with the following seventeen marchers. Several of these participants subsequently provided additional written testimony. As indicated in the endnotes
and bibliography, Pyarelal Nayar and Haridas Muzumdar gave a series of interviews,
then read or discussed my account of the march, either supplying detailed criticisms and
commentary on this account or complete references to their own extensive publications
on the subject. More biographical information on these and the other marchers is con-
tained in *Young India*, March 12, 1930, pp. 90–91
Abbasbhai (Vartegi), interviewed in Ahmedabad, Indian, July 1975.
Ashar, Prithvidas L., Bombay, August 1975.
Butch, Puratan J., Bombay, August 1975.
Dave, Bhanushanker, Ahmedabad, July 1975.
Desai, Rasik, Bombay, July 1975.
Desai, Valji Govindji, Vadodara, Gujarat, August 1975.
Harkare, Dwarkanath, Bombay, July 1975.
Joshi, Chhaganlal, Rajkot, Gujarat, March 1975.
Kalelkar, Satish D., Ahmedabad, March 1975.
Lalaji (Parmar), Ahmedabad, July 1975.
Mahimtura, Harilala, Bombay, July 1975.
Modi, Ramaniklal, Ahmedabad, March 1975.
Muzumdar, Haridas T., New York and New Jersey, 1976–1977.
Poduval, N. P. Raghava, Shoramur, Kerala, June 1975.
Pyarelal (Nayar), Delhi, 1966–1967, 1970, 1975.
Ratnaji (Boria), Ahmedabad, July 1975.
Zaveri (Jhaveri) Pannalal B., Ahmedabad, July 1975.
2. The following list regrettably includes only a fraction of those who gave gener-
ously of their time to answer questions in personal interviews relating to subjects raised
in this book:
Alexander, Horace, Gandhi associate, London, April 1968 and Swarthmore, Pa., June
1978.
Behn, Mira (Madeleine Slade), Gandhi associate, Vienna, August 1975.
Bhave, Vinoba, Gandhi associate and philosopher, Wardha, India, February 1975.
Bose, Nirmal Kumar, Gandhi associate, successive interviews, Calcutta and Delhi,
1966–67.
Dalal, Chandulal Bhagubhai, Gandhi scholar, Ahmedabad, July 1975.
Dave, K. M., journalist, Bombay, April 1975.

Gandhi, Kantilal Harilal. M. K. Gandhi's grandson. Bombay, July 1975.

Karnik, V. B., M. N. Roy associate, Bombay, November 1966.

Kripalani, Archarya, Gandhi associate, Ahmedabad, October 1966.

Lazarus, A. D., Gandhi associate, Durban, South Africa, August 1975.

Mehta, Usha, Gandhi scholar, Bombay, July 1975.

Nair, C. K., Gandhi associate, Delhi, July 1975.

Nayar, Sushila, Personal physician to M. K. and Kasturba Gandhi and biographer of both; successive interviews, Delhi and Sevagram January–July 1975; New York and New Jersey, July 1981, June 1984.

Parikh, G. D., M. N. Roy associate, Bombay, October 1966.

Park, Richard., M. N. Roy associate and political scientist, February 1965.

Patel, C. N., Gandhi scholar and editor of *MGCW*, Ahmedabad, July 1975.

Rajagopalachari, C., Gandhi associate and political leader, Madras, May 1967.

Ray, Sibnarayan, M. N. Roy associate and scholar, New York and New Jersey, October 1974.

Sinha, K. K., M. N. Roy associate, Calcutta, November 1966.

Spratt, Philip, M. N. Roy associate and Gandhi biographer, Madras, May 1967.

Swaminathan, K. K. Gandhi scholar and editor of *CWMG*, Delhi, November 1966.

Sykes, Marjorie, Gandhi associate, Philadelphia, June 1976.

Tarkunde, Justice V. M., M. N. Roy associate, Bombay, November 1966.

II. Collections of Source Material and Secondary Works: Published and Unpublished

Abernathy, Ralph D. *And the Walls Came Tumbling Down*. New York: Harper, 1989.

Acton, John F. E. D. *Essays on Freedom and Power*. Boston: Beacon Press, 1948.

Adler, Mortimer. *The Idea of Freedom*. 2 vols. New York: Doubleday, 1961.

Agerwal, S. N. *Gandhian Constitution for Free India*. Allahabad: Kitabistan, 1946.

Ambedkar, B. R. *What Congress and Gandhi Have Done to the Untouchables*. Bombay: Thacker, 1946.

Ambedkar, B. R. *Gandhi and Gandhism*. Jullundar, Punjab: Bheem Patrika Publications, 1970.

Amin, Shahid. "Gandhi as Mahatma: Gorakhpur District, Eastern UP, 1921–22," *Subaltern Studies II*, Ranajit Guha, ed. Delhi: Oxford University Press, 1984.

Anand, Mulk Raj. *Untouchable*. New Delhi: Orient, 1970.

Andrews, C. F. *Mahatma Gandhi's Ideas*, London: Allen and Unwin, 1931.

Andrews. Charles Freer. *Mahatma Gandhi—His Own Story*. New York: Macmillan, 1930.

Argov, Daniel. *Moderates and Extremists in the Indian Nationalist Movement, 1883–1920*. London: Asia Publishers.

Ashe, Geoffrey. *Gandhi*. London: Heinemann, 1968.

Bakshi, S. R. *Gandhi and Salt Satyagraha*. Kerala: Vishwavidya Publishers, 1981.

Bandyopadhyaya, J. *Social and Political Thought of Gandhi*. Bombay: Allied Publishers, 1969.

Basham, A. L. "Some Fundamental Ideas of Ancient India." In C. H. Philips, ed. *Politics and Society in India*. London: Allen and Unwin, 1963.

Bay, Christian. *The Structure of Freedom*. New York: Atheneum, 1965.

Behn, Mira. *The Spirit's Pilgrimage*. London: Longmans, 1960.

Berlin, Isaiah, "Two Concepts of Liberty." In *Four Essays on Liberty*. New York: Oxford University Press, 1984.

Bernays, Robert. *"Naked Fakir,"* London: Victor Gollancz, 1931.

The Bhagavad-Gita, New York, translated by Barbara Miller. New York: Bantam, 1986.

Birkenhead [2nd Earl of]. *Halifax: The Life of Lord Halifax*. London: Hamish Hamilton, 1965.

Bok, Sissela. *A Strategy for Peace*. New York: Pantheon Books, 1989.

Bok, Sissela. *Lying. Moral Choice in Public and Private Life*. New York: Vintage Books, 1979.

Bolton, Glorney. *The Tragedy of Gandhi*. London: Allen and Unwin, 1934.

Bondurant, Joan. "Satyagraha vs. Duragraha." In G. Ramachandra, ed. *Gandhi: His Relevance for our Times*. Bombay: Bharatiya Vidya Bhavan, 1964.

Bondurant, Joan. *Conquest of Violence*. Princeton: Princeton University Press, 1988.

Borman, William. *Gandhi and Non-Violence*. Albany, New York: SUNY Press, 1986.

Bose, Subhas Chandra. *The Indian Struggle: 1920–1934*. London: Wishard, 1935.

Bose, N. K. *My Days with Gandhi*. Calcutta: Nishana, 1953.

Bose N. K. ed. *Selections from Gandhi*. Ahmedabad: Navajivan. 1948.

Brailsford: H. N. "Rebel India." In *New Republic*: New York, 1931.

Branch, Taylor. *Parting the Waters*. New York: Simon and Schuster, 1988.

Brietman, George, *The Last Year of Malcolm X*. New York: Pathfinder Press, 1970.

Brown, Judith. *Gandhi's Rise to Power*. London: Cambridge University Press, 1972.

Brown, Judith. *Gandhi and Civil Disobedience*. London: Cambridge University Press, 1977.

Brown, Judith. *Modern India, The Origins of An Asian Democracy*. Delhi: Oxford University Press, 1985.

Brown, Judith. *Gandhi: A Prisoner of Hope*. New Haven: Yale University Press, 1989.

Brown, W. N. *The United States and India and Pakistan*, Cambridge: Harvard University Press, 1955.

Buber, Martin and J. L. Magnes. *Two Letters to Gandhi*. Jerusalem: Rubin Mass, April, 1939.

Burns, James MacGregor. *Leadership*. New York: Harper, 1978.

Calman, Leslie J. *Protest in Democratic India: Authority's Response to Challenge*, Boulder, Colorado: Westview Press, 1985.

Calman, Leslie J. *Toward Empowerment. Women and Movement Politics in India*, Boulder, Colorado: Westview Press, 1992.

Carson, Clayborne. *In Struggle*, Cambridge: Harvard University Press, 1981.

Case, C. M. *Non-Violent Coercion*. London: Allen and Unwin, 1923.

Casey, R. G. *An Australian in India*. Melbourne: F. W. Cheshire, 1947.

Cashman, Richard I. *The Myth of the Lokamanya*. Berkeley: University of California Press, 1975.

Bibliography

Chakravarty, Amiya. *A Saint at Work*. William Penn Lecture, 1950. Philadelphia: The Young Friends Movement of the Philadelphia Yearly Meetings, 1950.

Chandra, Bipan. *India's Struggle for Independence, 1857–1947*. Delhi: Viking, 1988.

Chatterjee, Margaret. *Gandhi's Religious Thought*. London: Macmillan, 1983.

Chaudhuri, Nirad. *The Autobiography of an Unknown Indian*. New York: Macmillan, 1951.

Chaudhuri, Nirad. *Thy Hand, Great Anarch! India 1921–1952*. New York: Addison-Wesley. 1987.

Churchill, Winston S. *India: Speeches*. London: Thornton Butterworth, 1931.

Cleaver, Eldridge. *Post Prison Writings*. New York: Vintage Books, 1969.

Coatman, John. *Years of Destiny: India, 1926–1932*. London: Jonathan Cape, 1932.

Coles, Robert. *Erik H. Erikson*. Boston: Little Brown, 1970.

Collins, Larry and Pierre Lapierre. *Freedom at Midnight*. New York: Avon, 1983.

Cone, James H. *Martin and Malcolm and America*. New York: Orbis Books, 1991.

Congress Presidential Addresses, 1911–1934, 2nd series. Madras: G. A. Natesan, 1937.

Coogan, Tim Pat. *Michael Collins: A Biography*. New York: Arrow Books, 1991.

Cruise, Harold. *The Crisis of the Negro Intellectual*. New York: Morrow, 1971.

Dalal, Chandulal Bhagubhai. *Gandhi's Struggle in South Africa* (in Gujarati: *Gandhiji Dakshin Africani Ladat*). Ahmedabad: P. Majumdar, Sabarmati Ashram, 1958.

Dalton, Dennis. *Indian Idea of Freedom*. Gurgaon, India: The Academic Press, 1982.

Dalton, Dennis. "Gandhi's Styles of Leadership." In B. N. Pandey, ed. *Leadership in South Asia*. New Delhi: Vikas Publishers, 1977.

Dalton, Dennis. "The Idea of Freedom in the Political Thought of Vivekananda and Aurobindo." *South Asian Affairs. The Movement for National Freedom in India*. St. Anthony's Papers No. 18, S. N. Mukherjee, ed. Oxford: Oxford University Press, 1966.

Dalton, Dennis. "The Gandhian View of Caste and Caste After Gandhi." In Philip Mason, ed. *India and Ceylon; Unity and Diversity*. London: Oxford University Press, 1967.

Dalton, Dennis. "Gandhi and Roy: The Interaction of Ideologies in India." In Sibnarayan Ray, ed. *Gandhi, India and the World*. Melbourne: The Hawthorne Press, 1970.

Dalton, Dennis. "Gandhi During Partition." In C. H. Philips, ed. *The Partition of India*. London: Allen and Unwin, 1970.

Dalton, Dennis. "The Dandi Drama." In Peter Robb and David Taylor, eds. *Rule, Protest and Identity*. London: Humanities Press, 1978.

Das, C. R. *Outline Scheme of Swaraj*, National Convention Memoranda, No. 2. Madras: Besant Press, 1923.

Das, C. R. *Freedom Through Disobedience*, Presidential Address at 37th Indian National Congress, Madras, Arka, 1922.

Das, Bhagavan. *Ancient versus Modern Scientific Socialism*. Madras: Theosophical House, 1934.

Das, Suranjan. "Towards an Understanding of Communal Violence in Twentieth Century Bengal." *Economic and Political Weekly*, 23 (35), August 27, 1988.

Das, Suranjan. *Communal Riots in Bengal 1905–1947*. Delhi: Oxford University Press, 1991.

Das, C. R. *India for Indians*. Madras: Ganesh, 1918.

Deming, Barbara. *We Are All Part of One Another: A Barbara Deming Reader,* Jane Meyerding, ed.. Philadelphia: New Society Publishers, 1984.

Desai, Ishwarlal I. ed. *Bardoli Satyagraha* (in Gujarati). Surat: Swatantrya Itihas Samiti, 1970.

Desai, Mahadev. *The Story of Bardoli: Being a History of the Bardoli Satyagraha of 1928 and its Sequel.* Ahmedabad: Navajivan, 1929.

Desai, Mahadev.*The Gospel of Selfless Action or the Gita According to Gandhi.* Ahmedabad: Navajivan, 1946.

Devanesen, Chandran D. S. *The Making of the Mahatma.* Madras: Orient Langmans, 1969.

Dhawan, G. N. *The Political Philosophy of Mahatma Gandhi.* Bombay: Popular Book Depot, 1946.

Diwakar, R. R. *Satyagraha: Its Technique and History.* Bombay: Hind Kitans, 1946.

Doke, Rev. Joseph J. *M. K. Gandhi: an Indian Patriot in South Africa.* London: The London Chronicle, 1909.

Draper, Theodore. *The Rediscovery of Black Nationalism.* New York: Viking, 1970.

Elwin, Verrier. *Dawn of Indian Freedom.* London: Allen and Unwin, 1932.

Erikson, Erik. "Identity, Psychosocial." *International Encyclopedia of the Social Sciences,* Volume 7. New York: Macmillan, 1968.

Erikson, Erik. *Identity Youth and Crisis.* New York: Norton, 1968.

Erikson, Erik. *Gandhi's Truth.* New York: Norton, 1969.

Essien-Udom, E. U. *Black Nationalism: The Rise of the Black Muslims in the U.S.A.* New York: Penguin, 1966.

Evans, Richard I. *Dialogue With Erik Erikson.* New York: Dutton, 1969.

Farson, Negley. *The Way of a Transgressor.* New York: Harcourt, 1936.

Fischer, Louis. *The Life of Mahatma Gandhi.* New York: Harper, 1950.

Gallen, David, ed. *Malcolm X: As They Knew Him.* New York: Carroll and Graf, 1992.

Gandhi, M. K. *Harijan. A Journal of Applied Gandhism* New York: Garland, 1973.

Gandhi, M. K. *The Collected Works of Mahatma Gandhi.* 90 Vols. Publications Division, Ministry of Information and Broadcasting, Government of India, 1958–1984.

Gandhi, M. K. *Delhi Diary.* Ahmedabad: Navajivan, 1948.

Gandhi, M. K. *Hind Swarajya,* (in Gujarati). Ahmedabad: Navajivan, 1969.

Gandhi, Manubehn. *The Miracle of Calcutta.* Ahmedabad: Navajivan, 1959.

Garrow, David J. *Bearing the Cross.* New York: Morrow, 1986.

Ghose, Aurobindo. *The Doctrine of Passive Resistance.* Pondicherry: Sri Aurobindo Ashram, 1952.

Ghose, Aurobindo. "Ideals Face to Face." In *Bande Mataram,* May 3 1908, as contained in Haridas and Uma Mukherjee, *Bande Mataram and Indian Nationalism* (1906–1908) Calcutta: K. L. Mukhopadhyay, 1957.

Ghose, Aurobindo. *The Ideal of Human Unity* In *The Human Cycle, The Ideal of Human Unity and War and Self-Determination.* Pondicherry: Sri Aurobindo Ashram, 1962.

Gilligan, Carol. *In a Different Voice.* Cambridge: Harvard University Press, 1982.

Goebbels, Joseph. *The Goebbels Diaries. 1942–1943,* Louis P. Lochner, ed. and trans.. New York: Doubleday, 1948.

Bibliography

Gokhale, Gopal Krishna. *Speeches and Writings, 1877–1913*, vol 1. R. P. Patwardhan, ed. Bombay: Asia Publishers, 1962.

Goldman, Peter. *The Death and Life of Malcolm X.* New York: Harper, 1973.

Gopal, S. *The Viceroyalty of Lord Irwin, 1926–1931.* Oxford: Clarendon Press, 1957.

Gordon, Leonard, A. *Bengal: The Nationalist Movement 1876–1940.* New York: Columbia University Press, 1974.

Gordon, Leonard, A. "Bengal's Gandhi." In D. Kopf, ed. *Bengal Regional Identity.* Michigan, 1969.

Gordon, Leonard, A. *Brothers Against the Raj.* New York: Columbia University Press, 1990.

Gordon, Leonard A. "Portrait of a Bengal Revolutionary." In *Journal of Asian Studies*, 27 (2), February 1968.

Gregg, Richard. *The Power of Non-Violence.* Amedabad: Navajivan, 1938.

Greenberg, Hayim. "An Answer to Gandhi." In *The Inner Eye. Selected Essays.* New York: Jewish Frontier Association, 1953.

Griffiths, Percival. *Modern India.* London, 1957.

Guha, R. "Dominance Without Hegemony and its Historiography." In *Subaltern Studies VI*, R. Guha, ed.. Delhi: Oxford University Press, 1989.

Haithcox, John P. *Communism and Nationalism in India. M. N. Roy and Comintern Policy, 1920–1939.* Princeton: Princeton University Press, 1971.

Hay, Stephen N. *Asian Ideas of East and West. Tagore and His Critics in Japan, China and India*, Cambridge: Harvard University Press, 1970.

Hay, Stephen N. "Jain Influences on Gandhi's Early Thought." In S. N. Ray, ed. *Gandhi India and the World.* Melbourne: The Hawthorn Press, 1970.

Hendrick, George. "The Influence of Thoreau's 'Civil Disobedience' on Gandhi's *Satyagraha.*" In Henry D. Thoreau, *Walden and Civil Disobedience*, Owen Thomas. ed. New York: Norton, 1966.

Hitler's Secret Conversations. 1941–1944, New York: Farrar, Straus, 1953.

Holmes, J. H. *My Gandhi* London: George Allen and Unwin, 1954.

Horsburgh, H. J. N. *Non-Violence and Aggression.* London: Oxford University Press, 1968.

Hunt, James D. *Gandhi in London.* New Delhi: Promilla, 1978.

Hunt, James. D. *Gandhi and the Nonconformists.* New Delhi: Promilla, 1986.

Huttenback, R. A. *Gandhi in South Africa.* Ithaca: Cornell University Press, 1971.

Halifax [Irwin, Lord Edward], *Fulness of Days.* London: Collins, 1957.

Indian Annual Register: January–June, 1930, vol 1. Calcutta: Annual Register Office, 1931.

Indian Year Book: 1930. Stanley Reed and S. T. Sheppard, eds. London: Bennett, Coleman, n.d.

Iyer, Raghavan N. *The Moral and Political Thought of Mahatma Gandhi.* New York: Oxford University Press, 1973.

Iyer, Raghavan N, ed. *The Moral and Political Writings of Mahatma Gandhi.* 3 Vols. Oxford: Clarendon Press, 1987.

Jesudasan, Ignatius. *A Gandhian Theology of Liberation.* New York: Orbis Books, 1984.

Jewish Resistance During the Holocaust. Proceedings of the Conference on Manifestations of Jewish Resistance, Jerusalem, Yad Vashem, Jerusalem, 1971.

Jha, Manoranjan. *Civil Disobedience and After.* Delhi: Meenakshi Prakasham, 1973.

Jugatram, D. "Shri Ramjibhai Gopalji Badhia." In *Vattavriksha,* May 1972 (in Gujarati).

Kabir, Humayun. "Muslim Politics, 1942–47." In C. H. Philips and M. D. Wainwright, eds. *The Partition of India.* London: Allen and Unwin, 1970.

Kapur, Sudharshan. *Raising up a Prophet. The African American Encounter With Gandhi.* Boston: Beacon Press, 1992.

Khosla, G. D. *Stern Reckoning.* Bombay: Claridge, 1952.

King, Martin Luther, Jr. "Letter from Birmingham Jail." In *Why We Can't Wait.* New York: Penguin Books, 1964.

King, Martin Luther, Jr. *The Words of Martin Luther King, Jr.* New York: New Market Press, 1983.

King, Martin Luther, Jr. *Where Do We Go From Here.* New York: Bantam, 1968.

King, Martin Luther, Jr. *Stride Toward Freedom. The Montgomery Story.* New York: Harper, 1958.

King, Martin Luther, Jr. *Strength to Love.* New York: Pocket Books, 1968.

Kishwar, Madhu. "Gandhi on Women." *Economic and Political Weekly* 20, (40), October 5, and (41), October 12, 1985.

Kling, Blair B. "Gandhi, Nonviolence, and the Holocaust." *Peace and Change* 16 (2), April 1991.

Kripalani, Krishna. *Rabindranath Tagore. A Biography.* London: Oxford University Press, 1962.

Kripalani, J. B. *Gandhian Thought.* New Delhi: Orient Longmans, 1961.

Krishna, Gopal. *The Development of the Indian National Congress as a Mass Organization, 1918–1923. Journal of Asian Studies* 25 (3), May 1966.

Kuper, Leo. *Passive Resistance in South Africa.* New Haven: Yale University Press, 1957.

Lambert, Richard D. "Hindu-Muslim Riots." Unpublished Ph. D. Dissertation in Sociology, University of Pennsylvania, 1951.

Lifton, Robert Jay. *The Genocidal Mentality.* New York: Basic Books, 1990.

Lincoln, C. Eric. *The Black Muslims in America.* Boston: Beacon Press, 1961.

Lincoln, C. Eric, ed. *Martin Luther King, Jr..* New York: Hill and Wang, 1970.

Lomax, Louis E. *When The Word Is Given,* New York: New American Library, 1963.

Lomax, Louis E. *The Negro Revolt.* New York: Harper, 1962.

Low, D. A., ed. *Congress and the Raj.* Missouri: South Asia Books, 1977.

Lumby, E. W. R. *The Transfer of Power in India 1945–1947.* London: G. Allen and Unwin, 1954.

MacCallum, Gerald C. "Negative and Positive Freedom." *The Philosophical Review* 76 (1967).

MacDonell A. A. and A. B. Keith, *Vedic Index of Names and Subjects.* London: John Murray, 1912.

Mahadev Desai's Diary (Mahadevabhaini Dayari, in Gujarati), N. D. Parkh, ed. Ahmedabad: Navajivan Prakasan Mandir, 1948–1949, Vol. 13, 1929–1931.

Mahatma Gandhi: Source Material for a History of the Freedom Movement in India. Vol. 3, Part III, 1930–1931. Bombay: Directorate of Printing and Stationery, 1969.

Majumdar, R. C. *History of the Freedom Movement in India,* Vol. 3, 2nd Revised Edition. Calcutta: Firma KLM Private, Ltd. 1977.

Bibliography

Malcolm X. *Malcolm X Speaks. Selected Speeches and Statements*, George Breitman. ed. New York: Grove Press, 1965.

Malcolm X. *The Speeches of Malcolm X At Harvard*, Archie Epps. ed. New York: Morrow, 1968.

Malcolm X. *The Autobiography of Malcolm X, as told to Alex Haley*. New York: Ballantine Books, 1965.

Malcolm X. *By Any Means Necessary*, George Breitman. ed. New York: Pathfinder. 1970.

Malcolm X. *The Final Speeches. February, 1965*. New York: Pathfinder, 1992.

Mansergh, Nicholas. *The Commonwealth and The Nations*. London: Royal Institute of International Affairs, 1948.

Mansergh, Nicholas. *Survey of British Commonwealth Affairs 1939–1952*. London: Royal Institute of International Affairs, 1958.

Masani, R. P. *Britain in India*. London: Oxford University Press, 1960.

McAllister, Pam. *You Can't Kill the Spirit*. Philadelphia: New Society Publishers, 1988.

Mehrotra, S. R. *Towards India's Freedom and Partition*. New Delhi: Vikas, 1979.

Mehta, Kalyanji Vithalbhai and Ishwari Desai. *Dandi Kutch* (in Gujarati). Ahmedabad: Gujarat Rajya Samiti, 1969.

Menon, V. P. *The Transfer of Power in India*, Princeton: Princeton University Press, 1957.

Miller, Barbara S. *Theater of Memory*. New York: Columbia University Press, 1984.

Miller, Herbert A. "Gandhi's Campaign Begins." *The Nation*, New York, April 23, 1930.

Miller, Webb. *I Found No Peace*. New York: Simon and Schuster, 1936.

Mohandas Karamchand Gandhi: A Bibliography. New Delhi: Orient Longman, 1974.

Monier-Williams, Sir M., ed. *A Sanskrit-English Dictionary*, New Edition. Oxford: Clarendon, 1899.

Montagu, Edwin S. *An India Diary*, Venitra Montagu. ed. London: Heinemann, 1930.

Moon, Penderel. *Divide and Quit*. Berkeley: University of California Press, 1962.

Moon, Penderel. *Gandhi and Modern India*. New York: Norton, 1969.

Moon, Penderel, ed. *Wavell. The Viceroy's Journal*. London: Oxford University Press, 1973.

Moore, R. J. *The Crisis of Indian Unity 1917–1940*. Delhi: Oxford University Press, 1974.

Moraes, F. *India Today*. New York: Macmillan, 1960.

Morris-Jones, W. H. "Mahatma Gandhi—Political Philosopher?" in *Political Studies* 7 (1), 1960.

Morris-Jones, W. H. *The Government and Politics of India*. London: Hutchinson University Library, 1971.

Morton, Eleanor. *The Women in Gandhi's Life*, New York: Dodd, Mead, 1953.

Muggeridge, Malcolm. *Chronicles of Wasted Time*. Vol. 1: *The Green Stick*. New York: William Morrow, 1973.

Muzumdar, Haridas T. *India's Non-Violent Revolution*. New York: India Today and Tomorrow Series, 1930.

Muzumdar, Haridas T. *Gandhi versus the Empire*. New York: Universal Publishing Co., 1932.

Muzumdar, Haridas T. *Mahatma Gandhi: A Prophetic Voice*. Ahmedabad: Navajivan, 1963.

Naess, Arne. *Gandhi and the Nuclean Age.* New Jersey: Bedminster Press, 1965.

Nakhre, Amrut. *Social Psychology of Nonviolent Action.* Delhi: Chanakya, 1982.

Nanda, B. R. *Mahatma Gandhi.* Bombay: Allied, 1958.

Nanda, B. R. *Gandhi and His Critics.* Delhi: Oxford University Press, 1985.

Nanda, B. R. *Gandhi, Pan-Islamisn, Imperialism, and Nationalism in India.* Bombay: Oxford University Press, 1989.

Naoroji, Dadabhai. *Speeches and Writings.* Madras: G. A. Natesan, 1910.

Narayan, R. K. *Waiting for the Mahatma.* Mysore: Indian Thought Publications, 1964.

Nathan, Otto and Norden Heinz, eds. *Einstein on Peace.* New York: Avenel Books, 1981.

Nayar. Pyarelal and Sushila. *Mahatma Gandhi.* Ahmedabad: Navajivan, 1965–1989.

Nehru, Jawaharlal. *India in 1930–31: A Statement Prepared for Presentation to Parliament,* Calcutta, Government of India Central Publishing Branch, 1932.

Nehru, Jawaharlal. *Discovery of India.* New York: Doubleday, 1959.

Nehru, Jawaharlal. *Autobiography.* Bombay: Allied Publishers, 1962.

Nehru, Jawaharlal. *Mahatma Gandhi.* Bombay: Asia Publishing House, 1965.

Nehru, Jawaharlal. *Selected Works.* S. Gopal, ed. vol. 3. New Delhi: Orient Longman, 1972.

Niebuhr, Reinhold. *Moral Man and Immoral Society.* New York: Scribner's 1960.

Nimocks, Mittie Jo Ann. "The Indian Independence Movement Under the Leadership of Mahatma Gandhi and the U.S.A. Civil Rights Movement Under the Leadership of Dr. Martin Luther King, Jr.: A Comparison of Two Social Movements to Assess the Utility of Nonviolence as a Rhetorical Strategy." Unpublished Ph. D. Dissertation, University of Florida, 1986.

North Robert C. and X. J. Eudin. *M. N. Roy's Mission to China.* Berkeley and Los Angeles: University of California Press, 1963.

O'Malley, Padraig. *Biting at the Grave: The Irish Hunger Strikes and the Politics of Despair.* Boston: Beacon Press, 1990.

Oates, Stephen. *Let the Trumpet Sound.* New York: Harper, 1982.

Orwell, George. "Reflections on Gandhi" in *A Collection of Essays.* New York: Harcourt, 1953.

Ostergaard, Geoffrey and Melville Currell. *The Gentle Anarchists.* Oxford: Clarendon Press, 1971.

Overstreet, G. D. and Marshall Windmiller. *Communism in India.* Berkeley and Los Angeles: University of California Press, 1959.

Pachai, Bridglal. *The South African Indian Question, 1860–1971.* Cape Town: C. Struick, 1971.

Pal. B. C. *The New Spirit.* Calcutta, 1907.

Pal. B. C. *Swadeshi and Swaraj: The Rise of the New Patriotism.* Calcutta: Yugayatri Prakashak, Ltd. 1954.

Pal. B. C. *Writings and Speeches.* Calcutta: Vugayatri Prakashak Ltd., 1958.

Pal. B. C. *The Soul of India.* 4th edition. Calcutta: Yugayatri Prakashak, Ltd. 1958.

Parekh, Bhikhu. *Gandhi's Political Philosophy.* Indiana: University of Notre Dame Press, 1989.

Patterson, Orlando. *Freedom.* Vol 1. New York: Basic Books, 1991.

Percival Spear. *Modern India.* Ann Arbor: University of Michigan Press, 1961.

Perry, Bruce, *Malcolm. The Life of a Man Who Changed Black America*. Barrytown, New York: Station Hill Press, 1991.

Perry, Bruce, ed. *Malcolm X. The Last Speeches*. New York: Pathfinder Press, 1989.

Pethwick-Lawrence, Lord, et al. *Mahatma Gandhi*. London: Odhams Press, 1949.

Plato. *The Republic*, translated by F. M. Cornford. New York: Oxford University Press, 1945.

Potter, Karl H. *Presuppositions of India's Philosophies*. New Delhi: Prentice-Hall of India, 1965.

Power, Paul, ed. *The Meanings of Gandhi*. Honolulu: East-West Center Press, 1971.

Prabhu R. K. and Ravindra Kelekav, eds. *Truth Called Them Differently*. Ahmedabad: Navajivan, 1961.

Prasad, Rajendra. *Satyagraha in Champaran*. Ahmedabad: Navajivan, 1949.

Pyarelal. *The Epic Fast*. Ahmedabad: Karnatak Printing Press, 1932.

Pyarelal. *Mahatma Gandhi: The Last Phase*. 2 Vols. Ahmedabad: Navajivan, 1958.

Pyarelal. *Gandhian Techniques in the Modern World*. Ahmedabad: Navajivan, 1959.

Pyarelal. *Mahatma Gandhi. The Early Phase*, Vol. 1. Ahmedabad: Navajivan, 1965.

Radhakrishnan, S., ed. *The Principal Upanishads*. London: George Allen and Unwin, 1969.

Raines, Howell. *My Soul is Rested*. New York: Penguin Books, 1983.

Ramachandran, G. and Mahadevan, T. K. *Gandhi. His Relevance for Our Times*. Bombay: Bharatiya Vidya Bhavan, 1964.

Rao, Raja. *Kanthapura*. London: Oxford University Press, 1963.

Ray, Heman. *Changing Soviet Views on Mahatma Gandhi*, Journal of Asian Studies 29 (1), November 1969.

Ray, Rajat Kanta. *Social Conflict and Political Unrest in Bengal, 1975–1927*. Delhi: Oxford University Press, 1984.

Ray, Sibnarayan, ed. *Gandhi, India, and the World*. Melbourne: Hawthorne Press, 1970.

Ray, Sibnarayan, ed. *M. N. Roy: Philosopher Revolutionary*. Calcutta: Renaissance Publishers, 1959.

Reynolds, Reginald. *A Quest for Gandhi*. New York: Doubleday, 1952.

Rigveda Brahmanas, The Aitareya and Kausitaki Brahmanas of the Rig-Veda, translated by A. B. Keith, Harvard Oriental Series, 30 Volumes, Cambridge: Harvard University Press, 1920.

Robinson, Jo Ann. *The Montgomery Bus Boycott and the Women Who Started It*, David J. Garrow. ed. Knoxville: The University of Tennessee Press, 1987.

Rolland, Romain. *Mahatma Gandhi. The Man Who Became One With the Universal Being*. London: George Allen and Unwin, 1924.

Rothermund, Indira. *The Philosophy of Restraint*. BombayL: Popular Prakashan, 1963.

Roy M. N. and Evelyn Roy. *One Year of Non-Cooperation*. Calcutta, 1923.

Roy, M. N. *New Orientation*, with Foreword by Philip Spratt. Calcutta: Renaissance Publishers, 1946..

Roy, M. N. *India's Message: Fragments of a Prisoner's Diary*, vol. 2. Calcutta: Renaissance Publishers, 1950.

Roy, M. N. *Reason, Romanticism and Revolution*. 2 vols. Calcutta: Renaissance Publishers, 1952.

Roy, M. N. *Crime and Karma, Cats and Women: Fragments of a Prisoner's Diary*, vol. 1, Calcutta, 1957.

Roy, M. N. *Politics. Power and Parties*: Calcutta, Renaissance Publishers,. 1960.

Roy, M. N. *Memoirs*. Bombay: Asia Publishers, 1964.

Roy, M. N. *India in Transition*. Bombay: Nachiketa Publications, 1971.

Ruddick, Sara. *Maternal Thinking. Toward a Politics of Peace*. New York: Ballantine Books, 1989.

Rudolph, Susanne and Lloyd. *Gandhi*. Chicago: University of Chicago Press, 1983.

Rushbrook Williams, L. F. "Indian Unrest and American Opinion." *The Asiatic Review* 26 (87) (July 1930).

Ruskin, John. *Unto This Last*. London: J. M. Dent, 1932.

Russel, Wilfred, *Indian Summer*, London, 1951.

Salt Tax: The Tragic Tale of India's Ruin (in Gujarati) compiled by K. N. Shah and C. N. Joshi. Ahmedabad: S. J. Shah, 1930.

Sarkar, Sumit. *Modern India. 1885–1947*: Delhi, Macmillan India Ltd. 1983.

Sarkar, Sumit. "The Logic of Gandhian Nationalism: Civil Disobedience and the Gandhi-Irwin Pact" *The Indian Historical Review* 3 (1), July 1976.

Sarkar, Tanikar. "The First Phase of Civil Disobedience in Bengal, 1930–1931." *The Indian Historical Review* 4 (1), July, 1977.

Sethi J. D. *Gandhi Today*. Durham, North Carolina: Carolina Academic Press, 1978.

Shah, Ghanshyam. "Traditional Society and Political Mobilization: The Experience of Bardoli *Satyagraha* (1920–1928)." In *Contributions to Indian Sociology*, no. 8, 1974.

Shakespeare, William. *The Complete Works*. New York: Viking, 1986.

Sharp, Gene. *Gandhi Wields the Weapon of Moral Power*. Ahmedabad: Navajivan, 1960.

Sharp, Gene. *The Politics of Nonviolent Action*. Boston: Porter Sargent, 1973.

Sharp, Gene. *Gandi as a Political Strategist*. Boston: Porter Sargent, 1979.

Sharp, Gene. *Social Power and Political Freedom*. Boston: Porter Sargent, 1980

Shils, Edward. "Ideology." In *The International Encyclopedia of the Social Sciences*. New York: Macmillan, 7: 69.

Shils, Edward. *The Culture of the Indian Intellectual*, University of Chicago Reprint Series, Reprinted from *Sewanee Review*, April and July, 1959.

Shimoni, Gideon. *Gandhi, Satyagraha and the Jews: A Formative Factor in India's Policy Towards Israel*. Jerusalem: The Hebrew University, 1977.

Shirer, William L. *Gandhi. A Memoir*. New York: Simon and Schuster, 1979.

Shivers, Lynne. "An Open Letter to Gandhi." In Pam McAllister, ed. *Reweaving the Web of Life*. Philadelphia: New Society Publishers, 1982.

Shridharani, Krishnalal. *War Without Violence*. New York: Harcourt, 1939.

Shukla, B. D., *A History of the Indian Liberal Party*. Allahabad: Indian Press Publishers, 1960.

Shukla, C. *Gandhi's View of Life*. Bombay: Bharaitya Vidya Bhavan, 1954.

Singh, Harnam. *The Indian National Movement and American Opinion*. New Delhi: Rama Krishna & Sons, 1962.

Sinha, Madan Gopal. *The Political Ideas of Bipin Chandra Pal*. Delhi: Commonwealth Publishers, 1989.

Sitaramayya, B. P. *The History of the Indian National Congress, 1885–1935.* Madras: Working Committee of the Congress, 1935.

Spear, Percival. *India.* Ann Arbor: The University of Michigan Press, 1961.

Spratt, Philip. *Gandhism.* Madras: Huxley Press, 1939.

Steinem, Gloria. *Revolution From Within.* Boston: Little, Brown, 1992.

Stokes, Newton Phelps. "Marching with Gandhi." In *The Review of Reviews,* New York, June, 1930.

Swan, Maureen. *Gandhi. The South African Experience.* Johannesburg: Ravan Press, 1985.

Sykes, Sir Frederick. *From Many Angles: An Autobiography.* London: George Harrap, 1942.

Syrkin, M. ed. *Hayim Greenberg. Anthology.* Detroit: Wayne State University Press. 1968.

Tagore, Rabindranath. *Gitanjali* (Song Offerings). London: Macmillan 1920.

Tagore, Rabindranath. *Reminiscences.* London: Macmillan, 1920.

Tagore, Rabindranath. *Letters to A Friend,* C. F. Andrew. ed. London: Geroge Allen & Unwin, 1928.

Tagore, Rabindranath. *Towards Universal Man.* London: Asia Publishing House, 1961.

Tahmankar, D. V. *Sardar Patel.* London: Allen and Unwin, 1970.

Templewood [Viscount; earlier, Sir Samuel Hoare]. *Nine Troubled Years.* London: Collins, 1954.

Tendulkar, D. G. *Mahatma.* 8 Vols. Delhi: Government of India Publications Division, 1960.

The Thirteen Principal Upanishads, Robert Ernest Hume. trans. London: Oxford University Press, 1962.

Thoreau, Henry David. "On Civil Disobedience." In *Walden and Civil Disobedience.* New York: Mentor, 1978.

Tilak, Bal Gangadhar. *Writings and Speeches.* Madras: Ganesh, 1918.

Tinker, Hugh. *Reorientations.* London: Pall Mall Press, 1965.

Tinker, Hugh. *South Asia.* London: Pall Mall Press, 1966.

Tinker, Hugh. *Experiment with Freedom.* London: Oxford University Press, 1967.

Tinker, Hugh. *India and Pakistan.* London: Praeger, 1967.

Tinker, Hugh. *A New System of Slavery.* London: Oxford University Press, 1974.

Tinker, Hugh. *The Ordeal of Love: C. F. Andrews and India.* Delhi and New York: Oxford University Press, 1979.

Tolstoy, Leo. *The Kingdom of God is Within You.* New York: The Noonday Press, 1961.

Tuker, Sir Francis. *While Memory Serves.* London: Cassell, 1950.

van den Dungen, P. H. N. "Gandhi in 1919: Loyalist or Rebel?" In R. Kumar. ed. *Essays on Gandhian Politics.* Oxford: Clarendon Press, 1971.

Venktachar, C. S. "1937–1947 in Retrospect: A Civil Servant's View." In *The Partition of India,* C. H. Philips and M. D. Wainwright, eds. London, 1970.

Verma, V. P. *The Political Philosophy of Mahatma Gandhi and Sarvodaya.* Agra: Lakshmi Narain Agarwal, 1959.

Vivekananda, Swami. *Complete Works.* Vols. 1–4. Calcutta: Advaita Ashrama, 1962.

Walton, Norman W. "The Walking City, A History of the Montgomery Boycott." In *The Negro History Bulletin,* October, 1956.

Watson, Blanche, ed. *Gandhi and Non-Violent Resistance. The Non-Cooperation Movement of India. Gleanings from the American Press.* Madras: Ganesh, 1923.

Weber, Thomas. "Kharag Bahadur Singh: The Eighth [sic] Marcher." *Gandhi Marg* 6 (9), December 1984.

Weber, Thomas. "Historiography and the Dandi March: The Other Myths of Gandhi's Salt March." In *Gandhi Marg* 8 (8), November 1986.

Wolfenstein. E. Victor, *The Revolutionary Personality: Lenin, Trotsky, Gandhi.* Princeton: Princeton University Press, 1967.

Wolpert, Stanley A. *Tilak and Gokhale: Revolution and Reform in the Making of Modern India.* Berkeley: University of California Press, 1962.

Wolpert, Stanley A. *India.* New York: Prentice-Hall, 1965.

Yeakey, Lamont H. *The Montgomery, Alabama Bus Boycott.* Unpublished Ph. D. Dissertation: Columbia University, 1979.

Zaehner, R. C. *Hinduism.* London: Oxford University Press, 1962.

Index

Index

Index